Human Services Management

OTHER WADSWORTH TITLES
OF RELATED INTEREST IN SOCIAL WELFARE

Clinical Social Work
Marion L. Beaver and Don Miller

Social Welfare Policy: Perspectives, Patterns and Insights
Ira Colby

Social Work Processes, Fourth Edition
Beulah R. Compton and Burt Galaway

Poverty and Public Policy in Modern America
Donald Critchlow and Ellis Hawley

Child Sexual Abuse
Danya Glaser and Stephen Frosh

Direct Social Work Practice: Theory and Skills, Third Edition
Dean H. Hepworth and Jo Ann Larsen

Social Welfare Policy: From Theory to Practice
Bruce S. Jansson

The Reluctant Welfare State
Bruce S. Jansson

Crisis Intervention Handbook: Assessment, Treatment and Research
Albert R. Roberts

Juvenile Justice: Policies, Programs and Services
Albert R. Roberts

Research Methods for Social Work
Allen Rubin and Earl Babbie

Human Services Management: Analysis and Applications, Second Edition
Myron E. Weiner

Introduction to Social Welfare, Social Problems, Services, and
Current Issues, Fourth Edition
Charles Zastrow

The Practice of Social Work, Third Edition
Charles Zastrow

Human Services Management

Analysis and Applications

SECOND EDITION

Myron E. Weiner

University of Connecticut

School of Social Work

Wadsworth Publishing Company

Belmont, California
A Division of Wadsworth, Inc.

Sociology Editor: Peggy Adams
Editorial Assistant: Karen Moore
Production Editor: Angela Mann
Managing Designer: Andrew Ogus
Print Buyer: Barbara Britton
Designer: Lisa Mirski
Copy Editor: Betty Duncan-Todd
Technical Illustrator: Alexander Teshin Associates / Romaine LoPrete
Compositor: G & S Typesetters, Inc.
Cover: Lisa Mirski

Printed in the United States of America 19
1 2 3 4 5 6 7 8 9 10—94 93 92 91 90

Library of Congress Cataloging in Publication Data

Weiner, Myron E.
 Human services management : analysis and applications / Myron E.
Weiner. — 2nd ed.
  p. cm.
 Includes bibliographical references.
 ISBN 0-534-12528-X
 1. Human services—Management. I. Title
HV41.W368 1990
361′.0068—dc20
                                          89-39406
                                           CIP

For my wife, Ruth, and our wonderfully expanding family,
Jonathan, Ethan, Adina, Jenny, Geoff, and Nathaniel.

Contents

Preface

Some of the best managed organizations and systems can be found in the public and nonprofit human services agencies of your community. Does this statement surprise you? Many people assume that state-of-the-art management exists only in high-powered business corporations and that human services organizations usually are poorly managed. This is a fallacy. Excellence in modern management stems from the work of a particular group of dedicated, talented, and skillful employees and managers and is not the automatic product of a particular type of organization. Human services managers should feel proud. They number among the best managers in our society—often while operating against overwhelming odds.

The challenge for the human services is infinitely more complex and difficult than that facing the vast majority of business organizations. The reason is obvious. As Peter Drucker, one of the world's leading authorities on modern management noted (1973), businesses have one clear-cut and dominant value that serves as their criterion for success: profit. For service institutions, multiple legitimate, worthy, and often conflicting values are the criteria for success. Successful management for the human services consists of continuous balancing and reconciling of the resulting tensions, while moving forward to accomplish what are often impossible tasks.

The second edition of this book is directed specifically to three audiences:

- Students of administration preparing to enter the field of human services management.
- Students preparing to become human services clinicians, who recognize that in the near future they may enter the ranks of human services management, or plan to do so.

■ Human services management practitioners who originally prepared themselves professionally as clinicians, and now find themselves carrying the responsibilities of management positions.

Management in the human services is different and distinct from management in other organizational and systemic environments. One difference, the continuous need to reconcile the tension among conflicting, equally worthy values, has already been noted. Another such characteristic is the continuous need to deal in a creative and timely way with a highly dynamic, kinetic environment. As we approach the twenty-first century, managing any type of organization or system is becoming more difficult because of the turbulence of the world around us. For the human services, this task is infinitely more complex because the problems and issues multiply and change rapidly, and have no easy resolution. Because of this complexity each human services manager must possess a deep understanding of a broad range of skills to respond to the rapidly changing needs of clients, and the demands of new situations and environments.

The purpose of human services management, therefore, is to create and maintain an environment of societal community services that are responsive to people, individually and in groups, as they strive to improve the quality of their lives. This is the distinctive role of the human services manager. It is a rewarding, but challenging and difficult mission.

This second edition is organized to help the human services manager acquire knowledge and skill in a number of important areas. Part I: The values that are inherent to human services organizations and systems that are often conflicting and require continuous reconciliation. Part II: The relationship between various ways of viewing the human condition and different models of organization and management; as well as the relationship and mutual influence of human behavior and organizational behavior. Part III: Dynamics of the organizational and systemic environment of the human services, including those specific to women and ethnic minorities in management. Part IV: Modern management concepts and techniques for institutional and organizational management. Part V: Modern management concepts and techniques necessary for systemic (strategic) management—the ability to analyze, design, change, and manage trans-organizational human services systems.

A stream of ideas, ideals, and caveats that permeate all these processes runs through the text as a theme. In addition to theoretical discussion, you will find a series of cases. These are completely fictitious as to place, person, and content, yet the situations and processes are based on actual cases to depict day-to-day realities, and help convey the feel and flavor of the field.

This book is written for you, the student preparing to enter the profession of human services management, and for you, the practitioner already there. Yours is a noble task. The institutions dedicated to the provision of human services will have to deal with problems of the highest priority for our society as we approach the twenty-first century. Whether we are capable of solving these problems is the challenge facing you, the managers.

This edition strives to achieve the same goals as the earlier edition: To provide in one volume a complete array of the needed knowledge and skills, as well as to integrate state-of-the-art management with the fundamental values and perceptions of the human services. This integration is fundamental to the management of human services organizations and systems.

It is my hope that this book will be of help to you on your difficult, challenging, and important path. I wish you success!

Myron E. Weiner

Acknowledgments

As I noted in the first edition, every author is a recorder of the thoughts and deeds of others. From that perspective, everyone that I have worked with, met, talked to, or read over the past forty years should be acknowledged as co-authors. In these past four decades, I have been fortunate to have had hundreds of colleagues, friends, students, and members of my family from whom I have learned so much. Thus, to you my colleagues, friends, and family, I am indebted. This is your book. You have shaped my thoughts and my insights. I hesitate to name you individually for fear I would slight one of you in oversight, but extend to you all my gratitude.

I want to also acknowledge the support I have received from my associates and students at the School of Social Work and the Masters of Public Affairs Program here at the University of Connecticut. Without their help, I could not have accomplished this task.

I further want to express my special gratitude to several human services managers who contributed directly to this second edition by providing me with the background for the fictitious cases included herein. They include Cathy Adair, Fran Anthes, Nancy Buckwalter, Cathy Daly, Betsy Loughran, Hanna Marcus, Marty Milkovic, Sarah Miller, Lorna Murphy, Nancy Rollins, and Carole Shomo. Each is a creative, dynamic human services manager who provides a model for others to emulate.

I wish to thank Dr. Thomas D. Watts, The University of Texas at Arlington; Thomas Packard, San Diego State University; and Michael Kelly, University of Missouri, Columbia, for their roles as reviewers. Their critiques and suggestions set the framework for this second edition and helped make the book more meaningful for the reader. I am equally grateful to Peggy Adams, Angela

Mann, and many others at Wadsworth Publishing Company for their outstanding support and assistance in the preparation of this edition.

For this second edition, I have worked closely with my wife, Ruth, an educator and human services manager, in shaping the ideas and language of this text. Her keen mind, sensitive insights, and skillful command of the language have been invaluable, and indispensible to the book. Chapter 7 dealing with women and minorities in management was essentially written by Ruth. This edition is truly a product of her unstinting effort and thus a joint product of our combined knowledge and experience.

PART

I

Values and the Human Services Manager

Human services management is unique: It has specific attributes that distinguish it from other forms of management; it is bedded on a foundation of values, each of which individually is critical and important and all of which collectively compete to dominate the decisions and actions of administrators. For the human services manager, the result is a career that can be one of the most challenging in the managerial profession—and one of the most frustrating.

Chapter 1 distinguishes human services management from other forms of business or public management and sets forth the book's thesis: There is a generic core that is universally shared by managers of all human services organizations and systems. Human services managers work in a broad range of disciplines (e.g., social work, health, mental health, education, and recreation) and in a broad set of environments (e.g., large federal and state social services departments, hospitals, mental health clinics, and senior citizens centers), but they all share this generic core of knowledge and skills. In addition, all human services managers share certain common values that provide the foundation for managing any aspect of this calling. The chapter also sounds several themes that will continue throughout the book. These themes delineate the distinctiveness of human services management and its dynamic, creative nature.

Chapter 2 focuses on the tensions that are created for human services managers as they attempt to reconcile competing values, each of which is important and legitimate, when several contend for simultaneous dominance. Managers in business organizations are also faced with a variety of values, but there is little conflict because one value clearly dominates: financial profit and thus success and survival. The goals of human services managers are not as direct, and so their decision-action processes are infinitely more complex and difficult. Survival becomes but one among competing values, each of which is vital. Thus, the role of the human services manager can be characterized as that of a mediator, continually reconciling conflicting values day to day and for the long term. Chapter 2 therefore details a number of these apparently irreconcilable value-tensions that are found in human services organizations and systems.

1

The Distinctiveness of Human Services Management

Who Is a Human Services Manager?

The Case for Generic Human Services Management

Commonalities in Human Services Management

Generic Core of Knowledge and Skills

Ever-Present Value-Tensions
Organization and System Perspectives
Dynamics of Organizational Environments
Institutional Management Techniques
Systemic Management Techniques

Generic Values

Humans: Things or Beings?
A Human Being: Animal or Godlike?
The Search for Uniqueness
The Search for Meaning
The Creative Potential of Human Beings

Challenge and Commitment: An Ideological Framework

Distinctive Characteristics of Human Services Management

Common Themes

Summary

Who Is a Human Services Manager?

Variations on a Theme: Human Services Managers

Dr. Janet Grant	Deputy Commissioner, State Department of Social Services
Morris Tyson	Vice President for Administration, Parkdale Hospital, Dallas, Texas
Dr. Alexander Hamilton	President, Mt. Ararat Hospital, New York
Molly Goldberg	Director of Human Resources, Everest Insurance Company, Hartford, Connecticut
Migdalia Ortiz	Director of Barton County Area Agency on Aging, Florida
Dr. Joseph Asner	Principal, Pulaski High School, Millville, Wisconsin
Joe Friday	Director of Parks and Recreation, Clearmont, California
Stella Dallas	Director, Visiting Nurses Association, Portsmouth, Maine
Guy Hawkes	Director, Community Action Agency, Lincoln, Pennsylvania
Dr. Daniel Auslander	Director, Northwest Community Mental Health Clinic, Sundale, New Mexico
Maria Montessori	Director, Medicare Contract Services, Everest Insurance Company, Hartford, Connecticut
Victoria Regina	Executive Director, YWCA, Green Belt, Washington

Who are these people? Their titles indicate that they manage organizations, agencies, or programs directed toward providing services to people. What do they have in common? Can we call them human services managers? Their academic credentials include M.D., M.B.A., M.P.A., Ph.D., Ed.D., M.S.W., B.S.W., a B.A. in psychology, and a B.S. in nursing.

Few have an academic degree in management. Their educational preparation and experience prepared them to be competent clinicians, although most have completed intensive seminars and workshops in management and are effective at what they do. If asked, most would identify themselves with specialized fields of management, such as hospital administration, education administration, social work administration, and not with the more general profession of human services management. Some would look puzzled when asked if they consider themselves human services managers: "I manage the processing of insurance claims for Medicare recipients and work for a proprietary insurance company!" "I'm the personnel director of that company; what do I have to do with human services?"

The thesis of this book is that there is a generic field of human services management. To support this thesis, this chapter presents its rationale, its distinctive qualities, a model for acquiring the generic core of knowledge and skills required, a set of generic values that serve as underpinnings and the challenge to our society of professionals who identify themselves as **human services managers.**

One hallmark of the twentieth century is the division of work in our society into specialized professions. To acquire the services that can enhance the quality of their lives, people must navigate through a maze of organizations that have dissected them into so many separate parts that rarely is there a single agency that deals with them as a whole person.

Practitioners specialize in narrow aspects of the larger field of human services management for several reasons. These include the following:

- The peculiar ecology of a specific organization and its culture—its dynamics, values, mores, and jargon
- The need for application-oriented knowledge—administrative techniques specific to hospitals or schools, for example
- The requirement for professional credibility and official accreditation

This specialization is both natural and legitimate, but it can also be confining. Movement from one specialized organizational environment to another, for even the most superior manager, can be difficult. Furthermore, concentrating on a specific environment within the broader field of human services generally distances the individual from the pertinent body of knowledge and skills shared by all human services managers.

My thesis of a generic field of human services management implies an explicit model of professional preparation. I suggest that the current approach to pursuing higher education only in a specialized field of administration is often dysfunctional. It may or may not lead to an awareness of being part of a much larger cadre of professional administrators—human services managers. A more reasoned approach would be initial preparation as a generalist human services manager, thus laying the broad foundation for a career that can lead to professional success in a variety of specialized fields of human services. To support the latter model, this book presents my case for generalist human services management, with highly specialized and updated skills acquired as necessary throughout a professional lifetime.

The Case for Generic Human Services Management

Let us begin with a profile of a human services manager whose work embodies a large number of the attributes of generic human services management. Meet Cathy Mendosa. Case 1.1 illustrates and supports the thesis of this book that the field of human services management has distinctive characteristics but that its foundation is a generic body of knowledge, skills, values, and ideology.

Case 1.1 _____

Cathy Mendosa: A Creative, Dynamic Human Services Manager

Bob Wise looked up from reading the program memo and commented, with a twinkle in his eye, "Here we go again, Cathy! You have a wonderful way of putting me on the hot spot. A year ago I had to get the city council to deal with the homeless, when most weren't willing to admit that our lovely suburb has such a problem. Then last winter, you and I went before them to request funds for a phobia self-help group, when most of them can't even spell phobia. Now, we bring up the issue of AIDS, in *this* community. At this rate, I may not be Glenville's city manager much longer!"

Cathy laughed, knowing that Bob would support her all the way. The two of them had developed a fine working relationship since he appointed her six years ago. He had a lot of confidence in her, and she could always depend on him. "Not to worry," she said. "They know no one can stretch a tight town budget the way you do. And by now they've probably gotten the message that AIDS has become a fact of life. So now, what's our strategy for getting council support for your proposal to provide supportive services to our AIDS patients?"

Bob knew they would probably be successful in gaining community support. The city had a good reputation in the area for its creative approach to human services. Six years ago he had reorganized the city's agencies by creating a city Department of Human Services with a twofold mission: to pull together all municipal human services under one roof (e.g., health, social, welfare, mental health, home care, and elderly services) and to serve as a catalyst for responding to the community's human services needs in a dynamic, supportive fashion by initiating programs that could become self-regulating and free-standing. Bob appointed Cathy, who shared his philosophy of responsiveness, as the director of the new department. As he had hoped, she turned out to be the right person at the right time.

Before the reorganization, the city's human services agencies were too segregated and focused on their own narrow professional specializations. Under the reorganization, they were to be less of a bureaucracy and more of an adaptive "adhocracy" responding to community needs in a more dynamic fashion. Cathy was appointed as the first director of the department. During the past six years in which the number of programs and resource investment in human services tripled, there was only a marginal increase in city employees. The additional human services initiated included

- Day care
- Shelters for the homeless
- Geriatric health services
- Phobia support group
- Dial-a-ride consortium
- Recreational services for the disabled
- Independent living for the developmentally disabled
- Community mental health services: shelters, prevocational training, social clubs, and managed care

Cathy worked very hard to create a team spirit among the department's staff. She successfully conveyed that they were the designers and initiators of new human services systems that could ultimately stand on their own. They knew that, although Glenville was a conservative community, the times were changing and human services had to be dynamic to respond to these changes. Together they developed a process for developing new human services systems. It used the following steps:

1. Monitor and sense the environment for priority needs.
2. Develop broad community support for new services and programs.
3. Create new programs that cut across organizational boundaries.
4. Acquire resources creatively from different sources.
5. Develop self-governance mechanisms for the new programs.
6. Support the new services in their infancy.
7. Take a backseat in taking credit for success; be the focal point for dealing with problems and conflicts.
8. Monitor progress and maintain liaison.

To create the new department, Cathy used patience, good interpersonal skills, a modern management style, and strong leadership. Her biggest problem, she had to admit, was in getting everyone to accept the department's fundamental role in creating and maintaining a community environment that was responsive and supportive to citizens as they struggled to deal dynamically with the issues and pressures in their lives.

Her training and experiences as an M.S.W. clinician and casework supervisor was a big help to her in managing the new department. She had to admit that her sense of commitment and personal strength kept her going during those times when it seemed she was the only one who believed in the department's mission. She was also thankful that she had a good, dedicated staff and a very supportive boss. It made the difference when things got tough.

The thesis of this book is founded on several timely propositions:

- Some of today's fundamental changes in our society require that institutions focus on each citizen in a comprehensive holistic fashion. Organizations that persist in the old narrow perception of highly specialized professions find themselves strained to the maximum to perform at minimum levels.

- Human services is a dominant growth industry in our society. It flows out of a more widespread concern for the quality of life.

- Like other modern industrial societies, we live in a modern-day welfare state that provides services that improve the quality of life for its citizens through three large systems: social welfare; tax welfare; and occupational welfare, for example, employment benefits.

- Thus, there emerges a need for all human services adminstrators to share a common mission, similar values, distinctive approaches, and a common ground for communication and coordination.

- The environment of human services organizations has distinctive qualities that call for a unique type of management.

- There is a body of theory and methodology that constitutes a generic core of knowledge and skills, peculiar to human services management.

Let us examine these assumptions further.

Commonalities in Human Services Management

As the United States reached for a level of material prosperity unrivaled in the history of civilization, it began to reach for a parallel increase in the quality of life. In less than half a century, this has brought about a shift from a product to a service economy. This shift is characterized by the proliferation of societal institutions devoted primarily to providing human services. The traditional division of organizations into business and public sectors of the economy has evolved so that there are numerous organizations that are neither clearly public nor private. At the same time, the relationships among all types of organizations have become so intertwined that confusion, conflict, and chaos often result, despite the fact that they are crucial to each other's effective operation. Consider the case of the Everest Insurance Company.

What Is This "Thing" Called Everest?

The Everest Insurance Company is a multibillion dollar insurance and financial services corporation. How does that make it a human services organization in the proprietary sector of our economy? Let us consider:

- What are insurance and financial services, if not fundamental human services?
- The ground rules, procedures, and even the profits of Everest are dependent on regulations by governments. Is Everest partially a quasi-public agency?
- Is Everest in the health-care business?
  They are a major owner and manager of health maintenance organizations (HMOs).
  They are a major provider of health insurance.
  They operate and manage Medicare for the federal government.
  Employment benefit packages are the basis of most peoples' human services: Everest manages benefit packages for a large number of corporations; and Everest provides benefits packages (30 to 35 percent of salaries) for their employees who number in the thousands nationwide.
- As a major corporation in the city of Hartford, Everest has a vigorous affirmative action program guiding their employment and purchasing practices. Has the company adopted fundamental human services values?
- Everest cannot escape the paradox of the coexistence of affluence and poverty in our nation. As one of the richest corporations in the United States, it is headquartered in one of the most impoverished cities in the nation, in a state with the highest per-capita income in the nation.
  Everest has a major "corporate responsibility" division that makes investment in the city of Hartford—directly and indirectly.
  Have they adopted the social commitment of a human services organization?

The Everest case illustrates that the normal division of organizations into three sectors (proprietary, public, and private-nonprofit) is not always clear-cut for human services managers. The provision of services to people spans the boundaries of organizations, creating a common mission, a common set of values, and a common set of distinctive approaches for all those responsible for managing human services.

This trend has been reinforced by two other major, worldwide trends. As human beings are viewed in a more comprehensive, holistic fashion, we see the rise of a systems perspective on societal institutions. This places pressure on human services organizations to stop fragmenting the individual and to find ways that integrate services performed for the same person. It is for this reason that the late twentieth century is a time of ferment and upheaval, reassessment and reform in the nation's human services. All institutions that provide services to human beings, regardless of their economic-legal-professional bases, now face a common challenge: how to best shape societal systems that deal with each person as a unique individual while providing effective and efficient services.

The provision of human services is one of the dominant growth industries in the United States today. The Everest case implies that all who are responsible for the management of human services organizations now share a common bond. This in turn raises some important questions about the distinctive foundation and characteristics of this common field of human services organization and management that we now share.

Generic Core of Knowledge and Skills

Human services management is by nature dynamic and multifaceted and thus demands a great amount of creativity and flexibility. Each human services manager therefore needs to acquire a generic core of knowledge and skills. These are the foundation for the continuous acquisition of further skills specific to different organizational settings: clinics, hospitals, schools, public and private agencies, recreation centers, residential facilities, and so forth.

The generic core of knowledge and skills for human services management consists of five elements. But, subdividing the generic core into elements may convey the impression that each element operates independently. The opposite is true. Dynamic, creative human services management is a totality that operates as an integrated whole. For the manager, the challenge is to integrate all distinctive human services knowledge and skills to achieve a powerful, synergistic, creative approach to organizational management.

Let us briefly survey the five elements that together form the core for generic human services management.

Ever-Present Value-Tensions

There is a generic set of unique values that serves as the bedrock of human services management decisions. These values must be internalized by the manager and inculcated into the organization. In addition, the human services administrator will be faced each and every day with making decisions and taking

Figure 1.1   Dynamic, Creative Human Services Management

Generic Core of Knowledge and Skills	**Generic Values**
constant presence of value-tensions organization and system perspectives dynamics of organizational environments institutional management techniques systemic management techniques	humans: things or beings? human being: animal or godlike? search for uniqueness search for meaning creative potential of human beings

Distinctive Characteristics

ideological framework

dynamic and creative

responsive, supportive environment

each client as a unique entity

effectiveness: primary outcome measure

self-management

fashioning unique management repertoires

two interrelated forms of management

continual coping with value-choices

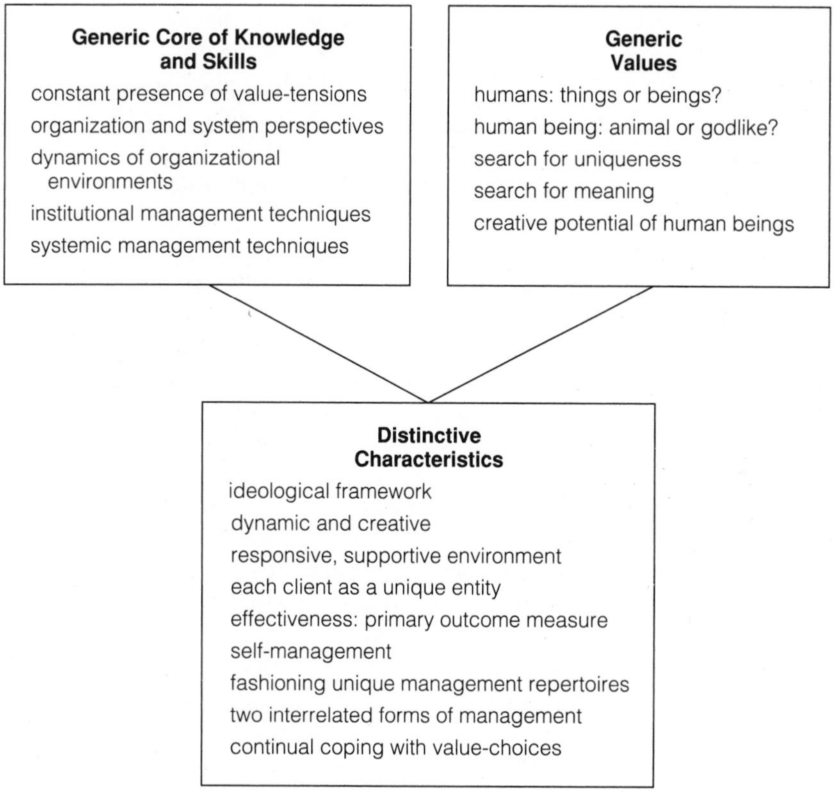

actions in situations in which there are two or more opposing values, each of them legitimate and vital. Reconciling these seemingly irreconcilable value-tensions is a primary characteristic, distinctive of human services management.

This is not to say that most other managers do not also have to struggle with value-tensions. But in commercial organizations, there is a clear, dominant value—making a profit. In public and private human services agencies, however, there are usually a number of conflicting values, and selecting one as dominant is problematic because they all are equally viable. Review Case 1.2 of the Woodhurst Agency, which moved from being a long-term care facility for the elderly and became a traumatic brain-injured (TBI) rehabilitation agency, mainly because it was more profitable. What are some of the value-tensions? Would you have made the same decisions as the managers in the case? Would you abandon one group of clients for another because the second group would be more profitable for the human services agency in which you work? How would you mediate between the conflicting tensions?

Case 1.2 _____

Woodhurst: An Agency for TBI Clients

Connie Czernick, Woodhurst's executive director, was upset with the drift
of the strategic planning meeting. The agency had been bought out recently
by New Horizons, a commercial health-care conglomerate based in Atlanta.
Woodhurst had an excellent record of professional quality services, at a profit,
for health care to elderly clients. It was a record of which Connie was justly
proud. But Rick Fisher, the finance director recently appointed at Woodhurst
by New Horizons, was presenting data that indicated greater profitability if
the agency were to switch to providing comprehensive services for TBI clients.

"But Rick," Connie pleaded, "Woodhurst has a great reputation in the
whole Southeast for both its high-quality service and its businesslike operations in elder care. It's a major pressing community need that we're meeting
effectively and productively."

"I won't argue with that, Connie," Rick responded, "but please don't take
my comments negatively in terms of the past. Woodhurst has an excellent
reputation. That's why New Horizons purchased the agency. But the whole
field of TBI care is an even more pressing community need. Often funded by
Medicaid and Medicare, it has a much more stable base, and, as my charts
indicate, it is three times as profitable as providing health care for the elderly.
On top of that, we would be getting in on the ground floor of a totally new
market in the human services field."

"What about our current clients, Rick?" Woodhurst's social work director Jim Cartwright asked, coming to Connie's defense. "What will happen
to them?"

"I don't think it's a problem, Jim," Rick was quick to respond. "We'll
stop taking new clients, phase out services to those who are healthy enough to
return home, and the few remaining clients will be transferred to other area
agencies. Believe me, they'll be happy to take them."

"Don't you think we should tell our patients?" Jim asked.

"Not only our patients," Connie added. "With our style of management,
we have always bounced ideas off our staff first and then our community
leaders. They're both great sources of creativity. Their ownership in a new
idea is valuable to effective implemenation of the new strategy."

"I respect that, Connie," Rick was quick to answer, "but staff and community participation in management is just not New Horizon's style. And
they've got a track record of excellent services and great profits during the
past five years. Seems to me that New Horizons is the model for modern human services management in the 1990s."

Chapter 2 examines in greater detail several of the irreconcilable value-tensions that each human services manager will have to deal with over the course of a career.

Organization and System Perspectives

Along with putting a human being on the moon and a television or two in every home, the twentieth century surely will be remembered for the proliferation of the number and types of proprietary, public, and nonprofit organizations that have been formed to maintain and sustain our complex society. It is therefore not surprising that the analysis and study of organizations has also expanded rapidly. This has resulted in a large number of different ways of thinking about organizations.

As managers we are influenced by our own images of the world and, in particular, the world of organizations and systems. Acute awareness of these internalized images is a prerequisite for improving the effectiveness of human services organizations and systems.

It is also important for human services managers to understand organizational behavior, the way in which organizations influence human behavior, and equally important, the influence that human behavior has on organizations. These essential topics are examined in Part II of the book.

Dynamics of Organizational Environments

The human services institutional environment is a web of constantly changing *inter*organizational relationships. Human services managers are caught between the tension of having to guard the resources and territory of their own environments and the need to span organizational, functional, and professional boundaries. *Transorganizational and interdisciplinary systems are the primary challenge for human services managers in the 1990s.* The goal: more productive and effective human services.

Part III examines the nature of the human services institutional fabric. It comprises countless numbers of segregated and fragmented structures arranged in categorical and bureaucratic fashion, each of which tends to have a highly specialized perception of the human being and client needs. Some of these structures place severe constraints on the delivery of human services, but they also serve as the loom on which human services managers weave a variety of strategies designed to develop systems of interrelationships that focus on the unique needs of people, as individuals or as groups.

The challenges, opportunities, and constraints of the rapidly changing environment of human services are examined, within the context of the changing demographics of the United States. Let us look at some of the significant changes. As a nation, we are moving from a *melting pot* to a *mosaic society,* and from *homogeneity* in cultural patterns to *cultural diversity.* By the year 2010, it is predicted that the majority of the population in the United States will be nonwhite. Increasingly, human services clients with the greatest priority of need are women and children. The staffs of human services organizations also comprise more women and members of minorities. This has profound implications and impact on the very nature of human services management, another phenomenon which is examined. We will turn to the writing of Mary Parker Follett, who is not only the progenitor of human services management but also of modern management itself. And for women who are human services managers, Mary Parker Follett provides an inspiring model (see Chapter 5).

There are new concepts and techniques for managing organizations and systems that deal with human behavior within a social environment. For dynamic, creative human services management, the manager is challenged to acquire experience in two simultaneous, complementary approaches to administering organizations: **institutional management** and **systemic (strategic) management**. The former focuses on managing the internal workings of a specific human services organization; the latter focuses on managing the interorganizational relationships that an agency has with other human services agencies and systems.

Institutional Management Techniques

Most traditional management techniques are developed in very narrow terms and are walled off from each other by technical jargon and narrow, disciplinary perceptions. A dynamic, creative approach to human services management comes from the recognition that techniques are dynamically interrelated.

Part IV of the book concentrates on techniques and tools that focus on managing the institution (organization). Fundamental processes such as finance administration and personnel administration are discussed, along with classic program management. Managing information and computer use, new and essential tools in human services operations, also are examined in this part of the book.

The discussion of administrative techniques for institutional management uses four paradigms (a set of basic concepts, perceptions, and propositions) that influence human services organizations. These include the

- Control paradigm
- Mission paradigm
- Client paradigm
- Staff development paradigm

Each emphasizes a different aspect of the environment. Each shapes the way in which human services are organized and administered.

Systemic Management Techniques

Peter Drucker (1988), one of the leading management thinkers in the United States, has noted that the newest form of societal institution is the **information organization**. It requires a systemic, strategic approach to management. Creative human services managers thus need to acquire knowledge and skill in this type of management, along with their abilities in institutional (organizational) management.

As our society increasingly struggles to fashion the delivery of human services to each person in a unique fashion, the design and development of **transorganizational systems** becomes a critical skill for the dynamic, creative human services manager. The number and range of administrative techniques available for this process has rapidly expanded and are examined in Part V of this book. It includes close scrutiny of computer and telecommunications technologies that have been used for applications to operations and practice. Their immense potential for enhancing the role and power of the human services manager in systemic management is still not widely understood or exploited.

The key to systemic management is more than just acquiring the understanding and skills demanded by state-of-the-art management technologies. It also requires skills in managing the change and transition from existing to newly designed systems. It further demands the acquisition of skills for managing change itself. For the creative human services manager, there is continual tension between maintaining the status quo and changing existing systems to more effectively respond to the human services needs of people. Skill in the design and operationalizing of more effective systems must be paralleled with skill in managing the change to the new system.

Generic Values

Every decision and action that you will take as a human services manager will be embedded in your beliefs, attitudes, and values. And whether it is a conscious or unconscious process, one must deal with the issue of these intrinsic *values*. Thus, in our search for the distinctive nature of human services management, we must face the question, *What generic values form the foundation of human services management?*

The goals of this book do not allow a discussion of more than a sampling of different perceptions of human behavior, but I will focus on five basic issues that help define generic values that underlie modern, dynamic, and creative human services management. They are

- Humans: things or beings?
- A human being: animal or godlike?
- The search for uniqueness

- The search for meaning
- The creative potential of human beings

Humans: Things or Beings?

As a professional person accountable for carrying out the mission of your agency, how would you react to being asked to develop and implement a system that would gas to death millions of human beings or to kill indiscriminately 347 people, including women and children, and destroy their small village in South Vietnam? Would your response be one of shock and distress? Two "responsible," highly regarded professionals efficiently and effectively carried out these assigned tasks. Their names were Adolf Eichmann and Lt. William Calley. Both were eventually brought to trial, but at the time they felt that they were carrying out the mission of their agencies, which was true.

Those are extreme examples of institutional philosophies that treated human beings as things. Now let's try an example closer to home and less clearcut. Proposition 13 in California and Proposition 2½ in Massachusetts were referendums presented to voters. In essence, each pitted property owners, genuinely concerned about reducing their taxes, against poverty-stricken people who needed services and income supports to provide a quality of life up to poverty-level minimum. At the heart of such a vote is a tough clash of philosophies, pitting thing-oriented values against being-oriented values in society. As a homeowner in one of these states and the manager of a human services organization, how would you have voted: in favor of restricting taxes or permitting revenue expansion to provide more public services to the needy?

The psychoanalyst Eric Fromm became concerned that in our society we not only deal with others as things but also frequently regard ourselves as things. He writes:

> Modern man has alienated himself from his fellow men and from nature. He has been transformed into a commodity, experiences his life forces as an investment which must bring him the maximum profit obtainable under existing market conditions. Human relations are essentially those of alienated automatons, each basing his security on staying close to the herd and not being different in thought, feeling or action. (1956, 86)

In response to this, other philosophies that stress the "beingness" of humans have received greater attention recently. One such modern philosopher, Martin Buber, a Nobel laureate, regards humans as unique beings. At the heart of his philosophy is the notion of I–Thou:

> I know three kinds of dialogue. There is genuine dialogue—no matter whether spoken or silent—where each of the participants really has in mind the other or others in their present and particular being and turns to

them with the intention of establishing a living mutual relation between himself and them.

There is technical dialogue, which is prompted solely by the need of objective understanding. And there is monologue, disguised as dialogue. (1970, 19–20)

In Buber's words, genuine dialogue is characterized by the basic term *I–Thou;* technical dialogue is symbolized by the basic term *I–It.* The former establishes the world of human relationships; the latter shapes the world of day-to-day experience.

In effect, Buber is saying that the only thing each of us really owns is our humanness, our sense of being, which we share very carefully with others. In certain situations, we develop personal relationships in which we give part of our humanness to another human being who reciprocates. In these rare situations, an I–Thou relationship exists. In other interpersonal relationships, we do not share this sense of being and only interact with others as objects. This is an I–It relationship. As Buber notes, most of our world of experiences is through these I–It relationships.

Despite the fact that we are surrounded by political, social, and economic theories that emphasize *things* over *beings,* one of the fundamental and generic values differentiating human services management must be the centrality of humans as special beings. This requires certain implicit behaviors:

- The nurturing of each human being as a valued, unique entity
- The dominance of being-oriented values over thing-oriented values
- The image of humans that fosters dealing with the self as a being and resists treatment of oneself and others as things

These are not abstract values. They seep into all of society's issues and even the climate of a nation. Applying them in concrete terms boils down to simple but tough questions: Assume that there is only an either/or choice in public use of tax money. Would you be willing to give up your tax deduction for owning a home in order to provide the funds needed to house the homeless? Would you accept a sales tax increase to fund care for AIDS victims? Would your neighbors? Most issues are not as extreme, yet both as a citizen and as a professional, a human services manager is faced with such value-choices daily: People as things versus people as beings.

A Human Being: Animal or Godlike?

The Levant religions (Judaism, Christianity, and Islam) developed a lofty concept of humanity, as illustrated by the following quotation from Psalm 8:5–6:

What is man, that Thou are mindful of him?
And the son of man that Thou thinkest of him?

Yet Thou has made him, but little lower than the angels,
And has crowned him with glory and honor.

In his book *So Human an Animal* (1968), René Dubos, the French humanist
philosopher, laments the dehumanization of people and examines the forces in
recent civilizations that have reverted to a conception of human beings as animals. The Holocaust in Europe during the 1940s and the mass slaughter in
Cambodia during the 1970s serve as grim examples that annihilating millions
of people can be acceptable to some as a political instrument. There are still
forces existing in the modern world that hold to a perception of humans as
being no different than animals. One noted author, Ernest Becker (1975), presents the thesis that all the evil over the course of civilization can be traced to
human beings trying to escape from one immutable fact: They are no better
than animals because ultimately every living creature will die.

Perceiving the human condition as a continuous process of growth and development is a fundamental value of human services management. Joseph
Campbell, the noted anthropological historian, undertook a study of mythologies throughout civilization, resulting in a four-volume work entitled *The Masks
of God* (1976). He notes that there is a cycle of development evident in all
mythologies that marks the maturing process toward humanness. It led Campbell to his notion of the struggle for creative mythology: All humans struggle
as mythical heroes trying to approach their own monomythical, monoreligious
existences. "All the gods are within: within you—within the world" sums it
all up (1976, 650).

The Search for Uniqueness

Abraham Heschel (1965), a modern-day rabbi and philosopher who survived
the Holocaust to march with Martin Luther King, Jr., during the 1960s, wrote
that no two individuals are alike and that every human being has something to
say, to think, or to do that is unprecedented. In this concept, he is joined by
Buber who also maintains that we each have within us something precious that
is in no one else. Finding that precious uniqueness forces everyone to search
deep within one's "inmost being."

If we accept as a fundamental, generic value of human services management the uniqueness of each human being, then we are led to two important
conclusions. First, each human must recognize the core of life that is fundamental and essential, distinct from the vehicle of life—the role and status that
humans play on the stage of life. This fundamental essence is unique, and the
only criterion for valuing the worth of one's life; the vehicle is the play-acting
role of life. Many humans live inverse lives—placing emphasis on their roles
in the societal drama of life—and get consumed by peripheral issues of status,
power, position, wealth, and the rest. A human services management philosophy that values this essential core helps managers deal with the basic authentic-

ity of human lives, those of their immediate primary groups, their colleagues, and their clients.

Second, if our roles as human services managers are a vehicle for our own unique existence, then tangential to this role is that of facilitating the same authenticity in the individuality and uniqueness of people to whom we relate—clients and colleagues alike. Our dedication to increased effectiveness of human services management has led us to new organizational strategies designed to provide a unique set of services to each client in an individualized way. Mainstreaming the physically and developmentally disabled in a barrier-free community environment is consistent with the mission and value base of human services management. While many would question the benefit-cost ratio of an elevator in a 1000 student high school that benefits 10 physically disabled students, our Declaration of Independence confirms this value for our society that is fundamental for every human services manager—the uniqueness of each human being in our society.

The Search for Meaning

After defining the nature of the individual, one comes naturally to the questions, What then is the meaning of life? Does it have meaning? In his book *Man's Search for Meaning,* Victor Frankl, a psychiatrist and another Holocaust survivor, answers:

> Man's search for meaning is a primary force in his life and not a "secondary rationalization" of instinctual drive. This meaning is unique and specific in that it must and can be fulfilled by him alone; only then does it achieve a significance that will satisfy his own will to meaning. . . .
> (1962, 99)

There are a number of philosophies presented by observers of modern life that propose the opposite. Life is absurd and devoid of meaning. Because there is no meaning to life, there is no point to hope for any future ideal or improved society. Thus, being creative or innovative toward building that better world is quite absurd. Rather than to try to construct a better world in a world that has no meaning, we might as well be *deconstructive.* Although not a "deconstructionist," Robert Bellah and his associates, in their book entitled *Habits of the Heart* (1986), note the difficulty people in the United States have in finding meaning in their lives. Our success as a society, Bellah notes, is that for 200 years we found "coherence" in our lives by connecting ourselves to the overall good of the collective society. The overemphasis on continuous acquisition of status, income, and security is viewed by Bellah as diverting us from finding the coherence necessary to convey meaning to life.

Human services organizations and systems are formed primarily to create an environment in which human beings are supported in their efforts to improve the quality of their lives, particularly where they suffer from trauma or deprivation. In this process, those dedicated to human services also strive to help people find meaning to their lives. As a by-product, working in the human services field contributes to one's own search for life's meaning, as one's own needs for giving and for contributing to the common good are actualized.

The Creative Potential of Human Beings

The fifth fundamental value of human services management concerns the creative potential of all human beings, the flowering of each individual. In recent times, it can be traced to the writings of psychologists Abraham Maslow (1954) and Carl Rogers (1977). The humanistic educator George Leonard states its fundamental premise clearly:

> But perhaps the most pervasive evil of all rarely appears in the news. This evil, the waste of human potential, is particularly painful to recognize, for it strikes our parents and children, our friends and brothers, ourselves. (1968, 23–24)

The recent neohuman potential movement was essentially a move toward a holistic approach to all of life and toward the realization of human potential in body, mind, and spirit. Carl Rogers, one of its leading spokespersons, wrote that he could see our society moving

- Toward the exploration of self, and the development of the richness of the total, individual, responsible human soma—mind and body.
- Toward the prizing of individuals for what they *are,* regardless of sex, race, status, or material possessions.
- Toward a more genuine and caring concern for those who need help.
- Toward creativity of all sorts—in thinking and exploring—in the areas of social relationships, the arts, social design, architecture, urban and regional planning, science, and the study of psychic phenomena.

> To me, these are not frightening trends but exciting ones. In spite of the darkness of the present, our culture may be on the verge of a great evolutionary-revolutionary leap. (1977, 282)

Others would use the term *social revolution* to describe the development of the human potential movement that was triggered by the civil rights movement of the mid-1960s. It continues to unfold as blacks, Hispanics, women, gays and lesbians, the elderly, the physically and developmentally disabled, and others form groups to seek recognition, acceptance, and their share of society's bounty. Based on the work of psychiatrist Elisabeth Kübler-Ross and the hospice movement, even the process of death and dying is being viewed and approached differently, thus perhaps answering Norman Brown's concern that "the inability to affirm death carries with it the inability to enter into life" (1974, 28).

The number of respected writers who subscribe to the fulfillment of human potential as a basic value seems endless. Many subscribe to the thesis that most human beings use a very small fraction of their capacities and potentialities. Again, a quote from Campbell:

> We yearn for something that never was on land or sea—namely the fulfillment of that intelligible character that only the unique individual can bring forth. This is what Schopenhauer called "earned character." You bring forth what is potential within you and no one else. (1974, 80)

Within the field of modern organization and management then, human services management can be distinguished by its unique set of generic set of value underpinnings:

- Humans are beings, not things.
- Human beings are godlike, not animals.
- Each human being is unique.
- There is meaning to life for each individual and for all of us collectively.
- Each human being has a creative potential that can and should be permitted to flower.

Each student and practitioner in this profession is faced with the challenge of identifying, internalizing, and expressing these values in the operations and management of their human services organization.

Challenge and Commitment: An Ideological Framework

Human services managers do not operate in a vacuum; they are the keepers and shapers of the modern welfare state. As such they need to have a clear vision of the ideological framework within which they operate. Regardless of personal political-economic philosophy, when accepting a position in human services management, one accepts a commitment to bring the highest quality of life to *all* inhabitants of our nation, particularly those with the greatest need. This requires a continuous analysis of the impact of the welfare systems unique to our society. It also presents a professional and personal challenge for the human services manager.

Some fifty years ago, we methodically set out to create a society where people would all be assured a fundamental quality of life—from cradle to grave. We may feel some pride that we have accomplished this task for 85 percent of our populace. But many elements of our current system are out of balance and are supporting a trend toward *two* U.S. societies—one for the privileged and one for the deprived. The goal of human services managers, and all of us committed to human services management as a profession, is to bring the highest quality of life and welfare for all, with the burden of such shared fairly by all.

Professionals must learn to balance their personal ideology with that of the organization in which they work and with that of their profession. The human services profession is committed to the continuous improvement of society for all inhabitants of that society. To carry out this commitment, human services managers are challenged to effectively manage their organizations, as well as to continually reshape and manage the large systems within which these organizations are set. The dynamic, creative human services manager therefore seeks proficiency in *institutional and systemic* management. The task at hand is complex and pressing: to sustain a strong economy and preserve our great health and welfare accomplishments while preventing a split America, which could put in jeopardy our form of social and political democracy.

Distinctive Characteristics of Human Services Management

The changes in our thinking and perception, the rapid growth in size and complexity of our society, and the quantum increase of the rate of change in our lives are symptomatic of three phenomena. Combined they form the essence of the distinctive features of all types of human services:

- All human services organizations deal with multifaceted and complex human beings who are increasingly being viewed in comprehensive holistic terms. Equally important, there is both the pressure and possibility for dealing with each person on an individualized basis.

- The natural setting for human services institutions is interorganizational in nature. It is difficult to find any human services manager who does not have to deal with interorganizational, interprofessional, interfunctional, and interdisciplinary relationships, processes, and mechanisms. Human services managers therefore manage with two simultaneous and coexisting forms of management: **institutional management** and **systemic management**. This is no mean task; it not only requires proficiency in each but also the artful balancing of one alongside the other.

- The environment and provision of human services opportunities is dynamic and changing at an incredibly rapid pace.

What can we conclude from these statements? First, the extraordinary character and mission of human services management necessitates a dynamic approach to management; second, dealing with such a continuously interactive environment of human and organizational relationships demands a creative approach to management. In other words, rather than thinking of human services management as a fixed set of knowledge, skills, approaches, and techniques, the management of human services organizations is something continually changing and evolving. Not only is the management of one human services organization different from another but also managing the same human services agency changes continually as its environment changes. For the human services manager, the implications are profound as each manager provides his own continually evolving definition and redefinition of human services management.

Creative is defined by Webster as *inventive,* based on the Latin *to come up, to discover.* Other words from Webster include *devise, think up, originate,* and *produce.* It therefore appears that a contemporary approach to human services calls for dynamic, creative management, which connotes a continuous process of creation: the act of originating or causing to exist *orderly processes* within a *constantly changing environment.* The former emphasizes *institutional* management; the latter, *systemic* management.

Dynamic, creative management is both old and new. It was set forth by one of the founders of modern management, Mary Parker Follett. As a human services leader during the first quarter of the twentieth century, she fostered the concept of dynamic management. In her book *Creative Experience,* she states:

> When we have really acquired the dynamic habit of mind which we boast of now, and think always in terms of process, we also think of both organism and environment, individual and situation, as activities, and that will make it easier to understand the activity of functional relating . . . the relating which frees and integrates and creates.
>
> We can now think of experience more as a creating than a verifying process. (1924, 129–30)

Throughout this text, Mary Parker Follett will be used as our model of the dynamic, creative human services manager. She was the first to point us in the direction of the distinctive nature of our field. Not only is the environment of human services organizations dynamic but more importantly, to deal with that environment, human services managers must employ management approaches that can truly be characterized as creative.

Common Themes

Several themes are at the heart of dynamic, creative human services management. They are worth remembering and will appear and reappear throughout this book. They are the following:

1. The generic mission of human services organizations is the shaping and maintaining of an environment that is responsive to peoples' efforts to improve the quality of their lives.

2. To achieve this mission, the human services manager sets the tone by creating an organizational climate that is supportive to professionals and staff as they foster the responsive environment.
3. There is no such thing as codified human services management. Instead, the human services manager fashions her own form of management creatively, almost day-by-day. This is achieved through the assembling of different administrative techniques and technologies that form **management repertoires**, uniquely fashioned and refashioned in response to the dynamic changes of the social and institutional environment.
4. Organizations and systems are self-regulating. They should therefore be designed to be self-managed by employees and clients as much as by managers.
5. The primary measure of effectiveness for human services management is the real impact such services have on improving the quality of clients' lives.
6. We now have the knowledge and technology for dealing with each client's case (individual or family) as a discrete organizational unit having a unique set of transdisciplinary services.
7. Human services organizations and systems are becoming so dynamic and complex that clients need to be educated to recognize that they are a major locus of responsibility for managing services that maximize effectiveness of outcomes.
8. The human services manager needs to be proficient in both organizational (institutional) and systemic (strategic) management.
9. The essence of human services management is coping with the continual presence of tensions between two or more equally legitimate but opposing value-choices.

Throughout the text, we will strive to continually emphasize, illustrate, and test these common themes of dynamic, creative human services management.

Summary

There is a generic professional field shared by managers of all human services organizations and systems, regardless of the setting or environment in which they operate. Because of commonalities in the field of human services management, a generic core of knowledge and skills are required for all managers who practice in this field. On this core, one can build an experiential base of additional knowledge and skills required for the specific environment chosen as a career: for example, social services, health, mental health, education, gerontology, developmental disabilities, and recreation—be it in public, nonprofit, or proprietary settings. In addition, managers who choose careers in this field bed their careers in the core, generic values that form the foundation of human services management: Humans must be treated as beings, not things; human beings should not be dehumanized or treated as animallike but can and should aspire to godlike qualities; each human being is unique; human beings can be aided in their search for meaning in life; and human beings can be aided in the efforts to achieve the full potential of their uniqueness.

There are several themes that occur throughout the book. Collectively, they identify the distinctive nature of human services management, that which sets it apart from other types of organizational and systems management. Because of the dynamic, even kinetic, environment of human services organizations and systems, continual creativity is a fact of life if one hopes to achieve effectiveness as a manager. The dynamic, creative human services manager seeks proficiency to preserve our society's great health and welfare accomplishments, while preventing a split in American society that could jeopardize our form of social and political democracy. This is the ideological challenge and commitment shared by all managers who seek careers in the human services.

2

Reconciling Conflicting Value-Tensions

Governance of Self by Self Versus Governance of Self by Others

I Shall Versus Thou Shalt
Freedom Versus Order
Democracy Versus Dominance
Anarchy Versus Totalitarianism

Equal Access Versus Specialized Treatment

Specialist Versus Generalist
Professional Versus Layperson
Calculative-Task Orientation Versus Intuitive-Relations Orientation
Providing Services Versus Educating for Self-Provision

The Tension Between the Universal and the Particular

Client-Specific Versus Client-Aggregate
Systems Maintenance Versus Systems Change
Political Versus Professional
Image Versus Substance
Career Future Versus Job Now

Summary

As this chapter's case illustrates, the human services manager faces a number of dilemmas when dealing with conflicting value-choices. You bring to the task of human services management a personal set of attitudes, beliefs, and values that will subtly but inevitably control the way in which you manage and influence the choices you make. Multiple sets of opposing pressures and tensions—all of them legitimate—will pull at you simultaneously. There are no clear road signs, and you will be so caught up in the day-to-day activities that you may be unaware of how your carefully developed human services value base is being eroded by the unrelenting pressures of the situation, sending you down paths you have no wish to travel.

Case 2.1 _____

Part 1: Managing a District Office
for the Department of Income Security

The clerical supervisors studied the memo listing the complaints and demands that the workers had sent Tara Mars, director of the district office. Finally, Janet Farrell, who had been working the longest in the office, spoke up: "What do you want us to do with this memo, Tara? It's like all the others I've read over the years."

"That's just it, Janet," Tara responded. "Some of these complaints can't be solved; they're an unavoidable part of our type of work. As we all know, we've been trying unsuccessfully for years to deal with them. Now, how do you think I should respond to the memo?"

"Well," Janet answered as she turned to the group, "let's start with the first one, case assignment. Anybody have any ideas about how to meet the workers' demands?"

"Sorry to interrupt, Janet," Tara broke in. "I think we need to take a different approach. Why should we deal with these demands? Why don't we talk instead about a process by which the workers can make their own changes around here, with our support?"

"You have to be kidding, Tara," Joe Adler, another supervisor commented. "We work for the ultimate in bureaucracies, we're about to be automated by computers, and you think the workers have the freedom to make their own ground rules?"

From their body language, it was clear that all of them agreed strongly with Joe. Turning to Joe, Tara answered, "Look, Joe, you've already seen other changes around here that you didn't think could be pulled off. Why not more?"

"Sure, Tara," Joe responded. "In the past two years we have completely refurbished this building, all two hundred and sixty-three of us have great ergonomic chairs; and the atmosphere is upbeat, positive, and cheery—that in itself is unheard of for a welfare office. But this is chiefly because of *you* and the way you are. And you are a boss who has the ear of the department commissioners. The system is simple: The workers complain to us; we cry on your shoulders; and then you go to headquarters and get what you can for us."

"That's just it, Joe," Tara said. "We just might have the freedom to turn this around one hundred and eighty degrees; we can put into place Tom Peters' inverted triangle organization that places the workers at the top of the organization and the bosses at the bottom."

Joe commented, "I know Peters is a popular management writer, Tara. But most of his work is with profit-making corporations. I don't think his ideas can work in public organizations."

"To a large degree, you're right, Joe," Tara answered. "But state and federal regulations and an automated computer system provide a great amount of order and rigor for our work. These create the conditions that give us the freedom to work out many of our internal processes."

"Actually, Tara," Janet joined in, "the biggest problem you've got is getting the workers to accept the responsibility for dealing with their own problems. They've had years of conditioning: Bosses call the shots, make all the decisions. So they let the bosses deal with the tough problems, find solutions, and make changes. Workers just pray that the bosses are nice enough and have enough clout with their own supervisors to make changes that will solve the problems."

"Janet, that's exactly the issue," Tara responded. "Now tell me, what *we* can do to turn this around one hundred and eighty degrees. How can we get the workers to buy into a process where they organize themselves to tackle tough problems themselves and use us to help them in this process?"

Janet looked at Tara and then at the other clerical supervisors: "Well, guys, any ideas how we can turn this around?"

Choices for any manager are always difficult. For the human services manager, they can sometimes seem almost impossible. The environment of human services management is complex and replete with a multiplicity of tensions, with one viable value pitted against another viable value. This chapter examines some of these value-tensions in order to emphasize a crucial point. The function of the human services manager is to cope with a dynamic set of seemingly irreconcilable value-tensions that challenge the societal institutions devoted to human-oriented services, and frequently the ideologies on which they are based.

For the dynamic, creative human services manager, the process of coping with irreconcilable value-tensions takes place within boundaries (Figure 2.1). One set of boundaries consists of generic values of human services management on the one side, and on the other, the values inherent in each situation

Figure 2.1   Boundaries of the Dynamic,
Creative Human Services Manager

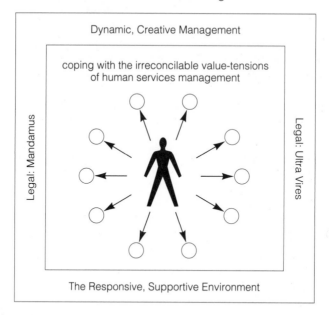

in which choices have to be made. In addition, along with all other professionals in human services organizations, the manager is bounded by two legal constraints:

- **Mandamus**: A legal writ issued by a court requiring that a specified action be taken by an organizational official

- **Ultra vires**: The potential for a citizen to demand in front of a court to know the legal power of an organizational official to take the action he has taken

These boundaries are a continual challenge. There is perennial pressure to be fully aware of the legal constraints of human services provision—those that force you to take actions against your best judgment and those that impede your decisions to take actions when judged necessary.

Besides legal boundaries, choices flow out of values. There is, on the one hand, the need to inculcate the organization and system with the fundamental values of human services. On the other hand, each decision and action will necessitate choosing among alternative values. Reflecting on the values inherent in the situation is therefore an ever-present task for human services managers.

Let us examine some of the value-tensions you will have to deal with as a human services manager.

Governance of Self by Self Versus Governance of Self by Others

The first basic tension we deal with is the fundamental American democratic concept of self-governance. This concept holds that an institution—whether a church, a civic association, a corporation, or a small-town government—can shape its own governance processes with minimum control from an external source. The self-governance concept is in counterdistinction to a concept of governance in which a strong central ruling body dictates the way in which all institutions will be governed.

In the 1960s and 1970s, we entered an era where the emphasis on self-governance shifted to the personal lives of our inhabitants. It is illustrated by the "revolution" of the 1960s and 1970s, which was directed at the empowerment of minority groups (e.g., blacks and Hispanics, women, the elderly, and the disabled).

The tension between self-governance versus governance by others is really the sum total of the following tensions:

- I shall versus thou shalt
- Freedom versus order
- Democracy versus dominance
- Anarchy versus totalitarianism

Central to all these tensions is the issue of power: the power over persons that is entrusted to the human services manager for the protection of the individual, the institution, and society.

To help us understand the importance of power in our personal lives and in our organizational role, we need to be able to differentiate between the different types of power as defined by Rollo May (1972), a noted psychotherapist and author:

- Exploitative (of others)
- Manipulative (over others)
- Competitive (against others)
- Nutrient (for others)
- Integrative (with others)

From a developmental point of view, if all humans matured as adults without any undue psychological need for exploitative-manipulative power, perhaps we could fashion both a political and organizational world based on the principle of governance of self by self.

Competitive and nutrient power both connote some level of imbalance in the relationships among human beings. Integrative power conjures up the image of an ideal sharing of power with others. But even if we accept the thesis that the flower of each individual's potential and creativity is in the hands of that individual alone, we must deal with the tension of the probable conflict between individual behavior and group behavior and the necessity at times for controls and limits exercised by others over the individual.

Let us briefly examine the tensions that represent different aspects of the classic human services management conflict between governance of self by self versus governance of self by others.

I Shall Versus Thou Shalt

In Part 1 of Case 2.1, Tara Mars continually tries to stress the need for every member of the staff to be responsible for shaping their own environment. Yet at every turn, she was frustrated by the pressures to have others govern staff behavior. It was a continual tension for her.

This tension is classic. It has plagued people from time immemorial. It can best be characterized by the monotheistic-ethical religions, which placed emphasis on "thou shalt," as opposed to the Greek ethical philosophers who stressed "I shall." The former focused on all members of society, whereas the latter addressed only a responsible, elitist element of society. Nevertheless, there is a tension between "thou shalt" and "I shall," and perhaps there is no solution.

The religions of the Levant (Judaism, Christianity, and Islam) would argue that ethical codes are easy to describe but difficult to apply in practice. Thus, millions of people, throughout history and currently as well, believe that the only realistic way to live an ethical, responsible, mature life is to follow a set of "thou shalt" commandments that reflect appropriate prescriptions of human behavior. "Thou shalt" connotes a source of norms that flows from religious or supraindividual sources—a notion of supreme being or the group norms of society, a concept that Joseph Campbell (1976) defines as the fundamental purpose of mythology.

Those who subscribe to an "I shall" philosophy of behavior, on the other hand, have an extraordinary level of trust in ideal human qualities. They also have strong faith that ethics in practice are clear-cut, when in fact they are often obscure and subject to wide interpretation. Assume, for a moment, that Tara Mars could issue a set of guidelines and then give each of the employees in her district office the discretion to make their own judgments about what type of income and service supports each client could receive. Would fraud occur? How could the federal government compute the "error rate" when decision-actions were based on the judgments of each employee and not on the rational application of detailed regulations? Would such a system end up in an inordinately extravagant Aid to Families with Dependent Children (AFDC) budget compared to current levels of expenditures?

The tension between "I shall" and "thou shalt" begs an even more fundamental issue: Can each human have a private mythology or religion to guide her own life, or must society continue to rely on group mythologies and group religions for the sources of everyone's norms? What implications will this have in a few decades as our society reaches the point where demographics will have changed drastically and cultural diversity replaces the current notion of a homogenous culture?

Like it or not, human services managers must deal with the tension between the recognition that most people need a "thou shalt" code and the desire to help people move toward an ideal "I shall" mode, with personal ethical-moral anchor points.

Freedom Versus Order

In *Matrix*—a book that describes conceptually and technically how to construct and maintain a **matrix organization**, a modern space-age form of organization—Stanley Davis and Paul Lawrence assert that

> All forms of social organization have two simultaneous needs that are often at odds with each other: freedom and order. Freedom springs from intuition and leads to innovation. Order stems from intelligence and provides efficiency. Both are essential, but are they compatible with each other? (1977, xi)

It would probably *not* startle you to realize that standard operating procedures (SOPs) are the foundation and framework of a human services organization. Along with legislative and administrative regulations, manuals, uniform procedures, checklists, and the like, SOPs create the conditions for regularity and order in an agency. And difficult as it may be to accept, order and regularity in a human services organization are a prerequisite for developing the environment for creative performance and management of human services.

When everyone—clients, staff, policymakers, and the public—can anticipate the fundamental processes to be carried out with dispatch and regularity, then the conditions are set for everyone to be creative and innovative in carrying out the agency's missions effectively and productively. The rationale that order creates the conditions for freedom and creativity is based on four premises:

- *First Things First.* Clients and staff alike expect an organizational environment that runs smoothly and in an orderly fashion, from the smallest detail to the most all-encompassing policy.

- *Conservation of Energy.* To devote physical and psychic energy to tracing a piece of paper that delayed services to a client or retarded the pay raise of an employee requires unnecessary energy expenditure. To meet once again to needlessly discuss an issue on which consensus was reached at a meeting three months ago is a wasted effort for all concerned. Clients, staff, and administrators all want to devote the maximum amount of time to those activities that are personally and professionally productive and important.

- *Clients and Staff Deserve an Optimum Environment.* In a perfect management world, clients and employees deserve a hassle-free environment in which everything works reasonably smoothly.

- *The Halo Image.* Like it or not, the image of efficiency that a manager achieves from order in the execution of fundamental processes creates a halo effect—the agency is considered, ipso facto, effective and efficient. It creates the climate for innovation. The opposite is even more true. "Sloppy" management creates a climate in which creativity is viewed negatively. "How can they be permitted to innovate when they can't even do the day-to-day work effectively?"

That order is the cornerstone for dynamic, creative human services management is paradoxical. It is also difficult to deal with the tension between freedom and order. The manager must be prepared to deal with the increased level of managerial complexity where such tension exists. Capturing the best of both is a classic challenge for human services managers.

Democracy Versus Dominance

If one traces modern administration in the United States back to its roots, one will discover a tension between democracy and administration. Democracy is dedicated to the elimination of dominance in political structures. But to be effective, democracy requires a cadre of people (administrators or "public servants") who are given special status—the power to dominate others in order to ensure the fruits of democracy for all inhabitants. It is not without reason that public servants in ancient Greece had to take the following pledge, known as the *Athenian code.*

> We will ever strive for the ideals and sacred things of the city. Both alone and with many, we will unceasingly seek to quicken the sense of public duty. We will revere and obey the city's laws; we will transmit the city not only not less, but greater, better and more beautiful than it was transmitted to us.

In modern times, Edward Lehan (1978) has noted that "making democracy work" is the lodestar of organizational professionals in a representative republic. Lawrence O'Toole (1977) traces the tension of democracy versus dominance to the dichotomy between policy formation (politics) versus policy execution (administration.)

In discussing "critical theory," Trent Schroyer (1973) considers domination as the coerced control of human behavior. The vehicle is the technocrat who is guided by an "instrumental notion of reason." There is no question that at times Tara Mars feels like a "technocrat." Despite her deep commitment to democratic and human services values, she is reduced to being an instrument of the power structure and establishment of society in carrying out the dictates that dominate the lives of so many thousands of people in her district.

Human services managers everywhere are left with the tensions of democracy versus domination. At the least, they must be sensitive to their special status in a society that has entrusted them with a special power to be used for the common good. It is therefore with great seriousness that I suggest that it might be fitting for all managers of human services organizations to be sworn into the profession with the pledging of the Athenian, or a similar, code. It is as desirable today as it was 2400 years ago and no less appropriate than the Hippocratic oath is to the medical profession.

Anarchy Versus Totalitarianism

Organizationally, this polarity exists between an environment of self-motivating, self-educating, self-judging people and a rigid hierarchical structure with prescribed behavior that leaves little choice to the individual. Whereas an **anarchic organization** might be characterized as "unfocused," "improvisational," and "unorganized," the **totalitarian organization** could be described as "rational," "objective," or "economizing"; yet there is no guarantee that the latter is more effective than the former, at least in the long-term sense.

It is worth noting that many "rational" management authors propose dual roles for administrators: one role within the bureaucracy as a detached specialist behaving in a dispassionate manner, dealing fairly with all citizens with no preconditioned biases; and the other role as an educator, engendering in coworker, colleague, and client alike a sense of duty, responsibility, sensitivity, and accountability. As James Charlesworth writes,

> Efficiency is not the prime desideratum in a republic form of government; efficiency within liberty should be the heart of the administrator's credo. The administrative instrument of education is conspicuously appropriate to this end. (1951, 699)

Perhaps it is ironic that like other human services managers, Tara Mars had to deal with the tension of installing new methods that some would characterize as authoritarian, while creating an environment that educates those in the environment to operate as self-guided, self-responsible, and self-accountable individuals.

In whatever form it takes, the tension between governance of self by self and governance of self by others is ever present for the creative, dynamic human services manager.

Equal Access Versus Specialized Treatment

As you will explore in the coming chapter, many respected organizational theorists view the organization as a carefully designed instrument that requires "functionaries" whose values have been neutralized. Instead of a natural system that developed organically, it is an artificial system of carefully constructed rules and roles that has made it possible for societies to provide the products and services necessary for modern-day life everywhere.

In a society dedicated to equality of opportunity, societal institutions are intended to be not only the vehicles for achieving that equality but also for ensuring that such equality is maintained. You want equal access to the opportunity, for example, of attending a university, driving a motor vehicle, receiving adequate health insurance for yourself and your family, eating in a restaurant, attending a movie, opening a bank account, and on and on. Equal access is important.

You want the "rules" for access to be open and fair; and once pronounced, you want the rules to be followed by an organizational employee who deals with you in a detached manner. You would not want to be denied a motor vehicle driver's license because the employee issuing the license does not like people with red hair, which you have. Such action would be arbitrary, denying you equal access. If you proved that denial of the license was based on the employee's own prejudice, you could appear and seek an overruling of the decision. You could even have hair color eliminated from the licensing procedure, if it was an official organizational criterion, by proving that hair color has nothing to do with the privilege or safety of driving. In a nation devoted to democratic ideals, we all want societal institutions to be based on equal access.

But let us now look beyond this relatively objective criterion. What about elements like humaneness and sympathy? Can the very rules and regulations designed to ensure equal access constrain a human services manager's ability to treat clients with dignity? This is the tension illustrated in Part 2 of Case 2.1 in which Tara Mars suggests that administrators can bend their own regulations. What if you were a working man with a wife and six children who will lose his job because his license was revoked for speeding—going 56 mph in a 55 mph maximum zone? If you were the person who had to decide to revoke or not to revoke in this case, how would you decide? If you decided *not* to revoke under these circumstances, how do you think a bachelor would feel when he hears about the decision if his license was revoked for also going 56 mph in a 55 mph zone?

Case 2.1

Part 2: Managing a District Office
for the Department of Income Security

By the time she got to the meeting in her office, Tara Mars found her top staff arguing loudly with each other.

"Whoa!" she yelled out. "Stop for two minutes, and somebody bring me aboard. I thought this meeting was to deal with the latest federal report on our error rate. It's obvious you're dealing with an even more emotional issue; all of you seem worked up. What's going on?"

"As you know, Tara," her deputy Jill Spahn said, "today is the last day for winter fuel energy-assistance applications. By the looks of the line right now, and it's already 3 PM, we'll never process everyone by the 4:30 PM quitting time. So we're split up over how to deal with it."

"What options have you spelled out?" Tara asked.

"Jack and I want to bring them all inside the building now and just complete the top part of the application, giving their name and address, and then set up appointments to complete the process," Jill responded. "Cal and Marian feel that we should process as many as we can by 4:30 and then tell the rest we're sorry, time ran out."

"In all fairness, Tara," Cal added quickly, "Marian and I feel that they had plenty of time to apply for energy assistance. They just procrastinated. This happens every year. By closing at 4:30 with many applicants literally out in the cold, we'll be doing them a favor and conveying a message loud and clear to all applicants in the future."

"Cal," Tara answered, "we've worked hard to create an upbeat, positive environment that treats our clients with dignity. This has been very hard, given a lot of factors. Sure, I agree with you; educating our clients is an ever-present role we need to play. But can't we teach a bigger lesson by showing them that we care?"

"What does that mean in practical terms, Tara?" Cal asked.

"We stay open, all night if necessary, until we process everyone of them," Tara answered.

"We'd be buying a lot of problems. Will our staff work overtime? Have we got that much budget for overtime? Can we even do this without front-office approval? What happens if we're still processing at midnight, when it's beyond the legal deadline?" Cal rattled off the questions.

"Let's take the last question," Tara responded. "Laws are our foundation and must be carried out; regulations, on the other hand, can be bent because we made them ourselves."

"Have *you* got authority for all this, Tara?" Marian asked.

"If we are all in agreement, we can inform headquarters that this is our best judgment and we have authorized it," Tara answered. "A bigger issue is can we sell the staff? What about incentives? We can bring in supper and offer comp time or overtime."

"But wait, Tara," Jill added quickly. "Our staff is too specialized; only around twenty can deal with the energy-assistance procedures. I'm beginning to wish I had supported the effort to make all the workers generalists. We've got over two hundred and fifty workers, each of whom is specialized to only process one of nine categories of programs. For any one category of program, we're limited in how many applications we can process each hour."

"Well, to tell you the truth," Cal added, "we can probably get another fifteen who used to process energy-assistance applications in previous years. They'll still remember the energy process. What do we do now?"

"Get out a memo informing staff," Jack answered.

"No, Jack," Tara responded, "for something this unorthodox and fast, we need a personal touch. Let's hit the hallways and see if we can't sell our approach to the staff who we will need to work overtime. Work up a list of who we have to talk to and ask to join us in this big push."

"Let's start with those we know will probably support the idea, then leave it up to them to sell the others," Jill pitched in. "And Tara, you're best for calling the front office!"

"Well, in this case, we have a lot going for us," Tara said, reassuring herself. "Our clients legally have access to this program; and this is consistent with the department's new effort to serve clients with dignity."

"Well," Cal responded, "if we can pull this off and come out with our skins intact, I'll be happy to treat for happy hour at the end of this week."

"That's a real first," Jack quipped, "and it sure provides us with the incentive to pull this off."

Such value-tensions are present in all our societal institutions. We have little or no differentiation among business, public, and nonprofit organizations on this issue. In a democracy, equal access versus privileged access is such a volatile issue (a holdover of the monarch bestowing favors on family, friends, or the wealthy) that all organizations are watched by the collective society for their equal- versus privileged-access behavior.

Yet the concern for human dignity is a counterpressure, favoring privileged access under certain conditions that are humane in the particular (the case of the working father with revoked driver's license) or in some generality (let us adjust rules for a certain group because they have been disadvantaged in the past). The pressure to "tilt" toward human dignity is strong and persuasive for human services organizations. As Eugene Dvorin and Robert Simmons stress, "The business of bureaucracy is not business on behalf of business. It is now business in the public interest on behalf of the individual . . . upon an overriding sensitivity for human dignity (1972, 46).

The tension between equal access versus human dignity can be better understood by examining what may be considered a set of subtensions:

- Specialist versus generalist
- Professional versus layperson
- Calculative-task orientation versus intuitive-relations orientation
- Providing services versus educating for self-provision

Specialist Versus Generalist

Long ago Harold Laski (1930) noted the problem with specialization in governmental organizations. It was his observation that practitioners whose vision becomes so intensely focused that it destroys their sense of proportion, and who place expertise above social need, are fatal to good government.

Laski's observation was restated by Herman Kahn and his associates (1976) in what they saw as an increasing problem of "educated incapacity." In other words, narrowly focused, specialized training and experience has a by-product: an acquired or learned inability to understand or see a problem, much less a solution.

There is concern among many writers that extreme specialization in modern society has led to technocracy, which has replaced democracy because the politician and the citizen becomes dependent on the technocrat. Jurgen Habermas, for example, feels that the roles of politicians and professionals have been reversed in modern society; the former have become the mere agents of a "scientific intelligentisia."

Many writers compare specialists with generalists: **Specialists** are concerned about efficiency, quantification, productivity, and serving institutions; **generalists** are concerned about care, quality, household, and community character. These writers argue that generalists are "nurturers" and specialists are "exploiters." Many writers are alarmed at the overspecialization in society, but Wendell Berry is perhaps the most critical, calling it a "disease of the modern character":

> Specialization is thus seen to be a way of institutionalizing, justifying and paying highly, a calamitous disintegration and scattering out of the various functions of character: workmanship, care, conscience, responsibility.
>
> Even worse, a system of specialization requires the abdication to specialists of various competencies and responsibilities that were once personal and universal (1977, 59).

Human services managers continually deal with the tension of specialization. It is a "you cannot live with them and you cannot live without them" type of tension: both the generalist's and the specialist's perceptions and skills are necessary. How can these individuals' viewpoints be balanced? Better still, how can each be trained to see the other's point of view? These are the challenges to managers of human services organizations.

Professional Versus Layperson

Seymour Sarason and Elizabeth Lorentz (1979) trace the rapid rise of a professionally dominated society and the problems it presents for people interested in maintaining control over their own lives. Noting that one of the strongest motivations for becoming a professional is the "quest for personal and social worth," the authors are very concerned with the phenomenon that defines a problem in such a manner that only professionals can be the solution.

Sarason and Lorentz's conclusion is one that will particularly haunt human services managers in their systemic management role (managing cross-organizational systems). In effect, Sarason and Lorentz conclude that a problem cannot be solved because there is either an insufficient number of professionals or inadequate resources for professionals required to solve the problem. They also are bothered by the unwillingness of professionals to share decision making with those most affected by their decisions. Society may well be unable to solve societal problems when they are defined solely from the professional's perspective.

Ivan Illich is perhaps the best known, if somewhat radical, critic of the overly dominant role of professionals in society's human services provisioning. He views the midtwentieth century as the "age of disabling professions": educators, physicians, social workers, and psychiatrists who disable their clients' ability to care for themselves. In four separate and well-documented books, Illich researches several themes, all of which have a common antiprofessional, prolayperson conclusion:

- "The needs of people in society are assessed by professionals primarily with an eye to assure continued need for professionals in society" (1978).
- "Learning would be returned to people if we would de-school society" (1971).
- "In developed nations, people spend one sixth of their waking hours as passengers and an equal amount of time to feed the fuel-dominant transportation system" (1973).
- "The greater the level of medical domination in our health care, the greater our inability to provide adequate, affordable health care for the majority of people" (1976).

Illich is concerned about balancing human dignity and societal economic productivity. Extreme professionalism, in his view, is counterproductive. At the base of his arguments is the concept of "conviviality": the return to **use-values** instead of dependence on **commodity values** in society; the return to our major societal resource—*people's energy to do for themselves.*

Professionals are the mainstay of the human services systems but they can also be the main enemy of these systems. Dealing with the tension between the professional and the layperson is an important element of struggling with the larger tension of equal access versus human dignity.

Calculative-Task Orientation Versus Intuitive-Relations Orientation

Human beings deal with every situation they face in one of two ways: thinking or feeling. At one level, when faced with a situation that requires a reaction or a response, each of us analyzes and examines it rationally, methodically calculating what different tasks or options are available to deal with the situation. At another level, our emotions deal with the same situation and, reacting intuitively, focus on human relationships. Usually, the two modes are combined, and together lead us to some conclusions of how to deal with the particular situation.

In organizational situations, there is a strong bias toward the **calculative-task orientation**. This is as true for human services organizations as it is for other institutions. But for many human services professionals, there is a strong bias toward the **intuitive-relations orientation**. Even though we all know that every problem-solving situation requires both a thinking and a feeling response, many human services managers find themselves torn between these two orientations. And too often, managers are accused of being biased toward the calculative-task orientation, while clinicians feel accused of being too biased toward the intuitive-relations orientation.

For example, in the situations described in the case of Tara Mars, the employees of the Income Security District Office might find themselves in great difficulty with state and federal government auditors if they were to respond to the question "On what grounds did you approve the eligibility to this case?" with "My intuitive reaction to the client's situation!" Indeed, determining eligibility for transfer payment programs (e.g., AFDC, Food Stamps, Medicaid) is so calculative that it can be programmed for a computer.

If Tara Mars's own brother were to appear at the district office requesting emergency aid, he would have to complete the forms and be subjected to eligibility criteria like all other clients. Yet, how would Tara react if her brother called her for emergency aid, at home in the evening? Would she be oriented to think in a calculative way, or would she react emotionally, using her own judgment that her brother needed her help and support, whether she approved of the reasons why such help was necessary? Theoretically, for Tara and her district office workers, if clients need emergency aid and if the request is authentic and urgent, assistance should be provided. Rules and procedures should be secondary in dictating human services organizational behavior.

But the reality of human services management is that Tara Mars knows she operates in an environment that for many reasons is biased toward the calculative-task orientation. She and her human services manager colleagues therefore devote time and energy to trying to work out other options and service pathways for clients who do not precisely meet the calculative-task criteria. It should be noted that there are nonprofit community agencies that can operate in environments in which the intuitive-relations orientation is stronger.

Another conflict between these two orientations expresses itself in a more personalized fashion. Some human services workers and managers have a tendency toward favoring the calculative-task orientation and expressing it in their day-to-day work: the job must get done, and one has to devote full energy to that effort, paying little beyond the minimum attention to interpersonal human relations with co-workers. In effect, "We're being paid to get the job done, not to be a buddy to those with whom we work." Other workers and managers favor the intuitive-relations orientation, with a leadership style that focuses on relationships with co-workers. An employee-centered leader is one who accepts the thesis that a group of employees who enjoy working together are more self-motivated and thus more productive. Thus, devoting time to interpersonal relationships in an organization is essential to organizational and management leadership.

To the task-oriented manager, spending time on employee relations is a waste of time; to the relations-oriented manager, a strict task orientation taps only a small portion of employees' motivation and energy. These values will tug at human services managers, who most likely will use a style that is a mix of both orientations. These orientations have received a great amount of attention from researchers and writers who focus on what is referred to as *situational (contingency) leadership* styles for managers, which we will explore further in Chapter 4.

Providing Services Versus Educating for Self-Provision

The primary theme of dynamic, creative human services management is *the recognition that the generic mission of human services organizations is the shaping and maintaining of an environment that is responsive to and supportive of peoples' efforts to improve the quality of their lives.* If this is true, there is a classic value-tension for human services manager: providing services versus educating for self-provision. The natural tendency for human services managers is to see service provision as their organizational and management strategy of first choice. In actuality, it should be the strategy of last resort.

A mix of value-tensions combines to form this sometimes irreconcilable value-choice. Like it or not, there is a natural tendency on the part of many managers to want to "expand their turf" and become "empire builders" by acquiring more and more resources to manage more and more programs. The larger the amount of resources under a manager's control, the greater his visibility, power, and influence over a particular human services system.

On the other hand, enabling people to use their innate energies and abilities to provide for themselves casts the human services manager as essentially an educator and guide. The primary tactics would be to become a community organizer, serving as a catalyst for energizing and motivating people, individually or in groups, to pull together their own resources and fashion their own human services institutions or systems. The manager applies her leadership skills to create the conditions by which people or institutions can work together so that new or improved services are available for the community.

Although the role of educator-guide is perhaps one of the primary roles for the human services manager, it generally requires the manager to take a low profile, while letting others take the credit for successes. While additional resources flow to the new institution or system, the manager-educator's power base is generally not expanded in the process. For that reason, unless a human services manager has an excellent reputation among the power brokers or is very secure in his position in the community, it takes a great deal of personal and professional fortitude to play the role of educator-leader-community organizer. The tension between the two opposing values, however, remains.

We have dealt with several tensions that arise from conflict between different values dealing with equal access versus human dignity. We move now to more sets of value-tensions, those dealing with the conflict between the universal and the particular in human services organizations.

The Tension Between the Universal and the Particular

The tension between the universal and the particular is actually a composite of a number of subtensions that represent this set, namely:

- Client-specific versus client-aggregate
- Systems maintenance versus systems change
- Political versus professional
- Image versus substance
- Career future versus job now

To illustrate a common situation in dealing with these tensions, let's take an example: Tara Mars's classic problem. As the boss, Tara must place primary emphasis on maximizing the quantity and quality of service opportunities available to the largest number of people; each of her workers places their primary emphasis on finding the most effective way to meet a particular client's needs. Generally, the universal needs of the total district office can be achieved as each client's needs are met. There are, however, situations where this is not possible. If there was, let us say, a significant decrease in workers in the district office assigned to the same number of clients, Tara would have to pressure each worker to spend less time with each case in order to deal with all of the district office's clients. Another reason why the universal-particular tension also operates in human services organizations is because the environment is primarily interorganizational. This means that agencies as a whole have to deal with tensions around boundaries and turf. To what extent should you or your agency work with others for more universal ends versus protecting your own turf, resources, and client base? In systems theory terms, this dynamic equilibrium between competing values illustrates the tension of balancing cooperation with competition so vital for all systems. These are the nature of the tensions being dealt with in Part 3 of Case 2.1.

Case 2.1

Part 3: Managing a District Office
for the Department of Income Security

Tara was having a hard time containing her impatience. A meeting had been called of top managers from three different state agencies. The agenda: to find ways to improve the "Job-Find" system, which had been set up to help AFDC families move toward economic stability by finding jobs. Tara recognized the source of her impatience. Because most of the other managers at the meeting had backgrounds as clinicians, Tara could sense that they were still thinking like clinicians. They had not yet made the transition to approaching the Job-Find system as managers.

Fred Hall, director of the southeastern district office of DSS (the Department of Social Services), was the first to comment: "I know you have all heard this before, but my workers complain that they aren't able to effectively deal with the clients they now have. And, on top of everything, we're pressuring them to work with Job-Find clients. It can't be done, particularly because working with Job-Find clients requires networking and case coordination, not casework. The former are more time-consuming."

"I have a feeling, Fred," Tara responded "that the Job-Find clients are just an additional workload for your workers. Can't you reorganize your office to deal with this new major system?"

"How could he, Tara?" Arlene Baker of the DES (Department of Employment Services) south central district asked. "It's up to our central headquarters to tell us how to reorganize."

"Arlene, I don't understand," Tara responded. "We all received the same memo signed jointly by the secretaries of our three departments. The memo directed us to implement Job-Find in an effective and efficient manner. The rest is up to us."

"I've been around long enough, Tara," Fred broke in, "to know that despite my secretary's go-ahead, our front office still likes to call the shots. But even if they gave me a total go-ahead, I still have an office full of workers who have caseloads much larger than they should have. They always have the feeling that they are cutting corners professionally with clients. And now, an additional workload. I doubt if it can be done. All we can do is try."

"Fred's right, Tara," Sam Hall chimed in. Sam was director of field services for Tara's Department of Income Security (DIS). "Even though we're putting our department's full energies behind the Job-Find system, no extra hands were given to us to implement the new system. So our options are limited."

Tara knew that Sam was in line for a top executive position in her department and didn't want to take any risks that would make him look bad with the secretary. Nevertheless, she responded: "But, Sam, one of our options is to look at what each of us is expected to achieve in our separate district offices and then redesign and reorganize the ways in which we get things done!"

"Are you suggesting that we're not as efficient or effective as we could be, Tara?" Arlene asked.

"No, Arlene," Tara answered. "I'm saying that a manager has several options available for achieving her office's goals and missions. The option selected is determined by the resources available. We'd all like to deal with each client in a professionally comprehensive fashion. But if our resources don't permit us to, we choose another management option."

"But our workers either aren't trained to deal with clients in a different way or would resist any change," Fred noted. "Our hands are tied by those below us and above us. Not only does my staff resist any major changes but also the private services providers in my district always go running to the department secretary whenever I make revisions to our programs. Tell me, Tara, would your staff go along with a radical change in their service-delivery system?"

"We've worked hard at getting an upbeat, positive environment in our district, Fred," Tara answered. "Most of the staff is with me; but as a realist, I know there will be some resistance. Still, it's my personal challenge: creating a level of self-confidence and ownership in the new system that would motivate everyone in the district office."

"Our bosses are really asking for the impossible," Sam added. "There will be major changes in the face of staff resistance; crossing of agency boundaries which creates all types of turf issues; workload increases in a situation where workload is already excessive. But we really have no alternative. We don't have time to sit back and be proud of what we've accomplished; the pressure is on to be more effective and productive. We've been directed to work out a new system, so what choice do we have?"

"That's true, Sam," Tara added. "But the real issue is that our professional image is on the line. We are all experienced and skilled managers. If for no other reason, we should design and implement this new system to prove to ourselves and our co-workers that we are not just another group of "incompetent state employees"! We're as talented managers as the executives of any business corporation. We can pull this off and prove that to ourselves and to our colleagues everywhere."

Client-Specific Versus Client-Aggregate

Many direct-service professionals move into managerial positions in human services organizations. Many have difficulty in making this transition. Their attitudes and skills have been oriented toward individual, specific clients, and so their loyalty is primarily to clients and to their profession. This is illustrated in Part 3 of Case 2.1. That the district office, the department, and even a cross-organizational system also have needs that require loyalty was not recognized and thus not important to many of them. Most difficult of all was the necessity to refocus their attention from one particular client (**client-specific**) to a group of clients who share similar needs (**client-aggregate**). The value stance of the direct-service professional and the manager are identical: the greatest good, the highest quality of life for clients. But the former's training and conditioning is to focus on the individual, specific client; the latter has been trained to focus on the aggregate client, that is, the generalized group of clients as a whole.

To think about devoting time and energy implementing a decision to restructure agency resources to benefit 1000 families headed by single mothers, at the expense of reducing intensive services to 200 current cases of disabled elderly clients, is difficult for the supervisor whose workers know each of the 200 clients intimately and who are focused primarily on meeting their respective individual needs.

Proficiency in benefit-cost analysis can raise some deep philosophical issues on the relative worth of human beings. Whether the human services managers agree or disagree with the value stance of quantifying the relative value of life, they must come to grips with the fact that, in and among the various human services, some clients will receive greater resources at the expense of others. We must therefore recognize and deal with the value-tensions as they exist for many human services managers who are called on to weigh the relative worth of two client-aggregate groups in order to choose the one who will obtain more resources than the other.

This irreconcilable conflict of values is perhaps one of the most haunting for human services managers, particularly those whose career paths to a managerial position led through a career as a clinician in a human services environment.

Systems Maintenance Versus Systems Change

Part 3 of Case 2.1 also illustrates the tension of two other opposing values: one that fosters **systems maintenance** for one in place versus the other that presses for **systems change** in order to adapt to changes in the environment. There are at least three basic reasons why maintaining the system is a natural bias in many human services organizations: (1) to guarantee equal access; (2) to maintain the status quo for the "establishment" (those who hold social-economic-political power); and (3) to minimize the psychic and physical energy output demanded of staff. Because we have dealt with equal-access tension already, let us briefly discuss maintaining the status quo energy-minimization rationale.

There is a tendency on the part of many agencies to attempt to maintain the existing system, but human services managers are continually looking for ways to change that system in marginal and major ways. Thus, one of their roles is that of a community organizer in the classic model:

Model	*Goal*
▪ Locality Development	Self-help; community capacity building and integration
▪ Social Planning	Problem-solving with regard to substantive community problems
▪ Social Action	Shifting of power relationships and resources; basic institutional changes (Rothman 1970)

Human services managers function as community organizers. They can (and should) be dedicated to systems change in the locality development and social-planning models. To what extent that can be totally dedicated to social action is situational. If you truly wish to agitate for changes in opposition to policies of the establishment (those currently empowered in the organization— e.g., a particular board of directors or group of legislators), in our society you might best do this by resigning your position. This would free you up to step outside the system to work in the best interests of your clientele and the public, without the encumbrance of being committed to representing official policy. Yet few professionals would choose to go this far.

Human services managers are thus committed to improving and thereby changing established systems. The tension is not over being dedicated to systems change per se but usually comes down to the rate of change and the extent of change. Some managers prefer incremental change, waiting patiently for an opportunity when the political climate is conducive. But incremental change slows the pace of systems change and may only result in marginal improvement in the face of the need for fundamental, perhaps even radical, change.

If you had been Tara Mars, would you have pressed as hard to change the department's system for more effectively implementing the Job-Find program that was failing because of cumbersome bureaucratic procedures? It required much staff time to make the changes to the system that Tara felt were warranted. She appreciated the fact that one of the strongest and most legitimate reasons for maintaining a system is the need to minimize use of staff time. The environment of human services organizations is dynamic. Once a new issue has been dealt with and routines developed to handle the issue on a regular basis, maintaining the new system is important for conserving the scarce energy and resources of human services agencies.

Reduction of energy requirements provides a good motive for maintaining the system once it is set. The danger is that the system may then no longer be responsive to the situation. Thus, human services managers need supersensitive antennas that constantly scan all routines to assess their ability to respond to clients' and the community's needs. When the mismatch between the need and the system's ability to meet the need is great, the human services manager must then be prepared to overcome the inertia of the currently maintained system and begin to change it.

The need for balancing the tension between systems maintenance and systems change is one that will be with the students of human services management over the course of their careers.

Political Versus Professional

Early in your careers, you will have to make some simple choices in how to approach your position. Will you be devoted primarily to your professional standards and code of ethics, will you mainly be devoted to the politics of the organizational situation, or will you find a way to mediate between the two when they are in opposition? This is another of the irreconcilable value-tensions with which human services managers must deal.

When you take an administrative position, the tension will be reflected by how you allot your primary energies: whom will you respond to first?

- Your *internal* environment—that is, your staff, your colleagues in the organization, getting your own "house" in order
- Your *external* environment—that is, your immediate superiors, your board or political body, your client-interest group, your community, the public

Some experienced human services managers would caution a new appointee to resolve this tension by focusing initially on the internal environment and, once good relationships with subordinates have been established, to then devote attention to the external environment because both are important. Two of the common themes that characterize creative, dynamic human services management reflect these two seemingly opposing values: creation of a community environment that is responsive to people *and* creation of an organizational climate that is supportive to direct-service professionals. While the former focuses on the political forces important for the organization, the latter focuses on the professional forces of the organization; because both are necessary, both must be balanced in some fashion.

There is another dimension to this political-professional tension: Managers may be under pressure to make appointments that are political in nature. Human services managers may place their future careers in jeopardy if they refuse to make appointments under such pressure. They find themselves in the same value-tensions when they are offered a political appointment.

It *is* possible for a professional to be appointed to a management position by a political leader. The professional guarantees loyalty to the politician in return for a guarantee of respect that professionals need to apply neutral competence to the common good and the public interest. Many good professional administrators have distinguished careers as political appointees. But when a professional begins to work with political interests, as an appointee or as an individual, there is the potential that she may cross an invisible and delicate line. If the professional is beholden to a political leader in any way that jeopardizes neutral, objective, and detached judgments on a particular decision or action, then the professional integrity of that individual may be compromised.

Political leadership in pursuit of human services goals is necessary and legitimate. But achieving political leadership requires the support of many interests and resources that usually involves a trade-off that potentially can bias an action or decision. Many professionals become politically active; that too is quite necessary and legitimate. But any professional, human services managers included, must be careful not to cross the fine line where political activism affects neutral competence or judgments. This then presents another often irreconcilable and always difficult value conflict.

Image Versus Substance

During the 1980s, we witnessed the escalation of image management to one of the primary techniques of administration. In our media-oriented society, an individual or an organization is frequently judged more on their image than on substance. In terms of the presidency of the United States, during the past decade the White House has been staffed with media specialists who carefully and skillfully manage the president's image. President Reagan, for example, had the image of being a strong advocate of the balanced budget. Yet, during his presidency, we had record deficits. Even when his vice president gained succession, the image, rather than the substance—although common knowledge—prevailed.

The human services manager has always had to struggle with the tension between devoting energy and skill to the substance of an agency's performance, maximizing the effectiveness of client services and outcomes, while devoting energy to projecting an image of proficiency and effectiveness. Use of media of all types is vital to provide to board, community, funders, and clients information that generates confidence and illustrates how the programs of the agency were managed economically and effectively, while maintaining factual integrity.

Some managers are very skillful at projecting an image of excellence to boards, legislative bodies, funding agencies, and client groups, whether it is supported by reality or not, sometimes at the expense of their staff, their clients, or the agency's mission. Rather than focusing on true quality in terms of client outcomes and employee relationships, not necessarily a "hot" media item, they focus on giving positive impressions to external groups. Other human services managers are excellent in managing the substance of the agency (i.e., the programs and services) but poor at building the agency's image. They focus on clients and staff foremost and only secondarily on the political and interagency dynamics of the environment, sometimes to the detriment of the image of the agency.

Because this is a classic tension for human services managers, one will recognize quickly that what is needed is skill in balancing both values. This is easy to say but hard to achieve.

Career Future Versus Job Now

Human services managers often have to make a choice early in their careers between being concerned primarily with the job at hand or with their future career. If it is the former, they devote a great deal of their energies to the tasks at hand, investing in strengthening relationships with their staff and their clients. If they were to set forth the criteria against which they could be evaluated, it would be in terms of quality and effectiveness of services to clients and in maximizing the impact of those services on clients' lives. Other criteria would also include the level of involvement, ownership, and enthusiasm of the staff in the agency's programs and services.

On the other hand, when a human services manager tends to be more concerned with his future career, there is a tendency to be careful about managing the task at hand to ensure "keeping your nose clean," "not rocking the boat," or "never stepping on anybody's toes." In addition, there is a tendency to focus on instant results in the current job, those that can be quantified easily to indicate a rapid increase of productivity in a relative short period of time. In recent years, the tendency for management in the United States to focus on immediate payoffs rather than long-term investment (i.e., on career future not job now) has received severe and justified criticism. Because of its concern for the job at hand and for long-term investment in the development of employees, Japanese management has become a model for American managers during the past two decades.

Each human services manager confronts this tension at many levels. Whose company, for example, will you seek on a day-to-day basis in the organization and socially? Co-workers with whom you have affinity or those who might be useful someday for upward mobility? In most organizations, professions, and communities, there is a power-position game. A manager will have one of two choices: to play the game or not. This seemingly simple decision sometimes determines the fate of your future career.

Human services managers must cope with this tension along with all the others: whether to throw oneself totally into today's job and be primarily concerned with professional quality and human relationships or to be more oriented to getting results that will receive the recognition of policymakers and superiors so that quick promotions are assured. In the former choice, recognition may never even come from clients or colleagues—only intrinsic rewards and your own self-awareness will give you self-satisfaction. In any event, the ultimate evaluator of your professional career will be you yourself. So you must deal with the tension between future career and today's job, as they interrelate and interweave, and seek to bring them into balance.

Summary

The environment of human services organizations and systems is complex and replete with a multiplicity of values, each pitted one against the other. The human services manager can never escape from having to cope with the tension between a dynamic set of seemingly irreconcilable values that challenge the human services agency and frequently the ideologies on which it is based. Each of these values is equally viable; most often they are in opposition to each other. The tension created over having to make a choice between two or more opposing but valid values is ever present for the human services manager.

This chapter examined several irreconcilable value-tensions, grouped into three sets: governance of self by self versus governance of self by others; equal access versus specialized treatment; and the universal versus the particular. For the human services manager, coping with these value-tensions takes place within the boundaries of two legal constraints (i.e., mandamus and ultra vires) and two conceptual driving forces (i.e., dynamic, creative management and the responsive, supportive environment). Collectively, these tensions and boundaries create the climate for one of the human services manager's primary roles: to reflect on the values inherent in a problem and to provide the organization or system with a solution based on fundamental human services values.

PART

II

Organizations and Systems: Some Dynamic and Diverse Perceptions

There are many different perceptions of organizations and systems. There are also many different ways in which they can be designed and managed. Each perception and approach depends on one's particular view of human beings and human existence. Furthermore, there is an intimate interrelationship between human behavior and organizational behavior. The three chapters of Part II examine what in essence determines the way in which human services organizations and systems will be fashioned and managed.

Chapter 3 discusses a number of different perceptions and interpretations of human behavior and how each of these influences the way in which human services organizations and systems are shaped and administered.

Chapter 4 describes several better known traditional and evolving theories of organizational systems, drawing on the works of major thinkers, researchers, and writers who have contributed their ideas to the field.

Chapter 5 examines the interaction by which human behavior influences the way in which organizations "behave" and vice versa.

Part II concludes with a case history of Mary Parker Follett, the progenitor and fountainhead of modern management perspectives and theories. It is included not only because she is a human services leader who was an early founder of the field but also because she serves as a model for human services management. She was a true dynamic, creative, gender-neutral, color-blind, androgynous manager.

Beyond providing an opportunity to broaden the foundation on which one can build a career as a human services manager, Part II challenges the reader to think critically and reflectively. For each individual, the starting point of human services management must be one's own finely honed perception of human behavior and existence.

3

Perceptions of Human Behavior and Organizations

The Nature of Human Beings: Different Perceptions

Humans as Economic Beings
Humans as Social Beings
Humans as Rational Beings
Humans as Problem-Solvers
Humans as Competitive Beings
Humans as Toolmakers
Humans as Complex, Self-Actualizing Beings

Images of Organizations

Marshall McLuhan: Media and the Perception of Phenomena
Stafford Beer: Stereotypes and Complexity
Orion White: Modes of Reality
Gareth Morgan: Metaphors and Organizations

Summary

The creative, dynamic human services manager continually shapes the way in which human services are organized and managed. This ability as a designer of human services institutions and systems requires fundamental skills and proficiency in organizational analysis. The baseline for this is a recognition that our underlying perceptions, images, and metaphors of human behavior and their interaction with the social environment are what shapes the way in which we organize and manage our society.

It is the purpose of this chapter to increase your skills as an organizational analyst and ultimately your ability to change and improve the way in which human services are organized and managed. To do this, you must examine your own images and metaphors of life and your self-awareness of the ways these shape your own perceptions of organizations and systems. This is an important starting point for becoming a skillful organizational analyst.

The Nature of Human Beings: Different Perceptions

Each of us carries around different perceptions of human beings that influence the way we see the world and go about carrying out our work. Most of these perceptions are very subtle and often not recognized. My recreation department professional colleagues might reject my claim that, despite all their friendly and warm relations with their participants, they generally view people as economic objects. They reject this notion even when I present one simple fact to prove my case: Most recreation departments do not attempt to keep individual participant records that indicate in which recreation program each person participated and what impact the program had on the participant. They simply count numbers to indicate success or failure.

This orientation toward "body counts" has subtly influenced many recreation professionals' perceptions of their human environment. They begin to view facilities, staff, material resources, and participants as *things* that are to be organized in economic terms: Let's provide the most recreation programming we can with the limited resources and facilities that we have.

The recreation professional is not alone. All of us, human services professionals included, have different notions about organizations and systems that are derived from our self-perceptions of how we fit into the social environment. Over the course of time, several different theories of human characteristics have influenced the way in which we view the world:

- Greek mythology suggests that there are four perceptions of human beings, each symbolized by a different god: Apollo, god of spirit; Prometheus, god of science; Dionysus, god of joy; and Epimetheus, god of duty.

- Classic theories of psychology offer different perceptions: pleasure-seeking (Freud); power-seeking (Adler); social status-seeking (Sullivan); seeking meaning in life (Frankl); and seeking self-actualization (Maslow).

Our attempt here is not to propose a final or full understanding of the nature of human behavior. Our premise is quite different. Regardless of the source, each different perception of human beings provides a different basis for understanding the way a society shapes the structures and processes of its institutions.

In Chapters 4 and 5, we examine different theories that present a diverse and dynamic range of organizations and systems. Each theory or school of thought flows out of a particular perception of the very nature of human behavior.

To understand organizations and systems therefore, it is necessary to examine briefly some of the different perceptions of the nature of human beings. Each gives us a unique way of viewing human existence; collectively, the different perceptions provide us with a more comprehensive view of humans that ultimately leads to a better understanding of organizations and systems we fashion in a complex society.

Just as our efforts to fully understand the nature of humans are elusive, so too are our attempts to fully understand organizations and systems of society. Human beings are complex; each of the following perceptions presents different aspects of human behavior, which are complementary in nature. As we strive for a more comprehensive view of human beings, we improve our ability to understand, analyze, and reshape the complex institutions needed to improve our society.

We begin our examination of this subject with Part 1 of Case 3.1, a study of Fern Anton and her efforts to manage programs dealing with teenage pregnancy and parenting services. As you read this part of the case study, try to identify two perceptions of human behavior—humans as economic and socially interdependent beings.

Case 3.1 _____

Part 1: Teen Pregnancy and Parenting Services

Fern Anton sat down after her presentation; she felt nervous. As program director for Progress, a health and social services agency for pregnant and parenting teens in southern New Hampshire, she was generally relaxed in such meetings. It puzzled her; was she going to have trouble today in getting the agreements she needed? She began to worry as she found that her intuition was correct.

"Fern," Joe Thompson, the superintendent of schools addressed her, "we obviously are sympathetic to your program, but we just don't have the staff resources to join in your planning committee and work up a grant for these new services. Frankly, our students who become pregnant and drop out of school are a real burden for us. If we were adequately funded by the state, we could set up our own program and take care of the problem."

"Dr. Thompson," Fern responded quickly, "that's the point. We'll relieve you of some of that burden by using community resources to assist over-whelmed school professionals—guidance counselors, nurses, and social workers. We'll coordinate services and work together on each case. In the schools where we have comprehensive health services, the professionals and administrators see us as an extra resource for themselves."

Bill Amos, the jobs-training coordinator of the Chamber of Commerce, quickly joined in the discussion. "Joe, this is a win-win situation for the school district. We all know that teen pregnancy translates into school drop-outs that translate into a reduced school population that jeopardizes teacher positions and state subsidies to your school district. This also translates into a reduction in the available workforce in the greater Ashton area, and our rapid growth means we need more qualified workers. We can't afford *not* to pitch in with Fern, and, with our participation, she can get a grant from the state and federal governments to subsidize the program."

Dr. Thompson was still dubious. "How do you feel about this, Peg?" he questioned his assistant for pupil services, Margaret Reilly.

"Bill is correct, Joe," Peg responded. "Economically, the schools can't lose on this one, and we get the grant money. I've talked with some of the other school districts that work with Progress, and I'm convinced it won't be any additional administrative burden for us. Besides, if we don't participate, we have a lot to lose. The chamber does want to help us train more students for the workforce, but I would hope we would join in for another reason. These pupils are part of our educational responsibility and represent a chal-lenge for us. The teenagers who become pregnant are trying to be adults be-fore they're finished being kids. If they get support from their families, we can educate them for life, and that education will make a difference to them and a difference to their children, who are also going to be our responsibility in just a couple of years."

"Peg, you know I agree with that," Joe responded, "but although Fern's program talks about health education and counseling, we all know it really is *family planning*. How am I going to sell that to this community and, more specifically, to my bosses, the school board. They're a pretty conservative bunch."

"This is your lucky day, Joe," Peg laughed. "Fern already has an advi-sory committee for the program that includes nearly all the clergy in the city. Admittedly, their primary interest is promoting healthy babies. Ashton has one of the highest infant-mortality rates in the state, and pregnant teenagers who have dropped out of our schools are particularly at risk. Community leaders are very concerned."

Fern jumped in. "Sure, we do have to deal with the issue of repeat pregnancy, Dr. Thompson. But our clients are already pregnant when they enter the program so that our primary services are health care and education, counseling, parenting education, child care and development, job preparation, and family management. We all know that the high school diploma is a vital first step to economic self-sufficiency. It's a shared goal for all of us."

Their eyes met. "Sorry I gave you a hard time, Fern," Joe grinned. "Public school management has gotten awfully complex these days. Whatever happened to the days of the Three *R*s? I hope you understand why I have to be so cautious."

"I don't envy your position, Dr. Thompson," Fern answered. "And thanks for your help." She smiled and noted that her nervousness had evaporated.

Humans as Economic Beings

Living in the United States in the last decade of the twentieth century, one cannot escape the perception that fundamentally we view each other in economic terms. We strive to increase and expand our material goods to increase our economic worth, to value ourselves and each other in terms of our net worth. Indeed, we evaluate our progress in life in terms of the amount and rate of increase in our economic equity and in terms of our accumulation of power and status in society. Are psychologist Alfred Adler (1927) and philosopher Friedrich Nietzsche (1976) correct? Do people have an innate drive for power and success?

If it were only in modern times that humans were viewed as economic beings, then we could perhaps be critical of our own times. But we know that the religious and philosophical stirrings of humans from the onset of civilization have been strongly influenced by material and economic rationales. In *Escape from Evil* (1975), Ernest Becker traces the way in which gold and other precious metals have been worshipped as gods and idols; and even after the transition to the concept of monotheism, modern-day idol worshipping of money, power, and status has persisted in society in subtler forms.

We view ourselves and others in economic terms. Should it be surprising therefore that we approach the design of organizations and systems with a perception that humans beings—both clients and staff—are primarily economic beings? Is there anything ethically or morally unsound when we view ourselves as making an economic contract with organizations: In exchange for some level of remuneration and economic benefits, are we willing to give our knowledge, abilities, and energies to an organization? By the same token, is there anything ethically or morally wrong when we place an economic value on human life when making investment of scarce and limited resources? Consider the following and see if you have difficulty in placing a dollar amount on the value of life.

The Economic Value of Life _____

In which of the following situations would you, as a human services manager, recommend the investment of scarce resources?

- Provide health and hospice services to 100 AIDS patients costing $2000 a week, knowing that the patients will most likely die within the next year.

- Initiate five new programs requiring an annual expenditure of $14.5 million that provide health and day-care services to 1600 teenage mothers to help them complete their high school education. Projections indicate that 40 percent will be successful and receive their high school degree.

- Fund five new, neonatal care units in the state, at an annual investment of $450,000 each, for an average of 100 infants a year per unit.

- For the same funds, provide a nutritional breakfast for 6000 infants and children who live in poverty.

For each of the above choices, which option would you select? Is it inappropriate to place an economic value on life, pitting one group of clients against another? Or is this a necessary process in a democratic society?

Humans as Social Beings

Most humans do not live in isolation; for that reason, human relationships are the foundation of civilization. Whatever your source—college textbooks on sociology and anthropology, the Bible, research studies of mythology or popular literature (e.g. the writings of Jean Auel)—the conclusion would be the same: Humans are more than just social beings; they are interdependent beings. People need to relate to each other and live in close proximity to each other, as families, clans, tribes, villages, and ultimately in communities. Throughout the course of civilization, humans have lived in groups that operated from the premise that their individual lives were interdependent to each other and to the group. In his study of mythology over the course of civilization, Joseph Campbell (1976) concludes that education was not primarily to learn but to create "communities of shared experience." The function of myth and ritual was to "engage" the individual in the local community.

Even a cursory analysis of different cultures indicates the extent to which the social interactions of people dominate and even control their lives. Our psychosocial needs find early expression in our families, among our peers, our school, and our community. As we become adults, our workplace, our professional lives, our leisure lives, our social groups (formal and informal), and formation of our own family unit serve as vehicles for meeting our social needs.

Some theorists hold that two people will only sustain interpersonal relationships as long as there is a **social exchange**—that is, each considers the relationship mutually rewarding. This has been criticized as being too economic in perception. People have social needs that are more important than economic needs. Material goods are a vehicle for the achievement of social needs, not vice versa. Too often the concern for status and position in the socioeconomic class system of society translates into an economic pursuit, with the goal being power along with wealth. But to a large number of people, wealth, power, and position are not what ultimately count in life. The true measure of quality of life is the number of sensitive and intense human relationships among family, friends, and community.

Robert Bellah and his associates, authors of the popular book *Habits of the Heart* (1986), maintain that our society suffers primarily from poverty of affluence. People may have a reasonable level of material well-being, but they still need a sense of purpose and meaning in life. This is achieved by being connected to others in cultural patterns that give *coherence* to life. Our psychic, even our physical, health is dependent on the culture of coherence. In the extreme, alienation and a sense of anomie can lead to depression or even suicide. In far too many situations, it leads to substance abuse—be it alcohol or other drugs.

In a modern complex society, people are totally interdependent. There is an implicit contract that creates a level of trust and expectations to support this interdependence. Each person carries out her task in society and is responsible for being concerned about the common good, the Indian philosophical concept of *dharma*—a sense of duty. A person who volunteers for a human services agency—whether as a Big Sister–Big Brother or as a board member—is someone who wants to share some of the responsibility for the common good of everyone in society. The same is true for someone who volunteers time to clean up a polluted stream or to raise funds that will benefit the community family services agency.

Living as a responsible individual in an interdependent society is an ideal that leads some people to foster the concept that self-governance of individual life is the only governance necessary in any society. A life of prescriptions, whether by a religion or government, is unnecessary.

Humans as Rational Beings

The accumulation and expansion of knowledge has always been a hallmark of human beings. It has led to a dominant way of thinking about the world and has been labeled variously as **scientific specialization** or **reductionism**. Essentially, it flows out of a perception that humans are primarily rational beings.

Along with the perceptions of humans as problem-solving and competitive beings, trace this perception in Part 2 of our case study of teen pregnancy and parenting services.

Case 3.1 _____

Part 2: Teen Pregnancy and Parenting Services

As she sat down to write her monthly report to the agency's director, Fern Anton reflected on her work. From her graduate work in social work adminis-tration, she had understood the importance of systemic management and the need to select a strategic role for her agency. But no one had ever hinted that her current managerial role could be included in the list of possible strategic roles for human services management. In a world of shrinking public services but expanding human need, she found that she had become a "cheerleader" for clients, for staff, for her board, for members of the community, and for professionals from other human services agencies. She decided that the tone of her monthly report should reflect that role. She wrote:

Progress: Monthly Report

Like other human services commitments, working with pregnant teenagers or those struggling in their roles as new parents is hard work. Increasingly, the environment's lack of resources and complicated bureaucratic regulations bring individual counseling days where there are far more "failures" in our work to help clients support themselves and love and nurture their children than there are "successes." Often I find myself becoming the cheerleader for staff in their work with clients.

Because we've learned enough about the obstacles that parents face and the systems that offer support and services, we can look to a number of clients as "successes": We provide the teen and her family with sufficient support and information for them to use their own self-governance and problem-solving abilities to work things out. Generally, this means using their own and community resources to

- Acquire health and nutritional care during pregnancy and for the baby after birth.
- Create the conditions such that a new family can be established with neces-sary family management supports in place.
- Work out ways for the teenager involved to complete her high school edu-cation, find employment, and use day-care services as appropriate.

When we are successful, everyone feels positive about our program: clients, staff, and community leaders.

Unfortunately, in many situations, our efforts encounter such obstacles of cyclical poverty and society's inadequate attempts to provide adequately for all needy citizens that success, as we define it, is an extremely long-term, if not impossible, goal. Some teens find their environment so hostile or negative that they do not receive the necessary nutritional and health care during pregnancy and their babies die at birth or are born in a frail condition. Some teens are not able to provide a home and create the family conditions that ensure continued quality health care or arrangements for day care for their infants, enabling them to complete high school and begin work. In these cases, the future is often one of poverty and welfare dependence for themselves and their babies.

In these situations, my role as cheerleader and validator of the importance of our work becomes critical for our staff, for our clients, for their families, and for other community agencies. Because of a tendency to blame the victim, our staff will often receive comments like these when working with other agencies' clients:

- Don't they know how to use birth control and not get pregnant?

- If they are pregnant, why don't they get health care for themselves? Don't they care about their babies?

- We're in the late twentieth century, not the dark ages! Where are their families in all this?

- Don't they realize that an abortion or adoption is better than a lifetime of poverty and welfare?

- If we help them too much, all we're doing is encouraging others to get pregnant.

- They got themselves into this situtation; let them get themselves out of it!

- It's not that we don't want to help. We just can't make exceptions in our educational program for anyone. We operate under strict state regulations!

- I made all the necessary referrals to other agencies for them; they just never kept their appointments once they were set up for them!

- It's a dog-eat-dog world; they have to learn that or they're never going to make it on their own. We can't hold their hands and coddle them!

- Please don't misunderstand. You're doing everything you can to help the young parent; that's great. Frankly though, we're worried about the infant; these kinds of parents become child-abusers!

When staff face ongoing comments like these from other human services providers, when they feel frustrated by systems that cannot respond to their clients' needs, when they do not receive community recognition or support for the difficult jobs they perform, and when they continue to be poorly compensated for their work in the nonprofit sector, it becomes difficult for them to stay motivated and feel pride in their work. My job as director, supervisor, teacher, appreciator, validator, and cheerleader is to help them feel good about the successes and determined to keep working with those cases that are more difficult to affect positively. We are all working hard.

Respectfully submitted,

Fern Anton

Societal institutions have been a primary vehicle by which humans methodically rationalize all aspects of life in the pursuit of making it more efficient and orderly. This process of rationalization has created a dominant role for specialists, experts, and professionals in society. This has in turn led societies to be dominated by **technocracies**, the ultimate organizational form that expands instrumental, rational orientation into the everyday, private and public, life of people. In our discussion of the irreconcilable value-tension between the specialist and the generalist in the previous chapter, we noted Jurgen Habermas's (1968) concern that people in society and their political leaders have become almost totally dependent on the **technocrat**—the ultimate form of the rational human being.

Karl Mannheim (1952) defined two forms of rationality: functional rationality and substantive rationality. **Functional rationality** is instrumental in nature, focused on the means of accomplishing a task. It never questions why something is being done. It only asks, How can it be done more efficiently and effectively? **Substantive rationality**, on the other hand, is directed toward questioning the ends: Should we even being doing what we are doing? As human services managers, which would you prefer to have on your staff? *Funcrats,* those who are seeking greater efficiency and effectiveness of services, or *sub-rats,* those who are searching for the answer to the question, What should the agency be doing to carry out its mission?

Scientific exploration into the workings of the human brain and in the way people think have led to the popular notion of *left-brained* and *right-brained* people. The former tend to think in methodical, linear, and rational forms and tend to become professional specialists; the latter tend to think in more holistic, intuitive, and nonlinear fashions, to operate more on feelings than thinking, and tend to become the artists and inventors in society. For anyone familiar with computers, the underlying design created by John VonNeuman was bedded in extremely rational, linear left-brained thinking. The results are the programmed large computers or, for those who use microcomputers, IBM-type personal computers. For those who use an Apple Macintosh computer with its icons, menus, graphics, and whole images, this more intuitive approach can be viewed as right-brained computing.

To the purist, rationality can be achieved by thinking from either side of the brain. One can manage organizations and systems "scientifically" or "intuitively" (see Rowan, *The Intuitive Manager,* 1986). Either way, it is an expression of rational behavior.

Humans as Problem-Solvers

Throughout the ages, humans have been curious about their world, trying to understand the wonders of their environment and of human existence itself. Whatever the barrier, whatever the unknown, or whatever the challenge facing people individually or in groups, humans have always strived to find solutions to the problems they faced. Driven both by the need to overcome some barrier or conquer some new frontier and by an urge for creative expression, civilization can be viewed as a continuous stream of human inventions.

To many people, life itself is a problem-solving process. It seems that everything we do in our daily life is dealing with or responding to a problem. You might find it useful or even humorous to take one day out of your life, from waking in the morning to going to sleep at night, and record all problems that you had to deal with and solve in the course of a day. While most may seem insignificant and be variations of problems that you have encountered before, your day could be viewed as one continual stream of problems that you had to solve. Add to this some desire or need that might arise (e.g., "How can I rearrange my work schedule so I can take off this Friday to go to an art museum or baseball game with a friend?"), you get a clue for the meaning to the adage "Necessity is the mother of invention!" A want, a barrier, or the frustration of a need is the source of people continually being problem-solving beings.

The creative energy locked within a human being seems to be almost limitless. Educators have sought to create environments or approaches that encourage use of such creativity as the impetus for human development and growth. The famous educator John Dewey (1933) was interested in fashioning learning environments for children and focused on the problem-solving nature of human beings. He explored the relationship between problem-solving and rational, reflective, and goal-directed thinking. He suggested that effective problem solving required an orderly sequence of "five phases of reflective thinking":

1. Recognizing the difficulty
2. Defining it
3. Identifying and exploring possible solutions (which requires skill in collecting and analyzing data)
4. Selecting the best of the possible solutions identified
5. Carrying out that solution

Because human beings are, or have to be, problem solvers by nature, it is important that they improve their knowledge and skills in problem solving.

Dewey was one of the many scholars and historians who have recognized this as a fundamental perception of human beings.

Humans as Competitive Beings

According to classic Indian philosophy, humans strive for three ends: *kama* (pleasure and love), *artha* (power and success), and *dharma* (lawful order and moral virtue). As noted in our discussion of humans as economic beings, Nietzsche and Adler would agree that a fundamental human impulse is the will for power and success. The human drive to conquer has not only been identified by psychologists but was found by Campbell (1976) in his study of mythologies to express itself in myths, gods, rituals of religion, supernatural means of self, and tribal aggrandizement.

Those who view humans as primarily competitive beings differ in explaining the reasons for such a perception of people. As already indicated, some subscribe to the theory that it is a basic drive of humans, or, as Darwin maintains, it is necessary for survival. It is the way in which humans are able to adapt to their changing environment. In the *Territorial Imperative* (1966), Robert Ardrey presents the thesis that, like animals, humans also have an innate drive for territory, setting and defending boundaries. It is connected to reproduction and survival. A species that has refined certain traits to survive the environment sets tight boundaries so that reproduction is within the species, to retain and strengthen the trait, not dilute it by reproducing with other species who were permitted to cross boundaries. This implies that where a human services manager encounters a professional who is overly concerned about issues of turf, that professional may be defending turf not for personal reasons but in defense of his entire profession or organization.

In searching for the source of evil in the history of humans, a history dominated by one group of humans killing another group and accumulating booty as symbols of power, success, and achieving "superrace" status, Becker (1968) maintains it is an attempt to deal with the inescapable truth that a human being cannot achieve immortality.

There are still other reasons for explaining humans as competitive beings. Many countries, the United States included, have accepted the ideas of Adam Smith who maintained that people engage in competitive games against each other at all levels of life. These games provide a great deal of energy that can be captured as a fundamental resource in any society. In essence, the human need to compete is innate. Although harnessing competition in an economy can lead to economic prosperity for a large number of people (and lead to a large number of societal problems), we noted in Chapter 1 that writers such as Eric Fromm (1956) suggest that human beings have transformed themselves into commodities. This has the effect of turning human *beings* into *things*.

Whatever the source of this perception, the image of people individually or in groups competing with each other is deep in our psyche. World conflicts everywhere are the ultimate expression of such perceptions, as are intergroup, even interfamily, conflicts and tensions. Whether a major or minor influence, the concept of people as competitive beings is one that must be recognized as playing some part in shaping your own perception of humans.

Humans as Toolmakers

Civilization is a flowing stream of human inventions. The history of humankind has been intricately linked with their tools. This is particularly true when viewing the centrality of work and production to people, with the continuous stress of humans as toolmakers (e.g., inventors of the techniques and technologies of human existence). Part 3 of Case 3.1 illustrates this view of humans, as well as the view of human beings as complex, self-actualizing beings.

Case 3.1 _____

Part 3: Teen Pregnancy and Parenting Services

Sitting at the teen-parenting council meeting, Fern found herself feeling very frustrated. Everyone around the table really did want to help. But they were so specialized that they viewed the issue too parochially, or they were encumbered with a system that was too inflexible. Her frustration was obviously shared by Molly Kutchen, one of the two parents on the council, who suddenly spoke up.

"Do you people have any idea how tough it is for my daughter's friend Kim, who is a sixteen-year-old teenage mother, trying to make it on her own? She gets up at the crack of dawn, gets her infant and herself ready for the day, grabs a bus, drops off the child at day care, goes to high school, takes the bus again, picks up her child, grabs another bus, gets home, takes care of the infant and her home, and then finally sits down—to do homework." Molly paused. "I know many working people in our community share this routine. But how many do it with such odds against them and so few supports to help them?"

Dead silence. Members of the council just sat looking at Molly. "What are you saying, Molly?" Fern finally asked.

"I guess I'm saying, Fern," Molly replied, "that all of you have to get beyond the problems you've got with your own agencies in getting them to change their systems for teen parents. You can't let the difficulty of your understanding how to work with each other slow you. Keep focusing on these kids; support them, and they'll respond."

"But, Molly," Kathy Brady, chair of the council, broke in, "most of the agencies say that the teens we deal with are different and thus almost too difficult to deal with! It takes a long time to work out special procedures to create a communitywide system to work with pregnant teens or teen mothers. We have to work out arrangements that cross agency boundaries."

"Well, teen parents may be younger, Kathy," Molly responded, "but they have the same kinds of needs that you and I have. Give them the chance, and they'll shape their lives like everyone else. But so far, the message to these teens is clear—you've made a mistake, and it has changed your life. You're different now, and you are out of it. Funny thing, down deep, all they want is to become part of the mainstream."

Fern thought for a few minutes and then, in a sober tone, shared her thought: "Molly has brought up an important idea. We need to reduce the odds that are stacked against our teen clients and increase the supports they need to help themselves. Seems to me this is a vital goal for the council. Could we sell the idea to the rest of the community?"

World history may be thought of as demarcated by the tools human beings fashioned to meet the challenges of their times. The fifteenth century, for example, is marked by the invention of movable type, a tool that eventually fostered a literate community, a middle class, and a mass culture. On the other hand, when posterity looks back on the twentieth century in terms of our accomplishments, it may find the century distinguished not by any specific tool but by technology or technique itself.

The perception of humans as toolmakers is important because of the debate over the impact of tools and techniques on values. Some claim that technology is value-free and neutral; others say this is not so. Everyone agrees, however, that tools help form societal values. It has been noted, for example, that farm cultures were nurturing in their attitude toward the environment. There was no adversarial relationship between the farmer's tools and the farm products, which were too numerous to develop any individual relationship. Individualism among human beings did not develop. From these cultures, the Eastern religions were fashioned; the gods were goddesses.

This was replaced in the West by the exploitive, plundering, male-oriented mythologies of herdsmen and hunters. The rider named his horse; the hunter knew the prey, almost by name. Out of this perception of life came the individual, being-oriented religions of the Levant (Judaism, Christianity, and Islam). Some writers have presented the thesis that these religions in turn fostered values (e.g., the work ethic) that encourage the use of their tools and thus the need to invent new tools to support economic perceptions of life. The Industrial Revolution of the seventeenth and eighteenth centuries was a result of these series of perceptions, values, and societal forms.

Techniques fashion the life perceptions of their users. The tools of the strip miner create an image of a *specialist* who exploits the land in order to extract an irreplaceable resource. The tools of the farmer, on the other hand, fashion a *nurturer* with generalized skills who invests in the land with concern for a cycle of regeneration of resources. The exploiter thinks in terms of efficiency, quantities and money (profits); the nurturer thinks in terms of care, quality, and the health and character of people.

Not only are the metaphors of life influenced by tools, so also are the institutions of society. Techniques, according to one social theorist (Ellul 1965), are being developed at a rate far greater than our ability to adapt, control, or even name them. In a subtle fashion, scientific-technical progress fosters the reorganization of social institutions. In modern societies, it leads to technocracies, an increase of technical control over objectified process of nature and society by specialists. As we have noted in other chapters, the politicians and people of a nation no longer fashion policies that technocrats implement. Technocrats shape and limit the policy options that people and their leaders endorse.

Human beings fashion their tools, which in turn shape the images of life of their inventors. It is another perception of people we cannot ignore.

Humans as Complex, Self-Actualizing Beings

As students in the human services well know, there are no shortages of theories of human growth and development. Whether we turn to the classic theories of Sigmund Freud (1935), Alfred Adler, or Carl Jung (1958), or more recent works of Erik Erikson (1959), Jean Piaget (1973), or Abraham Maslow (1952), there is general acceptance that humans have a complex range of needs that seeks expression.

The perception of humans as having a "hierarchy" of physiological, social, and psychological needs that serve as the very source of peoples' motivation is important for students and practitioners of human services management. It suggests that there are no simple or single perceptions of human beings. People are complex; this very complexity both complicates societal processes and in turn places emphasis on the need to deal with complexity. There is some agreement that people strive for a sense of self-worth, for identity, for meaning to life, and for an opportunity to be self-actualized—to find expression for that which is unique in each person. Whether we turn to theologians, psychologists, or philosophers, there seems to be a strong tendency to view human beings with this perception.

The perception of humans as complex, self-actualized beings strongly influences the field of human services. It is at the core of creative, dynamic human services management. As Table 3.1 suggests, one can easily construct a taxonomy of human services organizations in terms of Maslow's taxonomy of

Table 3.1   Maslow's Taxonomy of Needs and Human
            Services Functions

Basic Need	Vehicle for Satisfaction of the Basic Need	Functional Area
Survival	Food Clothing Shelter	Welfare Housing Manpower Corrections

Physical health	Preventative:
	  Diet
	  Exercise
	  Clean environment
	  Education
	Curative:
	  Access to care
	  Medicines
		Welfare
		Health
		Housing
		Recreation
		Education

Love	Relationships with others	Welfare Education Corrections Recreation
Belongingness	Family Friends Group association	Welfare Education Manpower Recreation Corrections
Sense of self-worth	Skills Opportunity for self-expression Education Belief system	Welfare Education Manpower Corrections Recreation Health
Efficacy	Achievement Participation	Manpower Education Recreation Corrections Politics

Safety	Preventative:
	  Laws and statutes
	  Safe environment
	  Education
	Curative:
	  Enforcement
	  Remedy
		Health
		Education
		Housing
		Corrections
		Justice
		Recreation

Self-actualization		

Source: City of St. Paul, Minnesota. *A Methodology for Systems Analysis in the Human Resource Development Subsystem* (Springfield, VA: National Technical Information Service, 1972). #PB 211 213.

human needs. In the search for continuous improvement of the human services in society, the creative, dynamic human services manager seeks to develop innovative, improved means for providing a full range of human services supportive and responsive to people striving to find self-actualization.

This perception of people also places demands on the inner workings of organizations and systems. Structures and leadership styles must be fashioned to provide maximum opportunities to motivate human services workers themselves to tap the full range of their creativity and to support them in their efforts to become self-actualized. Indeed, not only do societal institutions have the function of achieving their specific mission and carrying out their role in society, but they are also the vehicle through which most people will be able to find meaning and a sense of self-worth to their lives.

In rereading all three parts of Case 3.1, it is not hard to recognize that one of the dominant premises that guided Fern Anton in her efforts was self-actualization. It is a perception that is central to creative, dynamic human services management.

Images of Organizations

Everyone carries within their minds a set of images or metaphors about the nature of human beings. The way in which organizations and systems in societies are fashioned and managed can be directly related to these images. This is a vital insight for the dynamic, creative human services manager.

Before examining the relationships between images and metaphors *and* organizations and systems, let us define the following:

- Image   A mental picture; conception; idea; type; symbol (e.g., the human brain as a switchboard)
- Metaphor   A way of thinking or seeing (e.g., he is a devil; a saint)

To improve the human services, managers must understand and analyze the organizations and systems that serve as the foundation of human services provision. As a starting point, they need to recognize the way in which images and metaphors influence our perceptions of the organizations and systems of society.

The relationships between images and organizations-systems can be illustrated by four different theories or perspectives, each of which is briefly discussed: McLuhan's concept of the influence of media on perceptions; Beer's concept of our brain's programmed stereotypes; White's thesis that we organize and manage societal institutions strongly influenced by different modes of reality; and Morgan's premise that theories of organizational life are based on metaphors.

Marshall McLuhan: Media and the Perception of Phenomena

Marshall McLuhan (1967) proposes that there is a strong relationship between our perceptions of the environment and the media. For several centuries the printing press and the alphabet have influenced our thought patterns. We were conditioned to view the environment in terms of t-i-m-e and s|p|a|c|e. McLuhan notes that "With typography, the principle of the movable type introduced the means of mechanizing any handicraft by the process of segmenting and fragmenting an integral action" (1964, 160). What McLuhan is suggesting is that reductionism, or the scientific approach, in civilization was a result of the introduction of the Gutenburg press some 500 years ago. For example, something as simple as printing or typing one's name (M|Y|R|O|N) conditions one to view this phenomenon in a linear, ordered, and segmented fashion. Take a look at life around you and note the way that this process has influenced how we separate and segregate knowledge, the professions, work processes, our dwelling units, our vehicles for transportation, our organizations and institutions, even the way we mark time itself into hours, days of the week, years, and significant periods.

McLuhan went on to describe the new perception of the environment that has indeed taken place with our societal switch to electronic media. In our electronically configured world, all factors of the environment and of experience coexist in a state of active interplay, searching for recognition of patterns. We no longer shape institutional processes serially, block-by-block, step-by-step. Information interconnects humans instantaneously and continuously.

When you receive information from watching a TV documentary, you are processing simultaneous auditory and visual messages. These are further broken down into real-life images and real sound track, accompanied by graphics and supplementary images, commentary, and music. You are subject to the impact of editing and directing, timing and composition, and the perceptions of the reporter, camera-person, and producer, all within the space of a few minutes. Short of turning off the program, you have no means of control over this bombardment other than what goes on in your mind. Compare this with what happens when you read a newspaper item. It quickly becomes clear that McLuhan's prophetic vision has been realized—the medium has taken over to the point where it becomes part of the message, changing and reinterpreting its substance. This has implications not only for individuals, but also for their institutions.

In essence, McLuhan concluded that people are expected to manage modern, complex, highly interconnected and interrelated institutions with older concepts of specialization, segmentation, and compartmentalization. But the pre-twenty-first century world is a web of interrelated human responses to a highly technological environment, and these responses literally bombard our complex institutions with stimuli at a rate that is far beyond the symbol-manipulation capacity of one human's ability. Organization and concepts are in the process of growing to meet the fundamental change and challenge to current society: "We now live in a global village . . . a simultaneous happening" (McLuhan 1967, 65).

Stafford Beer: Stereotypes and Complexity

Stafford Beer was one of the founders of the current management-science movement. Like many other scientists, he turned philosopher, presenting a re-design of society in a book entitled *Platform for Change*. His theory flows from a fundamental thesis: "Man is a prisoner of his own way of thinking and of his own stereotypes of himself. His machine for thinking, his brain, has been pro-grammed to deal with a vanished world" (1975, 15).

As Beer sees it, in the old world, there was a need to manage *things;* in the new world, the need is to manage *complexity.* The trouble is that the tool for managing complexity is organization; but we are bogged down with concepts of organization and stereotypes of human existence that belong to our old world, and do not fit new realities.

Because humans cannot be deprogrammed like a computer, Beer maintains that we are stuck for life with the following stereotypes:

- Of Humans: Homo Faber . . . Humans are the creatures who invented work and the making of things to control the environment. Material wealth is the primary measure of achievement and work is the only "ethical" occupation.
- Of Culture: Totum-Quantum . . . Our culture conditions us to look at the universe as a whole (totum) which we subdivide into bits and pieces (quanta) which we attempt to assemble in order to understand the whole.
- Of Organization: Bifurcation . . . Fashioning organizations by cutting up the whole (totum) into pieces (quanta), calling the process *delegation.* Then nail the pieces together into a whole, and call the result *chain of command.* (1975, 24–37)

Beer notes that the stereotype of organizations looks like a hierarchy, a family tree showing at each level an increasing number of cousins. Horizontal linkages between cousins is very difficult.

To deal with the complexification of society, Beer suggests that we need to shift the stereotype of humans from *Faber* to *Gubernator* (steersman). We also need to change the organizational stereotype to one defined by the synthesis of information flow, not division of authority. The neurophysiology of the human body or the circuit diagram of a computer would be a better image of an orga-nization than the current one that views the organization as a family tree.

Orion White: Modes of Reality

Orion White (1973) has made a comparison of the influence of two different modes of reality on the organization and management of societal institutions. His analysis flows out of the premise that reality is socially constructed, and for centuries modern, industrialized societies have been dominated by one percep-

Table 3.2   Reality Modality and Human Services Provision

	Positivist Science	Symbolic Exchange
Perceptions of humans	Driven by need	Searching for identity
Essence of existence	Problem solution (reduce insecurity)	Interactions; moving on
Work	Labor; humans are appendages of machines	Intrinsic value of work (joy of creating)
Services	Rational solutions to problems; attempt to control	Move beyond present situation; creation, *not* control
Practice	Institutional action	Personal and responsible action
Role of service provider	Prescribed behavior of specialists and professionals dealing with each other as objects	Creation of process where all interacting entities strive to see each other in unobjectified terms
Perception of societal institutions	Consensual organizations based on normative order that ensures security	Network of relationships between people in whom mutual trust–responsibility must be placed

tion of reality that has been labeled *mechanistic, scientific, calculative, positivist,* or *economizing.* Lawrence LeShan (1976) calls this the sensory mode of reality: separating, contrasting, and defining things in space and time, based on our senses.

To illustrate the way in which the mode of reality influences the way in which we organize and manage societal institutions and systems, White compares the positivist science mode of reality with the symbolic exchange mode. He compares each mode as it influences the provision and management of human services. Table 3.2 summarizes this comparison. At the very least, White is suggesting that the creative, dynamic human services manager needs to recognize that the starting point of human services is an awareness of and sensitivity to the concept that human beings construct their own reality; therefore, difficult as it may be, one can manage in an environment of multiple realities.

This creates additional tensions within human services management—the tension between logical positivism (objective reality) *and* phenomenology (each person's own reality) and homogeneous reality *and* heterogeneous reality. What will it be like for you to manage a human services system in which the different actors (professionals and clients) operate with different realities?

Gareth Morgan: Metaphors and Organizations

Gareth Morgan (1986) suggests that there are some implicit metaphors that shape the way of thinking about or seeing the world around us and that influence the way in which we view societal institutions and systems. Morgan proposes that these metaphors are set within broad world views or paradigms. The most dominant paradigm is the *functionalist* paradigm in which "behavior is always seen as being contextually bound in a real world of concrete and tangible social relationships" (1980:608). On the other hand, Morgan notes that metaphors that are set within the *interpretive* paradigm start from the premise that reality is socially constructed:

> The interpretive social theorist attempts to understand the process through which shared multiple realities arise, are sustained, and are changed. Like the functionalist, the interpretive approach is based on the assumption and belief that there is an underlying pattern and order within the social world; however, the interpretive theorist views the functionalist's attempt to establish an objective social science as an unattainable end. Science is viewed as a network of language games, based upon sets of subjectively determined concepts and rules, which the practitioners of science invent and follow. (1980:608–609)

In his discussion of metaphors, Morgan starts from the thesis that better understanding of organizations leads to improvement in the way we analyze them and subsequently in our ability to design and fashion new, more creative forms of organizations. Given the dynamic nature of the environment of human services organizations and systems, this thesis is vital for the dynamic, creative human services manager.

Metaphors are very important for institutional processes and service provision. Police officers, for example, historically have had to struggle with two different metaphors: *law-enforcement officer* versus *peace officer.* Some analysts have suggested that 80 percent of what police do is human services. Why then do most police officers have the self-image of being in the criminal justice profession and not in the human services profession? In the answer to this question lies the heart of the phenomenon that organizations shape, and are shaped by, human behavior. It is obvious, therefore, that metaphors are critical in fashioning the way in which we shape and manage the human services.

Morgan proposes several metaphors for organization. They can be summarized as follows.

Organizations as Machines.   All elements of the organization—people, equipment, materials, processes—are fashioned as interrelated parts of a machine, arranged in a highly routinized but very specific sequence to be efficient and predictable. In this mechanistic view of organizations, human beings are turned into appendages of machines; thus, when robots can replace humans, this metaphor would reach its ultimate expression.

Organizations as Organisms.   This metaphor views organizations from a biological perspective. Just as organisms interact with their environment for growth, adaptation, and survival, organizations "behave" in the same fashion. Just as organisms seek the proper fit with their environment, so too must the organization adapt to find the proper fit with its environment.

Organizations as Brains.   Can organizations be designed to be as creative, inventive, flexible, and resilient as the brain? Can organizations be designed as information-processing, communicating, and decision-making systems like the brain such that information can be converted into thoughts and actions? If the metaphor of organizations as brains can be achieved they can be designed as self-regulating, self-learning systems.

Organizations as Cultures.   Organizations can be viewed as cultures that have unique shared beliefs, values, symbols, routines, and rituals. Just as the cultures of societies differ, one can move from organization to organization and experience different cultures. This metaphor leads us to recognize that through the culture of the organization, a distinct reality is socially constructed and imposed on organizational members.

Organizations as Political Systems.   Both in terms of their inner workings and in their interaction with their environment and society, organizations can be viewed as political systems. Since organizations represent power, this metaphor gives us greater insight into the behavior of individuals within an organization and the behavior of organizations themselves. As an arena in which humans express their desire or need for power and control, organizations can be viewed within a pluralistic framework in which different interests *compete, collaborate, compromise, accommodate,* or *avoid* each other to share and distribute power.

Organizations as Psychic Prisons.   Organizations are created and sustained by conscious and unconscious processes that help explain the hidden meaning of life. As a psychic prison, for example, organizations can be viewed as a patriarchal family that produces structures that give dominance to traditional male values. These self-contained views of the world can confine, even imprison, people, and shape the way in which organizational members see and act (or don't see and act) when interacting with their environment.

Organizations as Flux and Transformation.   Organizations are shaped by continuous processes of transformation that follow a fundamental logic of change. With this metaphor, organizations can be viewed as autonomous closed systems, that close in on themselves with the sole purpose of self-reproduction.

From this perspective, organizations view their environment as projections of their self-image or identity. In this process, organizations have to be aware of becoming too egocentric in asserting their identity. They might sow the seeds of their own destruction if they see the environment as a self-reflection. This metaphor suggests that there is an inner logic to the changes that shape our world and that, once understood, can improve our ability to manage organizational change.

Organizations as Instruments of Domination.   Many historians and sociologists conclude that organizations are instruments by which a selfish elite impose their will to dominate society. From this perspective, there is a close relationship between organization, class, and control. To some analysts this metaphor of organizations reinforces the phenomenon of the large number of negative effects of organizational life on employees. These include occupational work hazards and diseases, industrial accidents, "workaholism," conditions related to physical and mental stress, substance abuse, even suicides. Although this metaphor is fostered by "radical" organizational analysts, it helps all organizational analysts to appreciate issues that are the intended or unintended results of societal institutional formation and management.

Summary

Increasingly, the issue of how to improve our institutions is of paramount importance to our society. This concern is reflected in the belief that organizational and managerial techniques offer the optimal way of achieving our individual and collective goals in a society. For the professional human services manager, this places continual pressure to acquire new conceptual and methodological knowledge and skills that can lead to the improved management of the human services. One of the most important ways of satisfying this concern is to increase one's skills in organizational analysis.

The ability to perceive, diagnose, and critically evaluate the several different perceptions of organizations that exist simultaneously in the thoughts and actions of people interacting with a human services agency or system is both an art and a science. Acquiring and improving this capability is a lifetime challenge for the human services manager.

This chapter attempted to improve your skill as an organizational analyst by exploring a critical premise, one that serves as the baseline for human services management: *Organizations are an expression of the way we think of ourselves and the world.* Not only do we fashion organizations with our images of the nature of human-social environment interaction, but we also manage the societal institutions we shape according to the different perceptions of the very nature of human beings.

The next two chapters examine different perspectives and theories of organizations and systems relevant to the human services. As you study these chapters, you will recognize the ways in which different images and metaphors of human existence influence each of the different perspectives of organizations, management, and systems. This recognition is a sign that your skill in organizational analysis has begun to unfold and expand. Nurture that skill. It is one you will need continually throughout your career as a human services manager.

4

Organizations: Different Perspectives

The Rational Organization
Bureaucracy
Scientific Management
Administrative Management
Administrative Behavior

The Natural-System Organization
Human Relations
Cooperative Systems
Institutional Approach
Social Systems

The Open-System Organization
General-Systems Theory
Cybernetic Systems
Contingency Theory
Sociotechnical Systems

Summary

It has been suggested that three perspectives can be used to view the vast literature on organizations. Each perspective serves as a conceptual umbrella for several related schools of thought. W. Richard Scott (1987), a sociologist who is one of the leading organizational researchers in the United States, suggests viewing organizations from the following perspectives:

- **Rational organizations**: social groups exhibiting formalized structures oriented to pursue specific goals
- **Natural-system organizations**: informal structures whose participants engage in collective activities devoted to a common interest: survival
- **Open-system organizations**: coalitions of shifting interest groups strongly influenced by their environment

These perspectives are discussed by describing some selected schools of thought for each. Each is illustrated in one case vignette, which is separated into three parts. Two other case vignettes are presented as additional examples of the perspectives and schools of thought presented in this chapter.

The Rational Organization

Part 1 of Case 4.1 illustrates most of the different schools of thought that view organizations as rational social structures.

Case 4.1 _____

Part 1: The Family Development Center

The Family Development Center (FDC) prides itself as a community-based agency where "compassionate human services are integrated with sound business practice." Serving Brewer and Baker counties in western Pennsylvania, it has grown over a period of fifteen years to an $8 million operation providing diversified services to children and families, teenagers and adults. Its activities include

- Protecting neglected and abused children.
- Providing housing, training, and support to individuals with mental disabilities.
- Treating adolescents with emotional difficulties.
- Assisting court-involved youth.
- Providing an alternative high school for exceptional youth.
- Intervening in family crises.

- Providing shelter for the homeless.
- Finding emergency and long-term foster care for children and teens.

FDC has fourteen separate organizational units, each of which is a cost center. These are organized into two divisions—one for adult services and the other for youth and family services, with each division headed by an assistant executive director. There is also an administrative director, who directs a fiscal unit and a personnel unit, and a director of community relations. The four top administrators in turn report to the executive director.

FDC built its positive reputation in the community because of its professional expertise, caring staff, competent financial services and provision of services on a twenty-four-hours-a-day basis. It sees its mission as making the communities of western Pennsylvania "a more accepting and compassionate place for all people." To achieve this mission, FDC developed guiding principles for its staff, based on six values:

- Respect and dignity for all
- Community-based services
- Advocacy services
- Individual support
- Professional excellence
- Organizational excellence

FDC recognizes the need for a uniform set of programmatic and financial procedures as basic requirements for administering any program in the agency. FDC makes every attempt to have each program operate as an independent responsibility center; however, to maintain its standards and principles, the board and executives of FDC recognize the need for a basic chain of command for decision making and communications for everyone in the organization. This is important for separating decisions and actions that each member of the staff could make independently from those that need to be communicated to higher levels of FDC for their review, decisions, and actions.

The programmatic staff includes social workers, psychologists, nurses, educators, and specialists in the area of developmental disabilities, child and family development, vocational rehabilitation and training, and residential management. The administrative staff includes accountants, personnel specialists, secretaries, data-processing specialists, and public relations specialists.

Bureaucracy

Max Weber, a sociologist whose writings (1947) originally articulated the theory of **bureaucracy**, noted that power and authority in a society traditionally has been legitimated either by *tradition* (i.e., the divine right of kings) or by *charisma* (i.e., prophet, demagogue, or hero). But in modern industrial soci-

Table 4.1   Characteristics of a Bureaucracy

Division of labor	To foster specialization
Vertical hierarchy	To enable rational decision making
Rules and regulations	To prescribe worker behavior and citizen expectation of goods and services
Technical competence (for selection, promotion, remuneration)	To engender efficient, uninterrupted, and coordinated organizational activities
Career employment	To develop experience and expertise
Formalized channels of communications	To maintain emotional detachment of officials in dealing with citizens, other officials, and subordinates, thus preventing feelings that interfere with rational performance of duties

eties, the *rational-legal model* of power distribution is the best compromise for which any society can hope (i.e., a governance system of laws, norms, and principles). The bureaucratic model is the most dominant form of organization today. Its primary characteristics are illustrated in Table 4.1.

Although bureaucracies have many shortcomings, chief among which is often their negative impact on human dignity, it should be clear that in a large, complex society they are the institutional vehicle for providing equal access to goods and services of that society. Victor Thompson emphasizes this by pointing out that, as an artificial system of rules and roles, "the exclusion of personal elements from prescribed role-relations has made the modern organization possible and adequate to its logistical task of provisioning hundreds of millions of people" (1975, 17).

Scientific Management

From his work in steel mills at the turn of the century, Frederick Winslow Taylor concluded that work could be analyzed scientifically. The scientific application of knowledge to work has been acclaimed as one of the greatest philosophical events of the intellectual and social history of human beings.

Based on time-and-motion studies of work, Taylor developed *The Principles of Scientific Management,* which was published in 1911. These principles (see Table 4.2) have become the basis of productivity values and techniques in modern organizations. The foundation of Taylor's work was the perception that the pursuit of productivity through the scientific construction of work leads to mutual prosperity for both workers and management.

Table 4.2   Core Principles of Scientific Management

Scientific task analysis	To determine the one best method of doing a task
Scientific selection and training of workers	For standardized performance of tasks
Separate thinking about the job from doing the job	To divide responsibility between workers and management; the former undertake the work, and the latter plan, organize, and control the work

Table 4.3   Principles of Administrative Management

Coordination	
Scalar principle	Hierarchy: a pyramidal structure of control
Unity of command	Each employee reports to only one superior
Span of control	Limited supervision of subordinates
Exception principle	Subordinates deal with routine, leaving to the superior's discretion how to deal with exceptions to existing rules
Specialization	
Division of labor	Homogeneous groups of related tasks
Departmentalization	By *purpose* (e.g., social services, physical health) By *process* (e.g., eligibility determination) By *area* (e.g., district office) By *clientele* (e.g., developmentally disabled)
Line-staff principle	Operational units separated from support units

Administrative Management

Taylor attempted to rationalize the organization from the bottom up by analyzing work methods and processes to arrive at a logical organizational structure. Administrative management theorists, on the other hand, took a top-down approach. They modeled the best ways to subdivide and structure work to achieve the goals and missions of the organization and then proceeded to design the necessary organizational structure. Early administrative management theorists included Luther Gulick (a leader in the public administration movement in the United States), Lyndall Urwick (one of Great Britain's most respected organizational theorists), and Henry Fayol (a French industrialist).

These theorists attempted to develop administrative principles that could be used as universal guidelines for the rationalization of organizations. The principles they developed (see Table 4.3) attempted to guide two types of activities in organizations: coordination and specialization. In *Papers on the Science of Administration* (1937) Gulick and Urwick developed the acronym POSDCORB for the functions of executives (see Table 4.4); for several decades it has served as a guideline for public managers.

Table 4.4   POSDCORB: Fundamental Functions of a Manager

Planning	Preparing methodical plans for managing programs
Organizing	Creating the different subunits in an agency
Staffing	Hiring competent employees to fill vacancies
Directing	Issuing directives with time and performance criteria
COordinating	Interrelating employees' efforts efficiently
Reporting	Preparing reports for superiors
Budgeting	Preparing and executing budgets

Among the primary contributions of administrative management theorists was their conception of an "ideal" or "classic" organization structure consisting of **line units** (responsible for carrying out the tasks of the organization), **support units** (responsible for providing "housekeeping" or auxiliary support services to line units), and **staff units** (responsible for providing advice and technical expertise to executives). Figure 4.1 illustrates a classic model of organizational structure as conceived by administrative management theorists.

Administrative Behavior

Herbert Simon, in his book *Administrative Behavior* (1976), was critical of the principles developed by earlier administrative management theorists and of Taylor's assumptions about the nature of the human beings in organizations. He presented a different theory about the administrative behavior of human beings in organizations.

To Simon the actions that people take in organizations are determined by choices that have to be made in a complex environment in which it is difficult to be aware of all available alternatives, let alone predict the consequences of each alternative. Organizations can develop processes for searching, learning, and deciding, but the complexity is so great that limits to the decision-action process have to be set. The rationality of organizations is restricted by *value-premises* (e.g., assumptions about preferred ends) and *factual premises* (e.g., assumptions about the way the world operates). The higher an organizational participant is in the hierarchy, the greater the influence of value-premises; the opposite holds true for organizational participants lower in the hierarchy, where factual premises dominate behavior. This concept of **bounded rationality** was one of Simon's primary contributions to the theory of organizations as rational systems.

The structures of organizations serve to specify roles, positions, rules, and regulations that channel individual behavior toward the achievement of predetermined goals. Standard operating procedures, information systems, and training programs are developed to further limit and circumscribe the employees'

Figure 4.1   Classic Organizational Model

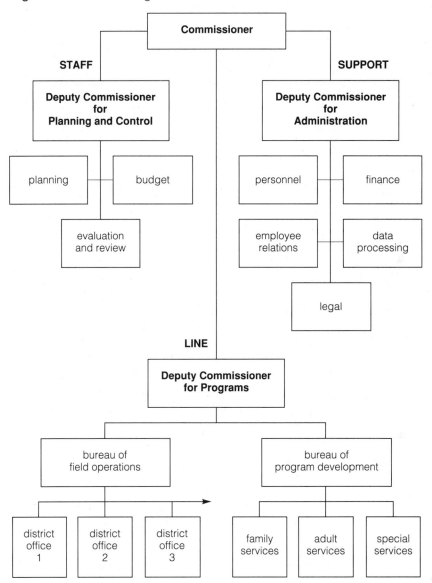

rationality. Although Simon viewed the behavior of people in organizations largely as decision making in nature, the administrative process was more correctly a chain of decisions resulting in required actions that led to more decisions that in turn resulted in more actions, on and on.

From this perspective, administrative behavior can be viewed as chains of decisions-actions, based on means-ends relationships, that move through an organization. These **means-ends chains** in a formalized structure promote consistency of decisions in all units of the organization. This process is illustrated by Case 4.2, which describes a *managed-care system* for developmentally disabled clients. A chain of decisions-actions ultimately results in the goal of the system: a unique set of community-based services for each client.

Case 4.2 _____

The Managed-Care System

Jim Dunn is a developmentally disabled client of the California Department of Mental Retardation (DMR) who was transferred from the state DMR institution to his home in region 3 of the department. He is now living at home with his parents, and receives a wide range of services from community agencies. Region 3 of the DMR has responsibility for his case.

A transorganizational system has been set up by the department to work with clients like Jim. At the outset an interdisciplinary team (IDT) assesses Jim's disability and develops a set of services that are specific to his situation. His parents take responsibility for managing his "services package" with the assistance of Cathy Davis, a case manager assigned by region 3. The service providers are a number of nonprofit, proprietary, and public agencies, each of which have a financial or bureaucratic contractual arrangement with region 3. Each contract is tied to outcome criteria that are the benchmarks against which his progress is measured. Although his individualized services package requires managing across several different organizational boundaries, Jim is a client of one agency: DMR.

The complete data specific to Jim's case are fed into an integrated computer system maintained by the DMR, with all transactions entered into this system by the IDT, providers, and Cathy as case manager. Data reports on Jim's progress are also available to everyone related to his case, his parents included. Technically, a telecommunication system permits anyone outside the department to interconnect by dialing the department's computer. Within the department, the terminals are interconnected by telephone wires. Procedures for limiting access and protecting confidentiality of Jim's data set are built into the computer system by means of identifiers and passwords, with levels of access depending on the type of data transaction.

The parents monitor Jim's progress and serve primarily as his advocate. Cathy, the region 3 case manager, also monitors Jim's progress for the IDT and deals with providers as problems arise. In addition, region 3 also has a systems manager who monitors the progress-performance of all clients assigned to the region. Performance "triggers" are built into each client's data set such that there are automatic alerts if IDT outcome criteria are not being met.

It is possible to view the managed-care system devised by the department for clients such as Jim as a chain of decision-actions that include:

- Interdisciplinary team diagnosis
- Specific services package
- Delivery of services
- Performance triggers–outcome measures

Specific services package
Services outcomes
Delivery of services
Performance triggers
Integrated computer system
IDT reassessment
Case management

In effect, each set of decisions leads to actions that require another set of decisions as the basis of new actions that trigger an additional set of decisions, on and on. The process is cybernetic; it feeds back on itself as a means of continually improving the outcomes and impacts on the client, who in this case is Jim Dunn.

The Natural-System Organization

In Part 1 of Case 4.1, were you able to identify and trace each aspect of the *rational* perspective of organizations? Reread it if necessary; then read Part 2 to compare it to the natural system's perspective.

Case 4.1

Part 2: The Family Development Center

Beverly Linquist, FDC's assistant executive director for family services, finished reporting to the board on FDC's three years of experience with the concept of the *parallel organization* (Barry A. Stein and Rosabeth Moss Kanter 1980). Their concept can be briefly described as

- A hierarchy that establishes financial and accounting procedures; policies and values for dealing with clients; quality-of-care policies; and professional and program standards, expectations, and accountability.
- Working committees that value people, emphasize excellence, and focus on decentralized decision making (an organizational culture); comprise a cross section of staff: professional, clerical, and managerial; deal with personnel policies, wage and salary, staff development, affirmative action, and client human rights; and use processes of shared leadership focused on goal setting and evaluation, hold meetings that are informal and inviting, use clear, shared-communication methods, and provide opportunities for resolving conflict by negotiation.

Beverly reported that the concept was working successfully. The Committee on Wage and Salary had, for example, used data collected by a consultant to develop a new compensation plan for FDC. The executive director had recommended it to the board, which accepted it. The Committee on Staff Development had initiated an employee satisfaction survey and had used the results to shape a new Professional Development program for FDC's staff. The board not only approved the program but also allocated the necessary funds for the first two years of its implementation. The Committee on Client Human Rights got so involved in the issue that they organized a network of agencies statewide and successfully lobbied for the passage of legislation in Harrisburg.

"I must admit, Bev," Peter said, "when you first presented your idea of the parallel organization, I had my doubts." Beverly knew she was lucky. A top executive of the Mallow Bank in Pittsburgh, Peter Brown as chairman of the FDC Board was willing to let the agency innovate.

She responded: "To tell you the truth, Peter, I had my doubts too. But I also had faith in the concept. As part of my doctoral program at Pitt, I've done a lot of research in participative management and democracy in the workplace. Centralized management and self-management can coexist. It is the order and rigor of the former that permits the creativity and innovation of the latter. The secret of our success is that members of these teams of employees feel vested in their committee. This means we have to clearly communicate to the staff in what areas FDC dictates policies and procedures and in what areas the staff can shape their own work environment. We have to pick tasks that meet three criteria: tasks that are clear, and can be accomplished in a reasonably short time; tasks that are highly valued by staff and organization; and tasks that demand creativity, providing members with a vehicle for personal growth."

"Peter," Bill Farrell, FDC executive director commented, "the parallel organization actually expresses the managerial philosophy that has helped us survive. Our annual report was more than just words when it stressed getting there on time, providing a caring environment, being there when needed, and seeing and responding to a need. We've been accepted by all elements of the community: business leaders because we use accepted business practices in our management; the human services providers because of our professional values and standards; and most of all, the people in the community who have firsthand experience in knowing that our motto of 'a caring and supportive environment' really describes our services, and is not just public relations."

Human Relations

The human relations school of thought developed in reaction to the then dominant organizational theorists' view of humans as "economic" or "rational" beings and the preoccupation with organizational processes that ignored the social aspects of work situations. The human relations theories grew out of the work of Mary Parker Follett—one of the pioneering giants in organizational and management thought—and of the research undertaken by Elton Mayo, F. J. Roethlisberger, and T. N. Whitehead at the Hawthorne plant of the Western Electric Company.

Follett lectured before leading business executives in the United States and in England during the 1920s. Although she is known primarily as the founder of the human relations school of thought, an examination of her writing and thinking indicates that she is the source of most modern management theories now practiced in developed societies. She should be considered a progenitor of human services management (see Case Study in Chapter 5). To Follett, the fundamental task of any organization is the building and maintenance of dynamic, harmonious human relations for joint efforts toward a specific purpose. Her writings focused on the dynamic, creative nature of human relationships that are the primary resource for any group effort, particularly in organizations.

Follett's philosophy was substantiated in the late 1920s by the work of Mayo and his group of researchers who were studying work in the Hawthorne plant of the Western Electric Company in Chicago. In attempting to further Taylor's scientific study of work, they undertook controlled research experiments that changed the work environment of employees and measured the results of productivity. They were surprised to find increases in productivity related to both improved work environment (e.g., better lighting) *and* deteriorating work environment (e.g., reduced lighting). Because the only constant in the experiments was the continuous attention devoted to the workers in the organization, the researchers concluded that social interrelationships affected productivity. The researchers decided to explore this phenomenon in greater depth and conducted thousands of interviews with employees of the plant. The effect of their research was twofold: The organization began to be viewed in terms of individuals, informal groups, and intergroup relationships; and behavioral science research methodologies for studying organizations were legitimized.

This provided a new thesis: Individual and human relations are the foundation of organizations (see Table 4.5). The human relationists provided the foundation for the perspective of organizations as natural systems and for the later work of organizational psychologists.

Cooperative Systems

Chester Barnard, an executive for New Jersey Bell Telephone, wrote *The Functions of the Executive* (1938), which was one of the first books devoted to the notion of organizations as natural systems. It contributed to the human relations school of thought and became the basis for the work of other organizational theorists during the decades of the 1940s and 1950s. Barnard viewed organizations as **cooperative systems** designed to interrelate the contributions of individual employees. This required the willingness of participants to contribute to the organization and required executives to direct these contributions toward a common purpose.

Table 4.5   Human Relationists' Perceptions of Organizations

- Organizations must be viewed from a social perspective.
- Workers are motivated by more than economic incentives; their psychosocial needs must be taken into account.
- The informal structure of an organization is as important as the formal.
- Democratic leadership styles of management, which involve workers, are important for effective organizations.
- Worker satisfaction is critical for organizational productivity.
- Both social and technical skills are important for managers.

In Barnard's view, directing the contributions of a large number of people toward a common purpose required (1) the inculcation of values, attitudes, points of view, and loyalties; and (2) securing, creating, and inspiring morale such that individual interests were subordinated to the good of the cooperative system. To this end, informal organization was as important as formal organization, and nonmaterial rewards as important as material rewards. In effect, Barnard was one of the first to identify the importance of **organizational culture** for managers.

Barnard was also one of the first to note that even more powerful than the common purpose of the organization is its tendency to perpetuate itself for the larger purpose of survival. This placed his **inducements-contributions theory** (e.g., the explicit or implicit contract between the individual and the organization of what each would contribute to the other and what each would receive) in a larger setting. It prescribed the behavior of individuals within the organization in return for the opportunity of building careers. Individuals are motivated to work for the survival of the organization as a means of protecting and enhancing their long-term careers.

One of the first to view the organization as a unit in interaction with its environment, Barnard contributed to the natural-system perspective of organization. From this perspective, the **natural-system organization** is viewed as a complex of interdependent parts that make up a whole, interdependent with a larger environment. Central to this approach is the concept of *homeostatis* (self-stabilization), which naturally keeps the system viable as it is buffeted by forces in the environment. As James Thompson subsequently articulated, *co-alignment is the basic administrative function* keeping "the organization at the nexus of several necessary streams of action; and because the several streams are variable and moving, the nexus is not only moving, but sometimes quite difficult to fathom" (1967, 148). To survive, Barnard noted, it is necessary to find the *strategic variables* that the organization can manipulate to achieve a viable co-alignment.

Barnard was not without his critics. In *Complex Organizations: A Critical Essay* (1979), the noted organizational scholar Charles Perrow critically analyzed the premises of Barnard's thinking. He began his analysis of *Functions of the Executive* by noting that it contained the seeds of three trends of organizational theory that were to dominate the field for several decades during the midtwentieth century (e.g., the institutional school, the decision-making school, and the human relations school). But Perrow then criticized Barnard for his insistence that organizations are superior to individuals because the former are rational, the latter irrational: "The organization is more rational than the individual because order is imposed upon members by those who control the organization, and the order is in the interests of goals or purposes established and guarded by those in charge" (Perrow 1979, 76). To Perrow, Barnard glorifies the organization and minimizes the person; in Barnard's thinking, the person is "as a slave voluntarily giving legitimacy to the authority of the master" (1979, 87). Organizations have a moral imperative, as defined by the executive, with apparently no participation by subordinates other than loyally accepting that imperative. Organizations are legitimized by their very definition; they are cooperative and pursue a moral purpose.

Despite the continued popularity of Barnard's conception of an organization as a cooperative system, Perrow's critical analysis is insightful. It underscores the fact that management is both an art and a science and that the manager must artfully and cautiously blend the various systems' perspectives in pursuit of human services organizational effectiveness.

Institutional Approach

In contributing to the perspective of organizations as a natural system, Philip Selznick, one of the leading organizational theorists in the United States, viewed organizations as adaptive institutions shaped by the rational and nonrational behavior of their participants and by influences from the environment. Just as individuals develop a distinctive personality over time, so too an organization develops a distinctive character over time through the process of institutionalization. "An *institution* is more nearly a natural product of social needs and pressures—a responsive, adaptive organism" (1957, 5). In his study of the TVA (the Tennessee Valley Authority created during the depression of the 1930s to deal with a range of economic and environmental problems of the entire Tennessee Valley), Selznick (1957) presented the thesis that organizations have a natural history in which they develop distinctive structures, capacities, and liabilities.

Despite the fact that organizations start out with what are considered clear and specific goals, over time these are adapted in order to survive and grow. One of the processes is the mechanism of **cooptation**. To gain legitimacy and political support from the environment, and thus to avert threats to its stability or existence, organizations incorporate external elements into the decision-making processes. In the case of the TVA, for example, public-interest goals were subverted to serve private interests. For example, land that had been reforested to serve as a watershed fell into the hands of lumber companies. As

Perrow, a student and follower of Selznick noted, the organization sold out its goals in order to survive and grow.

Selznick also viewed organizations as cooperative systems that have basic needs primarily related to self-maintenance. He suggested that there is a "Freudian model" of analysis whereby each organization, like each personality, is the result of adaptation to complex forces over a long period of time, which in order to understand requires intensive analysis not unlike that of psychoanalysis. In this respect, like other natural-systems theorists, he proposed a structural-functional perspective of organizations: the *structure* of an organization is shaped by its basic *functions* or needs.

Social Systems

You may have wondered how it is that an organization can have a turnover of personnel with different personalities and different positions and yet continue to function in the usual manner. To Talcott Parsons (1951), this can be explained in terms of four basic functions that organizations, like all social systems, must perform to survive (see Table 4.6).

Organizations are viewed as a network of interlocking subsystems that function to meet the needs of each other. Having both structure and function, the social system attempts to attain its goals by adapting and adjusting to changes in the direction of a new type of stability. This process is called *homeostatis,* a dynamic state of equilibrium.

By conceptualizing organizations as adaptive structures, Parsons broadened the focus of organizational theorists beyond individual or groups of workers to view the total organization as an element of an interrelated system of societal institutions. Social system organizations are related to the functioning of society. For example, from an *ecological* perspective, different organizations can be classified in terms of their primary societal functions:

- Economic-production organizations   Adaptation
- Political-government organizations   Goal attainment
- Integrative organizations (e.g., courts, political parties)   Integration
- Pattern-maintenance organizations (e.g., museums, religious and educational institutions)   Latency

Parsons also analyzed organizations as a social system, in terms of the AGIL functions, at what he calls the *structural level* of analysis and at the *social psychological level* (i.e., each subsystem in an organization is analyzed in terms of the four functions).

Parsons's analysis of organizations as social systems has one additional concept important for human services management. He identifies organizational structure in terms of the following three levels of systems: institutional,

Table 4.6   Basic Functions of Organizations as Social Systems

Adaptation	To acquire adequate resources
Goal achievement	To set and reach goals
Integration	To coordinate the elements of the system
Latency	To sustain the system's unique culture

Table 4.7   Parsons's Conception of Three Levels of Organization and Management

Institutional	To relate the organization to the larger society
Managerial	To mediate between the organization and the task environment
Technical	To service organizational clients (e.g., as clinicians)

managerial, and technical (see Table 4.7). As we note in subsequent chapters, this has become the accepted way of classifying levels of organization and management.

The Open-System Organization

By now you have developed your ability to identify different organizational perspectives in practice. Part 3 of Case 4.1 gives you an additional opportunity to analyze how a human services agency expresses, on a day-to-day basis, the different perspectives and schools of thought on organizations. The final perspective and its derivating schools of thought have become very influential in shaping modern human services organizations. See how you fare in detecting their presence in this part of the case.

Case 4.1 _____

Part 3: The Family Development Center

After the board meeting, Beverly sat in Bill Farrell's office and reviewed his annual report to the board. "They really ought to change our titles, Bill," Beverly remarked. "You and I, and the other FDC executives, work closely with other human services agencies in the community and form coalitions to deal with practically every issue that is pressing on society. That's why in the past five years western Pennsylvania has become more responsive to abused women, mental health patients trying to re-enter the community, the homeless, pregnant teenagers, and school dropouts. You spend a great deal of your time in Harrisburg working with the legislators of the commonwealth; I spend most of my time with community leaders. But both of us play roles of constructing new realities and forming new interorganizational structures and systems. Our titles say we're managers; aren't we really community organizers or community educators?"

Bill thought for a few minutes and then responded: "The key, Bev, is really our parallel organization. Without realizing it, we have really constructed intricate systems of people and technology in a way that they can continue to adapt to their environments, both within FDC and in the larger community. So I would say, more than just constructing new realities, we nurture an organizational culture in which those realities can be supported and sustained. We are role models for our staff: We stress professionalism and organizational competence. And I think you would agree that you also serve as a feminist model for the women in FDC, particularly the women administrators."

"That's true," Beverly responded, "but we also try to present models to other managers. We create the values and processes that serve as the rigor for all units in FDC and then let each administrator manage her own operation as an independent responsibility center. Maybe we get away with it because we limit the number of clients for each facility because of our personal, individualized approach to services."

"I must admit, Bev," Bill noted, "that I never thought about the interplay between our clinical values and our administrative values. But I think you're right. You know Jack Grant, director of our Lincoln homeless shelter? Well, he has a concept I like. Jack envisions himself as being the manager of a greenhouse: create a healthy environment in which people—clients and staff—can be protected from the bitter world and help them grow, learn, and develop."

"I think our staff likes the climate we've set," Beverly commented thoughtfully. "We're proud of what FDC has accomplished this past decade. But we're not alone. The community recognizes our achievements; so does the board, obviously. And in our recent survey of FDC employees by the Staff Development Committee, 85 percent liked working for FDC and liked the way it's being run. Do you think we can rest on our laurels?"

"Sure," Bill quickly answered, "for about sixty seconds. After that our environment will change, and we have to start searching again for ways of improving FDC!"

General-Systems Theory

Some historians consider the period between the Renaissance and World War II as the mechanical age during which theorists focused on *reductionism,* explaining the whole in terms of the parts. The end of World War II marked the beginning of the systems age, in which researchers attempted to explain the

Table 4.8   Common Characteristics of Open Systems

Importation of energy	Deriving energy from the environment
Through-put	Transformation of energy into outputs
Output	Exporting some product into the environment
Systems as cycles	Cyclical nature of the energy exchange
Negative entropy	Importing more energy than required, in order to survive
Information, negative feedback and coding	Positive and negative feedback of information inputs, in order to keep the system on target
Dynamic homeostatis	Tendency toward a steady state in which the system is preserved through growth and expansion
Differentiation	Specialized functions performed by different components of a system or subsystem
Equifinality	Reaching the same final state from differing initial conditions and by a variety of paths

Source: Adapted from Daniel Katz and Robert L. Kahn, *The Social Psychology of Organizations* (New York: Wiley, 1966).

parts in terms of the whole. The work of Ludwig Von Bertalanffy in general-systems theory (1956) served as the catalyst for the 180-degree turn in our perception of phenomena.

General-systems theory (GST) views an organization as a system of interdependent parts to be viewed holistically and that are interrelated through the processes of communication, feedback, and control. Central to GST are the concepts of closed and open systems. **Closed systems** are highly structured and relatively unresponsive to the external environment. **Open systems** react readily to changes in the environment; they tend to be self-regulating systems. It is suggested that bureaucracies tend to the closed-system philosophy, whereas open systems are viewed as adhocracies (e.g., adaptive, temporary systems that are organized around issues or problems—e.g., a task force on teenage pregnancy). Daniel Katz and Robert Kahn (1966), two leading social psychologists, were among the first to analyze organizations as open systems. They described nine characteristics that seem to define all open systems (see Table 4.8).

To the organizational theorist, one of the important characteristics of open systems is that they have a *nesting* quality. Like a set of Russian dolls, systems are made up of subsystems and in turn are themselves contained within larger systems.

GST can be viewed as a search for law and order in the universe: an order of order. Kenneth Boulding (1956) classified systems in terms of levels, which established what is generally accepted as the hierarchy of systems (see Table 4.9).

GST has strongly affected human services provision as well as human services management. The conceptual roots of the ecological and life-model perspectives of social work practice, for example, are traced to GST. The medical model of treatment, if not replaced by a systems model, is at least being seri-

Table 4.9   Ordering of Systems by Complexity

Level	Characteristic	Example	Science Classification	Nature of System
Frameworks	Static structures	Geography	Physical	Closed
Simple dynamic	Predetermined motions	Clockworks	Physical	Closed
Cybernetic	Self-regulating	Thermostat	Physical	Closed
Self-maintenance	Resource transformation	Living cell	Biological	Open
Genetic-societal	Blueprinted-growth	Plant	Biological	Open
Internal-image	Self-awareness	Animal	Biological	Open
Symbol processing	Self-consciousness	Humans	Social	Open
Social systems	Organizations	Society	Social	Open
Transcendental	Inescapable unknowns	Theologian	Social	Open

Source: Adapted from Kenneth E. Boulding, "General Systems Theory—The Skeleton of Science," *Management Science* (April 1956): 197–208.

ously challenged. GST has initiated a holistic view of human existence in all of its dimensions.

Cybernetic Systems

Have you ever wondered how the staff of a human services organization—clerks, professionals, and administrators—can stay on top of all the countless number of details involved in operating a complex societal institution? Difficult as it may seem, the process of communication and control that keeps an organization functioning with large volumes of operations, decisions, and actions each day is the same process that permits the human body to make thousands of decisions daily in an automatic, self-regulating fashion. This process is called **cybernetics**.

In the 1940s, Norbert Wiener proposed the theory that the self-regulating processes of control and communications in humans and machines can be viewed as a common body of science. He called this process cybernetics, a Greek word for *steersman*. In other words, whether talking about how human beings are able to bring a glass of water to their lips successfully (without looking in a mirror) or how a jumbo jet can land using a computerized automatic pilot, the processes are the same: (1) a detector, (2) a selector-transformer, and (3) an effector, all tied together with (4) a control and feedback loop that permits the system to control itself against some preset or dynamic condition (see Figure 4.2).

Stafford Beer (1975), one of the leading management science theorists, maintains that the science of cybernetics conceives of organizations as complex systems that, if properly managed, can be self-regulating and self-controlling.

Figure 4.2   The Cybernetic Process

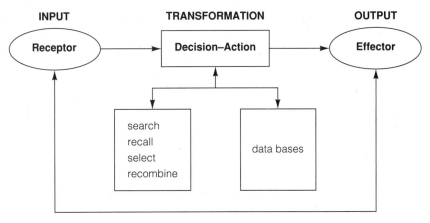

Organizations can be designed to deal with the enormous complexity of modern society. The measure of complexity is variety. For human services managers, the challenge is the design and management of organizations that can function with ultimate variety—dealing with each client in an individualized fashion. In effect, the human services manager's function would be to become a "variety engineer."

The ability to develop self-regulating systems that can deal with the complexity of modern society in a way that treats each client uniquely is important for modern-day human services management. For this reason, the concepts and techniques of cybernetics are vital to the design of today's **sociotechnical systems**. For example, when a fire dispatcher enters the location of a fire into the department's computer system, prestored data can automatically communicate to the video screen in the fire engine the location of the room of a disabled person living in the burning building. With this type of cybernetic system, firefighters can be more responsive in carrying out their primary mission: the saving of human life.

Wiener's book on cybernetics was entitled *The Human Use of Human Beings* (1950, 1954) because he was convinced that machines can enhance human dignity if we combine our know-how with our know-what and if we have a clear understanding of the type of society we want to fashion and how best to go about achieving that ideal. He understood that cybernetics could lead to machines, even robots, that could free human beings from having to be automatons in their work or home life. But this leads to a crucial challenge: What would replace work as the central focus of people's lives? Are most people in human services organizations used as automatons today? What would a society look like in which the majority of people would be able to consider leisure as the main focus of their daily lives?

Contingency Theory

One of the most dominant schools of organizational thought that emerged during the third quarter of the twentieth century was **contingency theory**. It is based on the assumption that the best way of organizing depends on the organizational environment. In essence, it derives from the recognition that the forms and processes of organization are not static but are instead highly situational.

Originally identified in the 1920s by Follett as **situational management**, contingency theory emerged some four decades later as a result of the work of sociotechnical systems designers. It subsequently influenced those theorists working in the fields of organizational leadership and organizational decision making. Their combined work points to the situational or contingency nature of organization and management.

Situational Organizational Forms.   During the 1950s and 1960s, a number of organizational scholars began to propose that there was no one best way of organizing. They argued that different organizational structures are needed for different technological environments. The degree of internal differentiation and the modes of integration of differentiated parts of an organization depended on the environment. In stable environments, for example, integration can be achieved by hierarchy, rules, and procedures. For uncertain and turbulent environments, integration required interdisciplinary project teams and coordinators skilled in conflict resolution.

The work of a large number of sociotechnical systems researchers had a particular influence on the development of contingency theory. Their work pointed to the need for adapting the social and technical aspects of organizations to meet the situational needs of an organization.

Situational Leadership.   Initially, researchers in organizational leadership attempted to isolate and identify those traits that effective leaders displayed. Over time, the currently popular situational approach to leadership began to emerge. Working on the assumption that leadership style is the single most important influence in an organization, several scholars began to focus on the contingency nature of leadership. Studies indicated that leadership styles varied from situation to situation and were dependent not only on work environments but also on specific interpersonal relationships between leaders and their individual followers.

Even though contingency leadership theories focus on specific situations, most tend to view a mix of leadership styles. A number of organizational psychologists have developed specific theories and approaches that range from emphasis on the job-task to emphasis on employee relationships; they include the following.

Author-Researcher	*Theory-Approach*
▪ Douglas MacGregor	Theory X–theory Y
▪ Rensis Likert	System 1–system 4
▪ Robert Blake and Jane Mouton	Managerial grid
▪ Paul Hersey and Kenneth Blanchard	Situational leadership

These approaches are treated more fully in the Chapter 5 discussion of organizational psychologists.

Situational Decision Making.   Most managers have innate styles of decision making. Moreover, managers from specific environments either develop specific ways of making decisions or have reputations for such styles (e.g., physicians, police chiefs, generals, social workers, and educators). But during the past two decades, we have recognized that there is a relationship between successful decision making and the particular situation. There are some situations when it is proper for a manager to make a decision without consulting other members of the organization. The opposite is also true; there are situations in which it is best to call a meeting of all those in an organization who are affected and turn over to them the task of making a decision. Effective decision making is considered to be the task of matching the demands of the situation with the proper decision style.

Victor Vroom (1973) was one of the first scholars to undertake research in the area of situational decision making. In his research, he employed five alternative decision processes:

Make the Decision Yourself

1. Using available information.
2. After acquiring information from subordinates.
3. After sharing the problem with each subordinate and acquiring their ideas and suggestions.
4. After meeting with your subordinates as a group, sharing the problem, and acquiring their suggestions.

Shared Decision Making

5. Arrive at a consensus with your subordinates after meeting with them as a group, sharing the problem, and acquiring their ideas.

Vroom analyzed the attributes of decision situations to arrive at key questions that would lead to a situational decision-making model. These questions relate the degree to which the problem is structured, the speed with which a decision must be made, the availability of sufficient information to make the decision, and the importance of subordinate ownership in the decision for it to be effectively implemented.

Contingency theory, regardless of its particular expression, is generally accepted as the dominant current approach to the organization and management of societal institutions. Although not the "magic bullet," nevertheless it is a move toward dynamic management. The knowledge and skills that have evolved from the contingency school of thought are therefore important to the human services management student and practitioner.

Sociotechnical Systems

Working in England during the 1950s, Joan Woodward (1965) found that organizational structures and processes are dependent on the technology and environment of work itself. Industries involved in mass production, where efficiency and productivity were the central organizational issue, had formal bureaucratic hierarchies. On the other hand, for companies concerned with product development, where creativity and innovation were the primary organizational issue, nonbureaucratic structures were more appropriate. Her work indicated that technical systems placed different demands on organizations. Thus the premise that there existed a universal set of principles of how to organize and manage was invalid.

Woodward's findings were supported by many colleagues who also focused their research on organizational structures, processes, and technology. In general, they found that organizational structure depends on the technology and technical system used for work. Eric Trist (1981), for example, found that miners using small hand tools work together as small groups with a great deal of independence and autonomy as a group. But with the introduction of mechanical coal-cutting methods, the work groups were eliminated. A change in organizational structure was required to recapture the work-group notion. Sociotechnical systems researchers began to view organizations as open systems that must dynamically react to the different demands of changing technologies and work environments of organizational structures. The best organization form for any particular institution depended on a *goodness of fit,* balancing the various subsystems: human-cultural, technological, structural, strategic, and managerial—all as they interact with their environments.

The recognition that organizations are sociotechnical systems emphasized the need for managers to have good skills in **systems design**. Interrelating workers, technology, and environment is a very complex process that is critical to the effective and efficient functioning of societal institutions. An eligibility management system (EMS) for transfer payments to impoverished families is a good example of a complex, sophisticated sociotechnical system. It illustrates the way in which the design of technical systems in the services industry will ultimately alter the organizational and managerial structures-processes of human services management. As Case 4.3 discusses, it anticipates a number of significant impacts on the organization and management of the Connecticut Department of Income Maintenance. Because it uses state-of-the art technology, the design and development methodically sought the best fit between organizational structure and processes, employee and client needs, and the interorganizational and intergovernment systemic environment of eligibility determination.

Case 4.3

Part 1: Eligibility Management System*

In 1984 the state of Connecticut began to design an automated, client-based, on-line eligibility management system (EMS), which was actualized in 1989, in a district office. When fully operationalized, EMS would provide integrated processing for the following areas:

Function

- Determination of client eligiblity
- Issuance of benefits
- Management support

Programs

- AFDC
- Food Stamps
- State Supplements
- Refugee Assistance
- Energy Assistance

Connecticut is one of several states to have an EMS; some others include Alabama, Alaska, Arizona, Colorado, New Mexico, North Carolina, Ohio, Pennsylvania, Utah, Washington, and Wisconsin.

EMS is a carefully designed, sophisticated sociotechnical system. It consists of several subsystems where people, processes, and technology all interact with each other and with their tasks and general environments. This interaction in turn influences the way in which each subsystem is designed.

EMS represents more than a sophisticated computer system, although it does use state-of-the-art computer and telecommunications technology. It represents a new approach to the organization and management of the Connecticut Department of Income Maintenance, and also creates new role definitions for the staff of the department, particularly for the eligibility workers who operate the system. And perhaps, most important, it provides a new way of interacting with clients, improves the way in which services are provided, and perhaps even defines how clients are perceived.

In terms of department organization and management, EMS has had the following impacts:

- A new management philosophy
- Changes in organizational structure
- Rewriting of policies
- User involvement in planning and design

- Eligibility workers handle *all* assistance programs, with no specialization
- Client works with *one* eligibility worker for case maintenance

The primary objective of EMS is to serve clients more efficiently and more accurately. In addition, there are several other benefits that are anticipated from this major investment in change. They include

- Faster, cost-effective delivery of benefits to clients.
- Reduction of error-prone, burdensome paperwork.
- Uniform application of policies.
- Support for administrative and management activities.
- Enhanced client referrals to other programs.
- Enhanced interfaces with external human services agencies.
- Supported quality control.
- Increased workers' job satisfaction.
- Reduced error rates.

EMS has three subsystems: client certification, financial information and control, and management information and control. It also contains four generalized functions: systems help, data validation and control, electronic mail, and systems security.

With the exception of sociotechnical systems designed by the military or NASA, EMS is one of the most complex, sophisticated systems to be designed and operationalized by any organization—public or private.

*Note: Parts 2 and 3 of the EMS case appear in Chapters 13 and 15, respectively.

Summary

Is it possible to identify and describe different schools of thought and theories of organizations and systems? Does each have distinctive and recognizable features that lead to specific impacts on human services organizations—for both employees and clients? Both these questions have been answered in the affirmative by this chapter's brief review of the three perspectives of organizations and systems used by scholars today to examine the field. But as the student and practitioner of human services management realize, there are overlaps and interrelationships among these perspectives. The study of organizations and systems can be likened to a visit to an aquarium. There are several windows from which spectators can view fish in the tank; and although different spectators view the fish from different perspectives, the contents and behaviors in the tank remain the same. We just see them differently. Even more critical, what we see has changed almost before we have recorded our particular perceptions.

People in many areas of life are concerned with the issue of how to improve our societal institutions and systems. This concern is reflected in the belief that effective organizational and managerial techniques offer the optimal path to achieving our individual and collective goals. For the professional human services manager, this places continual pressure to acquire new conceptual and methodological expertise for the improved organization and management of the human services. A search for the roots, the conceptual bases of human services management by examining the vast literature devoted to perspectives, schools of thoughts, and theories of organizations and systems is the starting point for professional management of the human services. It is also the point of departure for responding successfully to a dynamic environment that continually requires more creative ways of improving the organizations and systems by which human services are managed in our society.

The reader should feel sufficiently familiar with the perspectives of organizations and systems presented to recognize them, to understand their implications, and finally, after further study, to exploit the potentialities of each. Dynamic, creative management of the human services can only be undertaken within the context of a body of conceptual and theoretical constructs, which, over a lifetime, the human services manager must continue to expand and refine.

5

Human and Organizational
Behavior: Some Interactions

Behavior is a function of the interweaving between activity of organism and activity of environment, that is, response is to a relating. By this interlocking activity, individual and situation each is creating itself anew, thus relating themselves anew, thus giving us the evolving situation.

To free the energies of the human spirit is the high potentiality of all human association. (1924, 303)

These words, which resound with such clarity, significance, and contemporaneity, are neither new nor orginal. They are the words of an individual who wrote in 1924—at a time, in fact, when the term *human services* did not even exist. They are offered here not only to indicate what shapes the behavior of human beings as they interact within an organizational environment but also to serve as a motto for all who seek careers as dynamic, creative managers. They are the words of Mary Parker Follett, little known by most people but recognized as one of the founders of modern organization and management theory and of human services management.

The Influence of Organizations on Human Behavior

People act differently when working in an organization. For a number of complex reasons, this phenomenon is true for all of us. Why? Let us explore some theories or perspectives that might help find the answer to this question. Searching for this answer will help provide a view of the way in which the interaction between people and organizations shape individual and collective behavior. Let us look at Case 5.1.

Case 5.1 _____

The Resignation of Cindi Sherwood

As she watched Nan Taylor, director of her agency, read her letter of resignation, Cindi thought back over the sequence of events that led to her decision to leave. When she was appointed assistant director of the Arizona United Services Appeal Association (AUSAA), she had been both excited and proud. It was more than a great career move, it was an opportunity to actualize some of her deepest human services values and ideals. But her enthusiasm lasted only a few weeks; it dropped sharply with her first clash with Nan.

"Organize campaigns among the Mexican–American communities?" Nan had exclaimed. "That's not the direction of the innovations we need, Cindi. First, most of those people are taken care of by community action programs. Second, it would take up too much time and energy to help them organize.

Their notions of community involvement are different than ours. Besides, where's the money in Arizona these days? In the new corporations, the yuppies, and the well elderly who are moving here for retirement. That's who we need to organize. Working with Mexican–American councils is a great idea, but not right now and not for us."

"Can't we at least bounce the idea off of our board's Long-Range Planning Committee?" Cindi had responded. Nan's answer was curt and final: "It's out of the question right now. You need to spend your time modernizing the way we manage our office. The staff in the office have been pushing me for months about modernizing our procedures and systems. That's a much higher priority for me right now."

That was the first sign to Cindi. It came as a shock. When she was hired, she and Nan had talked about the role of the assistant director as being essentially strategic and program planning. Statewide, the AUSAA was losing its market share of fund-raising. Because Arizona was a growth area, long-range planning was vital. Working with the Mexican–American population was only one of several new programs Cindi had suggested. But the suggestion got no further than Nan, and Nan turned Cindi into an office manager.

That soon bogged down. Nan spent 90 percent of her time working with board members who were very impressed with the way Nan ran the monthly board meetings and with the briefing materials she prepared for these meetings. She also spent a lot of time meeting with individual board members in between the monthly meetings.

It didn't take long for Cindi to size up a number of problems she hadn't recognized before she was hired. Like many managers, Nan had two personalities. Although she had excellent political skills in the community, she had poor interpersonal skills when working with colleagues and subordinates. Her style inside the office was autocratic, even though verbally she preached involvement and participation.

Nan was good at understanding the culture of the "old guard" of AUSAA. The board's understanding of the agency was limited to the reality that Nan constructed for them because they only received data and briefings that Nan wrote. They really only wanted to make modest changes. Nationally, the organization was in trouble, but in Arizona they were still growing. So Nan let the board call the shots; after all, the previous director had tried to implement change and had been rejected. His resignation led to Nan being appointed to the position on a permanent basis, and the lesson was not lost on her.

Even after approving Cindi's plan for changing office procedures to tighten up controls and put the agency in a more flexible position, Nan undercut each change as it was about to be implemented. More important, the finance director was her eyes and ears for the day-to-day operations, and the rest of the staff resented it. They saw Cindi as an ally but soon recognized that Nan did not give up any of her authority to Cindi, although holding her responsible.

Nan looked up from reading the resignation letter. "Any chance of your reconsidering this, Cindi?"

"Well," Cindi responded, "are you willing to reconsider my new marketing plan for the agency, at least take it to the board for their consideration?"

Nan was quick to answer: "It just won't work, Cindi; this is Arizona, not your southern California. Maybe in a few years; but we're doing fine as is."

Cindi smiled, but it was a sad smile.

Role Theory

Consider how many different roles each of us plays in our lives: mother–father, son–daughter, mate, student, professional, lover, friend, organization member, and so forth. Do each of these roles prescribe different behaviors for us? What happens when two different roles prescribe different types of behavior that contradict each other?

Social work clinicians play a number of different roles that Harold Weismann and his associates (1983) document with case studies: diagnostician, expediter, case manager, colleague, advocate, program developer, organizational reformer, supervisor, practice researcher, and employee. Human services managers must play some of these roles and still others: executive, change agent, evaluator, public relations person, promoter, planner, educator, entrepreneur, systems negotiator, broker, network manager, facilitator, and so on. And all these are added to their primary organizational role as boss, subordinate, and co-worker.

Because roles are important to organizations, sociologists and psychologists have made them the focus of research. A body of literature, definitions, and constructs known as **role theory** has been the result.

When sociologists and psychologists use the term *role,* they generally mean a set of behaviors that the individual—as an occupant of a position within the social system—perceives of himself, that are perceived toward others, and that are shared expectations of others. The literature employs a number of terms as part of role theory: *role set, status set, status sequence, role expectations, sent and received role, role behavior, role episode,* and *role conflict.* Of these, **role set** is one of the most important—it refers to an assortment of role relationships that are acquired through occupying a particular social status.

For human services management, the role set of different positions in an organization shapes the way the occupants will behave. This becomes more complicated when two or more roles that one person has are in conflict with each other. For example, Betty Barry's role as school social worker at Winfield High School carries with it a set of organizational and professional expectations that are similar to any high school social worker. They are further affected by the fact that Betty is married to David Barry, principal of Winfield High School. There is potential for conflict if the two disagree about a particular student problem at the school. Betty's activity in the school employees' union generates potential for conflict at three levels: professional, organizational, and personal. This is further complicated by her colleagues' perceptions because of her special relationship as the boss's wife. This could be an advantage or a detriment to their **role relationships**.

There is yet another aspect of role theory. How we as human services managers fashion human services is a direct result of our own role image. When that role image and the activities in which we engage are unclear, tensions result. We begin to ask basic questions: Who am I professionally? What is my role? Take the following example: Which do you consider the appropriate role?

Two Different Role Images of a City Human Services Director

1. Providing the most efficient execution of the municipal social services department's services, including such activities as family services, youth services, food bank, general income assistance, services to the disabled, and senior citizen services
2. Attempting to achieve the optimal conditions for residents in the city to acquire human services as needed, at the least aggregate expenditure of physical and psychic resources: for the residents; for the taxpayers; for the city's economy

Contrary to conventional thought, the management of human services organizations begins with the human services manager's definition of role image, in all of its dimensions. (See the discussion of the human services manager's role perceptions in the Epilogue of this book.)

People play a variety of different roles, which can conflict in complex ways, that affect their behavior. It is obvious why a good understanding of role theory is important for the human services administrator who is trying to manage in a dynamic, creative way.

Managing Change and Transitions

If you were asked to make a prediction about the world, your life, or your human services agency ten years from now, there would probably be at least one certain response: There will be a lot of changes when compared with today. Because change is the only constant in today's society and the only certainty in our future, it is natural that the dynamic, creative manager should devote a great amount of time, thought, and energy to the subject.

We have already noted (in Chapter 2) several irreconcilable value-tensions that relate to the issue of change. One way of viewing the field of human services management, for example, is to characterize it as the tension between systems maintenance and systems change. In actuality, both order (systems maintenance) and freedom (systems change) are necessary for creative management of human services organizations. Thus, it is appropriate to view change management as very relevant to human services management.

Can the human services manager sort out all the knowledge and skills on the subject of change? It is indeed a difficult task. The terms are not precise, and there are overlapping areas of interests of theorists and practitioners. Warren Bennis and associates' book, *The Planning of Change* (1961), symbolized two separate streams of intellectual thought—that of organizational psychologists interested in managing the process of change and that of planners who, bedded in an entirely different professional value, were concerned with refashioning the institutional fabric of the United States.

In the literature and practice of planning, one can find many different approaches and tensions. One of the classic tensions is between the concept of long-range planning and incremental planning. **Long-range planning** subscribes to a methodical, rational approach to planning, involving collection of data, assessment of needs, consideration of alternative plans for the future, selection of the best plan, and identification of the resources and processes required to achieve the selected plan. **Incremental planning** suggests that change is best accomplished in small increments, which are achieved when the opportunity presents itself in the social-political-economic environment. This tension is one that human services planners and managers face continually over the course of their careers.

As I noted in opening this chapter, Follett was one of the first to write on the subject of change and conflict management. At the very heart of the subject was her conception of human interaction as a *creative experience:* "I relate to you; you relate to me; we both relate to the relationship of you and me. By the very process of meeting, we both have become something different" (1924, 62–63). It was her perception that because conflict cannot be avoided it should be used to work for our benefit. As Follett viewed it, just as friction is necessary when the wheel of a locomotive conflicts with the track in order to haul the train, so also does conflict bring us the music of a violin.

Follett considered three possible methods of dealing with conflict: domination, compromise, and integration. She concluded that integration is the best method because it involves invention, the creation of something anew: *The basis of all cooperative activity is integrated diversity.*

This was Follett's concept of **constructive conflict**. In today's terminology, domination would be considered a win-lose option; compromise would be considered a lose-lose option; and integration would be considered a win-win situation. Some fifty years later, we use the term *creative conflict* to refer to the process of change that grows out of conflict resolution and, interestingly enough, conflict stimulation. The latter is now viewed as much of a process for managing change in organizations as is the former.

One of the classic studies of the literature dealing with planned change suggested that there are three groups of change strategies: empirical-rational, normative-reeducative, and power-coercive (see Table 5.1).

Concepts of change have also emerged from work in the field of knowledge of technology transfer. The term generally used for this process has been **diffusion of innovations**, where *innovation* has been defined as "an idea, prac-

Table 5.1   Change Strategies

Type	Thesis	Methodology
Empirical-rational	Humans will follow their rational self-interest	Universal education Basic and applied research Systems for diffusion Mass communications Psychometrics Merit personnel systems
Normative-reeducative	Change will occur as the people involved change their attitudes, values, skills, and relationships	Integration of differences Nonrational action Social intelligence Analysis of utopias Psychotherapy Counseling Action research National training labs
Power-coercive	Humans will change mainly because of the application of some form of power	Political institutions Changing power elites Conflict confrontation Nonviolent strategies Judicial process Interest groups

Source: Adapted from Robert Chin and Kenneth D. Benne, "General Strategies for Effecting Changes in Human Systems," in *The Planning of Change,* 3d ed., edited by Warren G. Bennis, et al. (New York: Holt, Rinehart & Winston, 1976).

tice, or object perceived as new by the individual." Essentially, there are four categories of innovations: product–service (e.g., home care), production process (e.g., computer systems), organizational structure (e.g., task force), and people (e.g., female administrators).

The process of diffusion of innovations moves through five stages: awareness, interest, evaluation, trial, and adoption. Adopters of innovations have been characterized by Everett Rogers and Floyd Shoemaker (1971) as follows:

- Innovators are venturesome.
- Early adopters are respectful.
- Early majority are deliberate.
- Late majority are skeptical.
- Laggards are traditional.

This suggests that people have different attitudes toward change, with an inclination toward resisting change, particularly in its early stages.

There are a large number of barriers to rapid diffusion of innovations in public and nonprofit human services organizations; they include poor incentive systems, short-term horizons of policymakers, inflexible merit systems, and inadequate or inflexible budgets. This presents an enormous challenge to human services managers who must continually press for improved effectiveness and productivity of services. Knowledge and skills relating to planned change and diffusion of innovations are therefore vital for human services management.

Group Dynamics

The work of those in the field of **group dynamics** has had a profound impact on modern organizational management. The concepts and technologies of group dynamics represent a major trend in practical tools for modern society. They include such techniques, approaches, and institutions as action research, force-field analysis, sensitivity training, "T" groups, encounter groups, minority-group relations, democratic-participative management, the National Training Laboratory (NTL), group decisions, self-management, leadership training, problem-solving laboratory method, and data collection and feedback. All can be traced to the work of those in the field of group dynamics.

The pioneer in this field was Kurt Lewin (1951) who fashioned the concepts of dynamic psychology and developed what is known as **field theory**. He posits that actions cannot be understood on the basis of the personality of the individual or the nature of the social environment alone, but that *group behavior is a function of the dynamic interaction between the individual person and the social situation*. Along with his colleagues, Lewin was dedicated to democracy in the relationships of human beings and to here-and-now change in the workplace, particularly if it would humanize organizational behavior.

Group dynamic researchers were the first to describe different approaches to organizational management, such as autocratic, laissez-faire, and democratic leadership. Their work and actions served as the springboard for a technique known as Organization Development (OD), which established the fact that organizational effectiveness, productivity, and efficiency require knowledge and skill in both the management sciences and the behavioral sciences.

Perhaps more than any other single perception, the group dynamics concept of **action research**—that change is best managed by those most directly affected by the change itself—is of profound importance to the dynamic, creative human services manager. The case of the EMS (eligibility management system) is presented in three parts, the first of which was introduced in Chapter 4. (See Chapter 13 for Part 2 and Chapter 15 for Part 3.) It illustrates how the action research approach was used to deal with the organizational, technological, and systemic issues of such a major change. The action research approach is of infinite value for improving the effectiveness and productivity of human services agency functioning. The work of Lewin and his colleagues emphasizes the vital role that group dynamic concepts and techniques play for human services managers. Bedded in his dynamic notion of human psychology and his dedication to humanistic values, Lewin's mark on modern, dynamic, creative human services management is profound.

Interorganizational Relations

The environment of modern human services institutions has been characterized as the organizational version of the "survival of the fittest." It is the very nature of our current society that all societal institutions, particularly in the human services, operate in a network of relationships and transactions with other organizations. Interdependence has become the major characteristic of modern human services management. To get anything accomplished, the human services manager needs to be knowledgeable and skillful in interorganizational relations. Several of the cases presented in this text illustrate this phenomenon.

A large number of researchers have concentrated on the field of interorganizational relations. Some have concentrated on defining the organizational set, that is, the network of organizations that interacts with a particular agency (see Figure 6.2). Others deal with different configurations of interaction. These include cooperation, coopting, coordination, coalitions, affiliation, and networking.

Other researchers are concerned about identifying the unique and specific factors in human services organizations that create problems for the management of interorganizational relations. They identify four such factors:

- A human services organization often provides multiple services, thereby increasing its dependence on other human services agencies.
- The increased specialization of some agencies forces the client to interact with a wide range of other organizations for complementary services.
- Special interests pressure for segregated, specialized services, and this intensifies difficulty in interorganizational coordination.
- Change in the environment of one human services organization generally forces other such agencies with which it relates to accommodate.

The *organizational set* is referred to as the **task environment**: those organizations with which an agency interrelates. First and foremost in its interrelations with the organizations of its task environment, an institution must achieve consensus around its domain. *Organizational domain* defines for an agency, and for all other organizations in its environment, the human problems that will be dealt with by that agency, the population it will serve, and the services it will provide. In more popular terms, an organization defines its boundaries and stakes out a claim of its "turf."

An institution achieves *domain consensus* through a complex process of negotiations, agreements, resource acquisitions, and the like, particularly from

Table 5.2   Exchange and Organizations

Social exchange	Human interaction is an exchange of material and nonmaterial goods; as long as both parties in the exchange perceive that the exchange is mutual, the relationship will reach a dynamic equilibrium and be sustained.
Organizational change	Any voluntary activity between two organizations that has consequences, actual or anticipated, for the realization of their respective goals and objectives. Such exchanges can include information, services, personnel, or even clients.

those organizations that provide the necessary resources. It is an organizational expression of what researchers identify as the territorial imperative, an innate tendency of behavior in the animal kingdom by which boundaries are clearly established and defended. There are a number of factors that influence the ease or difficulty of achieving domain consensus. But once having been achieved by an organization, the steady flow of resources from the environment is more stable.

As Table 5.2 indicates, some researchers have applied the sociological theory of social exchange to develop the concept of interorganizational exchange.

Yeheskel Hasenfeld (1983) has noted that, with each exchange a human services agency has with another organization in its task environment, a *power–dependence relationship* is created. In effect, when one agency is dependent on another agency—say, for resources—then the latter has power over the former. Ideally, there should be a balanced exchange between two agencies so that their power–dependence relationship is equal, but generally this is not the situation, and this gives one agency a power advantage over the other. A number of strategic options can be used to change the power–dependence relationship: authoritative, competitive, cooperative, contracting, coalitions, cooptation, and disruptive.

This is an age when the creative, dynamic human services manager has to fashion improved human services systems that cross the boundaries of several human services organizations—what will be referred to in this text as transorganizational systems. This *spanning of the boundaries* of one's agency requires skillful managing of the task environment. There are a number of *bridging strategies* (Scott 1987). They include bargaining, contracting, cooptation, joint ventures, mergers, associations, and government connections. As you will note, these are similar to the strategies identified for changing power–dependence relationships because bridging requires developing relationships that have dimensions of power–dependence.

Practically all human services organizations operate in an environment requiring high-level interorganizational interaction. This profoundly affects the behavior of every person working in this environment; conversely, the behavior of individuals influences and shapes the "behavior" of the organization, which because of its interorganizational nature is both unique and complex.

Political Economy

There is still another perspective in which human behavior profoundly influences the organization. It is known as the *political economy perspective* of human services organization. From this perspective, organizational and individual behavior is fashioned by the nature of the exchange relationships between a number of different interest groups working internally within the organization and externally in the environment.

All human services organizations, particularly those of a public and nonprofit nature, interact with the political, economic, and social forces in the environment. Through this interaction, the structure and processes of an organization are shaped and systems fashioned. At the heart of these interactions are issues of resources, power, values, and legitimization. The distribution of power and resources to interests holding a specific set of values is a critical outcome of these interactions.

From this perspective, a creative human services manager needs to acquire skills in dealing with a broad range of interest groups within the organization and in the environment. Within the organization, these groups would consist of a coalition of professionals and managers who have sufficient power, status, or resources to permit them to influence the distribution of power, decisions, and actions in the organization. In very large organizations, there are several such coalitions. The creative, dynamic human services manager strives to become part of what is referred to as the *dominant coalition* in an organization, without sacrificing personal integrity.

The dominant coalition obviously seeks to form strong bonds with those in the task environment who have greatest influence over the distribution of power and resources. In the case of a state government human services department, this could be relationships directly with the governor's office and the governor's finance or budget office. This would also include relationships with key committees in the legislature and the individual leaders of the legislature. Good ties with interest groups—for example, the business community and client advocates—are also important. In addition, members of the coalition may include other human services executives; relationships with various economic and business groups are also very critical, particularly where they influence resource distribution or play important roles in the economic life of the community or state.

Human services organizations are highly dependent on the environment for legitimization and resources. The political-economy perspective, with its focus on the power relations among the various political and economic interests in a community, therefore is vital for understanding the dynamic nature of human services organizations. The necessity for the managers to acquire knowledge and skills in managing their organizations is fairly well recognized. It is what this text calls *institutional (organizational) management*. What is not always understood is the fact that the dynamic, creative human services manager must also acquire knowledge and skills in *systemic (strategic) management*. The political-economy perspective focuses attention on this second managerial role—helping to improve the human services systems in the environment by skillfully managing the political and economic environment of the human services agency.

Critical Theory

You have already been introduced to the image of the organization as an instrument for domination. The critique of the processes by which societies create structures where the few dominate the lives of the many has in our time been identified with the Communist blueprint for world revolution. This perception comes from the fact that in relatively recent times the leading theorist in critical theory was Karl Marx who is also identified with the Communist movement. Actually, the reflective critique of unnecessary constraints of human freedom can be traced to classic Greek philosophy; in modern times, the intellectual roots of critical theory include such German social theorists as Max Weber, Edmund Husserl, Jurgen Habermas, and Martin Heidegger—all widely respected philosophers. They all write about the unintended domination by coerced control of human behavior through our collective belief in instrumental reason and management.

The critical theory perspective is the source of the irreconcilable value-tension between democracy and domination that we examined in Chapter 2. As already noted, democracy is devoted to the elimination of domination in political structures. But to be effective, a democratic society requires institutions, with a cadre of people who have been entrusted with the power and responsibility to protect the common good and given special status—the power to dominate others to ensure that the fruits of democracy will be shared equitably by all. In effect, democratic institutions are a paradox: to ensure the elimination of domination, we must create societal institutions charged with the power to dominate the lives of others for the purpose of protecting the public interest.

The Greek philosophers recognized this paradox as did the modern sociologist Max Weber (1947). He recognized that, given a choice for structuring societal institutions, a system based on rational laws and rules was a preferable option to placing power into the hands of a charismatic leader or a king. But this had to be accomplished at the price that these rational-legal structures (bureaucracies) would still be staffed by people with power to dominate and control the lives of everyone, although their power would be bounded and prescribed. Weber too was critical of such domination by one group over others in a society dedicated to democracy, but he saw bureaucracies as the best of the three options, none of them ideal.

To Marx and those in modern times who adhere to his philosophy, the issue was one of social class. Bureaucrats are in effect the puppets of those who control the power and resources of the society. This is particularly true, Marxists argued, for human services organizations that provide a range of services fashioned by capitalists to provide support to workers who must be pacified and kept ready to provide an available labor pool for the capitalist system.

Critical theorists challenge a creative, dynamic human services manager to improve his skills as a systemic manager—to analyze the current human services systems in order to reform the human services systems in our nation such that we can (1) achieve a more equitable distribution of resources to all citizens in society and (2) minimize the extent to which one group of humans can dominate and control the lives of others. The human services manager probably can influence the latter more than the former. Mimi Abramovitz (1988) examines the way in which social welfare policy from colonial times to the present has regulated the lives of women. She argues that human services professionals have an opportunity to change this. We are currently witnessing the growth of a two-tier human services system in the United States. In the dominant system, which serves the majority of people, human services professionals are cast in the role of facilitating the provision of services. In the secondary system, consisting largely of impoverished or working poor women, human services professionals are forced to behave primarily as regulation enforcers. For this group, critical theorists present to human services managers a challenge of enormous proportions.

The Influence of Human Behavior on Organizations

Thus far we have examined a number of perspectives of the ways organizations influence the behavior of employees in the human services. Let us now look at the other side of the coin and examine a number of theories and perspectives of institutional processes in which the behavior of human beings influences the behavior of organizations.

Decision Theory

Is there a way of predicting how organizational decision makers will behave when required to choose from a variety of options for action? To decision theorists, led by Nobel Prize winner Herbert Simon, an organization is a decision machine. In 1946, he wrote that "administrative processes are decisional processes"; by 1960, Simon used the term *decision making* as if it were synonymous with the term *managing*.

Decisions are usually divided into two types: programmed (routine, repetitive) or nonprogrammed (novel). **Programmed decisions**—aided by the rapidly expanding knowledge and skill base in operations research, quantitative analysis, information sciences, and cybernetics—have been increasingly automated with computer-based sociotechnical systems. **Nonprogrammed decisions**, on the other hand, have been influenced by the work of organizational psychologists and group dynamic theorists who stress intuitive, creative, and heuristic ("rules-of-thumb") decision processes.

Decision theorists helped shape the perspective of organizations as rational systems. As we noted in our discussion of contingency (e.g., situational) decision making in Chapter 4, researchers such as Victor Vroom (1973) also concentrated on categorizing decision-making situations. Vroom, for example, suggested the following ways of deciding:

- Make the decision yourself.
- Obtain the data from others but make your own decision.
- Share the problem with subordinates, individually or collectively, to receive input, but make your own decision.
- Arrive at a group consensual decision with your subordinates.

The major influence of decision theorists has been the widespread acceptance of their thesis that organization and management processes are indeed decision processes. This is best observed by noting the necessity for human services organizations to design, develop, and maintain computer-based, automated systems for operations and for management information systems (MISs). Already, expert systems are being designed for some social services agencies. Could a child-protection social worker, for example, use a computer to analyze data and indicate whether a child is at risk of being abused by parents and therefore should be removed from the home? To date, such expert systems are only experimental. But it represents a step in the direction of artificial intelligence—the use of technology for the decision–action processes of human services agencies.

The dynamic, creative human services manager cannot escape the world of decision theorists. On the one hand, the normative rationalist will lead us to consider a range of new techniques: quantitative analysis, operations research, decision trees, decision tables, models and computer simulations, probability, payoff matrices, and so forth. But as human services professionals grounded in the behavioral sciences, we will be continually concerned with the underlying value systems, group decision making, problem-solving methods, brainstorming, and judgmental decision making of the descriptive decision theorist.

Whatever our persuasion, whether we acquire modern technologies or rely on traditional techniques, the human services manager is central to the decision-making process and ultimately bears responsibility for the decisions made.

Game Theory

While not always aware of it, public managers are always in competition. Human services managers' professional careers are marked by competition, whether against other professional colleagues for the same vacancy or for increasing their unit's budget, competing against another human services agency for the same grant or for influencing legislation, or competing with private companies or interest groups who are resisting the agency's policies, plans, or programs.

For these reasons, it is important for human services managers to be familiar with **game theory**—the study of competition between factions. When used by large organizations, it is based on mathematical models that indicate gains or losses for each strategy taken in the face of unknown strategy choices of an opposing group. Most medium-size and small agencies apply game theory in an informal fashion. For example, in applying for a grant, a human services organization will assess the various programmatic approaches to the funding source, keeping in mind the probable approaches of other agencies applying, and looking for an approach that will win the largest grant at the expense of other potential grantees.

A human services manager needs to be aware of the terminology, techniques, and rigor of game theory in order to improve the benefit (payoffs) that can accrue to her agency when faced with a competitive situation (see Table 5.3).

Gaming requires skills in identifying opposing interests and their strategies, developing payoff matrices for the different strategies, formulating decision rules concerning minimal or maximum payoffs, and devising methods of mixing strategies. Whether applied formally or informally, when human services managers use game theory to maximize their agency's expected payoffs, they need to assume that the opposing group of "players" is equally rational in what it seeks.

Gaming strategies can be focused on competition (introducing new services), conflict (a labor dispute), or leisure (chess). They can also be used for training purposes (e.g., simulation of an emergency response to a major disaster in the community). Increasingly, the environment of human services, both for organizations and for managers, is one of internal and external interactions that necessitate strategies of conflict, competition, compromise, and cooperation. Difficult though it might be initially to comprehend, game theory has an influence on the micro- and macro-processes of human services organizations and thus necessitates our awareness and understanding of its concepts and techniques. Table 5.4 illustrates how game theory can operate simultaneously at a number of levels.

In practice, human services managers soon learn that growth and improvement in human services depends on the development of strategies and tactics to combat different factions, interests, or agencies that are in competition or in opposition to a human services organization. Acquiring greater formal knowl-

Table 5.3 Some Game Theory Terminology

Term	Definition
Strategy	A plan so complete that it cannot be upset by opposing interests
Payoffs	The benefit (or losses) that can be anticipated by each interest or faction in the game situation
Zero–sum game	When what one interest wins is equal to the total losses of the other interest
Min-max	A strategy that protects an interest's minimum payoff while attempting to strive for a greater payoff
Max-min	A strategy that will prevent an interest from getting anything less than a minimum payoff
Mixed	Use of only one strategy permits the opposing interest to develop a response strategy to neutralize your gains; you may have to mix strategies to keep the opposing interest guessing at your next move

Table 5.4 Simultaneous Levels of Gaming in a Human Services Agency

Levels	Examples
Global-organizational	Human services professions form a coalition with labor groups to oppose the American Medical Association's attempts to defeat national health system legislation
Local-organizational	The state department of social services needs to develop strategies to prevent the passage of legislation, introduced by commercial long-term-care institutions, that would eliminate state agency review of rates
Intraorganizational	Several of your professional colleagues are competing for appointment as director of the agency
Interorganizational	Several private agencies in your community are competing for the same federal demonstration grant

edge and skills in game theory may prove not only worthwhile but also may be a necessity for survival.

Market Theory

It may seem out of place to include market theory in this presentation. But, increasingly, human services agencies—public and nonprofit included—are recognizing that marketing and market theory are a basic necessity for improving and expanding services or, perhaps, even for insuring survival. There is a strong debate over the privatization of social and health services. Regardless of the outcome of that debate, in many situations the most effective human services manager is one who exploits market and economic dynamics to improve human services in the community. For this reason, **market (public choice) theory** has a natural place in human services management.

Marketing is relevant in all situations in which there is a client group and products–services that are desired. In essence, marketing is the process whereby wants and needs of consumers are matched with the productive and distributive capacities of providers.

For the human services manager, the application of market theory can take several forms: improved skills in marketing services (e.g., community recreation or care for the disabled), arranging for contract services on a competitive basis (e.g., family services or home nursing care), and exploiting the natural market dynamics by providing services directed at identified citizen needs (e.g., child and adult day care).

Public human services agencies operate in a fishbowl; their activities are open and thus monitored closely either by the legislature, comptrollers, the media, or client advocate groups. This may exact a price by inhibiting creativity and risk taking.

One of the themes of this text is that direct delivery of services by an agency should be considered a strategy of *last* resort. The first choice of fashioning a responsive, supportive environment focuses on other community strategies, including delivery by business or nonprofit organizations operating in the marketplace. Under these conditions, the role of the public agency is that of a contractor, to monitor the carrying out of contracts and monitor the quality and effectiveness of services delivered. This has become a major strategy for many state government human services organizations.

Whether a service organization is operated as a business in the classic sense (paid for by the consumer) or as a budget item (paid out of a budget allocation), sooner or later market conditions will determine the existence of the service. Human services management therefore is dependent on conditions or events created by prevailing and changing markets and must embody the theory and techniques of marketing.

Most human services organizations actually need to organize and manage marketing to several different groups. Marketing methodologies require strategies and tactics for dealing with product definition, pricing, distribution, advertising and publicity, personal contacts, and sales promotions for each identified market segment.

During the 1980s, there was increased emphasis on exploring more areas of public-private initiatives for the purpose of improving human services effectiveness. Whereas it was once considered a requirement only for business managers, today it is taken for granted that proficiency in marketing is a skill for human services managers in public and nonprofit agencies. Market theory provides a foundation for many applications and techniques that have potential for human services reform.

Organizational Psychologists

The rapid growth of the field of organizational psychology supports the thesis of this chapter: *the behavior of human beings influences the structures and processes of organization, and, conversely, organizations influence the way in which human beings behave.* It is important therefore to briefly review the work of this group of organizational scholars and researchers.

Following World War II, a group of "neohuman relationist" researchers, writers, and theorists had a major impact on the expanding body of knowledge and skills in organization and management, concentrating on the behavior of people in organizations. Their expressed purpose was to introduce purposeful changes into organizations to make them more responsive to human needs. They became known as **organizational psychologists**. Their approaches were diverse, but they shared some common conceptions:

- Organizations can be viewed as open systems.

- Human beings have a complex hierarchy of needs, with the need for status and self-actualization being ultimately as important as safety and physiological needs (the Maslow hierarchy of needs).

- Although there is conflict between individual worker needs and organizational goals, this conflict can be reduced through employee participation in organizational processes, open communications, and nonbureaucratic structures.

Daniel Katz and Robert Kahn (1966) were among the first to focus on the common characteristics of open systems. They noted that organizations were a social system composed of a set of interdependent behaviors of people in different roles. These roles, along with norms and values, furnish the three interrelated bases for the integration of social systems, one of an organization's primary subsystems. They analyzed several different approaches to organizational change, namely, information, individual counseling and therapy, the influence of peer groups, sensitivity training, group therapy, feedback, and systemic change (direct manipulation of organizational variables).

Rensis Likert (1961), a researcher–writer who had a major influence on organizational psychology, became director of the Center for Group Dynamics following the early death of Kurt Lewin. The Center was then moved from MIT to the University of Michigan. Likert began to expand early conceptions of patterns of organizational leadership. He developed a continuum of management styles, which he labeled system 1 through system 4. Essentially, system 1 represents a highly structured authoritarian, task-centered management style; system 4 represents the opposite—a management style based on trust, teamwork, and employee interrelationships. Systems 2 and 3 represent styles of management between the two extremes.

A similar approach was taken by Douglas MacGregor (1960) who theorized that leadership operated from two different perceptions of human behavior. He

Table 5.5   Theory X and Theory Y

Theory	Perception
X	Employees do not necessarily like work, are not ambitious, have little desire for responsibility, are motivated by money and/or threat of punishment. They prefer to be directed and are not interested in participating in organizational processes beyond their specific work tasks.
Y	Employees find work as natural as leisure and are strongly motivated by social, esteem, and self-actualization needs. Having creative potential and self-control, employees can be self-directed, requiring a minimum of managerial direction.

called these theory X and theory Y (see Table 5.5). MacGregor's work strongly influenced the field in two ways. First, studies of leadership styles shifted from studying the *traits* of effective organizational leaders to that of studying the variables in different *situations,* which require different approaches to leadership. Second, studies began to explore two inclinations in organization and work situations: job-centered, task-oriented leadership and employee-centered, relationship-oriented leadership. As we noted in the Chapter 4 discussion of contingency (situational) leadership, organizational psychologists concluded that there is no one best way to influence the behavior of people in organizations. It all depends on the specific employee in a specific organizational situation set within a specific organizational environment.

As can be anticipated, this approach to leadership places a greater demand on managers to acquire knowledge and skills in identifying the variables of each situation and selecting the appropriate leadership style to fit each set of variables. Generally, the leadership style calls for a combination of two types of leader behavior:

- **Task behavior** organizes and defines the tasks, duties, and responsibilities of employees—what to do, when, where, how, and who is to do it.

- **Relationship behavior** focuses on maintaining relationships with individual or groups of employees, concentrating on interpersonal communications and facilitative–supportive behaviors.

Paul Hersey and Kenneth Blanchard have taken the contingency leadership approach even further. They developed what is known as situational leadership, which they define as the following:

> According to Situational Leadership, there is no one best way to influence people. Which leadership style a person should use with individuals or groups depends on the readiness level of the people the leader is attempting to influence. (1988, 171)

This led them to describe four different leadership styles: S1—telling, guiding, directing, and establishing; S2—selling, explaining, clarifying, and persuading; S3—participating, encouraging, collaborating, and committing; S4—delegating, observing, monitoring, and fulfilling. Where the readiness level of employees is low (e.g., unable, unwilling, or insecure), then leadership styles S1 and S2 are appropriate; where the readiness level of the employees is high (e.g., able, willing, or confident), leadership styles S3 and S4 are better suited.

Working Life (Quality of Work Life).   Organizational psychologists, such as Chris Argyris (1964), have studied the mismatch between the needs of a mature adult employee and the needs of an organization. He believes that the demands of the organization are incongruent with the needs of the individual and the conflict leads to employee frustration. This leads some employees to develop defense mechanisms, such as rationalizing, projecting, or becoming ambivalent in their approach toward their work; others seek to escape from their work situation by either not coping, daydreaming, or other escape mechanisms; still others become alienated, have a high rate of absenteeism, or have major stress-related illnesses. His work, and that of others pursuing similar research, has led to a movement known as the Working Life (Quality of Work Life—QWL), which attempts to fashion work environments that deal with these issues.

QWL has been defined as a way of thinking about people, work, and organizations. It flows from a view of workers as capable of learning and of organizations as learning environments. During the past several decades, three primary strategies have been adopted by researchers and organizations concerned with improving the QWL of their employees, namely, autonomous work groups, job restructuring, and structural changes. The latter includes reducing the number of hierarchical layers, broadening the span of control, and simplifying role relationships.

Organizational Culture.   It has been accepted for some time that the culture of a society influences the way in which that society organizes and manages its institutions. The same culture also has a way of creating homogeneity among employees that serves as the foundation for fashioning the rationale for management. But do different organizations really develop different and peculiar cultures that influence the behavior of people working in the organization? There is a growing body of thought that would answer that question in the affirmative.

To observers of the human services, it has always been clear that when comparing one type of human services organization to another (e.g., a hospital with a mental health clinic or a public high school with a recreation center), one experiences a significant change in the culture of the organization. But it has only been in recent years that organizational psychologists have begun to concentrate on organizational culture in order to better understand the interaction and influence of human behavior on organizations and vice versa.

The term *organizational culture* can have different meanings for writers focusing on this issue, such as norms, dominant values, philosophy, rules of the game, or climate. To Edgar Schein, one of the leading organizational psychologists during the past several decades, culture in this context is

> A pattern of basic assumptions—invented, discovered, or developed by a given group as it learns to cope with its problems of external adaptation and internal integration—that has worked well enough to be considered valid and, therefore, to be taught to new members as the correct way to perceive, think, and feel in relation to these problems. (1985, 8)

Schein identifies three interacting levels of culture in organizations: (1) basic assumptions (e.g., nature of reality, nature of human beings and their relationships, and relationship to the environment), (2) values (e.g., beliefs and habits), and (3) artifacts and creations (e.g., the physical and social environment, overt behavior, and written and spoken language).

In essence, organizational culture is a process of reality construction that gives employees shared meaning and understanding of behavior in organizations. Some organizational psychologists would go further and say that organizations develop unique cultures as a way of enacting the shared reality necessary for the effective functioning of the organization. As a student or practitioner of human services management, an understanding of the perspective of organizations as cultures is important (1) to acquire an appreciation of the distinctiveness of the organization in which you work, (2) to gain increased understanding of other institutions and systems with which you will interact and (3) to participate in the shaping of a reality conducive to the effective achievement of your human services mission and responsibilities.

The work and influence of organizational psychologists are extensive; over the course of their careers, most human services managers find the need for pursuing continual professional development training in the knowledge and techniques developed by organizational psychologists. Do you think you can now analyze the Cindi Sherwood case from the perspective of organizational psychologists and identify the difference in leadership approaches between Cindi and the agency director, differences so significant that Cindi felt she had only one option after nine months—to resign?

Summary

People who work within an organizational setting engage in different behaviors. Conversely, organizational processes are shaped by that human behavior. Why? The obvious answer is that organizations and systems are in essence groups of people working together for some common purpose. As Lewin and Follett have pointed out long ago, "group behavior is a function of the dynamic interaction between the individual person and the social situation" (Alfred Marrow

1969, 17), "an interweaving between the activity of the organism and the activity of the environment" (Mary Parker Follet 1924, 89).

Several different schools of thought and theories of human–environment interaction therefore are important for the human services manager. They hold the key to better understanding of the nature of this interaction and lead to improved management skills drawn from these bodies of thought. The literature dealing with role theory, change management, group dynamics, interorganizational relations, and critical theory help us better understand the ways organizational processes can shape and even change human behavior. The writings and research of scholars in decision theory, game theory, market theory, organizational psychology, and organizational culture contribute to the human services manager's understanding of the ways in which human behavior shapes organizational processes. Because the starting point for improving the management of human services is acquiring skills for analyzing organizations and systems, understanding these schools of thought and theories is part of the generic core of knowledge and skills of human services management.

Case History: ───────────────────
Mary Parker Follett
The Human Services Leader and Early Founder
of Modern Management

The quotation at the beginning of this chapter introduces the reader to the motto of our field: creative, dynamic human services management. It is for this reason that I feature the author of those words and the progenitor of the concept, Mary Parker Follett. Although still little known by most people, she is recognized by those truly informed as one of the founders of modern organization and management science and of human services management.

Life History

Mary Parker Follett was born in Quincy, Massachusetts, in 1868. The two formative experiences of her childhood seem to have been her assumption of her invalid mother's role in the household, and the fine education she received in a private academy. Thanks to an inheritance, she was able to enter the Harvard Annex that would later become Radcliffe College. Due to various interruptions that included a year at Newnham College, Cambridge University, England, and time spent caring for her mother, it was 1898 before she graduated (summa cum laude) from Radcliffe. She had already published her first book *The Speaker of the House of Representatives* (1896), indicative of her interest in government and constitutional law at that time.

By 1900, however, she was already moving from her theoretical studies into the then emerging field of social work. Her first efforts were on behalf of a settlement house in Roxbury, a neighborhood in Boston, at a time when such places were playing a crucial role in the integration of the new and poorest citizens into American society. Follett—thanks to her independent income— was able to devote many of the next years to this project, helping provide educational, social, and recreational activities for the Roxbury neighborhood. She branched out into other areas, such as getting Boston to open its school buildings in the evenings for educational and community activities—a practice soon copied elsewhere in the country (half a century ahead of the community school concept) and developing vocational guidance and job-placement services for young people. She also served on the Massachusetts Minimum Wage Board, where she came into direct contact with representatives of employers and employees. All these experiences helped shape the ideas of her book *The New State* (1918), in which she argued that the future of democracy lay less in political parties and the ballot and more in organizations at the neighborhood level.

These activities brought Follett into increasing contact with industry and business, and her thinking broadened to incorporate ideas about industrial relations, as well as social work and political theory. This resulted in her book of 1924, *Creative Experience*. Moving beyond her emphasis on neighborhood groups and drawing on her belief that all problems at all levels were ultimately psychological, Follett's thesis was that there could be no genuine resolution of problems—in government, in business, in society at large—until the problems inherent in human relationships were worked out sensibly and sensitively.

As a result of the reception of this book, Follett became known in widening circles, both in England and in America, and she was increasingly consulted by businesspeople about both specific and broad problems in organization and management. As she increased her own knowledge and expertise in that area during the 1920s, she also began to give lectures and courses in that emerging field. In 1929, she moved to England, where she had long maintained strong links, and concentrated on problems in industrial relations there.

Follett returned to the United States in the Fall of 1933 and died in December of that year. At her death, she was eulogized by those who had worked with her, but much of their praise focused on her influence on social work and social legislation. The field of organization and management was still too new for people to recognize her contributions. Sadly, her reputation went into eclipse in the following years, in part because so many of her most prescient ideas were in articles, papers, and lectures scattered in little-known periodicals. In 1940 many of her lectures were collected in the volume *Dynamic Administration;* another volume, *Freedom and Coordination,* appeared in 1949. These finally established her justified reputation as an early advocate of the human relations theory of management.

In the years since, the explosion in the field of human services with its new authorities, schools, theories, and perspectives, plus her own inevitably dated vocabulary, have tended to deny her the prominent position she deserves as one of the founders of modern management. But over the years, serious researchers in the organization and management sciences have recognized Mary Parker Follett as one of the field's most original and stimulating thinkers.

Follett: Progenitor and Fountainhead of Management Thought

We do not need to argue that Follett is the source of most management perspectives or theories: writing in the first three decades of the twentieth century, she had neither the research tools nor the literature base to have achieved such a distinction. But in reading her seminal works, one finds certain themes that can be used as guideposts for the distinctive constructs of the management of organizations. She viewed organization and systems as a total reality. She used simple words and commonsense notions to express this totality (and there is no denying that we must occasionally look beyond her sometimes dated terminology and even her time-bound attitudes). She is not a founder of any specific theory, and indeed we should resist those who would try to classify her simply as a founder of the human relations school of thought of management, discussed briefly in Chapter 4. One should examine her role from a special point of view: as an anticipator, forerunner, precursor, and progenitor—usually unacknowledged—of much that is current in thinking about organizations, systems, management, and the human services. This seems most appropriate for an individual who sought to integrate thought and action in the contemporary world. Beyond singling out her pioneering ideas in theory, we also want to establish that Follett's writings still offer directions for all human services professionals, particularly for dealing positively and creatively with the ever-present tension between relating to people as human beings on an individual, service-oriented basis and dealing with people as things, subjected to processes of complex, bureaucratic, societal organizations.

There are a number of schools of thought, theories, and perspectives of organizations, systems, and management that her thinking addressed. I will review several of them to illustrate her genius and creativity.

Contingency Theory

One of the dominant current organizational theories is that known as contingency or situational management. Its historical antecedents can be found throughout Follett's writing, particularly in the cornerstone of her philosophy, her "law of the situation" (e.g., different situations require different kinds of management). Follett set before us a goal to which we still aspire in organization and management: a natural and commonsense understanding of the process of human experience in which no two situations are ever alike and in which the inherent dynamics of situations require a continual sensitivity to and understanding of continuous sets of interrelationships—humans to other humans, humans to their environmental settings, and, simultaneously, all elements to each other.

Follett, in other words, presented a challenge that theorists and managers in the human services as well as other organizations have yet to satisfy: how to manage a totally dynamic environment. Because situations change faster than anyone's ability to report, she called for a "dynamic habit of mind" toward the "evolving situation." A manager's own behavior helps create and develop the situation to which he responds. Therefore, "we should work always with the evolving situation and note what part our own activities have in that evolving situation" (1940, 49).

Systems Perspectives

Follett anticipated modern areas of cybernetics, industrial dynamics, decision theory, and systems perspectives. Her works are replete with concepts that today are considered hallmarks of these schools of organization and management thought (e.g., holism, interrelationships, interdependence, and feedback). Noting that the whole cannot always be deduced from the sum of the parts, she wrote that "the whole is itself interweaving with the parts at the same time that the parts are interweaving to make the whole" (1924, 94–102).

While her writings do not use today's terminology, her concepts of "cross-functions," "cumulative-collective responsibility," and "pluralistic authority" are essentially the bases of new adhocratic forms of transorganizational systems, such as task forces, teams, coalitions, or matrix organizations. The general-systems theory (GST) notion of subsystem components that are interdependent and interrelated is contained in her notion of "total relativity": a total where every part has been permeated by every other part.

Organizational Psychology

It has already been established that Follett has been recognized as contributing to the foundations of today's neohuman relationists: organizational psychologists. She offers basic insights into both grand strategies and specific techniques for effective management of organizational change. Various specific components of the technologies of organization development (OD) may be traced to Follett's ideas of "participative management," "self-management," consensus building, and equal concern for process as task. Perhaps her most fundamental contribution to OD is her conception of the management of human beings in an organizational setting—namely, her perception of the potential for development of every human being.

Conflict Management

One aspect of management closely related to OD—planned change and organizational psychology—is "conflict management," and Follett's insights into this have also been recognized. Conflict management receives considerable attention today from management theorists, and many of their ideas are anticipated by her writings. She felt that conflict not only cannot be avoided but should also be used to work for us in the same way that the mechanical engineer uses friction for transmitting power through systems of belts and pulleys or a train is hauled by the friction of the locomotive's driving wheel against the track. As she noted often, "the music of the violin we get by friction" (1940, 30–31).

Follett considered three possible methods of dealing with conflict: domination, compromise, and integration. After dismissing the first two, she concluded that integration is the best method, in life as well as in organization: "Integration involves invention . . . creating something anew. The basis of all cooperative activity is integrated diversity" (1924, 174). Her book *Creative Experience* has a great deal to say about contemporary ideas on "constructive conflict," which is now recognized by human services managers as an important element of their function.

Social Work Practice

It would be misleading to give the impression that Follett offers insights only into different schools of thought or perspectives of human services management. In fact, she provided quite practical guidance in the practice of social work decades ahead of her time. Today, for instance, at a time when the influence of GST on casework is apparent in both the literature and in practice, with *ecological perspective, life model,* and the *family systems* models popular—in contrast to the older *medical model*—it is instructive to see that Follett's keen mind dealt with these progressive concepts a half-century ago. Social workers, she felt, deal with the interaction of clients with all the different elements of an "environment complex":

> What the social worker tries to do is to bring about the *kind* of interweaving from which it follows that further responses from environment, further responses from individual, will mean a *progressive* experience . . . which shall make the child's life more happy and fruitful and also make the social environment contain more possibilities for all young people. (1924, 106)

Even the conclusion that "services integration" was a direction to explore did not escape her keen analysis of social work practice. When writing about a child guidance clinic, she noted that clients had to deal with several specialists (i.e., social workers, physicians, and psychologists); the clinic needed to find, she wrote, some technique for uniting these separate approaches.

A Model for Our Times

There is another—perhaps less explicit but no less crucial—motive behind our use of Follett as a model for human services managers. Follett grew up, studied, worked, thought, wrote, and moved in what was an almost 100-percent man's world. What makes her achievement doubly impressive is that she not only thrived in this world but, at least in her public writings, seems never to have felt it necessary to refer to her extraordinary situation. All the more reason for us today to recognize that, through her personal experiences and work, Follett helped establish the central role that women play in management in many areas. And if in the late twentieth century the subject of women in management remains an issue, it is because all of us—particularly men, but women also—did not heed the force of her message, implicit but no less clear: Management is androgynous and should be practiced in a gender-neutral, color-blind fashion. Mary Parker Follett created a role model for all of us, regardless of sex, in the human services—one to which we can all aspire, to become dynamic, creative professionals.

There remains still another area where her work would yield timely insights: her concept of "personal power." This is of particular importance to women or minority administrators who are often made to feel less powerful, by their white, male counterparts. Her concept of personal power, which she expressed in many ways, was the cornerstone of her approach to management:

> The only genuine power is that over the self. When you and I decide on a course of action together and do that thing, you have no power over me nor I over you, but we have power over ourselves together. . . . Genuine power is power-with; pseudo power is power-over. (1924, 186, 188)

PART III

Dynamics of the Organizational Environment

CHAPTER 6

The Organization and Its Environment

CHAPTER 7

Women and Minorities in Management

CHAPTER 8

Organization as a Strategy: A More Dynamic Approach to Managing the Human Services

The primary requirement for human services management is that it be continually dynamic and creative. The reason: Human services organizations and systems are set in an environment that can best be described as kinetic. The implication of this phenomenon is profound. The administrator needs to manage human services organizations and systems in ways that meet the unique needs of each situation and each client. The continual refashioning of human services management demands rich repertoires of management approaches and techniques.

Part III consists of three chapters that both describe and discuss the dynamic nature of the human services organizational environment and strategies for achieving creative human services management.

Chapter 6 deals with the almost revolutionary societal changes that have occurred and are occurring in the United States and worldwide. Fundamentally, nations are struggling with the issue of recasting their institutions and systems so that they can meet the primary challenge of the twenty-first century: managing the tremendous complexity of societal processes.

Chapter 7 discusses that, for the human services in the United States, the most significant change during the 1990s will be demographic in nature: women and people of color are becoming the largest proportion of the work force and also the largest percentage of clients for human services organizations. Within the next decade or so, white males, who have traditionally dominated the ranks of human services managers, will suddenly become a minority. For human services management, this is a challenge of immense proportions.

Without our realizing it, most of us are programmed at an early age to view human existence in a segmented, sequential stereotype that limits the way in which we shape and manage societal institutions (organizations) and systems. Chapter 8 describes an alternative way of viewing the world—in a strategic, systemic way that builds on the simultaneous, comprehensive, and integrated interaction of all environmental phenomena. That chapter also sets forth the approaches and technologies needed to manage human services organizations and systems as strategies.

The chapters of Part III lead to a major conclusion: The human services manager needs to be knowledgeable and skillful in two simultaneous and interrelated forms of management—institutional (organizational) management and systemic (strategic) management. The former concentrates on the management of the particular institution in which the human services manager finds herself; the latter deals with the increasing number of interorganizational and transorganizational systems that human services organizations need to achieve their mission and to meet both the unique and comprehensive needs of their clients.

6

The Organization
and Its Environment

The Organizational Environment
Intraorganizational Dynamics
Interorganizational Dynamics

The Task of Serving Human Beings
A Taxonomy of Human Services Organizations
The Elusive Unit of Service
The Services-Provider Spectrum

The Kinetic Nature of Human Services Environments
The Momentous Nature and Pace of Change
Demographic Changes
Cultural Change
Economic Change
Technological Change

The Human Services Organizational and Systemic Environment in Transition
Some Fundamental Assumptions
Strategic Targets and Opportunities for the 1990s

Summary

The Organizational Environment

From solo practitioner to large institutions, human services are provided in an organizational and systemic environment. Webster defines *environment* as "a surrounding or being surrounded." Everyone who relates to human services organizations—clients, professionals, clerical staff, managers, policymakers, volunteers, and citizens—are surrounded by people, processes, and physical objects that make up the social, economic, psychological, and political environment within which human services are made available, acquired, and provided.

The human services manager therefore needs to have a good understanding of the dynamic relationships between the organization and its environment. This is an important point of departure for human services management, particularly because fashioning a **responsive environment** is its mission. As noted in Chapter 1, contrary to traditional notions, the primary purpose of a human services organization is not delivery of services. Rather, it is

1. The creation of an environment that is responsive and supportive of people as they use their innate, creative potential and avail themselves of human services opportunities and resources.

2. The development of a climate within the organization in which professionals and workers will be motivated to create the widest possible options for a responsive, supportive environment for clients.

For the purpose of examining the organization and management of human services organizations, it is helpful to conceive of the dynamic interaction between organization and environment (see Figure 6.1) in the following manner:

- D1: Intraorganization—the task of serving human beings. We refer to this dynamic as *task setting.*

- D2: Interorganization—the interactions with other organizations that uniquely identify the human services organizational environment. We refer to this dynamic as the *organizational set* or *task environment.*

- D3: The interactions of the human services organization(s) with the social, economic, and political environment of society. We refer to this dynamic as the *systemic environment.*

Intraorganizational Dynamics

Figure 6.1 graphically describes the intraorganizational dynamics of a municipal youth services bureau and focuses on **D1**, the **intraorganizational dynamic.** In classic management terms, the director of the youth services bureau must manage in three directions:

- Down: Managing the task setting. In essence, this involves the management of work, workers, and other managers.

Figure 6.1 The Dynamic Interaction of Organization and Environment

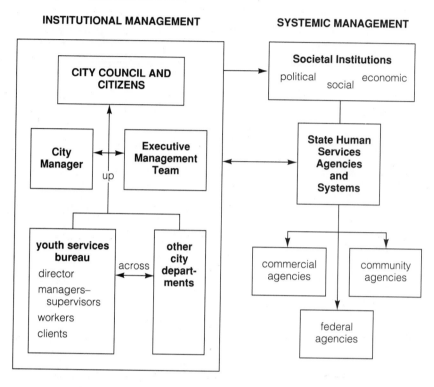

- Up: Helping the chief executive and the executive management team (EMT) manage the total organization (in this case, the municipal government).
- Across: Supporting other bureau directors in managing their organizational units (social services, recreation, police, health).

In this example, the chief executive is a city manager who is assisted in city management by an EMT made up of all department or bureau directors. The aggregate of knowledge and skills required for this collection of tasks is referred to in the remainder of this text as **institutional**, or **organizational**, **management**.

Interorganizational Dynamics

By now you have concluded that the function of the human services manager is quite complex. To be accurate, we must describe additional functions that only increase this complexity. These relate to the **D2 (interorganizational)** and **D3 (systems) dynamics** of the organization—environmental interaction.

Figure 6.2 The Task Environment: Youth Services Bureau Interorganizational Set

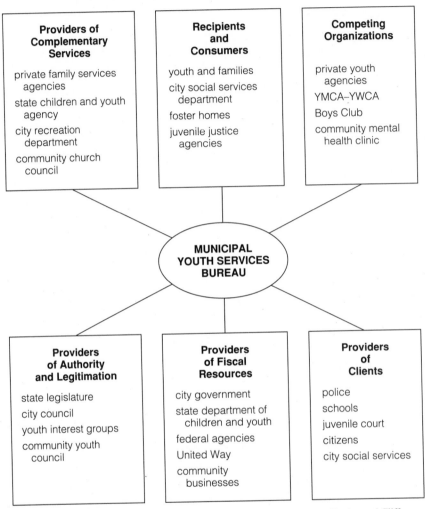

Source: Adapted from Yeheskel Hasenfeld, *Human Services Organizations* (Englewood Cliffs, NJ: Prentice-Hall. 1983), 63.

Figure 6.2 illustrates the task environment of the municipal youth services bureau. Each element of the task environment consists of complex, interrelated systems. It focuses the youth services director on managing

- Out: *Spanning the boundaries* of the youth services bureau and the municipal government to interrelate with a large number of other organizations and systems. Different *bridging strategies* are required to effectively manage in this direction.

Essentially, the youth services director must fashion, manage, or participate in transorganizational systems that cross the boundaries of a number of different human services disciplines, organizations, jurisdictions, and systems. The aggregate of knowledge and skills required for this collection of tasks is referred in the remainder of this text as **systemic**, or **strategic**, **management**.

Throughout the text, we attempt to sharpen the multiple tasks of the human services manager to illustrate the necessity to simultaneously manage with two hats: that of an institutional manager *and* that of a systemic manager.

We initially focus on the task of serving human beings, the intraorganizational-environmental dynamic. We then move on to examine the forces buffeting the general environment of human services organizations and the resulting changes put into motion to alter the framework within which we have traditionally viewed human services provisioning.

The Task of Serving Human Beings

A Taxonomy of Human Services Organizations

Is there a classification scheme for human services organizations that might advance our understanding of the peculiar task of serving human beings? We examine a number of approaches to a *taxonomy* (e.g., the science of classification) to acquire an appreciation of the extent and complexity of the subject.

Generic Taxonomies.   Yeheskel Hasenfeld (1983) classifies human services organizations according to two dimensions: (1) by *type of client*—those requiring support that will enhance their well-being and those who have some state that needs control, amelioration, or remedy; and (2) by *transformation technology*—people processing, people sustaining, and people changing. Table 6.1 provides examples for this typology.

Table 6.1   A Typology of Human Services Organizations

Type of Client	People Processing	People Sustaining	People Changing
Normal functioning	Job training	Social Security	Public school
Malfunctioning facility	Hospital emergency room	Long-term care	Correctional

Source: Adapted from Y. Hasenfeld, *Human Services Organizations* (Englewood Cliffs, N.J.: Prentice-Hall, 1983).

Size of the Organization.   The number of employees in an organization and the number of clients dealt with is another way of classifying human services organizations, for size must be understood as reflecting more than the obvious quantitative factor. For example, one way of categorizing by size could be the following:

- A center has a set of programs and services that generally are neighborhood-based and has a few employees. Centers' budgets can range from $xx,xxx to $y,yyy,yyy; they attempt to foster family–neighborhood values; and they are formal to informal with simple administrative mechanisms. EXAMPLES: Churches, YWCA/YMCA, and neighborhood outreach programs.

- An agency has a few employees who provide a specific and limited set of services. Agencies' budgets can range from $xxx,xxx to $y,yyy,yyy; their structure generally connotes informality, familiarity, and accessibility; and they are formal, but not complex, administrative mechanisms. EXAMPLES: Family services, health clinic, and Hispanic council.

- An institution is a structure that physically houses clients; the staff is large. Institutions' budgets can range from $xxx,xxx to $yy,yyy,yyy; they imply anonymity and a regulated, formal environment; and they are formal, complex administrative mechanisms. EXAMPLES: Medical or mental health hospital, prison, nursing home, halfway house, and shelters.

- A bureaucracy is a monolithic organization with many employees who provide or manage a range of services. Bureaucracies' budgets generally range from $x,xxx,xxx to $yyy,yyy,yyy; they imply anonymity and a regulated, formal environment; and they are formal, complex administrative mechanisms. EXAMPLES: Government departments (health, education, and social services) and private health insurance.

Economic-Legal Bases.   Human services organizations and their tasks can be classified by the factors related to their economic and/or legal foundation. This would produce the following taxonomy:

- Business: Commercial, proprietary companies interested in making a profit from human services. These can be solo practitioners (physicians, psychiatrists, social workers, dentists, psychologists) or they can be corporations (profit-oriented nursing homes, hospital conglomerates, insurance company-owned health maintenance organizations [HMOs], health-recreational centers).

- Public: Federal, state, regional, county, or municipal government.

- Nonprofit: Nonprofit, not-for-profit, private, voluntary, quasi-public agencies.

We have noted earlier that the lines between organizational and jurisdictional boundaries are blurring. A business organization can be under contract from a public agency; a nonprofit agency's revenues may include government grants, fees collected from clients, fund-raising by volunteers, and United Way allocation; a proprietary long-term rehabilitation center can receive payments from Medicaid and Medicare.

The Elusive Unit of Service

Several attempts have been made to find a taxonomy of services units for human services organizations; to date there is no universally accepted standard taxonomy. There are instead a number of different approaches to defining a unit of service in human services organizations, the most common of which is **professional specialization**.

Human services have expanded to include all skills and talents devoted to humans in our society. The following list is only a sampling of the variety of human services functions:

- Gerontology
- Physical health
- Mental health
- Youth services
- Police
- Social work
- Psychology
- Recreation
- Cultural arts
- Physical education
- Education
- Family development
- Child development
- Developmental disabilities
- Employment development

Some of these may not seem to be human services professions. But some analysts would maintain that most functions or professions have a human services dimension. Police functions, for example, have traditionally been perceived as criminal justice and law enforcement. But they also include vital human services: dealing with substance abuse, suicide attempts, sexually related assaults, marital disputes, people abuse, and so on.

The complexity of human services is readily apparent when one considers that each specialized profession has human services technologies that can be viewed as unique within the totality of the field. These technologies have different, often diametrically contradictory, philosophies and techniques of providing services.

In a fairly "new" area of education—special education—some twenty-three "problem–status" areas have been identified, each cross-classified with twenty-five different services. The health and mental health fields have large, printed volumes classifying illnesses and conditions. In the past two decades, there is almost a totally new medical marketplace because of the widespread use of several hundred **DRGs** (diagnosis related groups—"a set of categories based on patient diagnosis, procedures, and age").

In the field of social work, Albert Alissi (1980) identifies some thirty-eight different comparative approaches and methods to group work, broken down as follows:

- Medical clinical approaches   (14)
- Group counseling guidance   (7)
- Psychological self-awareness   (8)
- Social work approaches   (6)
- Emerging generic models   (3)

Each has specific schools of thought, literature, training, and, in some cases, professional associations.

In our attempts to find a common classification scheme that helps us better understand the task of human services provisioning, we can quickly conclude that the number of different, specialized, functionally oriented professions dealing with human-oriented problems number in the hundreds. It is quite complex.

Classifying organizations by the particular service technology in each of the human services functional fields presents a classic problem for human services management: To what extent must a human services manager be familiar with the specific service technologies of the organization? At one extreme is the opinion that only a practitioner–professional should be appointed to administer a human services organization. At the other extreme is a generalist administrator with no prior experience in the specific service technology for the human services organization to which he has been appointed. There is no single solution to this issue.

But every human services manager has a responsibility to become familiar with, and stay familiar with, the particular service technologies of her organization. We would even go as far as to take the position that, where possible, every administrator should continue to practice with a small group of agency clients in order to maintain a dynamic touch with the operation and services aspects of the organization.

The Services-Provider Spectrum

In the 200 years since the founding of the United States, the manner of services provision may have come full circle. The cycle has moved from a broad spectrum of services providers to a narrow one and then back again. In a pioneer society, individuals relied on the development of their skills for survival. As we became more industrialized and more urbanized, we constructed complex systems in which the dominant provider element was that of the professional and the highly trained specialist. But more and more individuals have begun to question the need and desirability of the specialist and are seeking to again become more self-sufficient.

A number of researchers, critics, and analysts are beginning to argue for a broadening of the services-provider spectrum, as are a number of grass-roots movements and alternative life-style adherents. Feminist health centers, which train women in basic techniques of self-care and attempt to confront the problems traditionally slighted by male physicians, is one illustration of this phenomenon. Deinstitutionalization and half-way houses are other examples.

The pressures to broaden the spectrum of services providers are both economic (e.g., an all-professional staff of providers is too expensive for our economy) and philosophic (e.g., professionals breed bureaucracies, are unresponsive to human needs, and provide an immature transactional analysis model [parent–child]).

It is now common to find a spectrum of professionals, paraprofessionals, and volunteers in a number of human services (education, health, mental health, and developmental disabilities). In addition, a growing number of professionals are recognizing the need to concentrate on developing self-help or mutual-help groups. A large number of groups have formed in the past two decades and continue to grow. They include groups developed in response or reaction to

- Personal crises: Alcoholics Anonymous, Parents Anonymous, National Society for Autistic Children

- Technological advances: United Ostomy Association, Make Today Count (cancer), National Dysautonomia Foundation

- Social change: National Sudden Infant Death Syndrome Foundation, Widowed Persons Service, Parents Without Partners

The movement toward this broader spectrum of services providers includes more than just those calling for paraprofessionals and mutual-help groups. It also includes respected scholars and leaders calling for inclusion of the client as a full partner in the helping process.

It is too early to speculate about the outcome of the movement to broaden the spectrum of services providers. It may be a feeble attempt to counterbalance the continued move toward greater specialization of human services professionals, a trend that Mark Yessian (1978) feels should greatly concern human services managers. Or it can represent the client's recognition that the only possibility for dealing with an ever-increasing complex human services environment is to take over responsibility for managing one's own care.

The Kinetic Nature
of Human Services Environments

Historians will debate why the mid-1960s experienced worldwide upheavals that included such phenomena as major changes in our social patterns, our dress, our arts, our life-styles, and an expanded tolerance of deviation from group norms. Even our industrial culture is in transformation. Notions of mass production characterized by a 1920 Ford assembly line are being challenged with new techniques for individualized production of automobiles and other products and services (see Chapter 8).

The world of the human services manager has become bewildering. It has reached the point where probably the manager of the 1990s will use a lexicon that would appear—to the management student of the 1940s—to be written in a foreign language. The rate of change in the human services can only be characterized as **kinetic**, that is, in constant motion. One of the popular management writers of the 1980s, Tom Peters, marked the period by entitling his book *Thriving on Chaos: Handbook for a Management Revolution* (1987).

The Momentous Nature and Pace of Change

Several authors have been heralding the move from one phase into a much different phase. Whether we refer to Alvin Toffler's *Third Wave* (1980), John Naisbitt's *Megatrends* (1983), R. Buckminister Fuller's *Spaceship Earth* (1978), Marshall McLuhan's *Global Village* (1968), Dennis Gabor's *Mature Society* (1972), or Daniel Yankelovich's *New Rules* (1981), the prognoses agree with Stafford Beer (1975): The world has gone through radical change in recent times and has become extremely complex. The issue—how to manage complexity in our individual lives and collectively in the societal institutions we have created—is for us all.

One need not belabor the rapid, geometric rate of change in the United States. What is important instead is to note the significant changes in every aspect of societal life and the difficulty many organizations and systems are having in adjusting to a new world characterized by complexity. Perhaps the greatest irony is the tendency to listen to leaders who offer simple answers. For the field of management, this has been paralleled by the appearance of "quick-fix management" literature. While many political and community leaders criticize what they consider a poor state of public management, other more thoughtful critics point to the demise of business management in the United States because of its inability to adjust to the growing complexity of the world.

Professionals who enter the field of human services management are faced with a challenge and an opportunity of immense proportions—fashioning organizational and management responses that can meet the needs of this new, more complex world. Our existing organizations and institutions provide an anchor in a turbulent world, a stable foundation from which adaptation to a changing environment can be made. The issue, more precisely, is not only adapting to an increasingly complex world but also blending the fundamental value of collective order, represented by stability, with the value of individual creativity and variety, which is represented by change and complexity. The future holds both frustration and excitement for human services managers willing to face these enormous challenges.

Even the casual observer can note the phenomenal changes that have occurred in the United States and elsewhere during the four decades from 1950 through the 1980s. On every level—demographic, cultural, economic, and technological—the changes can be called revolutionary. They are highly interrelated, and we examine each briefly because they set the conditions for our hypothesis: *We now live in a complex society that will only survive and evolve if we can organize societal institutions to manage complexity in a way that blends the values of stability and order with those of creativity and change.*

Demographic Changes

Demographics has suddenly become an important starting point for human services strategic planners. For example, there are two "bulges" in our age groups that have important implications for strategic thinking: members of the "baby-boom" are now in their forties and approaching what is popularly called midlife crisis, and there is a continuing rise in our "mature adult" population, particularly those over age eighty-five. But perhaps the most important demographic fact that concerns most human services planners is the increase in families that are now headed by single parents, primarily women. Where the single parent is a woman under the age of twenty-five, mother and children are probably living in poverty. There is a great likelihood that if there is no systemic change the majority of these families will stay poor. Poverty is increasingly affecting women, usually from a minority group. A sizable portion of U.S. children are living in poverty. The health, education, child development, and employment problems that this will ultimately present led ABC journalist Peter Jennings to pronounce that "we have a generation of children in jeopardy."

In their proposal for "welfare reform," the American Public Welfare Association and the National Council of State Human Services Administrators pick up the same theme: "One child in four is born into poverty in this country today. One child in five spends his or her youth in poverty. Among blacks and Hispanics the numbers are even starker. One in two black children are poor. Two of five Hispanic children are poor. America's children are at risk and so, too, are their families" (Heintz 1978, 1).

As we are moving increasingly to a service and information–knowledge economy, women and minorities are the dominant labor force for the service economy at pay levels significantly lower than men. The large number of school dropouts, particularly among minority youth, and the increased numbers of youth in societal institutions (correctional and noncorrectional) have created the probability of our having a large, functionally illiterate labor pool, at a time when we are moving into a decade of labor shortages. Economic opportunities that come from being in upper-management positions of commercial and public organizations are essentially still not available to women and minorities; the decline in black and Hispanic college students will only exacerbate this problem.

Perhaps the most startling demographic data relate to the likelihood that by the turn of the century, or soon after, the majority of people in the United States will be nonwhite. In California this phenomenon is already evident for school-children in the lower grades.

Demographically, the United States of the 1990s will be a far cry from that of the 1950s.

Cultural Change

U.S. society in the early 1990s is fundamentally different from that of the 1950s, in any way you wish to measure it. But contrary to popular opinion, some fundamental values have been retained. For example, the family has not "disintegrated"; instead, we now realize that alongside the nuclear family of a working father, domestic mother, and two children, we now accept a wide range of additional family structures. They include

- Working father, working mother, and children
- Working mother, domestic father, and children
- Single parent (female or male, previously married or not) and children
- Single adults (all ages)
- Gay or lesbian couples with or without children
- Childless couples (same or different sexes) living together or married
- Blended families: married couples with her-his-their children
- Widowers and widows living together or remarried
- Families with disabled parents–children of all ages who live at home rather than in an institution
- Families of unrelated people: communes; half-way houses for correctional inmates, mentally ill, alcoholics, developmentally disabled, traumatic brain injured (TBI); unrelated people living together in same house
- Foster homes for children or the elderly

The United States has always been a nation dedicated to self-governance, which in the first 200 years of its history was interpreted on an institutional basis (we want to run our governments, churches, social groups, and businesses in our own way). But in the 1960s and 1970s, individuals began to view self-governance on a personal basis: I want to govern (shape) my own life. Initially, the beneficiaries were members of minorities and women, but this movement has also benefited many other groups, including the disabled, unmarried single adults, the elderly, native Americans, middle-aged persons seeking new ca-reers, and homosexuals. The traditional "linear" life plan (school, work, and retirement) is giving way to many alternatives.

Yankelovich and his associates undertook studies to discover the extent of cultural change in the United States. They discovered that 80 percent of people are adopting "new rules" for governing their lives in their search for self-fulfillment. The result is significant change in social norms. The traditional "giving-getting compact" (i.e., the unwritten rules governing what we give in marriage, child rearing, work, community, and sacrifice for others and what we expect in return) is in the process of being reinterpreted.

Although home, community, religion, and workplace still are important centers for our value-systems, there has been the beginning of a shift toward social, personal-oriented, inner-directed values that emphasize people over institutions, quality over quantity, individualism over conformity, diversity over uniformity, experiences over things, and participation over authority.

Culturally, we live in a new society.

Economic Change

Where once our economy was symbolized by blue-collar workers producing material goods, we emerged from the depression of the 1980s in a radically different fashion than we did from the 1930s depression. We are now symbolically a white- and pink-collar economy, oriented toward services and information. There have been major geographic—economic relocations, some international in scope; our growth industries are in the fields of biotechnology, robotics, computers, laser and fiber optics communications, health care, geriatrics, and leisure.

Although our work force has continued to grow, we continue to be plagued by the problem of a relatively large number of underemployed people (particularly, inner-city youth and minorities). In addition, women and minorities are a much larger percentage of the work force. The number of well-paying factory jobs is significantly reduced, or going to underdeveloped countries, while the number of service-oriented jobs is growing. As a result, the number of full-time employed workers making less than a poverty-level income is growing and equally alarming, the dream of working hard to get ahead economically and socially is fading for larger numbers of people who do want to work hard but are pessimistic about the outcome.

The most revolutionary feature of our economy is the dramatic shift *from* mass production of uniform products and services *to* a rapid-response, flexible-systems process of customized, individualized products and services. Although the takeover of business management by finance and legal experts has produced a trend toward mergers, and raised questions of paper entrepreneurial contribution to the real gross national product (GNP), there is growing recognition that the U.S. economy must compete in a worldwide market to retain the leading role we have enjoyed as business management leader, a role we lost during the 1970s.

In 1969 Edward Lehan, a noted public-budgeting theorist, forecast that the rise in real wealth in the United States would increase, rather than abate, the pain of choice in the allocation of public resources. Both in the home and at the workplace, goals for individuals and organizations are now focused on improving the quality of life. But we now live in what is called a zero-sum economy—what one segment gains is at the expense of another segment.

While the vast majority of families in the United States has attained an economic standard of living that far exceeds that of the rest of the world, there are increasing numbers who reside below the poverty level. The latter group are considered an economic underclass because their form of transfer payments are *welfare* in nature (AFDC payments, Medicaid, and food stamps), whereas transfer payments to the middle class (Medicare, Social Security, veterans' benefits, pensions, public-support jobs, and educational subsidies), to the wealthy (tax shelters and tax breaks), and to corporations (subsidies and write-offs) are considered socially and economically sound.

We have entered into a significantly different, world-oriented economy that soon will have few similarities to the 1950s.

Technological Change

The reader may question what implications technological changes have on the environment of human services organizations. If this were being written in the 1910s and the subject of the impact of the telephone and automobile technologies was being discussed, the reader then might also have been puzzled. But in hindsight, the telephone and the car changed the very way we live and suburbanized our nation. Most human services organizations, incidentally, could not survive without telephones or cars, and a large number of these agencies are located in communities that would not even be in existence without these technologies. We are now in the midst of another technological revolution that will have as profound an impact on human services management during the next two decades as the car and telephone had 70 years ago.

For most of the twentieth century, electrical-mechanical devices dominated the driving force of our means of productivity, and paper was the medium by which we processed and retained the data necessary to control and shape our lives, both in our factories and in our homes. But we are on the threshold of an environment, electronic in nature, in which the means of productivity *and* the medium for data storage and processing will be identical—the electron. Whole images, digital data, voice, music, pictures, and documents—everything that represents a means for the retention and processing of culture and work—will be electronic in form. Commuting to work can be replaced with communicating with work. With the increase in robotics and artificial intelligence (expert systems), we will be able to extend our capabilities by forming partnerships with robots that cannot only undertake home and office chores but also help us extend our brain power, if we can handle the cultural shock they represent.

The electron transmits instantaneous and simultaneous stimuli. It provides the opportunity for great freedom: we are no longer bound to an 8:00–4:00

workday, five days a week. We can interrelate in real time—with anyone, any-where—within split seconds. This can be a boon for the quality of our work and leisure lives. For example, the electronic medium of television improves the quality of our leisure lives (culture, sports, etc.) by bringing events that would be impossible to attend (in time, energy, and resources) into the home "live" as they are happening, to all of us regardless of economic status.

But electronic technology can also be a bane. We were held hostage by Ayatollah Khomeini in Iran who staged demonstrations as media events for broadcast at dinnertime. The management of images by our leaders frequently distorts the reality of problems and issues of life with which our nation must deal. Our youth even think differently, deal with reality differently, and process data differently because media imprints the way in which humans perceive and shape their world. The jet airplane and electronic communications industries are teaming up to make the United States and the world a global village. We can project ourselves thousands of miles away within seconds and if necessary propel our bodies anywhere within hours. And in addition to all this, we are on yet another threshold: space travel.

Technologically, we now live in a new world.

The Human Services Organizational and Systemic Environment in Transition

Is it possible to provide human services managers with a comprehensive set of trends in humans services organizations and systems that reflect a changing or newly structured set of assumptions, concepts, and propositions as we approach the twenty-first century? This is our task for this section.

There is no better starting point for this discussion then to examine Case 6.1, a story of two human services managers, Lydia Martinez and Carol Davis. Not only does this case illustrate the kinetic nature of the human services environment but it also indicates some of the types and rate of changes that can be anticipated in the environment of human services organizations and systems for the remainder of this century. Both women have prepared themselves for the world of human services management; both are part of the executive management team of their state government agency—involved in reshaping human services systems at the highest level. These systems deal with such issues as deinstitutionalization, community-based services, the homeless, TBI, teenage pregnancies, and comprehensive services to the disabled. Both work to link several different disciplines, programs, and organizational units within their own departments, with other state agencies, with local governments, and with community agencies. Both have to deal with legislators, legislative commit-tees, and the judicial system. Definitely a kinetic human services environment!

Case 6.1 _____

Dealing with the Kinetic World of Human Services Systems

Carol Davis was beginning to unwind after another hectic day. Meeting Lydia Martinez for dinner was a great idea. "Glad you called me, Lydia," Carol remarked. "We haven't matched notes for a long time. Besides, I needed respite. The pace of our jobs is frenetic. Is this what human services management is about?"

"To tell you the truth, Carol," Lydia answered, "we hold graduate degrees as human services managers, but I'm not sure what we do qualifies us for the title. Here, let me show you something," she said, pulling a chart out of her briefcase. "Here's what I'm involved in right now. Compared to just seven years ago when we graduated, the world of human services is rapidly changing, even while we speak!"

As executive assistant to the secretary of the Department of Human Services for the State of Missouri. Lydia's chart analyzing her current tasks listed the following:

- Member of the EMT of the department: regular meetings, management development, management retreats, and brainstorming
- Redesign statewide delivery systems for the homeless, deinstitutionalized clients, comprehensive services for disabled, teen parents, AIDS patients, TBI patients, independent-living arrangements, community-based services, day care, and family support services
- Managed-care systems: interdisciplinary team assessments, case managers, services packages, and integrated computer systems
- Preparation of request for proposals (RFPs) for legislatively mandated studies; evaluation of proposals and new systems development
- Act as legislative liaison: meet with legislators, draft legislation, monitor legislation, attend committee meetings, testify at committee meetings, and prepare budget-hearing comments
- Work on cross-organizational teams or task forces: strategic planning, consensus building, planning for change and transition to new systems, and program planning
- Complete staff work for the secretary: analyze issues and respond to governor's requests
- Policy development: assess and write policy and give technical assistance on policy implementation

Carol studied the chart carefully and got excited. "This is unreal," she remarked. "I do almost exactly everything you have listed here. That's why I asked the question, is this human services management? As special assistant to the secretary of the Department of Mental Retardation, I'm responsible for the implementation of the consent decree, which mandates the transfer of most clients into the community and out of the institution. I don't have as many different client groups; but I get involved with the same type of day-to-day tasks—with one big addition. I have to deal with the court system, with the magistrate who handed down the consent decree, *and* with the court-appointed monitors and their staff."

"How many cross-organizational task forces are you on right now, Carol?" Lydia asked.

"You won't believe this—four right now," Carol answered.

"I'm on about five tasks forces right now," Lydia responded. "The trouble is, it takes constant meetings with middle managers of the department, trying to link them up with these cross-organizational systems. It's exciting but draining."

Carol sighed. "Do you think we'll get a nameplate on our doors that says 'Human Services Manager'?"

"If we do," Lydia responded, "they'd better change the textbooks we used. The field sure has changed radically, in less than a decade."

We are currently on the brink of a major transformation in human services systems in our society. Such transformations seem to come in thirty-year cycles. When someone writes a book entitled *The Fashioning of the Welfare State in the United States,* the 1990s will be compared to the 1930s and the 1960s. The 1990s will see major and fundamental changes in our human services systems. We could sit by as observers, only reacting to systemic changes fashioned by forces and groups that do not share our values. Or we could choose the role of primary architects of human services systems in our society.

Assuming that all of us would prefer to be proactive players in this transformation, let us use the important organizational theorist James Thompson's "opportunistic surveillance" (i.e., scanning the environment for opportunities that anticipate institutional trends) to identify "strategic opportunities" for the human services in the 1990s (1967).

Some Fundamental Assumptions

A number of assumptions serve as the underpinnings to seeking out strategic opportunities in the refashioning of human services systems over the next decade. Briefly they are the following:

1. We are dealing with success, not failure. Most people in the United States enjoy a quality of life that far exceeds that of the majority of the world's nations. Our standard of living can be traced to half a century ago when human services professionals like ourselves struggled with another ma-

jor transformation in human services systems and fashioned today's welfare state. For the vast majority in our nation, these systems have been successful.

2. The *primary* focus of most of our individual and collective efforts is an ever-increasing quality of life. The vehicle for this achievement is Richard Titmuss's (1956) welfare paradigm: social welfare, tax welfare, and occupational and corporate welfare.

3. During the past decade, we have seen two opposing trends: an increase in affluence and an increase in poverty. Currently, 85 percent of those living in the United States are considered the "haves" in society; the remaining 15 percent are the "have-nots," those who are considered to be living in poverty. As human services professionals devote themselves to refashioning today's human services systems, their goal should be quite clear: drastically reducing poverty in the nation.

4. The major roadblocks to the redesign of human services systems are threefold:

   a. Systems designed for one set of demographics (e.g., the 1930s) become *the* primary constraint for redesigning systems based on a new set of demographics (e.g., the 1990s).

   b. As Figure 6.3 illustrates, instead of a "tighten the belt" ethic, our society opted instead for a "credit-card economy." Even in the face of astronomic federal deficits and the weakening of our economy internationally, the upper and middle classes refuse to reduce the level of benefits and services received from our current welfare system.

   c. Until our economy makes a quantum increase in GNP, if a redesign of human services systems is focused on priorities—improving the quality of lives of those who need it most—such redesign essentially pits the "haves" against the "have-nots" in society. Because most human services professionals are part of the "haves" in society, this presents most of us with a personal versus professional dilemma.

5. Most human services systems analysts would agree that there is a major danger that we are fashioning *two-tier* human services systems in the United States. The lower tier is characterized by services of a poor quality, services in which human services professionals are cast in roles as probation officers, not facilitators or helpers; even total lack of services. (It is estimated that 34 million U.S. citizens do not have health insurance; of this, 18 million are in the work force.)

6. What is perhaps more disturbing, there are indications that we may be moving toward a *two-class* system in the United States, perhaps even a permanent underclass. Our move away from a product economy toward a service economy is damaging the traditional "American dream" of upward socioeconomic mobility through hard work. The key is college. A recent, important study on this issue concluded: "This nation may face a future *not* divided along lines of race or geography, but of educational at-

Figure 6.3   Tax Decreases and Deficits (in billions of dollars)

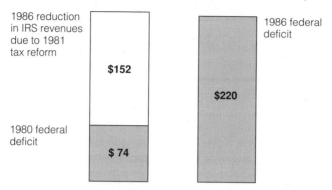

tainment" (Halpern 1988). It would appear that our enormous school dropout problem (particularly in our urban centers) is now a subset of a much larger issue facing our nation today—those young adults not going on to college.

7. Human services are sociotechnical systems. For those of us devoted to systemic design or redesign, our task is to integrate two types of change-making: technology change and interpersonal change. The latter is extremely difficult, particularly when we are currently faced with some fundamental cultural issues in our society, namely:

   a.   Fifty years ago, we were a society proud of our ethic of self-reliance. Today, venality, or greed, is often the dominant ethic: Get everything you can from the system, regardless of how it may impact on your neighbor. It is an unfortunate by-product of the social welfare systems designed half a century ago.

   b.   In fifty years, we have also attempted to create a "no-risk" society, shifting the natural individual or corporate risks of life from ourselves or our families to others in society. This is another by-product of the systems designed during these past five decades.

   c.   To Ivan Illich (1978), this is the "age of disabling professions." The more human services professionals do for people, the more we take away their ability to do for themselves and the greater the need to "provide services" to others becomes.

These assumptions are the starting point for applying strategic thinking to the remainder of this century.

Strategic Targets and Opportunities for the 1990s

When one begins to think strategically about the 1990s, there is a mixture of opportunities, priorities, and trends that seems to emerge.

A National Agenda of Priorities.   A fundamental revision of our welfare state emphasizes the need for a national priority agenda. Currently, many experts are placing child care and youth development for families of all socioeconomic classes as the highest national priority. We need top quality and comprehensive day care and latch-key care, as much for a "welfare" mother whom we want to help acquire a permanent job, as for a single-parent "high-tech" professional. We need to muster a program as major and as comprehensive as the GI bill of rights of the 1940s and 1950s to bring into the mainstream of our economic and social life the undereducated children and noncollege youth everywhere. They represent a vital human resource for our labor force, as the United States struggles to maintain a leadership role among world economies.

Compared to some fifty countries worldwide, the United States lags in having a **comprehensive national policy toward families** that is focused on universal quality child development and child care. Programs would range from child subsidies to quality day care, early childhood development to maternal and child care. It also would include parental leaves and guaranteed employment for new parents during pregnancy and following childbirth. It also would be a catalyst for an adequate supply of affordable and safe child care provided in a range of options, based on sound child development principles.

In terms of cost–effectiveness, the expenses incurred by society for the unwillingness to place high priority on a comprehensive child and family policy are enormous. It would be an interesting exercise to total the costs for human services systems currently in place that deal with the results of inadequate child development—be it costs in our educational, health, mental health, correctional, employment-unemployment, substance-abuse, and people-abuse systems. We know well the adage that an ounce of prevention is worth a pound of cure but honor it more in the breach than the observance. One effect of this is that the productivity of our economy during the 1990s will depend on our ability to deal with significant labor shortages. Our major labor pool for the 1990s is the 25 percent of children now in poverty, who, if left economically deprived, will be functionally illiterate and unemployable.

We need, for example, an integrated approach to child and youth development for all classes that integrates the knowledge and skills of what heretofore have been segregated disciplines, professions, and bureaucracies: for example, child care and development, public school education, social work, recreation, health, mental health, job and vocational training, employment, youth services, and parenting care. Our major systems require comprehensive reevaluation leading to new policies and approaches that would include family support and stabilization; lifetime education with emphasis on career development and more creative use of leisure time; broader options for long-term care; more balanced health-resource allocation, which emphasizes prevention, to provide affordable health care for all ages; and housing for young families, the homeless, and the disabled.

There are other priorities that fall quickly behind the above: more comprehensive, less costly health care for all. Anne Stoline and Jonathan Weiner

(1988, 1) note that U.S. medical-care expenditures will reach 11 percent of the GNP by 1990: "The escalation of [these] costs has prompted an evaluation of benefits obtained from our massive commitment of resources to health care." Such evaluation includes looking at a number of health-care allocation issues. For example, saving one baby's life with neonatal-care technology costs over $100,000 per child. The same resources could be applied to hundreds of infants and children under age five who currently are receiving inadequate nutrition and maternal and health care. Our current health and human services are replete with examples of extreme costs per client: $100,000+ at one extreme; less than $100 at the other.

Other top priorities include continued efforts to turn the corner in fighting life-threatening diseases such as cancer and AIDS. Long-term and catastrophic care are also high-priority human services, not only for today's and tomorrow's elderly but also for a large number of people of all ages, from high-risk infants to hospice patients. Housing is still a top priority for young people first starting out, for the homeless, for the disadvantaged, for the disabled, and for many elderly. Given the significant changes in the demographics of our population, priorities are, and should be, a continuous agenda-setting process.

Steady-State Public Funding.   Since the mid-1960s, we have witnessed periods of incremental (expansion) and decremental (contraction) public funding of the human services. We are now in a period of what could be called steady-state public funding. In actual outlays, federal spending for human resources, for example, went from $62 billion in 1985 to an estimated $79 billion in 1990. But its percentage of the GNP will remain the same during that period.

In other words, increased resources will remain steady (proportionate) with the growth of our economy. All indications point to the same public finance trends in state and local governments. With growing state economies, there will be increased resources available for human services. The issue then becomes one of priorities. Even more important, will the priorities be decided by a comprehensive, strategic planning process? By different human services professionals joining forces with interest groups to foster a more parochial approach to priority setting? Or by competing groups? This may be a period in which strategies of community organization and advocacy are of prime importance for human services managers.

As the federal government places the burden of improvement in human services on other levels of government, this shift toward decentralized systemic design of human services provides an opportunity for state and local government strategic planners between now and the turn of the century. There is some danger of disparate quality of systems nationwide, but there will be a larger number and variety of systems designs. This could lead to greater creativity in finding the best possible systemic solutions to extremely difficult human services issues.

Decremental and steady-state public funding has apparently brought a change in the relative roles of government human services agencies versus commercial and voluntary (private) agencies. Increasingly, the former are operating as contractors and the latter as contractees. Knowledge and skill in purchase of services and contracting are thus vital for both parties to the contract.

System Redesign or Reform?   The design of new human services systems for critical client groups is complex; their operationalization is quite difficult. We need a comprehensive redesign of our welfare state, not incremental alteration of small subsystems. Consider, for example, the issue of the increasing numbers of homeless people. To some, the preferred solution might be putting into place, most often with volunteer resources, a larger number of community-support systems. But to others, the system should have three tiers: emergency shelters, transitional shelters, and permanent housing. Actually, rather than provide housing subsidies for the residences and vacation homes of the middle and upper classes, which currently are still built into our tax-welfare system, our nation also needs to channel adequate housing subsidies to the homeless, to the poor, and to young families moving to their first home, to solve this problem. The issue requires both community-organization and systems-design skills on the part of human services professionals.

Whatever the national priority, a fundamental and comprehensive redesign requires analyzing and reshaping all mechanisms that currently are the cornerstones of our welfare system: direct and indirect resource transfers and subsidized services provision. Increasingly, we must move from systems that attempt to minimize individual and collective risks by finding a more balanced level by which individuals and society share life's risks.

The cornerstone of a comprehensively redesigned welfare state should be *occupational welfare,* the fringe benefits that come with employment. This means therefore that job acquisition and career development are central to the system. This also means that such benefits should be designed as "flex-benefits" or "cafeteria-style" benefits: each employee can pick and choose what would be the unique mix of benefits best suited for his particular age or stage of life. Occupational welfare could be the basis of nationalized health services, administered and financed at the place of employment, and regulated and monitored by the federal government under uniform standards and guidelines. It would have to include systems for providing quality of services to those not covered by occupational welfare, which currently represents 15 percent of the population—over 40 million citizens.

One-Tiered Services and Two-Tiered Financing.   There could be *one set* of health and human services for all with, however, a *two-tier* financing system: universal and fair-share. Those who elect a **universal system** would pay a greater amount of their income for the costs of services, whether it be in terms of the cost of service to a profit-making organization or taxes to a government jurisdiction; in return, there would be no limit on their use of the services provided by the system. Those who elect the **fair-share system** would pay a lower amount of taxes to government jurisdictions, in a reformed tax system that only very selectively uses tax regulations for policy purposes (e.g., stimulates homeownership for young couples). However, when they need a specific health or welfare service, fair-share taxpayers would pay a higher cost of service or receive a reduced set of benefits.

In the fair-share system, the focus would be on establishing the true and actual cost of services (health, education, mental health, home care, etc.) and then finding a level of recipient cost sharing that balances individual with community responsibilities. Today, for example, a young adult motorcyclist who is badly hurt in a severe accident receives services valued at many hundreds of thousands of dollars. TBI therapy is comparatively successful today, but the cost is often borne by all of us—out of Social Security funds, incidentally, an unfair burden on those least able to pay. If the patient or his family do not have the immediate resources for such care, should their neighbors bear the full cost of such services, or is there a lifetime fair share that the client and family should shoulder? The cost of a community-based program for the developmentally disabled is significant, and as a nation we need to provide the highest quality of such services. But is there some fair-share payment system for these families? If we lived in a Scandinavian country where their welfare system design includes high-level taxation to provide universal services to all, there would be no issue. But the United States has chosen a different welfare state design, which requires two levels of financing.

Once again, our single, most effective payment–accounting system is the Internal Revenue Service (IRS), particularly with our exploding state-of-the-art technology of information processing. Our ability to design computer systems to calculate financial impacts—be it for insurance ratings, investments, or programmed stock transactions—is perhaps the most sophisticated in the world. Thus, when individuals attempt to switch from fair share to universal and perhaps back again to avoid the risks of life, the IRS would have no problem in creating tables for accountants to recalculate payments due. For example, if the children of an older, retired, disabled parent switched to the universal payment system after a lifetime of being in the fair-share payment system in order to qualify for Medicaid to support long-term care, a portion of the parent's estate (including proceeds from the sale of his home) would be paid to the IRS to repay for the shift from one payment system to the other.

Trends in the Design of Human Services Systems.   A number of interrelated trends in human services systems are increasingly becoming design standards. They flow out of a fundamental change in the way in which societal institutions and processes are being organized and managed. These trends include managed care; quality assurance; comprehensive, unique sets of services; client-managed services; cross-organizational-disciplinary systems; integrated service-delivery technologies; and multiple strategies to achieve the same goal. They are briefly discussed next and are expanded in Chapter 14, a chapter devoted to the analysis and design of transorganizational human services systems—the starting point of systemic management.

Managed Care.   Increasingly, health and human services systems are being designed to "manage" the care process. In the health field, HMOs and preferred provider organizations (PPOs) are becoming the standard, as is case management for the mentally ill and developmentally disabled. Case managers most likely will be found in every human service by the 1990s. Whereas the services integration movement of the early 1970s was essentially focused on more *effective* delivery of services, the managed-care trend has a powerful resource-conservation impetus. Many view the move in public agencies away from direct-service provision to one of directing, managing, and coordinating client services (e.g., case management) as a diminution of professionalism. Indeed, this change is used as an excuse to replace professionals with lesser credentialed employees in order to reduce costs. However, where such a move is client- and community-oriented and is focused on treating each client in a unique fashion, case management by professionally qualified people is an important systems-design specification.

Quality Assurance.   We are in a period where there is increased privatization in a broad range of human services; corporate medicine is a good example. To many people this is alarming and even threatening. Regardless of our professional and personal attitudes about this trend, it is clear that a very high priority for human services strategic planners is the design and operationalization of quality-assurance systems to monitor privatized services.

Traditionally, our form of a welfare state encourages the design of societal systems in which the public, commercial (private), and nonprofit sectors of our economy are integrated. The proper use of well-designed privatized human services systems is legitimate for redesigned human services systems. Currently, however, these systems are being fashioned at the marketplace, not in public human services planning offices. Narrow-casted interest groups are reaching state government policymakers more effectively and more quickly than are human services professional planners serving those same governments. Whatever their roots, quality assurance for privatized systems is recognized as necessary.

Comprehensive, Unique Sets of Services.   For physical and mental health and for services to the developmentally disabled, there has been an increasing commitment to "packaging" a unique set of services specific for each client. In most situations, the services are provided by a number of different professionals or even different organizations. This trend is now spreading in efforts to "reform" child welfare, youth development, and family services systems.

Client-Managed Services.   It is preferable that people manage their own delivery of services, both from a therapeutic perspective and out of necessity because they have to deal with a number of different professionals, institutions, and systems. In some systems (e.g., the mentally ill or physically-developmentally disabled) where they are dependent on others (e.g., members of the family or professionals), clients are assisted in managing service delivery by advocates or surrogates.

Cross-Organizational and Interdisciplinary Systems.   It is almost impossible to design a human services system today that is not interdisciplinary or cross organizational in nature. The spanning of jurisdictional, organizational, or professional boundaries is both intergovernmental and intragovernmental in nature (linking federal, state, and municipal agencies, as well as linking several different state agencies) *and* intersectional (or interjurisdictional), linking public, nonprofit, and proprietary organizations. This is true even when one state agency—for example, a state department of mental health—creates and controls its own system that links itself to several different state agencies and several different community agencies.

Integrated Service-Delivery Technologies.   Integrated service-delivery technologies include these components: assessment of client needs by an integrated team of professionals; development of a unique "package" of services usually from a variety of providers; specificity of outcome criteria; designation of a case manager with responsibilities for client mentoring, case monitoring, and systems-change agent; and an integrated client-information system. All these are essentially managed by the client or client's surrogate.

The design, or redesign, of human services systems are the means by which strategic plans are converted to implementation strategies and ultimately to systemic management. In the first instance, sociotechnical systems require sophisticated design and development planning that use state-of-the-art cybernetic principles and technologies. While this is largely a high-tech field, more important is the need to focus on the systems-design process. Because many systems are bedded in laws and administrative regulations, a close working relationship must be established between the executive and legislative branches of governments. Although legislators may not have systems expertise, the vast majority accept the advice and guidance of their professional staffs. Today, the quality of professional staffs in both the legislative and executive branches is excellent. Where a systems-design team effort is undertaken, the result will be state-of-the-art human services systems.

Summary

Complexity is the very stuff of today's world. The tool for handling complexity is organization. But our concepts of organization belong to the much less complex old world, not to the much more complex today's world. Still less are they adequate to deal with the next epoch of complexification—in a world of explosive change. (Beer 1975, 15)

The management of the human services has become quite complex. The move from simplistic to complex management is a challenge that can be met with an investment of energy and creativity. The challenge must be accepted because the stakes are high; but this challenge is exciting, for it can lead to a new conception of the role and function of the human services manager, as we strive for an improved society for *all* of our inhabitants.

To meet this challenge, one must have an understanding of the dynamics of both the intraorganizational and interorganizational dynamics of the human services, as well as the nature of the task of serving people. As noted, the rate of change in the human services can best be characterized as kinetic, that is, in constant motion. Understanding the nature and pace of change is a starting point for creative, dynamic human services management. It must be coupled with a recognition of the momentous transition currently taking place in the human services organizational and systemic environment. Already one can detect a number of strategic opportunities that this transition will provide for the human services manager during the 1990s. What is at stake is nothing less than our form of democracy. Should current trends continue, we will not only have a two-tiered human services system, one for the privileged and one for the disadvantaged, but we will also have two societies in the United States. For a profession dedicated to the ideals of those who founded the nation over 200 years ago, the human services manager's mission is quite clear.

7

Women and Minorities
in Management

Demographic Changes: Implications

Institutional Barriers Facing Women and Minorities
Recruitment, Selection, and Appointment
Promotions
Personnel Policies

Interpersonal Barriers: Attitudes and Actions
The Power of Images and Stereotypes
Sexism and Sexual Harassment
Racism
Other Affected Groups

Personal Barriers: The Roadblocks Within
Management Styles

Strategies for Dealing with Barriers
Personal Strategies: A Practical Approach
Institutional Strategies

Summary

This chapter is a paradox for many reasons. Ideally, human services organizations should be neutral in terms of gender, race, class, and ethnicity. Are they? Ideally, agencies whose clients are disproportionately female and nonwhite and whose staffs comprise mainly women should reflect these realities in the makeup of their management. Do they? It is a further paradox that the white male managers who presently dominate the field of human services management in numbers, values, styles, and techniques thus provide the norm by which others who will ultimately replace them are judged. To avoid the same paradox and to broaden the perspective, this chapter includes the insights of a number of female and minority administrators. And while many of the issues are discussed primarily in the context of female administrators, the dynamics described share significant commonalities with all minorities.

This chapter is also about power. Power is something that is rarely shared willingly and never relinquished gladly. Our field is no different from others. The barriers and barricades that we discuss are designed to protect the "haves" and to keep the "have-nots" out—a simplistic explanation of a complex strategy. How to overcome this strategy for the empowerment of all is our problem as managers. Rosabeth Moss Kanter (1977) has pointed out that power should not mean domination, tyranny, control, or power for its own sake. Rather, it is the capacity to "get what you need to get the job done," that is, power in the service of performance. Kanter also defines the powerless as "people who can be bypassed or left out." Though fully competent, they do not play a critical role and may be bypassed in the organization in terms of their own authority. When this occurs, everybody loses. This chapter identifies some of the barriers that the "power-haves" erect, their impacts and implications for many, and how, once understood, they may be broken down for the good of all.

This is a chapter then for all human services managers, regardless of gender, race, class, and ethnicity. If professionally we are dedicated to developing a more just society, then a deeper understanding of the issues raised in this chapter is essential for all of us. Although the past two decades have seen some progress, much still needs to be done as the United States moves toward the day, just past the turn of the century, when the women and nonwhites in the work force will outnumber men and Caucasians. Adapting to these changes will present a challenge of immense proportions and equally immense possibilities for human services management. If we are to be successful at replacing the discredited "melting pot" notion of a homogeneous society with the far more realistic one of a well-integrated, harmonious "mosaic of diversity," then the place to begin is within our own organizations. If the leaders of the human services fields, attuned as they are to the betterment of the human condition, cannot find the way to resolve these issues within their own circles, then who will?

Limited space does not allow us to provide as in-depth and detailed a treatment of some of the complexities of this broad topic as we might like, and there are many, solid, serious presentations by other authors available to those seeking more information. But no responsible text addressed to the future leaders of this field can ignore the need to sensitize, to build awareness and recognition of disabling injustices, and to point the way to gender-neutral, color-blind human services management. That is the purpose of this chapter. Let us begin our examination of the issues with Case 7.1.

Case 7.1

Breaking the Glass Ceiling: Women as Executives

Van Tracey closed the door behind her and walked quickly down the hall after her meeting with Dr. White, president of the hospital. She was elated, confused, and mostly in shock. Because of her outstanding success in working with the hospital's Employee Assistance Programs (EAPs) for local companies, Dr. White had said, they were offering her the position of director of program development for the hospital, starting immediately. Caught by complete surprise, Van was ready to accept on the spot. But something restrained her, and she told Dr. White that she would like to talk it over with Reggie, her husband, and would give him her answer tomorrow.

Walking back to her office, Van's head was whirling. Her first reaction to Dr. White's offer was pure joy—the goal she had struggled so hard to reach was finally in her grasp. She made herself a cup of coffee, sat down at the desk, and pushed her papers aside. She needed to think clearly. What lay ahead? Despite the fact that she loved the day-to-day work with patients, joining the hospital's executive management team had been her career goal from the moment she took her first management position.

She picked up a pencil and decided, in her usual meticulous style, to make a list—pros on one side of the fresh white sheet of paper, cons on the other. She began to write:

Pros

- I've always felt that a capable woman who really wanted to work hard enough could succeed in a "man's world." I think I've just proved it, and I'm so proud!

- Mama will be so happy! After all her years of work to get off welfare and help Savannah, her baby, get that hard-won B.S.W. Now I'll not only be the first college graduate in the family, but I'll also be the first executive.

Cons

- How will Reggie feel? His job hasn't been going well. As it is, our relationship is feeling the strains of my long hours. And he doesn't much like having to pick up Randy at day care on the days I have to work late. How will he handle my having to work late all the time?

- Randy is only seven. He still needs a lot of my time and attention. And also, I'm not getting any younger—that big three-oh birthday came as a shock—and I really do want another baby. Could I really manage that? Maternity leave now? Forget it!

- EAPs can do great work in improving the quality of people's lives by upgrading their health care—particularly in the areas of preventive care. This job will really give me a chance to make them available to many more working folks.

- I'll be the first black on the executive team. It's about time! About half the hospital's employees are black, and they need somebody to speak for them.

- We could use that nice increase in salary, all right. And I sure wouldn't mind getting out of this stuffy cubicle into my own office—with a window!

- I loved working with patients—it seemed to bring out the best parts of me! I missed that when I began working with the EAPs, but at least there was still some one-on-one and direct supervision. Am I suddenly going to be a high-class salesperson?

- I've met the people on the executive team—they're a nice enough bunch. But they're all white, middle-aged guys who've been working together since the year one. They all have master's degrees or Ph.D.s or M.D.s. I'll be the only B.S.W., only woman, only black. Come to think of it, is that why I got picked? Double points for affirmative action?

- I know I've got the smarts, I know I work harder than most, and I certainly put in the effort and the money to look "packaged" for success. But will I really be able to hack it? That executive team is heavy-duty!

Van's phone rang, and she answered it. When she finished the conversation, she picked up the sheet of paper, sighed, and put it into her briefcase. This decision wasn't going to be easy.

Demographic Changes: Implications

In Chapter 6 we examined some of the momentous demographic changes in the United States during the past two decades. Foremost among these are (1) that the majority of families living in poverty are headed by women; (2) that shortly after the turn of the century, the majority of the population in the United States will be nonwhite; and (3) that soon women will outnumber men in the work force. A by-product of these demographic changes is that women are increasingly being impacted by the intensifying pressures of their competing roles as homemaker, wife, mother, breadwinner of necessity, employee, and caretaker—daughter of an elderly parent, with major implications. These implications are discussed in detail later.

Marie Weil (1987) has noted that during the 1990s both the work force and the client groups for human services agencies will be increasingly women and nonwhite. This will place demands for new insights, new sensitivities, and new knowledge and skills, as well as new systems, approaches, and policies on everyone in the area of human services. Professionals, managers, executives, and policymakers alike will be pressed to make the necessary changes, which will probably not be easy for a number of important and complicated reasons:

1. As Mimi Abramovitz documents, from historical times to today, welfare policies regulate the lives of women. Yet even with the clear necessity for women in the labor force of today's U.S. economy, the policies of our modern-day welfare state perpetuate a family ethic that "accepts female economic dependence on men, the sex segregation of the labor market, the gender division of society, or otherwise supports the conditions that underpin female subordination in both the public and private sphere" (1988, 8). This is further reflected in societal institutions that continue to foster "patriarchal hierarchies," with the value and status of women's waged labor regarded as inferior both in terms of the policies and structures.

2. Despite the major efforts to eradicate both sexism and racism during the past few decades, they are still deeply entrenched in many organizational cultures. Due to affirmative action legislation, progress has been made in the number of women, nonwhites, and different ethnic groups who are now in the work force. The numbers in professions and in management positions have also significantly increased. Efforts to deal with such issues as comparable worth (equal pay for work of equal value) and sexual har-rassment have brought these matters into the public consciousness. And although there is some real progress, it can be described as "chipping away at the tip of the iceberg."

3. Many scholars have identified the phenomenon that societal institutions, human services organizations included, *mirror and help sustain the strati-fication patterns of the society in which the organizations exist.* Thus, the attempt to apply a neutral standard of gender, race, or ethnicity in human services agencies will probably not be completely successful until it also occurs in society in general.

4. Recent data indicate that the number of female human services managers is increasing, particularly in middle-management positions. At the same time, there are indications that the increase in the number who will move on to fill top executive positions may not be as large as would normally be projected. This is partly due to external barriers, but also because the women involved are beginning to ask a crucial question: Are the benefits for achieving such a promotion worth the cost in personal trade-offs?

All these demographic, economic, cultural, and technological changes dur-ing the past decades have raised a number of critical issues concerning women and ethnicity in the human services. Collectively, as we have noted, they represent a challenge for *every* human services management professional, male as well as female. These challenges are examined in this chapter.

Institutional Barriers Facing Women and Minorities

Weil (1987, 24) defines institutional barriers as "obstacles embedded in organization policy, structure and behaviors which disadvantage women or minorities." Let us examine several of the major institutional barriers that fit this definition.

Recruitment, Selection, and Appointment

Most human services organizations operate within a merit personnel system. This is highly formalized in public agencies, particularly those within the civil service, and may be more informal in private, nonprofit agencies. Technically, this means that there are in place rigorous policies, procedures, and mechanisms to assure that people with the highest merit will be recruited, selected, and appointed to all positions covered by the system. Federal, state, and municipal affirmative action and equal opportunity laws and regulations exist to monitor these systems and to assure anyone who is deemed qualified an opportunity to be appointed on the basis of merit. In addition, these laws actively seek a balance in appointments that reflect the demographics of the jurisdiction.

The problem is that the policies, procedures, and mechanisms for recruitment, selection, and appointment often have built-in biases and are subject to informal processes that can create subtle but formidable barriers for women, nonwhites, and people from different ethnic groups. Management positions in human services organizations represent opportunities for career advancement and for higher pay. In making appointments to these management positions, the first decision the human services agency makes is whether to promote from within or to conduct an open search, recruiting candidates from other areas as well as from within the agency. Both approaches have their pluses and minuses.

Appointments from within can be used by a human services organization as a positive strategy for providing women and minorities opportunities to advance their careers by training them for success in more challenging roles, and encouraging them to compete for the higher-level positions. But it can also be used to "wire" the appointment—that is, going through the merit system process and knowing in advance that, if the hand-picked candidate can make it to the panel of top three or five persons, the appointment will be automatic. The agency goes through the motions and appears to meet the merit system, affirmative action, and equal opportunity regulations and procedures, when in reality these have been bypassed.

Appointments based on an open search are used when the agency wants to find talented people who may have experience in other jurisdictions and who bring new perspectives to the agency. Recruitment is directed at qualified people from other human services organizations in the same geographic area and might include a nationwide search. Competition can be quite keen. Opportunities for attracting talented minority candidates may be broader in an open search if this is truly the aim. The opposite is also true if the aim is to manipulate the process.

Close scrutiny can reveal manifestations of institutional barriers in either of the two approaches to recruitments and selection:

- The application for the position may include questions or requirements that are inappropriate because they seek data that may potentially bias the process; this includes questions about gender, age, marital and family status, race and religion, and physical condition. (Many such questions, incidentally, are illegal.)

- The specifications–qualifications for the position may be skewed in a way that reduces the likelihood of a woman, nonwhite, or person from a minority ethnic group qualifying for the position. Usually, these limitations relate to prior education or experience requirements and in some fields, such as corrections or public safety, include physical attributes required at entry level. This ultimately limits the pool from which managers are selected.

- The nature of the recruitment-and-selection process may be exclusionary or not sufficiently proactive or aggressive. Selection may include a written examination that is skewed toward a particular group of candidates in terms of their ability to provide the desired answers. Even the use of a written examination that relies heavily on language skills can sometimes be restrictive and inappropriate if written language skills are not an essential part of the job description.

While formal institutional barriers can limit the opportunities for being among the top candidates selected for consideration, informal barriers inherent in the appointment process or the values of the appointing person or group will also influence the final appointment. The latter, the informal barriers, may be the most insidious and the most frustrating to identify. They generally are subtle and sometimes not consciously recognized by those who hold them.

For those who survive the initial steps, the appointment process then usually includes a personal interview between the candidate and the appointing authority. While some minority candidates are very successful in such one-on-one encounters, others who are less adept in the interview process, particularly when there is a cultural mismatch, may not be able to generate the necessary rapport. And beyond interviews, some appointment processes also have a political dimension, whether through "cronyism" or party politics. This can place many women and nonwhites at a decided disadvantage; and although often illegal, it usually occurs in a gray area that does not lend itself readily to legal recourse.

Promotions

In most public agencies, promotions to upper- and middle-management positions in human services organizations are also based on merit and guided by the policies, regulations, and procedures of the civil services system. All barriers discussed thus far apply. Promotions to higher executive positions, however, usually do not follow as formal a set of policies and procedures. Although merit is the official standard for appointments to significant and important upper-management posts, these appointments are also influenced by images, perceptions, and biases on the part of the appointing authority.

Besides the structural barriers noted in the discussion of recruitment, selection, and appointment, a subtle but important handicap to promotion occurs early on, by defining who will qualify for consideration. The specifications are often written in such a way as to exclude otherwise qualified women and minorities, who therefore never become part of the promotional pool. An example of this would be a specification setting forth the length and type of experience of the candidate, for example, ten years of significant administrative responsibility similar to that required by the open position. Again, this may be legitimate, or it can be a subtle way of skewing the promotion toward white males who "have paid their dues," that is, have been in middle-management positions for several years.

While statistics do indicate that an increasing number of women and members of minorities have been appointed to middle-management positions during the 1980s, there does not appear to be a great deal of upward mobility for these new human services managers. The barrier here may be more legitimate. Because the group presently clustered near the top of the organizational pyramid will not retire until they meet the requirements of the public pension system, there is no place for these middle managers to go until that time. While the requirement of highly advanced preparation for some top positions is also usually legitimate, it too may pose a barrier. A major investment in time, energy, and resources may be necessary to obtain the required credentials such as an advanced degree or special certificate. This can militate against those who possess the talent but are prevented by their situation from investing the time and resources, thus creating a "double-whammy effect." The net result of such legitimate barriers is that even in a well-intentioned human services organization where sexist and racial attitudes, biases, and prejudices might be at a minimum, women and minorities can nevertheless frequently be excluded from promotions to upper-management positions.

Personnel Policies

The United States lags far behind the rest of the world in terms of personnel policies that are supportive to employees who want to balance their work life with their family life, although recent legislation is being addressed to this problem. While parenting leaves are covered by most personnel policies in the United States, they are minimal at best; and in most instances, they are more directed at conforming with the letter of the law than embodying its spirit. In many situations, to take additional time necessary during the latter months of a pregnancy or during the early months of caring for the infant, the mother must resort to taking leave without pay. Attempts to return to work on a part-time basis after such leaves are not usually made easy except in the case of irreplaceable employees. During a period of shortage of nurses, for example, hospitals liberalize their policies concerning family leave. In nursing management positions, the policy is not so liberal: "It is almost impossible to get someone to manage your organizational unit while you are on maternity leave and then expect your replacement to step aside so that you can resume your responsibilities" is a frequently heard report from female managers in most fields, not only nursing.

Progressive organizations are exploring a system of "flexible benefits" or a "menu plan" in their management of fringe benefits for employees. This means that these benefits can be tailored to the specific needs of the employee, with expanded choices that include options such as child care, respite care, and day care for an elderly parent, besides the traditional offerings. But at the same time that more women enter the work force, the family responsibilities of these women grow at a faster rate. Besides the traditional need for providing child care, older parents who are living longer now also need special care, and this is a responsibility that usually falls on women. Further, the number of households headed by women is steadily increasing, with nearly twice as many non-white women in the work force in this situation, and thus doubly vulnerable. It must be strongly emphasized that, although these are usually raised as women's issues, they impact strongly on men as well, whether as primary parent or as an involved father in a two-wage-earner household. Such concepts as the four-day work week, flex time, job sharing, working at home, workplace day care or shared cost of day care, and other creative efforts at addressing these problems are increasingly finding their way into personnel policies. But in general, we in the United States still have a very long way to go before such enlightened policies become common place enough to have impact or even find acceptance as an attainable goal for most organizations. That these policies can be beneficial to all has been proven in a number of other nations, with Canada and the Scandinavian countries providing ready examples.

Interpersonal Barriers: Attitudes and Actions

Although institutional barriers are difficult to overcome, even more problematic are the subtler interpersonal barriers that many women and minorities
face. Sexism and racism are potent, multifaceted, subtle, and expressed in
many ways.

The Power of Images and Stereotypes

The issue of images and stereotypes is a very difficult one for all women,
nonwhites and members of minority ethnic groups. Research indicates that
for all women, regardless of their color, these stereotypes generally fall into
several categories:

- Family role
- Gender role
- Power roles

Traditional, historical family models and stereotypic roles, while certainly
changing, are still pervasive: fathers are the primary breadwinners and
"bosses"; mothers are the child caregivers, homemakers, and general nurturers. Women are also daughters who are protected and supported by their
fathers and are therefore expected to be grateful and obedient. And the male
"birthright"—that is, power—is transmitted from male to male. These simplistic images have prevailed for centuries. It is not surprising therefore that
cultures imprinted with this patriarchal stereotype and societal institutions
that have been inherently patriarchal are not instantly responsive to changing
social mores.

The notion of gender carrying with it distinctive traits is another stereotype
that has survived throughout the ages and is only being openly challenged in
recent times. Table 7.1 lists a number of traits different writers characterize as
gender related. There is no solid research to support these stereotypes as a
scientific assessment of women's innate characteristics or organizational behaviors, or of males for that matter. But true or not, these stereotypes have a life
of their own, which creates a problem for female administrators and, in fact,
for all administrators. Can a woman, for example, be decisive, assertive, and
authoritative? Those are "male" traits. How will male and female subordinates
accept and respond? On the other hand, can a male administrator be gentle and
nurturing and still be seen as a strong manager, or will he be branded a
"wimp?" These are issues of managerial style and are examined further in this
chapter in that context.

Many men feel uncomfortable with women in high positions of power,
particularly as a colleague on the management team or as their subordinate.
And rather than dealing with either the feelings or the realities of a situation

Table 7.1   Stereotyped, Gender-Related Leadership
             Characteristics and Traits

Female	Male
Cautious	Decisive
Conciliatory	Direct
Subjective	Rational
Accommodating	Exploitative
Submissive	Assertive
Dependent	Independent
Acquiescent	Ambitious
Process-oriented	Impact-oriented
Nurturing	Authoritative

that requires that power be relinquished and redistributed, they resort to earlier life stereotypes. The women are then "cast" in roles like "Mom," "Sis," or "old-maid schoolteacher," all roles that are inappropriate to collegial working relationships. These games serve their players as a temporary "out" that offers neither resolution of the tensions or a solution to the problem. And many times, even when women are promoted to upper-management levels, they are steered to staff positions that are relatively powerless, for the same reasons. Thus, when a woman is appointed to an upper-management position, the conventional wisdom often assumes either that she was twice as good and worked three times as hard as her competitor or perhaps that sex was part of the process. This brings us to our next topic: sexism.

Sexism and Sexual Harassment

As they enter the ranks of human services management and move up the ranks of human services organizations, women face *sexual discrimination,* which is usually very subtle, although it may occasionally be blatant. This form of discrimination may appear in the form of not being selected in the first instance, being passed over for higher executive positions although qualified, or by being sidetracked to positions of lesser managerial power. It may manifest itself through less pay or "perks" for the same work as men, in being treated as "second-class citizens" in terms of membership on the management team, or in subtle ways in which ideas are ignored or coopted. A female manager may be treated as a token who will never be a member of the "old-boys" network or part of the locker-room culture. Most instances of sexism are subtle, hard to pin down, and difficult to document. And worse, many well-intentioned male administrators buy into the comfortable fiction of denial that sexism is operative in their agency. After all, it's nobody's fault that the female administrator on

Table 7.2 Types of Racism and Manifested Behavior

Types	Manifested Behavior						
	Overt—Conscious	Overt—Unconscious	Subtle—Conscious	Subtle—Unconscious	Lack of Interest or Dissociation	Ignorance	"Cultural Blindness" or Ethnocentricity
Institutionalized racism: supported by official policies or legislation—example, apartheid regulations	Exclusion of discrimination sanctioned in social policy	Policies or agency procedures that exclude or discriminate without overt intent	Barriers to employment such as height requirements	Culturebound employment or aptitude tests	Failure to mandate interpreters for services and court actions	Policies or procedures that violate cultural or religious taboos	Refusal to allow ethnic foods or religious objects to be brought into hospitals by patients or families
Institutional racism: present in policy, administrative regulations, program access, or opportunity	Refusal to take cultural or ethnic factors into account—overt discrimination	Location and scheduling so that they are not accessible to high-risk groups	Application of inappropriate, i.e., insensitive "treatment" models	Assumption that ethnic variables will not affect service	Absence of outreach programs	Absence or refusal to use a family-oriented service model	Failure to provide for special population needs, i.e., hospital translation or failure to address cultural norms of behavior
Individual racism: beliefs and actions of individuals or groups based on prejudice or racist attitudes	Bigotry or active efforts to discriminate against a group	Avoidance of members of racial groups and failure to include groups in milieu and other treatment	Use of derogatory terms	Refusal to learn to pronounce names correctly	Insensitivity to culturally patterned responses	Ignorance of central cultural or religious beliefs	Lack of recognition of cultural differences among groups—on the assumption that all "should" behave like one's own group

Source: Adapted from Marie Weil, "Southeast Asians and Service Delivery: Issues in Service Provision and Institutional Racism," in *Bridging Cultures: Southeast Asian Refugees in America* (Los Angeles: NIMH and the Asian-American Community Mental Health Training Center, 1981).

the team had to pick up her baby from day care after work, while the guys went for a quick game of racquet ball and managed to transact some business while they were in the locker room. Female administrators therefore must develop keen "radar" and adopt a strategy for combating sexual discrimination in their own work lives, without becoming consumed or compromised by it. And all administrators must adopt strategies for eradicating it wherever it exists because it will not disappear by itself.

As noted earlier, besides sexism that is usually subtle, 50 percent of all women at the workplace have reported some *sexual harassment* episode. It may have been low-key, taking the form of seemingly good-natured banter that clearly conveyed the message that male colleagues viewed them as sex objects, or overt by the way they were addressed or even propositioned. And there are sufficient documented accounts of women being harassed physically—whether by a "playful" touch or, more seriously, by being promoted for tangible sexual favors—to indicate that this is a very real problem. Further, a female manager is at a serious disadvantage in bringing these matters to light, particularly if the offending man is her superior, which is frequently the case. Once again, it behooves both male and female human services managers to be on guard against the exploitation and victimization represented by this type of behavior.

Racism

As the population in the United States becomes increasingly nonwhite, which includes Blacks, Hispanics (Puerto Rican, Chicano, Cuban, and Central-South American), and diverse ethnic groups from Asia, the issue of racism will grow. Racism, like sexism, occurs for two fundamental reasons. The underlying one, which drives the erection of barriers and all other mechanisms of exclusion, is the unwillingness to relinquish and share power, a very deep-seated drive. The second is *xenophobia*—the fear of the strange, which in its milder forms is expressed by rejecting or ignoring the unfamiliar group. And these are compounded by the great degree of *ethnocentricity,* the "We're the Greatest" syndrome that prevails among mainstream white Americans. As a result, even when the often expressed policy in an organization is nonracist, racist behavior often abounds in subtle ways. There have been many excellent treatments of this topic, and a particularly succinct overview is provided by Weil (1981). Her chart on types of racism presents the full range of behaviors against which human services administrators must guard within their organizations (see Table 7.2). Once again, the first step toward bridging differences and of making an asset of diversity is a heightened sense of awareness and a strong will to begin the journey to gender-neutral, color-blind human services management.

Other Affected Groups

No concerned treatment of the difficult subject of interpersonal barriers due to prejudice would be complete without considering two more subgroups. The "groups" that we discuss are not really groups. They are rather an aggregation of individual human beings who happen to share one particular common attribute that is used by others to lump them together for easy identification. It is essential to remember that people do not "lump" well and that vast differences exist, and managers attempting to treat these groups monolithically do so at their peril.

The first such subgroup, and it frequently includes individuals who in other ways are part of the dominant majority, are people who have a physical disability or a major illness that carries with it some disabling features. The word *barrier,* which we have used liberally throughout this chapter to denote more abstract concepts, becomes a very concrete phenomenon for these people. Many buildings legally deemed as "disabled accessible" are nothing of the sort, and we won't even discuss those buildings not in conformity. Simple things such as a high curb, a steep incline, or an out-of-reach elevator button can render a dynamic but wheelchair-using manager on his way to a meeting virtually dysfunctional, and a long slippery corridor can stop someone using crutches or a cane dead in her tracks. Other physical barriers, equally self-evident, present major and usually unnecessary obstacles to people who have visual or auditory disabilities, although the technologies for overcoming virtually all of them are readily available.

What is not always available is the determination and energy on the part of co-workers and those in authority to exert the effort necessary to remove these barriers. The dynamics in this instance are somewhat different than what has been described. Most human services managers have a clear commitment to the notion of equal access and to adapting work situations to accommodate disabilities, but the day-to-day implementation often falls far short of the mark. Every disabled professional striving to maintain high standards of effectiveness has horror stories to tell. These include such simple things as lengthy meetings with no possibility of getting to the only barrier-free toilet facility on the premises, of being trapped on the third floor of a building when the only elevator goes out of commission, of being bowled over by heavy swinging doors, and other such mishaps.

Subtler but no less treacherous are the attitudinal barriers. Although sympathy or pity are the accepted overt response, these often mask an underlying unease and fear on the part of a surprising number of people. This is particularly true in interactions with individuals who have a deformity that is apparent, with conditions like cerebral palsy or other spasticity, with amputees or people requiring orthopedic devices. And an even greater degree of discomfort, sometimes to the extent of a documented phenomenon referred to as "shunning," occurs when a colleague is dealing with cancer, epilepsy, AIDS, and certain other illnesses that allow people to continue to work for long periods between bouts.

Precisely because no one in the field intellectually condones such attitudes, these behaviors in all their potential cruelty and destructiveness are very subtle and exceedingly difficult to isolate and confront. They come from the primeval human prejudice against anomaly or disease that exists in our society and to some extent in each of us. And these attitudes defend us against the feelings of vulnerability that few like to admit having. As with other barriers, it is the people most affected who have provided the most courageous and enlightened leadership in the battle to eliminate them from our institutions, and it behooves all human services managers to heed and join the process.

There is another aggregation of human services managers who also face subtle but insidious barriers growing out of very deep-rooted societal prejudices. Certainly nothing is more private and personal than an individual's sexual preference and practice. It has not traditionally been a workplace concern. The notion of "between consenting adults" was the enlightened overt criterion for sexual behavior, something not usually discussed openly. Homosexuality was usually kept "in the closet," as the popular expression describes it, by those who practiced it. Recent years have brought about a far more open and honest way of expressing and talking about one's sexual practices and thus have seen many homosexuals "coming out." While this has been liberating for some gay and lesbian professionals, for others it has brought them face to face with the deep homophobia that exists within our society and that, like the dynamics discussed previously, sometimes leads to highly paradoxical behavior on the part of otherwise enlightened human services professionals. What should be a completely personal choice for a competent person performing in a professional role evokes the same dynamics of subtle but very real prejudices and barriers we have been talking about in the previous contexts and requires the same response if we seek a truly equal opportunity workplace.

Personal Barriers: The Roadblocks Within

We have discussed a series of common and serious barriers that exist in the human services workplace and the way of dealing with them. But some of the most difficult barriers to overcome for women, nonwhites, and diverse ethnic groups who aspire to careers as human services managers exist within themselves.

Management Styles

Three types of potential personal barriers that relate to management style have been identified as related to **gender**, **culture**, and **clinical perspectives**.

Gender-Related Management Styles.   One of the most difficult decisions that faces many female administrators upon accepting a new appointment in a human services management position is often: What style of management will I use to be effective? (See Table 7.3.) Marilyn Loden, in her book *Feminine Leadership or How to Succeed in Business Without Being One of the Boys* (1985), maintains that organizational life in the United States has values, traditions, structures, and behavioral norms that are linked to masculinism. For most female managers, working in such environments is like visiting a remote part of the world, with a quite foreign culture. She suggests that the differences in leadership styles are "rooted in the basic facts of biology and physiology as well as in the fundamentally different ways in which boys and girls are raised and socialized within our culture" (63).

Loden presents two models of leadership, based on gender, which she categorizes and describes in Table 7.4. Feminine leadership style uses personal power, whereas males depend on position power. Women frequently are more concerned for people, include intuition as a legitimate management approach, and use creative problem solving. Loden therefore encourages women to pursue their innate feminine leadership style because the different views and approaches of male and female managers will enrich the quality of work life for all. She feels that these differences can be used in a complementary way to improve organizational effectiveness.

Loden joins other recent writers who describe the feminist approach to management. Among them is Roslyn Chernesky (1983) who has proposed what she calls a feminist approach to traditional social work supervision. This includes the following principles that differ from the traditional view and express some of the qualities noted in Table 7.4.

- Individual workers have the capacity for self-direction, self-discipline, and self-regulation.
- Workers can assume responsibility for the quality of their work.
- Leadership and worker roles can be assumed and shared by all employees.
- Expertise is not positively correlated with hierarchical positions.
- Authority need not reside in a hierarchical arrangement.

Another model is proposed by Alice Sargent in *The Androgynous Manager* (1987). She proposes a blend of typical female and male behaviors that can lead to an androgynous model of a manager. (In Greek, *andre* is the root for male, *gyne* for female.) Sargent suggests that women are particularly skillful at things like compromise, interorganizational cooperation, negotiation, and mediation. Men, she notes, are primarily competitive, entrepreneurial, analytic, and logical. By blending all these characteristics, the androgynous model leads to qualities that can achieve order, harmony, maximum productivity, and employee satisfaction for both workers and managers. And the liberating message for both men and women would be that each one's special qualities are needed and recognized no matter where they fall on a gender-role spectrum.

Table 7.3   Some Alternatives for Management Styles for Women*

Style	Implications and Risks
Strong, masculine style	Be as "macho" as your male colleagues. Risk being isolated from both male and female colleagues.
Feminine style	Express your innate female characteristics. Risk resistance and being viewed as ineffective and weak.
Androgynous style	Be a pathfinder searching for a style shared by both women and men and enhancing for both. You still risk being excluded from the dominant management coalition, if its style is strongly male.
Your own unique style	Be sufficiently self-confident to build on your strengths and work on your weaknesses; risk being beset by self-doubts and possibly being passed over for top positions if you haven't conformed sufficiently.

*Based on reports from female managers.

Table 7.4   Masculine and Feminine Leadership Models

Element	Masculine	Feminine
Operating style	Competitive	Cooperative
Organizational structure	Hierarchy	Team
Basic objective	Winning	Quality output
Problem-solving style	Rational	Intuitive–rational
Key characteristics	High control	Lower control
	Strategic	Empathetic
	Unemotional	Collaborative
	Analytic	High performance standards

Source: Marilyn Loden, *Feminine Leadership or How to Succeed in Business Without Being One of the Boys* (New York: Time Books, 1985).

It is the bias of this text that when answering the question of managerial style, all human services managers must follow the same dictum: *Know yourself—be yourself—be a unique manager.*

Human services organizations must be managed in a creative fashion, with the ability to adapt to an extremely dynamic environment. Management of this fluid environment must therefore be defined differently by each manager, with integrity—cognizant of the environment—and in a continually changing fashion. A superior management style is one that flows out of *your* unique talents and characteristics, without reference to labeling. It asks that you be acutely aware of your strengths and weaknesses as a manager and be prepared to build on the former while taking steps to overcome the latter. It requires a great deal of inner security to express one's unique style of management, particularly if it is different from the dominant style in the organization. Upon assuming a new position, a minority or female administrator may have to acclimatize and adapt to the specific culture of the new organization, at least for the period of adjustment. In time, as one's managerial position becomes more secure, it hopefully will be possible to begin to blend one's unique style with that dominant style in the culture of the organizational management team and to bring about changes beneficial to both, in a climate of understanding and respect.

Culture-Related Management Style.   For Black, Hispanic, or Asian-American managers, the issue of male versus female management styles is often secondary. The indigenous cultures of different races and different ethnic groups foster norms and values that may be foreign to the dominant managerial culture in the United States. This can easily create misunderstanding and tensions, particularly because the U.S. culture is known to be ethnocentric. Take, for example, the simple situation of managers greeting each other. In the United States, managers measure each other when first meeting by the strength of the handshake and maintain steady eye contact throughout the meeting. When someone from a Far Eastern culture meets a colleague of equal or greater authority, he lowers the head and averts the eyes as a sign of respect, although not necessarily deference, and clasps his hands together with a slight bow. In the U.S. management culture, these could both be perceived as signs of weakness, and it becomes mandatory for the minority person to adopt U.S. behaviors.

Weil (1987) has noted that Asian–Americans have been socialized to behave in "a very role-fixed and deferential manner" when dealing with organizational superiors. In management meetings in the United States where free and easy exchange, at least superficially, is typical among all present regardless of their hierarchical position, such managerial behavior may be considered by the Asian–American as "curious, disrespectful, and downright rude." Many managers of Asian-American descent therefore would not speak out at a management meeting unless asked directly to do so. They might find it difficult to partake in the ongoing banter that is a normal component of the interaction, while learning to observe the subtle rules that control the underlying dynamics. All these customs in our culture carry messages that are essential to organizational communication patterns.

Clinician's Management Style.   Most human services managers come to their first managerial position because they were outstandingly successful at a clinical job. But the professional preparation and experience that made them a superior, direct-service clinical worker can be a barrier that creates tension and places them at a disadvantage to management colleagues trained formally as administrators. The world of clinicians consists mainly of clients and colleagues, on whom all energy and loyalty is focused. To redirect their primary energies to an organization and its outcomes requires a major shift of professional priorities, particularly when clinicians often view organizations as hostile environments.

Further, many human services clinicians have internalized a deep, fundamental value that people need to make their own decisions over issues that affect their lives. Regardless of decision styles, however, there will be some situations that require human services managers to make decisions that will strongly affect the lives of colleagues and workers. For many managers with a clinical perspective, this also can present a major barrier. It is worth noting that, although this is a problem that pertains equally to all, female or minority practitioners are more likely to have followed the "work-up-the-line" route to management and are therefore more likely to arrive with a well-internalized, clinical approach to management.

Strategies for Dealing with Barriers

Are there distinct strategies that people who feel powerless can adopt to deal with the various barriers to entering the ranks of human services management and to proceed up the career ladder? Those who have "been there," as well as the literature, suggest several, all of which are designed to increase personal and organizational power. Power has a cyclical, synergistic effect: It enables effective leadership, and it attracts supporters, which in turn produces more power. These strategies can be categorized into two groups: personal strategies and institutional strategies (see Table 7.5).

Personal Strategies: A Practical Approach

The two personal strategies that appear to be the most important for a female or minority administrator are developing **mentors** and **peer support**. Either as a way of breaking into the ranks of human services management or upon assuming an administrative position for the first time, a female or minority administrator should find and develop a mentor, who should be asked to take only a limited risk. Preferably, the mentor should be another female or minority manager, who can serve as a sponsor and role model for those who are moving into managerial positions. Another important step is to actively seek and participate in support and alliance networks. They are important for support and enhancement of self-confidence; they are equally vital for sharing of information, advice, and experience. Support networks are also useful in improving the individual and collective power of female and minority administrators in an organization and can bring valuable benefits for others in the organization as well.

Another personal strategy that is considered essential is the preparation of

Table 7.5   Personal and Institutional Strategies for Dealing with Barriers that Confront Female and Minority Human Services Managers

Personal Strategies	Institutional Strategies
■ Find a female or minority manager who will serve as your mentor; be willing to be a mentor, sponsor, or role model to others.	■ Help women and minorities adjust to "alien" norms and behavioral requirements.
■ Prepare a well-developed career plan: clarify personal and career goals, weigh the pros and cons of being an administrator, have realistic expectations, and document and promote your skills and strengths.	■ Participate in agency-sponsored training and development that includes sessions to deal with issues of sexism and racism, provides workshops on affirmative action issues, provides women and minorities with opportunities to develop and expand managerial knowledge and skills, and sponsors cross-cultural seminars for all employees.
■ Use knowledge as a source of strength in pursuit of professional goals.	■ Provide a forum to deal openly with incidents; invite participation.
■ Use positive attitudes to enhance self-confidence.	
■ Develop self-awareness through self-analysis.	■ Participate in agency-sponsored organizational development, i.e., team building, job enrichment, sensitivity training, and support groups.
■ Seek work groups that welcome women and minorities.	
■ Have adequate preparation skills and knowledge.	■ Make clear that sexual harassment will not be tolerated; develop clearly understood complaint procedures and processes.
■ Seek and participate in support and alliance networks.	
■ Deal openly with role casting as it occurs, being careful not to feed into it.	■ Undertake continual examination and analysis of recruitment processes for women and minorities, career patterns and career ladders, the organization's opportunity structure, and organizational patterns that disadvantage women and minorities.
■ Confront racism, sexism, and sexual harassment openly.	
	■ Actively attempt to change any existing exclusionary masculine ethic.

a well-developed **career plan**. It has been said that if you don't know where you want to go, it doesn't much matter which road you take. Such a plan forces female or minority administrators to clarify both personal and professional goals and to develop a realistic set of expectations. It also requires some self-analysis that can lead to awareness of one's strengths and weaknesses. Both become the basis for promoting one's skills and talents, on the one hand, and for shaping a realistic management-development program, on the other. Further, the self-analysis necessary for a career plan also helps one to clarify and assess the positive and negative aspects of becoming an administrator. Although there are obvious benefits and payoffs from being a manager, there are also some costs. These can range from redefining the role one plays in the lives of clients to placing pressures on one's personal or family life. The ultimate choice of both destination and road can only be made by the enlightened individual.

Closely related to a career plan is the **professional management development program** noted above. Many female and minority human services professionals begin their careers as clinicians, only to find themselves attracted to or propelled toward management positions. Education is a source of strength and power in pursuit of professional goals. Therefore it is important to acquire the additional knowledge and skills necessary for managers as one begins to move into an administrative position, as well as the prerequisite academic qualifications. This often takes time.

The last personal strategy deals with **clarification of personal values**. Harriet Braiker (1986), a noted psychologist, has identified some of the psychological traps of success:

- Competition forces one to stress achievement, which may place one's self-concept in question.
- Being an administrator may call for certain traits (e.g., assertiveness, ambition, and autonomy) that may clash with one's own innate characteristics.
- Emphasis on results and impacts requires an orientation that may leave feelings of inadequacy in terms of "process."
- There is a tendency to discount one's own abilities and undermine one's sense of self, lowering expectations for success.
- There is a tendency to filter out positive feedback and amplify negative feedback.

If female or minority administrators can take credit where it is due, if they see failures as having less to do with skill and more to do with lack of resources and support, and if they correctly process information, then their expectations for success would rise, and self-concept and achievement would be more consistent. This would lessen personal stress and avoid some of the potential pitfalls.

Institutional Strategies

Most writers and researchers in this field seem to indicate that one of the most important institutional strategies for dealing with barriers that confront female and minority administrators deals with the mentor strategy. Successful female and minority administrators should become mentors, helping their mentees adjust to the "alien" norms, behavioral requirements, and culture of the agency. Recognizing the importance of mentors–mentees, a human services organization should institutionalize and support this practice as a way of nurturing more female and minority administrators and as a way of removing or reducing the barriers that prevent this group from making their contribution to the agency.

The second most important institutional strategy concerns the development of **agency-sponsored training and development programs** and a **forum for addressing sexist-racist issues**. Such a program should provide knowledge and skills to women and minorities that are directed toward providing the opportunities to enter and excel in managerial positions. Equally important are programs that provide cross-cultural training for **all** employees. An ongoing forum for addressing affirmative action issues and dealing openly with resolving issues of racism, sexism, and sexual harassment helps prevent these problems from arising and can rectify and defuse them if they do.

In conjunction with a training and development program, a human services agency needs to have a well-planned and implemented **organizational development program**. From an agency point of view, as well as from the more obvious personal-professional perspective, team building, job enrichment, sensitivity training, participative management, and support groups are vital for men and women, whites and minorities alike in a human services organization. This is an important institutional strategy for the agency that is sensitive to the need for creating a barrier-free organization.

Most human services organizations have clearly stated **policies** that oppose racism, sexism, or sexual harassment, but most are less clear in communicating that these attitudes will not be tolerated in any form. Clearly understood complaint procedures and processes should be in place and communicated to everyone in the organization. When problems do occur, the actions taken must be firm and decisive. The old adage that actions speak louder than words must be the real policy of the agency, both in letter and spirit.

Despite all of the good intentions of a human services manager to rid the agency of racism, sexism, and sexual harassment and to be dedicated to affirmative action, **continual examination and analysis** of these issues must be an integral element of human services management. Recruitment processes, career patterns, career ladders, and management-accession plans must all be subjected regularly to close scrutiny and data analysis to identify agency patterns that de facto place women and minorities at a disadvantage. The best of intentions, while praiseworthy, are not sufficient. Actual practices are what counts when it comes to eliminating barriers that prevent women and minorities from rising into the managerial and executive positions of an agency.

Summary

Despite the significant progress made by women, nonwhites, and people of diverse cultural groups to advance as human services managers, there is still a long way to go. Existing strategies for dealing with and eliminating structural, interpersonal, and internal barriers must be strengthened, and new strategies for redistributing power must be found. What is the likelihood for improvement in this aspect of human services management?

Perhaps the greatest hope for impetus in bringing about progress lies in the demographics of the United States during the decade of the 1990s. Human services organizations, along with all institutions, will increasingly face a shortage of workers. Two-thirds of the new entrants into the job market are women and minorities, and it is estimated that 80 percent of new female employees are of childbearing age and 90 percent of these will become pregnant. As the 1990s and the first decade of the twenty-first century arrive, the labor shortage in the United States will place women and minorities increasingly in a more powerful position to demand that the work environment be improved to meet their multiple needs and requirements. Thus, necessity may succeed where loftier motives do not.

Recognizing the substantial investment necessary to train new employees, retention will become a major goal of organizational personnel systems. Significant inroads will be made to remove major structural barriers that will indirectly affect interpersonal and internal barriers. Already, new and expanded forms of benefits fashioned specifically to the changing demographics of the new work force are being developed, and new attitudes are emerging.

It remains to be seen to what extent this major demographic trend will shift the masculine, patriarchal bias in organizations and systems to one that is more encompassing. Certainly, moving toward such a fundamental change will require perseverance, sensitivity, dedication, and commitment to the notion of the intrinsic value of the individual, as well as active effort on the part of all concerned.

8

Organization as a Strategy: A More Dynamic Approach to Managing the Human Services

What is the key to good, modern organization? Can human services managers take advantage of the newer approaches to organization? What are the structural and strategic views of organization, and how can they be interrelated? Is there a scheme to follow to produce an organization that uses the advantages of good organizational structure and yet can still adapt dynamically to an ever-changing environment? What are the two forms of management that must coexist and be used simultaneously to meet both the stable and the dynamic requirements of an organization? To address these issues, let us first compare the two organizational charts in Figure 8.1.

Organization A (Figure 8.1a) is a traditional, municipal government structure. It represents an image of an organization that is known by a term introduced earlier, namely, *bureaucracy*—fixed organizational divisions and subdivisions managed by sets of officials following fixed routines. Organization B (Figure 8.1b) is a task force of community agencies who have a common concern: teen parents. This joint effort represents a different image of organization: an *adhocracy*—rapidly changing, adaptive, temporary systems, organized around problems and issues and made up of groups of relative strangers from diverse professional and disciplinary backgrounds.

Many readers might automatically assume that organization A is more efficient and effective than is organization B. The series of boxes connected by direct lines depict clear-cut roles, relationships, and responsibilities and convey required management principles of command, authority, and communication channels. But one should not make that assumption so quickly. In today's environment of rapidly changing human services demands and requirements, organization B can become an equally effective model, if modern organizational and management mechanisms are used to clarify roles, responsibilities, relationships, communications, command, and authority.

For many human services managers, organization A may appear preferable to organization B. There are essentially two reasons for this preference. Organization A depicts the traditional view of organizations, one that flows largely from a structural view of phenomena. From this point of view, organization B is difficult to comprehend; it appears complicated, confusing, and difficult to maintain.

Often there is a lack of awareness or understanding of the modern management mechanisms and techniques that permit organization B to function smoothly, productively, and effectively. Yet organization B represents an equally viable strategic approach to managing the provision of human services. It generally involves several agencies crossing the boundaries of their organizations and forming a transorganizational system. And it is an approach that is becoming more frequent because of the increasingly kinetic nature of the human services organizational environment.

Currently in the United States, the organizational pattern of human services is characterized by vast numbers of segregated and fragmented structures arranged in categorical and bureaucratic fashion, each with a highly specialized set of services. These separate, unconnected agencies make it very difficult to provide a comprehensive, integrated set of services that meet the unique needs

Figure 8.1   Two Different Organizational Designs: (a) Organization A
—Bureaucracy; (b) Organization B—Adhocracy

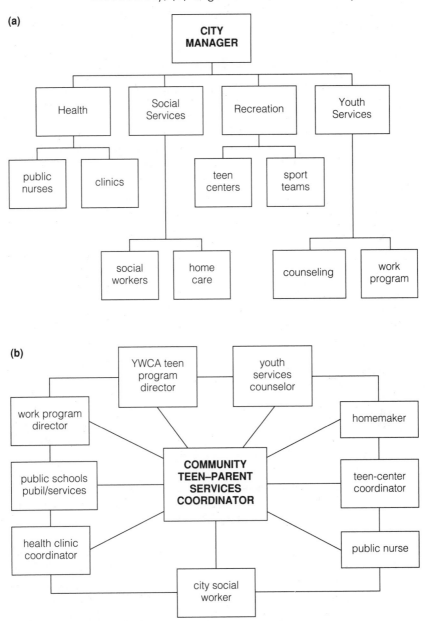

of one client. But these separate and unconnected agencies are a fact of life.
They therefore are the framework on which the human services manager must
weave a variety of strategies designed to develop transorganizational systems.

A state government, for example, that has twenty-one different agencies providing separate but overlapping human services does not have to combine them into one huge bureaucratic superagency to avoid chaos. What it does have to do is weave a well-designed and well-functioning network that interrelates the various functions, using the new management techniques available and focusing sharply on individual clients or specific community problems. *The seminal twentieth-century concept that carries the seeds for significant improvement of human services is the image of organization as a strategy.*

Two distinguished management thinkers have expressed notions that are important for us to understand. Let us examine their statements:

> We have learned that "structure follows strategy." Organization is not mechanical. It is not done by assembly, nor can it be prefabricated. Organization is organic and unique to each individual business or institution. We realize now that structure is a means for attaining the objectives and goals of an institution. And if a structure is to be effective and sound, it must start with objectives and strategy. (Drucker 1977, 173)

> In our view, the central function of administration is to keep the organization at the NEXUS of several necessary streams of actions; and because the several streams are variable and moving, the nexus is not only moving but sometimes quite difficult to fathom. . . . The configuration necessary for survival comes neither from yielding to any and all pressures nor from manipulating all variables, but from finding the strategic variables. (Thompson 1967, 147–48)

Both writers confirm the necessity to view organizations as strategies focused on defining desired end results and proceed to put into place mechanisms that will best achieve the defined mission. The key organizational and management problem of our society today is not the lack of available strategies and mechanisms—never before have we had such a large number and variety of administrative techniques. The problem is that people—workers, managers, policymakers, and clients alike—must be weaned away from a singular image of organization and management. They must recognize that a simultaneous approach based on strategies of interrelationships is the essence of organizing and managing a complex society for the effective acquisition of human-oriented services. What is required today of human services managers is nothing less than managing with two simultaneous and coexisting forms of management: **institutional** (organizational) and **systemic** (strategic) **management**. This is no mean task: It not only requires proficiency in each but also the artful balancing of one alongside the other.

In the first section of this chapter, we review two conceptions of organization: the first we label the **structural-lineal** view of phenomena; the second, the **strategic-integrated** view. The former refers to bureaucracies, the latter to adhocracies.

Two Complementary Views of Organization

In Chapter 3, we discussed various, different images of organization. Let us re-examine two that have important implications for human services management.

The Structural-Lineal View of Phenomena

As we have suggested in previous chapters, for several centuries those from the Western tradition have tended to accept a structured view of human existence. This view is relatively simple:

1. Segment all phenomena.
2. Classify and categorize each segment.
3. Place each category into a separate, lineal stream.
4. Repeat the process for each separated, segmented category.

This process flows out of the perception that people are rational beings. It has been labeled variously as *scientific specialization, logical positivism,* or *reductionism.* For the human services, the process is portrayed graphically in Figure 8.2.

This structural-lineal approach to human existence impacts every aspect of our lives. The way we separate work from leisure or value individual dwelling units and private cars—whatever the aspect of our life, the process is the same. Our society's lock-step educational system or our specialized health-delivery system are two more pertinent examples.

Frederick Taylor's (1947) scientific management and its stress on compartmentalization of work is based on the structural approach to phenomena. As we noted in a previous chapter, Marshall McLuhan (1967) maintains that Taylor, and most scholars, were influenced by the printing press: All of life (leisure and work) is segmented in much the same fashion as the alphabet is used, one element at a time . . . c,o,n,t,i,n,u,o,u,s and c-o-n-n-e-c-t-e-d.

Regardless of the historical basis of our structural-lineal conceptual image of life, the foundation for organizing and managing our complex society is reductionism—developing expertise in specialized bodies of knowledge and skills. It represents a centuries-old process that only recently has been challenged as being extreme, compulsive, and even oppressive because it has created several institutional defects. Let us look at some of these and how they are manifested:

- **Boundary calcification**: Governments, businesses, professional groups, and unions that are more concerned with defending their boundaries and self-interest from intrusion than with national concerns that would require cooperating action

Figure 8.2   The Scientific, Reductionist Process

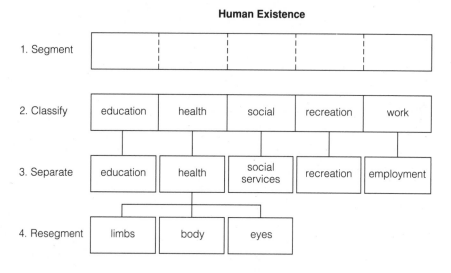

- **Fragmented services**: The necessity for clients to receive piecemeal rather than comprehensive services and to adapt themselves to institutional processes instead of the opposite
- **Segmentation of the whole**: Officialdom that deals with the "rational person" who is supposed to operate according to prescribed rules, when in reality people have a motivational hierarchy of needs
- **Difficulty in focusing on multifunctional problems**: The number of separate organizations and professional specialists that try to deal with different aspects of the same client-group's problems, often in conflicting ways

The structural-lineal view of organizations is the foundation of today's human services organizations. The challenge for human services managers is refocusing overspecialized workers, professionals, programs, agencies, and systems into new, multitask systems.

The Strategic-Integrated View of Phenomena

In the twentieth century, there has been a growing awareness that the structural-lineal conception of our social structure is limiting and to some degree dysfunctional. We have been forced to see the interconnections between different social functions and institutions in order to coordinate and control these organizations. Thus, we no longer believe we are isolated individuals performing narrow functions but instead see ourselves as integrated within a complex net-

Figure 8.3   Child Abuse Treatment from a Strategic-Integrated View

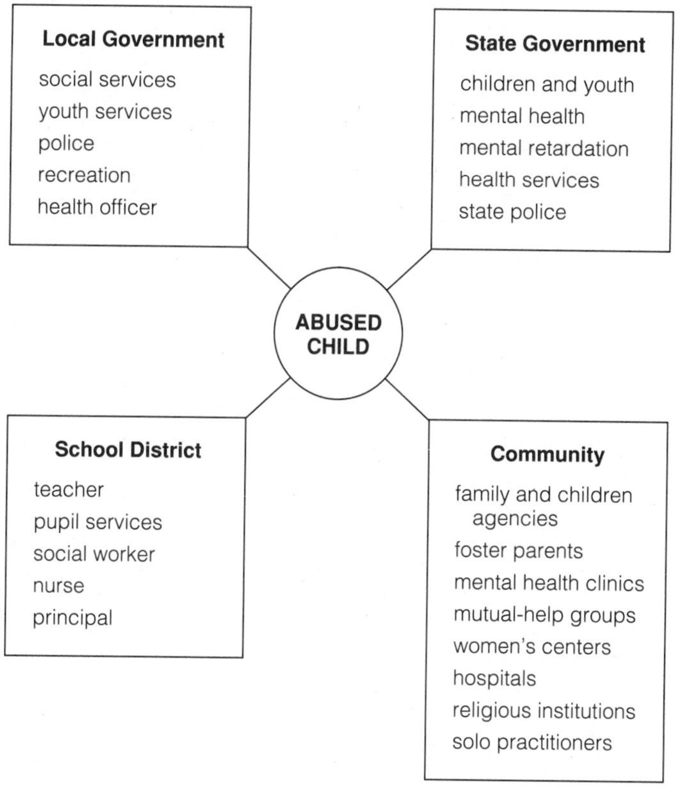

Local Government

social services
youth services
police
recreation
health officer

State Government

children and youth
mental health
mental retardation
health services
state police

ABUSED CHILD

School District

teacher
pupil services
social worker
nurse
principal

Community

family and children
   agencies
foster parents
mental health clinics
mutual-help groups
women's centers
hospitals
religious institutions
solo practitioners

work of people and processes: a **social system** in the fullest sense. It is the dynamic interaction of the system's parts that is essential to service delivery, not the system's static structure (see Figure 8.3).

As we noted in an earlier chapter, McLuhan (1964) interpreted our shift from a reductionist to a holistic, systemic approach to the environment, as one related to the shift from a print-oriented society to an electronically configured world. From this perspective, all factors of the environment and of experience coexist in a state of active interplay searching for recognition of patterns.

In a holistic, total system, strategies configure every role, resource, process, and technology in an *intricate network* of critical interrelationships, each to the other. In the strategic perception of an organization as a system, organizational responsibility must be joint and overarching.

To understand the strategic approach to human services management, examine the several illustrations of different strategies for providing day-care services and note the implications for organization and management, keeping in mind Drucker's principle that "structure follows strategy."

Strategic Options for Day-Care Services

- Government grants: A federal or state categorical grant program is used for the creation and maintenance of day care. Administrative regulations are formulated to specify the target population, the services eligible, the professional criteria for the staff and services, and the amount available per grant.

- Community-based: A nonprofit organization is formed with funds from a number of sources such as community fund-raising, United Way funding, local government, and parent fees. A public agency (health, education, or human resources) is responsible for licensing and monitoring.

- Corporate-based: A corporation sponsors the formation of a day-care center for children of its employees. Resources are a mix of corporate subsidies and parent fees. A regional public school agency sends child development professionals into corporations to provide technical assistance.

- Tax subsidies: Government agencies develop a range of tax incentives for parents and corporations for day-care expenditures. Such incentives can include IRS regulations governing income tax deductions; other incentives could include reducing property tax burdens for a corporation that provides day-care services for its employees.

Each of the above strategic options has strong implications for both institutional and systemic management.

Implications of the Two Views of Organization

To better understand the implications of these differing perceptual images of organizations for the human services, let us examine a number of practical issues.

From the inception of organizational theory, people have had to deal with apparent conflicts that flow out of different ways of structuring organizations. Traditionally, we have organized by

- Function—health, education, social services, and mental health
- Process—counseling, advocacy, contracting, and case management
- Client group—at-risk children and youth, disabled, and elderly
- Geography—district or area office, region, or municipality

Conflicts may occur within organizations structured on the basis of a function, for example, between the maternal and child-care bureau of a state health department and the district offices of the same department. Or they may occur between different functional organizations having some common interest, for example, municipal social work, health, school, recreation, and youth services professions all concerned with child and youth development.

Table 8.1   Two Models of Human Services Systems

Vertical	Horizontal
monolithic and bureaucratic in nature with each component operating from separate, categorical, specialist, and discipline bases (*examples:* state and federal agencies and institutions)	arrangement of community-based agencies using an interrelated comprehensive multifunctional approach to the needs of people living in a common geographic area (*example:* community youth council)

For human services organizations, the issue is critical because it characterizes the nature of the field. The problem is classic: how to organize both on a basis of function, capturing the expertise and efficiency of specialists, and on a basis of services, which focuses resources effectively on a specific problem, client group, or geographic area.

When human services organizations are faced with the problem of needing to organize both on a functional basis and on a service basis for one client group or one common geographic area, the structural-lineal conceptual image of organizations has serious limits. As the remaining sections of this chapter describe, the strategic-integrated view of organizations provides a far greater range of options for addressing such conflicts. In other words, using some of the mechanisms provided by the strategic-integrated organizational approach, it is possible to have a highly structured bureaucracy composed of several separate functions such as education, health, social service, and recreation, yet interrelated to focus on a single client group such as the developmentally disabled.

Without attempting to trace their historical evolution, it is helpful to conceptualize human services in the United States today as organized in two separate but mutually supportive systems (Table 8.1). Let us examine these further.

Vertical System.   The basic pattern of human services in the United States is strongly influenced by federal categorical programs that are vertically structured within an intergovernmental framework. This pattern is the result of (1) historical developments (new problems led to new solutions that led to new programs), (2) practices and trends, and (3) the principles of scientific management that stressed functional specialization and subdivision of work requirements and procedures.

The vertical system has certain undeniable strengths. It is relatively easy to finance the various levels of control. In addition, the simplified channels of communication allow for intrafunctional and interorganizational flow of funds. This is because, at each level of government, there is an agency that integrates the plans, budgets, reports, and services of several agencies. Equally important, under a categorical funding system (even when in block-grant form), fast initiation of new programs is possible. It is also easy to specify and direct legal and program responsibilities and to disseminate information relating to policy and procedures.

The words *vertical* and *categorical* are appropriate because services result from a specific category of separately funded programs administered by a discrete organizational unit in the federal government. The funds for these services are funneled through another discrete administrative unit for each of the states, which must administer the funds according to specific guidelines. The state government funds in turn are provided to the appropriate community-level agencies, either a department in the municipality or a private, voluntary agency. The vertical human services system can also be labeled as "functional" in nature because the flow of funds and services relate to organizational units of the same function.

Horizontal System.   The community-wide human services system has become popular in recent years because the vertical system has a number of weaknesses at the point of impact on the client. Some of the weaknesses are that services at the local community level are poorly defined and often inaccessible to the client who must negotiate a maze of service facilities and complex subsystems; services may also be competitive, fragmented, and isolated, resulting in poor or inadequate response or minimal opportunity to provide referrals and follow-up. They may also be ineffective because they overburden individual and community resources, and frequently there is a lack of communication between services providers that limits the capability for comprehensive management and narrows the perspective of interfunctional planning.

The communitywide system is referred to as *horizontal* because it attempts to link and create a network of different functionally based organizational units funded from a variety of categorical sources. It also focuses on individual clients with a multiple set of problems, living in a common geographic area. Multiservice centers created for a specific geographic area of an inner city are an example of the community horizontal human services systems. Task forces to deal with the homeless or drug abuse are other examples of horizontal systems.

Both models are legitimate; it is important to recognize that the essential issue is one of interrelationships and interfaces that exploits the strengths of both systems. The issue is not primacy of one system over the other; it is the productive interface between the two coexisting organizational arrangements.

Interrelating Vertical and Horizontal Systems.   Interface is the issue between the monolithic, vertical human services system and the community-wide, horizontal system. Positive interrelationships are important for mutual, complementary strengthening of each. This calls for great sensitivity and understanding of our form of democracy, in which the *municipality* or *county* serves as a *general-purpose government*, the link for distribution of public power and resources. They thus should serve as the primary, integrating focal point for the community-oriented human services system.

But in the vertical-oriented human services system, this fact of political life is often ignored and is replaced by organizational power politics. Thus, both federal and state agencies often bypass the local government, dealing directly with private and proprietary human services agencies, thus treating local government providers as just another agency, along with all other community services providers. This is not only a poor interface between the vertical and horizontal human services systems but also a debasement of the process of democratic governance. Direct involvement by a categorical program with community human services agencies can ultimately be counterproductive.

Interrelating the vertical and horizontal human services systems requires great technical and interpersonal skills. For example, in recent years, the Reagan approach to federalism focused on the creation of block grants for states, leaving them to make their own judgment of service priorities. One of these block grants, the Social Service Block Grant (SSBG), was an attempt to find a better interface between the vertical and horizontal human services systems. In the state of Connecticut, this interface was strengthened by the use of a strategic management technique known as the *negotiated investment strategy*. A tripartite negotiating committee made up of an equal number of representatives from state agencies, municipalities, and private, nonprofit agencies met to negotiate the amount of the SSBG that would be allocated to each program and jurisdiction in the state.

The negotiated investment strategy is an excellent model for interrelating the vertical and horizontal human services systems. It also illustrates that relating these two systems is a continuous creative challenge, one that emphasizes the reality that human services managers wear two hats, as the next section illustrates.

Two Coexisting Forms of Human Services Management

As we have emphasized in the chapters in Part III, human services administrators manage with two simultaneous and coexisting forms of management: institutional *and* systemic management (review Figure 6.1 on page 137). For institutional management, the administrator is primarily concerned with managing down, up, and across. As the reader recognizes, this deals with the intraorganizational dynamics of the human services environment. For systemic management, the administrator manages out, dealing with the interorganizational dynamics of the environment. Each form of management requires different sets of skills and values. The human services manager not only needs to have proficiency in each but also skills in the artful balancing of one alongside the other.

It would be incorrect to assume that the division between the two is crystal-clear because these are simultaneous and coexisting forms of management in which different strategies and approaches have a mixture of both. In the past two decades, there has been a move by most states toward a "comprehensive" or "semicomprehensive" human services agency. These agencies usually have the following characteristics:

- They may be *integrated*—that is, a highly centralized single agency that provides an integration of administrative and program authority for all or most human services programs.

- One often finds *consolidation,* where an agency organizes along traditional program lines, with an agency management and administrative unit that assists the agency head in establishing policy and goals.

- Common also is a *confederation,* where autonomous program units retain most of their administrative and program authority, in one agency that coordinates service delivery of the various programs.

The move toward giant, public human services organizations can be seen in some large cities that have created "super" departments of human services or designated an assistant city manager for human services, with authority over all human services-oriented municipal departments.

But simply creating large human services organizations, whether integrated, consolidated, or confederated, is not sufficient for effective reform or improvement. Of greater importance is developing understanding and skill in systemic (strategic) organization and management. Let us therefore examine this form of management further to deepen our understanding of its potential.

Managing with a Strategic-Integrated Style

If you are persuaded that there is a fundamental relationship between images and organization, then it follows that you will need to adapt your own images of the organization and of administration to meet the challenges faced by human services organizations. Thus, one of the most critical challenges facing professional human services managers is understanding and acquiring the strategic conception of phenomena and relating it to our traditional structural image of an organization.

Strategies focus on defining desired end results and then proceeding to put into place mechanisms that best achieve the defined outcomes. To help you understand the "strategic, organic, network, adhocratic" concept of an organization, consider what occurs when you decide to travel to your favorite sun-filled island by air transportation.

Regardless of the airline used, countless different organizational structures (commercial-public-nonprofit) instantly form an interlocking network organized around one *temporary* organizational focus . . . YOU. These include the airline, the airplane manufacturer, air controllers, airport officials, and baggage handlers in at least two airports, food-service companies, gasoline companies, maintenance and security companies, land-transportation companies, weather-reporting agencies, possibly a travel agency and a major credit-card company, and many others. And all these entities are managed by one person—you, the occupant of your seat on the flight, until the goal of a completed trip is met.

Let us identify and enumerate the bodies of knowledge and skills required to design and operationalize similar organizational forms and processes for the provision of the human services. They include

- New organizational forms
- Flexible-systems production
- Implementation strategies
- Management repertoires
- Cybernetic management
- Integrated computer-based information systems

To help illustrate our discussions of these strategic technologies, let us draw on Part 1 of Case 8.1 of River City, Inc., an excellent example of systemic management.

Case 8.1

Part 1: River City, Inc.*

They sat with the papers all spread out on the conference table: grant applications, affiliation agreements, and organizational design—standard forms everyone would use. Jim O'Neill, executive director of River City, Inc., looked up and noticed Nan frowning. Nan Rogers was the agency's director of adolescent services. "Why the serious look on your face, Nan?"

She laughed. "I'm becoming an academic, Jim. I've been invited to lead a seminar on organizational design at the University of Tennessee's School for Human Services. And the question going through my mind is: Are we a human services agency with many different creative programs, or are we a collection of different programs, each of which has its own unique, creative, organizational design?"

Jim laughed. "How about both?"

"Seriously though, Jim," Nan continued, "look at the papers in front of us. A totally new, very creative organization built around traditional-type programs packaged in a totally unique fashion—Teen Health Centers. The director will be an assistant school principal from Tucker county's school district. We've pulled together doctors from the hospital's clinic, the local VNA, the state's district office of human resources, a private group of pediatricians, and a number of consulting specialists. And the city's gluing us all together with their regional human services computer system. We've even incorporated— our official name is Teen Health Centers, Incorporated. So, tell me, Is THC, Inc. a program of River City or is it a unique organization that River City created, together with other organizations?"

"Well," Jim responded, "maybe that's not even the key question, Nan.

Had River City stayed like it was—a traditional child and family services agency—could we have survived these past ten years? Hey, all the partners in THC were around ten years ago, but all of us have had to adapt to the rapidly changing human services environment. Maybe this sounds a little macho, but tell those graduate students that human services management these days is like being a pro-football offensive back: just keep zigging and zagging all over the field, moving closer and closer to the goal."

"I'm a football fan, too, you chauvinist. But I have to ask, What's the goal—our survival or a human services environment that is responsive to our community?"

"Both, Nan, you know that. Sure we've survived, but take a look at this brochure listing the thirty-two responsibility centers we have—none of these were in existence ten years ago. Is the fact that all these programs are being used to the max any proof our goal was responding to people's human services needs? Look at this!"

River City Family Center
- Clinic
- CSAT (Child Sexual Abuse Treatment)
- Substance-abuse programs

TAP (Tucker County Adolescent Program)
- Adventure programs
- On-site school counseling in six separate schools
- Outreach family counseling
- Home support
- Parent groups

JPTC (Job Preparation and Training Center)
- Work–study program
- Apprenticeship program
- Information and referral

Project START (teen parenting)
- Day-care centers (2)
- Mother and child clinic
- Outreach
- GED programs
- Family-life education

Elderly Parents Programs (EPP)
- Family-life planning
- Outreach counseling
- Nursing home services

Coalition of Adolescent Programs

Nan scanned the brochure, thought for a few minutes, and then looking at Jim, commented, "There's a pattern here, Jim. You've taught us to scan the horizon for a need and an opportunity. Then we come up with a design so we can shape a unique organization to meet that need and opportunity, pull together the different pieces, and glue them together with legal and procedural mechanisms. Next, we go after the money, set up shop, focus on each individual client's unique needs, and give each operation the framework to manage itself as an independent responsibility center. What's more, the organizational form depends on the situation: we're a holding company; we're shareholders in several not-for-profit corporations; we're a nonprofit agency; we're members of several teams, task forces, and coalitions; we're contractors and contractees; we have countless affiliation agreements; sometimes we deliver services, other times we're catalysts for service delivery. We're the organizational version of a chameleon."

"There you go, Nan," Jim smiled. "Not quite as simple as you put it; and you left out the fact that our computer system, performance and productivity targets, and rigorous accounting systems also link us together. This permits each responsibility center to manage itself. And most of all, the key is involving the community right from the start. But doesn't all of this describe the way human services management is today?"

*Parts 2 and 3 of the River City case can be found in Chapters 11 and 16, respectively.

New Organizational Forms

Seven new organizational form options have been proposed as useful in moving from bureaucracies to adhocracies (Galbraith 1977). They range from the simple to the complex in the following order:

1. **Direct contact** is an informal relationship between two agencies or professionals within the same structure or between different organizational structures.
2. **A liaison role** designates specific professionals in different organizational units to serve as official liaison for a specific purpose such as services for the "frail elderly."
3. **The task force** is a temporary organization, which is formed by a large number of professionals from different agencies. The term *project management* is often interchanged with the term *task-force management*. The task force usually has a single issue (e.g., a particular problem of the homeless) whose final resolution will result in the disbanding of the group.
4. **The human services team** is a more complex, transorganizational structure. Choosing this option comes from accepting the interdependent, interorganizational nature of most human services provision, particularly if there is a desire to create opportunities for an integrated, comprehensive approach to client groups. The *team* option requires professionals to have dual loyalty to both their primary organization and to the team. Substituting team action and team decision making requires relearning administrative styles; it therefore must be supported with team-building mechanisms.
5. **The integrating role** is assumed by someone who operates as an extension of the chief executive; the title can be "coordinator" or "planner."

Integrators do not supervise or direct any service provision; they primarily coordinate the decision process. They usually have no formal authority; thus they must establish a climate of mutual trust while influencing those who have the power of decision. They are facilitators of the decision process. There is implicit power for the integrator through the ability to report to a higher authority.

6. **A linking role** increases the hierarchical power and authority of the coordinator because problems have occurred where different organizations have not been willing to work with each other. This need not mean the creation of a single, *super*department of human services; it could mean giving the assistant to the chief executive an overview function that, when necessary, invokes the full authority of the chief executive.

7. **The matrix organization** is a powerful, complex but flexible form of organization that has become popular in recent years. This form of organization is a combination of the project and the functional form of organization and is graphically portrayed as a mathematical matrix of columns and roles, hence its name.

In the matrix organization, every employee is part of two streams of authority and communication, one oriented around the functional department and the other around a specific service, client group, or geographic area. It breaks a traditional rule of hierarchical organization; in place of the concept of "one worker, one boss" is the "two-boss" rule, a multiple-command system. When applied with care and understanding, the matrix organization has significant potential for the human services manager.

Consider the River City case. Can you identify some of the new, strategic organizational forms? Why do you think certain types were selected over other options? What were the specific administrative techniques used to implement the new form?

High-Volume, Standardized Production
Versus Flexible-Systems Production

In the nineteenth century and the early part of the twentieth century, the industrial mode of production emphasized fragmentation, specialization, and mechanization. Production was a result of separate structural entities made up of highly specialized workers and processes placed in a lineal stream; the end result was the final, completed product. It represented the zenith of the structural-lineal conception of organization and management. Whereas a skilled shoemaker once performed all tasks from start to finish to produce a shoe, in a shoe factory each task was separated for the purposes of specialization (and thus efficiency), and the shoe moved from one task to another until it was completed. Automobile production epitomized this process. There were a limited number of models and options: thus, the famous statement by Henry Ford

Figure 8.4   (a) Mass Versus (b) Flexible Systems
             Production of Automobiles

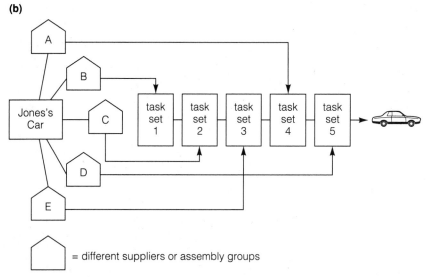

(a)

**PRODUCTION
PERIOD**

**Weeks
1 and 2**   task set A → task set B → task set C → task set D → task set E → etc. → Model T

**Weeks
3 and 4**   task set M → task set N → task set O → task set P → task set Q → etc. → Model A

(b)

A

B

Jones's Car   C   task set 1 — task set 2 — task set 3 — task set 4 — task set 5 →

D

E

⬠ = different suppliers or assembly groups

that one could have any color Model T, as long as it was black. Mass production of automobiles could be viewed as shown in Figure 8.4a, it is a model for
the high-volume, standardized production of services in most hospitals, clinics,
or welfare offices.

In 1946 one of the most important events, designed to produce goods or
services, occurred in the history of the management of societal institutions.
The president of Ford Motors hired a group of World War II veteran officers to
analyze the then existing production approach and to design a more modern
approach to automobile production. The "whiz kids" (as they were subsequently called) developed what has now become known worldwide as **flexible-
systems production**. This shift represented a new conceptual image of or-

ganizing and managing auto production, the strategic-integrated view. The customer could choose from hundreds of options in models, accessories, colors, interiors, and so forth. Production lines were intermixed because all options were integrated at the point of final assembly (see Figure 8.4b).

The shift from uniform to customized flexible-systems production was created by new processes, not the least of which was the creation of a temporary organizational team of specialists from a number of different supplier organizations devoted to a single client—the Jones family. Eventually, the team came to be held together by a computer–telecommunication system, which regularly provided a comprehensive, integrated report on the Jones's car, in accordance with its special, preordered optional features, which held all team members to a rigorous schedule in order to accurately coordinate the completion of specialized tasks such that final assembly was integrated simultaneously. This rigor has spawned what today is called *just-in-time inventory:* Do not stockpile parts needed for production—have them delivered to the production line just as they are needed for assembling the product.

The earlier example of flying between two places is an excellent illustration of how this new flexible-systems approach to producing goods and services permitted an explosion of individualized opportunities for people in a society. Indeed, the air-travel options available to people are now so numerous that it is almost impossible to keep track of them. But it illustrates how countless different specialists, operating from different organizational bases, provide individualized services for each specific air traveler.

If we can produce goods on an individualized basis with the strategic-integrated conception of organization and management, so too with services. The services-integration movement in the 1960s and 1970s and the current emphasis on managed care express attempts to shift to a flexible-systems approach of human services delivery for each client. Examples of the flexible-systems model of managed-care services are discussed more fully and graphically portrayed in Chapter 14. They are typical of what a number of state governments are moving toward in such services as mental health, developmental disabilities, school dropouts, and others.

Implementation Strategies

There are a number of important definitions that can help the human services manager more clearly understand the many dimensions of strategic organization and management of human services:

- **Strategy**: Determining long-term goals and objectives of an organization, followed by the adoption of courses of action and allocation of resources to best achieve these goals.
- **Strategic thinking**: A way of approaching issues that are sensitive to the "big picture," long-term implications of actions, the basic mission of an

enterprise, a comprehensive view of societal trends, basic changes in the environment, the maximization of benefits from available resources, and the interrelationships among different activities.

- **Opportunistic surveillance**: Monitoring behavior that scans the environment for opportunities and that anticipates institutional trends.

- **Strategic planning**: Scanning the interaction between the organization and its environment, to arrive at the ideal state, where the organization *should be,* compared to the actual state, where the organization is *currently.*

- **Classic governance strategies**: A fundamental construct for the organization and management of human services organizations, which managers sometimes do not appreciate. These are, in order of application: (1) *strategies of education and persuasion;* to demonstrate to the public, the people in a democratic society, that it is to their benefit to do for themselves; (2) to *regulate* others; and (3) to use strategic roles that only in the last resort require *direct provision of service,* beginning with *nonservice*-delivery strategies (e.g., advocacy, mutual-help groups, tax-policy changes).

- **Strategic goal**: Some future desired state.

- **Strategic role**: The organization's concept or image of its mission–function in the environment. These lead to a variety of vastly different implementation strategies.

- **Strategy-formation process**: The process by which the interaction between the agency and its environment is scanned to compare *what is* with *what should be* in terms of the organization's missions and activities (see Chapter 10 for expansion of the discussion of this process).

These terms, used accurately, provide the communications code for development of effective implementation strategies.

Management Repertoires

Traditionally, there has been a tendency to apply management tools narrowly and to expect a single management technique to correct an organizational problem. But in reality, that's not the way effective human services managers operate.

To manage reality, one must assemble a variety of techniques and mechanisms that, when used in concert, produce a *repertoire* (e.g., a specifically chosen collection) of management tools. The task of managers is to assemble, reassemble, and arrange clusters of applied theories and techniques in dynamic configurations that, when implemented, will achieve the strategic goal(s) of the organization at any given moment.

As an organization attempts to shape or reshape its environment, there is continual pressure to form and reform management repertoires. For example, in today's human services environment, temporary groups most often are

Figure 8.5 Management Repertoire: Network Management

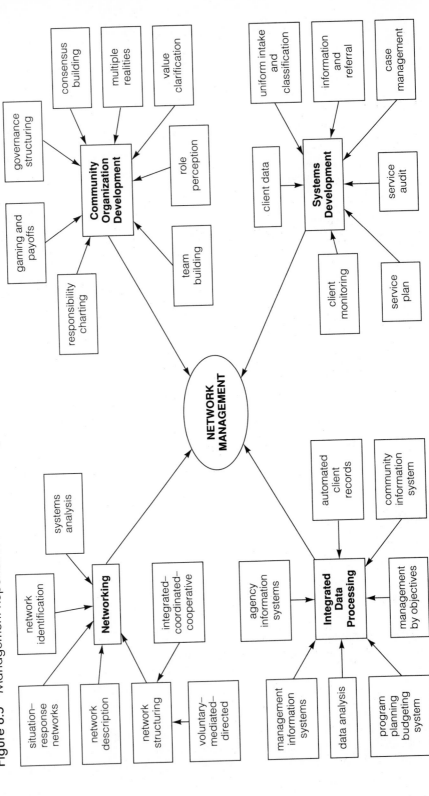

formed to manage a special cross-organizational project for a particular set of clients who need specialized services. The result is a new system in which several different agencies are interrelated so that management of a network of organizations becomes the focus of effort. Multiple management repertoires for managing a network of agencies and providers are called for, as illustrated by Figure 8.5. The implications of management repertoires for managers are several, but most important is a recognition that the choice of the components and deployment of the resulting cluster of techniques continually changes over time in accordance with the changing needs of the organization's environment, emphasizing the creative, dynamic nature of human services management.

Cybernetic Management

In Chapter 4, we discussed cybernetics, the process of control and communications that permits systems to be self-regulating. In less than fifty years, this theory and the technology it spawned has fundamentally altered the field of management. It has not only changed the technology of management but has also eradicated old organizational perceptions and substituted new ones. Systemic management, which is founded on the cybernetic processes of control and communications, can permit sociotechnical systems to be self-regulating. Its utilization, however, requires a major shift of managerial habits and thought patterns. For example, the concept of span of control—that assumes that a supervisor can only coordinate a limited number of other workers or cases—is no longer operative. With cybernetic management, such coordination is automated, and thus the numbers that can be coordinated by one person are significantly increased.

To manage cybernetically, one must no longer view organizations in hierarchical layers. Instead, much like the nervous systems of humans or the electronic circuits of a computer, organizations should be viewed as a series of interrelated systems, nested one within the other, much like wooden painted dolls. Each system interacts and affects each other. When carefully designed, these interlocking systems are self-regulating and self-controlling and capable of responding to a variety of stimuli in a highly individualized manner.

The emergency room of a hospital is a good example of a modern cybernetic system. Staffed by a wide variety of different health specialists, it is poised to respond quickly and specifically to each individual patient who has an emergency. Because there are identifiable patterns to the types of emergencies with which hospitals have to deal, systems of humans interacting with machines (e.g., medical technology) can be specifically designed to deal successfully and effectively with almost any conceivable emergency that might occur. Not unlike football or basketball teams that continually practice to achieve perfection, emergency room teams even simulate emergencies to practice and perfect their responses so that the system can be self-regulating. No one needs to be in charge. When a patient is rushed to the emergency room, the team moves into action in an automatic-response manner. For the past several decades, these systems even begin their activity out in the field through the use of emergency medical technicians (EMTs) in the field who communicate to the emergency room with sophisticated telecommunications and telemetry equipment, for continuous, uninterrupted care of the patient.

Emergency medical systems are also a good example of cybernetic systems nested one within the other. First, there is the system of the patient and her doctor. Second, there is the community's emergency response system (whether private or in the municipal police or fire departments), which relates to the patient. The community response system is interrelated to hospital emergency room systems. Often several hospitals interrelate to arrive at a more responsive system, whether it be a helicopter-based medevac system or a regional mobile neonatal crisis response system. And within the hospital itself, the emergency room systems are closely related to all other units of the hospital. The system can be accessed at any point, as the situation demands.

The management of cybernetic systems has become critical for the creation and maintenance of an environment that is responsive to and supportive of the human services needs of people. Because the needs are increasingly crossing the boundaries of several human services agencies, it is not surprising that cybernetic management is at the heart of strategic (systemic) management.

Integrated Computer-Based Information Systems

The River City case illustrates how computers and telecommunications are a fundamental specification for the strategic-integrated approach to management. This is true for several reasons:

- The electron is being harnessed as both the energy source and the medium for institutional-systemic processes and memory.

- Organizations are dependent variables; data are independent variables. In effect, the computer-related electronic technologies create the cybernetics necessary to manage adhocracies and bureaucracies simultaneously.

- The continual bombardment of data on a human services manager is so massive and rapid that only electronic extensions can permit the manipulation and display of data so that patterns can be perceived and understood.

- The missions of human services organizations can be most effectively and productively dispatched when the work tasks and systemic processes are automated.

The electronic technologies are the means by which adaptive organizations can be interrelated for flexible-systems provision of individualized products and services. Such an integrated system has at least three requirements:

- A *common, shared data set* for each client's individualized service plan, complete with techniques for protecting privacy

- A *dual-reporting system* that aggregates data in terms of reporting needs for each professional's bureaucratic agency *and* in terms of reporting needs for the adhocracy itself
- *Data analysis* and *feedback capabilities* that include both internal and external data bases

In effect, an integrated computer–telecommunication system, available to all involved, thus becomes the skeleton that holds a transorganizational system together, as well as the nervous system that allows it to function as an organic whole.

Summary

Two complementary views of organizations are vital for the human services manager. The first, the *structural-lineal view,* was a by-product of scientific specialization that dominated Western thought for centuries. It resulted in the development of the bureaucracy as the ultimate form of organization required to manage societal processes. The second, the *strategic-integrated view,* evolved and matured as a by-product of the twentieth-century shift toward viewing phenomena in a holistic, comprehensive, and interrelated fashion. The systemic view of societal processes led to the conception of temporary organizations (e.g., adhocracies) as an additional, necessary form of a societal institution.

During the past several decades, there has been a fundamental worldwide shift in how goods and services of a society are produced and how to organize and manage institutions that produce these goods and services. Mass production and bureaucracies are not the only available managerial options. We now fashion the production of goods and services in an individualized fashion through the means of flexible systems, organize that production with a variety of temporary forms of organizations, and manage both with integrated computer-based information systems. Combined, these changes represent a new strategic approach to management.

Viewing organization as a strategy is the key to a more dynamic approach to managing the human services, namely, *systemic management.* With traditional skills of institutional (organizational) management, the human services manager now learns to blend skills in the strategic approach to management. This is particularly important because there have been two separate human services systems that need to be integrated. This requires an understanding and mastery of new organizational forms, flexible-systems production, a variety of implementation strategies, cybernetic management, and integrated computer-based information systems. Increasingly, the task of human services managers is to assemble repertoires of management techniques in dynamic configurations that, when implemented, will achieve the strategic goals of the human services agency at any given moment. Dynamic, creative management of the human services has not only become a possibility for the manager, it has become a necessity.

The new approaches to the organization and management of human services institutions represent new capabilities that come at a time when we need them most—as a society struggles to provide human prosperity, along with material prosperity, to all.

W e now turn our attention to the specific tools, techniques, and technologies needed by human services managers to carry out their task. Part IV addresses the fundamental processes: the management of programs, finances, people, and information. Knowledge and skill in each of these areas are at the heart of managing human services institutions and organizations. There are other aspects of institutional management that do not fall directly within the scope of this book, but are of practical importance to human service managers in the field. Two in particular are office and facility management, and image management. A brief treatment of both these topics may be found in the Appendix, pages 467–472.

Fundamental management processes can be applied in significantly different ways, depending on the particular set of assumptions, concepts, and propositions, or paradigms that one holds. There are at least four such paradigms that a manager will find in human services organizations, with the most dominant being the control paradigm. As a framework for applying all fundamental management processes, Chapter 9 discusses each of the four paradigms, stressing the need to strive for a balance in how they collectively shape human services management. The Appendix also provides a brief overview of office management and image management. Both are fundamental institutional management processes that the human services manager must eventually master.

The first fundamental process deals with the management of programs. Chapter 10 describes program planning and control in great detail. It is an interrelated set of technologies that needs to be common place in every human services organization. It is the means by which a human services organization (1) formulates strategies for achieving its mission, (2) designs tactics (programs) for implementing strategies, (3) monitors progress toward meeting intended outcomes, and (4) evaluates the effectiveness of program and employee performance.

Chapter 11 provides an overview of the body of knowledge and skills necessary to manage the finances of an agency. Bookkeeping and accounting, budget preparation and execution, cash and debt management, and revenue generation are all covered in this chapter. Institutional management of a human services organization does not require the administrator to carry out the details of these tasks, but the human services manager must be intimately involved in these processes because she is ultimately responsible for their correct and effective application.

The third fundamental management process necessary for institutional management deals with the management of people. Chapter 12 focuses on the formal techniques and technologies necessary to put into place an approach to managing people in a human services organization. A large number of orderly processes are necessary to recruit, select, motivate, and retain top-quality personnel. This chapter deals with the traditional personnel management techniques as well as those that indicate a shift toward human resources development—authentic concern for the people employed in a human services organization and their professional-personal development.

Knowledge and skill in use of computers for a wide range of information–management processes are the subject of Chapter 13. The discussion and descriptions are comprehensive and broad, dealing with a large number of trends in the technology and with different aspects of computer-based information management: for example, management information systems (MIS); decision support systems (DSS); information resource management (IRM); office automation (OA); and artificial intelligence (AI). Specific examples are provided of computer technology application to human services information management—for operational employees, professionals, clinicians, managers, and most of all, for clients themselves.

9

Fundamental Management Processes

Every societal institution has some fundamental processes that relate to the management of programs, finances, people, data, and the work environment. For the human services manager, these basic management processes have specific emphases that flow out of the peculiar environment and mission of human services organizations. Other chapters have indicated (or will indicate) underlying values that shape the management of human services; these include such values as

- Primary focus on effectiveness of agency services.
- Dealing with each client in a unique fashion.
- Maintaining a quality of humanness in the organizational environment.

These various values often create ambivalence for which solutions do not come easily:

- Lack of resources that heightens the need for increasing use of technology, while machines are resisted as being inhuman
- Personnel systems that pit workers against clients in terms of who has highest priority for greatest consideration in humane treatment
- Resistance to "sound business practices" for what they represent symbolically, while there is increased pressure for a quantifiable results orientation

Is an efficient, orderly approach to management incompatible with the value-underpinnings of human services organizational missions? Does managing with limited resources negate any possibility for creative management? The response to the above questions is clear: There need not be any incompatibility between effectiveness and efficiency. The chapters in Part IV attempt to point out that such value-conflict need not be present if a human services manager uses the best of administrative knowledge and skills. These chapters attempt to provide insights into administrative techniques and technologies that are *fundamental* to managing the program, financial, personnel, and information functions of human services organizations. Because they are too specialized for this text, an overview to office management and image management, two additional fundamental management processes, are included in the Appendix, pages 467–472.

But before dealing with the fundamental management processes in the next four chapters, we need to reflect on two concepts that have a significant influence on these processes:

- The need and rationale for order
- Organizational and management paradigms

The first subject may come as a surprise to the reader because order appears to be the antithesis of creative management. A close reading of all case studies in this text reveals that the opposite point of view is maintained: **Order** is the basis for the *creative* management of human services agencies. To achieve creativity, the human services manager has to exert an increased amount of effort to establish the order necessary for such creativity to thrive.

The creative manager will also face a large number of forces (people and institutions) that are shaping his human services organization with a set of **assumptions**, **concepts**, and **propositions** (i.e., a **paradigm**) that can impede or aid efforts to achieve good human services management. In the following pages, four of these paradigms are discussed because they will shape and influence the fundamental management processes presented in the next four chapters. The reader must recognize and be sensitive to these paradigms as a starting point for using them for purposes of improving human services management.

Both of these concepts need to be discussed and analyzed before we deepen our knowledge and skills in the fundamental processes required for program management, financial management, human resources (people) management, and information management.

Order: The Framework for Management Processes

Order and Regularity for Freedom

Order develops a positive organizational environment that promotes a responsive, creative human services organization. But as our discussion of the value-tensions between order and freedom in Chapter 2 indicated, there is no glamour in creating order; indeed, it requires attention to the same details day-after-day. What, if anything, will the following daily tasks have to do with the important policy and program issues that will affect hundreds or thousands of your agency's clients?

Orderly Processes in Human Services Management

- Clean restrooms
- Courteous telephone manners
- An efficient interoffice mail system
- Timely payment of bills
- Preventive maintenance of motor vehicles
- An attractive client-waiting room

For the human services manager concerned with accusations that she is more concerned with systems maintenance than with systems improvement (another of the classic value-tensions discussed in Chapter 2), such details seem not only unimportant in terms of allocating time for their management but they also create philosophical problems: We are all adults; thus we all can take mutual responsibility for details (a basic value-tension).

To suggest that the basic framework for every human services organization should be the creation of standard operating procedures (SOPs)—complete with daily, weekly, and monthly checklists that assure their dispatch—raises the image of a paramilitary organization. For most human services professionals, this model is the antithesis of democratic values that should not only permeate our society but also our human services organizations. But the cold, impersonal nature of order serves a purpose—creating the conditions for effective and efficient dispatch of human services organizational missions.

Rationale

As we first noted briefly in Chapter 2, the case for SOPs and checklists can be stated simply.

First Things First.   Clients and staff alike expect an organizational environment that runs smoothly, providing the necessary artifacts in support of service provision. Therefore, the first basic administrative task of the human services manager is to see that SOPs create performance standards that are commonly understood and accepted. These run a full range. Are restrooms inspected hourly? Is a procedure in place to assure that the telephone is answered every day, for twenty-four hours, and messages are properly recorded? Is there a procedure to assure that calls are returned within twenty-four hours? Are client requests-complaints answered within twenty-four hours? Are payroll changes processed by the next pay period? Do clients wait less than twenty minutes for appointments? Are building maintenance standards clear (e.g., waiting-room carpet will be vacuumed daily; staff carpets vacuumed every other day)?

This rationale is particularly appropriate when a human services manager first assumes a new position. His first task is crystal-clear: Get your own house in order before turning your attention to the external environment of the organization.

Conservation of Energy.   In a human services organization, all clients, staff, and administrators want to devote the maximum amount of time to those activities that are personally meaningful and professionally important. To devote physical and psychic energy tracing a piece of paper that delayed services to a client or held up the pay raise of a staff member requires unnecessary energy expenditure for all concerned. To meet with accounting personnel to discuss the subject of slow-payment procedures—when the same discussion was held two weeks ago—is wasted energy for all concerned. To have an agency worker stranded with the agency's car broken down on a highway because attention was not paid to preventive maintenance of the vehicle is inexcusable.

To conserve everyone's energies so that the maximum amount of time will be devoted to the achievement of client and organizational goals, the human services manager is expected to deal with fundamental management processes, regularize them, and then monitor them through SOPs.

Clients and Staff Deserve an Optimum Environment.   In a perfect management world, clients and staff deserve the best—the best furnishings, the best supportive services, the most attractive and pleasant environment within which to operate, and so on. The human services manager should strive for a hassle-free environment in which everything works smoothly: supplies are on hand when needed; there are no unexpected shortages; walls–furniture–floors are attractive, neat, and clean; and so forth. Although SOPs for fundamental management processes tend to be mundane and uninspiring, when performed with excellence they set a high standard from which program achievement can be launched.

The Halo Effect.   As a nice by-product, the image of efficiency that a manager achieves from a track record of excellence in the creation of fundamental management processes creates a halo effect—the human services manager and all program managers related to the agency are considered, ipso facto, effective and efficient managers. But the opposite can be even more true. If there is one minor lapse of good fundamental management, the whole agency may be considered inefficient.

Consider Case 9.1. Most people in the community are not aware of Bob Williams's distinguished twenty-three-year career and reputation as an effective social services director for the city of Bridgeton, as he generally keeps a low profile. But the auditor's negative report of a relative minor fund will leave a bad image. Bob will have to work months to restore the department's excellent management track record. The irony: The audit of the department's primary budget, with all its complex program financing, was spotless.

Case 9.1 _____

The Case of the Missing $300

City manager Greg Sullivan just shook his head. "Bob, this is crazy. How could you let this happen?"

"I have no excuse, Greg," Bob Williams, Bridgeton's social services director responded. "This is a special bank account that was set up years before I ever came. It has discretionary money for the director to use in emergencies. For all I know, the missing three hundred dollars happened before I came."

"What's crazy about all this," Greg noted, "is that the auditors find total conformity with your budgeted accounts of one million, four hundred and thirty-five thousand dollars. But they are going to report that in their audit of your eight-thousand, seven-hundred-dollar discretionary fund, they can't find the three hundred dollars. It's really peanuts."

"But when it hits the press, my good reputation in the community will be in doubt," Bob lamented. "No one will even notice that the accounting for my million-and-a-half dollar budget is perfect *to the penny.*"

"I hate to ask, Bob," Greg said. "What kind of accounts do you keep for the discretionary fund?"

"I inherited the books," Bob commented. "It's just a ledger book that someone purchased at the drug store. I enter all deposits when donations are received from local citizens or companies; I enter all checks issued. The funds are kept in a separate NOW account in the Bridgeton Savings and Loan Association. I attempt to reconcile the ledger book whenever I get the chance, which I admit is usually a few months late."

"Do you make the deposits?" Greg asked.

"No," Bob answered. "I make sure that my secretary actually makes the deposit."

"Well," Greg continued, "at least the auditors gave us advance notice of their report that goes to the council next week. We'd better prepare a letter to the city council. I'll talk to the mayor and get her advice as to who is going to talk to the reporter. Darn. We've got more important things to spend our time on than dealing with a press reporter eager to make a mountain out of a mole-hill. But we have no choice. Unlike our colleagues in private business administration, we live in a fishbowl. I almost wish it was three hundred thousand dollars that was missing; that would be worthy of public involvement. But three hundred dollars!"

"Bite your tongue, Greg," Bob responded quickly. "If it were three hundred thousand dollars, I'd have no choice but to give you my letter of resignation."

It is unfortunate if an auditor reports that your agency has poor fiscal controls over petty cash or failed to insist on proper travel-reimbursement documentation or if staff complains to the press about a leaking roof and this results in a dramatic newspaper picture; but no matter how effective or efficient the management of your programs or services, the public and other professionals will consider your agency ineffective, not to mention inefficient. Your agency's image will be marred.

Although the halo effect can be irrational and perhaps irrelevant, it must be taken seriously. The effect is a reality, and a human services manager should take advantage of it: match effectiveness of program management with the efficiency of performing fundamental management processes. (See the discussion of "Image Management" in the Appendix.)

Standard Operating Procedures

When everyone—clients, all members of the staff, policymakers, and the public—can anticipate fundamental processes to be carried out with dispatch and regularity, then the conditions are set for innovation in carrying out the agency's missions more effectively and productively. **Standard operating procedures** (SOPs) are the foundation and framework of a human services organization.

Most human services management students and practitioners recognize the role of formal legislative and administrative regulations, uniform procedures, and manuals in creating the conditions for regularity and order in an agency. In recent years, there have been moves to reduce the number of regulations, to write them in "plain English," and to simplify procedures and manuals. Among the various approaches for simplifying procedures is that known as playscript developed by Leslie Matthies (1961) (see Table 9.1).

But if the importance of SOPs is generally recognized, the role and function of simple checklists is not as appreciated as a vehicle for regularity and order. A more detailed discussion of this topic, therefore, seems appropriate.

Checklists

There are several different forms for checklists (see Table 9.2). The most important checklists from the standpoint of the human services manager are known as **management-monitoring checklists** of which there are two categories: monitoring potential improvements and monitoring compliances to SOPs.

The former is extremely helpful; examples can be found in handbooks, textbooks, and professional journals, or they can be prepared and updated periodically by the individual office manager. Quarterly or semiannually, the office manager should refer to this type of checklist, to explore further improvements that can be made in office productivity and effectiveness (see Table 9.3 for an example). Items checked indicate areas of potential improvement and the manager develops plans to improve the office operations.

Perhaps the most important type of checklist is the one devoted to monitoring *compliance* to SOPs. This type of checklist flows out of the need to ensure order and regularity in an organization. The key phrase is *to ensure* that SOPs are in effect. Thus, checklists that a human services manager can use to monitor compliance with SOPs should

- Be in question form.
- Provide indication that a condition is present; using checkboxes for yes or no.
- Be time-specific: generic—daily, weekly, last week, end of month—and include actual date and hour of day.
- Indicate who is/was responsible to see that the condition is present or was achieved.

Table 9.1 Playscript Procedures Manual: Subject—Personnel Changes

Responsibility	Action
Employee	Complete form 15C "Changes in Employee Status–Benefits"
Supervisor	Sign and send copies to department personnel
Department personnel	Add effective date of change: • Sends copies 1 and 2 to comptroller–payroll division • File copy 3
Comptroller	Adjust master payroll record Forward copy 1 to state personnel Forward copy 2 to data processing
Data processing	Change computer payroll master file Return copy 2 to comptroller–payroll division Verification prepared by computer Verification sent to employee
Comptroller	File copy 2
State personnel	Adjust employee master record File copy 1

Note: For detailed instructions for preparing playscript-style procedures manuals, see Leslie H. Matthies, *The Playscript Procedure: A New Tool of Administration* (Stamford, Conn.: Office Publications, 1961).

Table 9.2 Different Forms of Checklists

Form	Description	Examples
1	Steps prior to (or after) an event	Response to request for proposal Recruit and select Training conference Recontracting with state agency
2	Tasks, responsibilities, and duties	Budget preparation Payroll process Hiring process (e.g., secretary, therapist) Staff development and training
3	Tasks and time in order for A to accomplish X	Orientation for new employees Getting out newsletters Process request for new position Preretirement conference
4	Signoff sheet—X has been accomplished	New employee completed orientation Grantor's accounting requirements met Periodic checking of rest rooms Preparing for annual special event
5	Activities to be undertaken to accomplish X	Improve communications Decrease turnover Prepare budget Process monthly reimbursements

Table 9.3   Checklist: Monitoring Potential Improvements

Check Items of Potential Improvement in Your Office

Employee–employer relations

☐ Have productivity incentive contracts been explored for some or all municipal employee groups?

☐ Are there other means of sharing productivity improvement savings with employees?

☐ Are there adequate incentive programs for municipal employees?

Procedures and methods

☐ Have supervisors been trained with basic skills of work simplification: procedures analysis, work distribution, work measurement?

☐ Is there an active effort to simplify forms and their flow between citizens and municipal departments and between departments?

☐ Is there a system to measure work and compare with performance and cost standards?

Location

☐ Can services be provided from locations other than the agency?

☐ Should cost of office space (new construction or refurbishment) influence the choice of service locations?

☐ Can you find ways to interrelate the services of your department with those of other departments or other community organizations where they are intricately tied to your services?

Modern office technologies

☐ Are citizen service requests–complaints computerized with an on-line system for citizens and employees?

☐ Are nationwide data banks available through computer terminals for employees searching for technical data?

☐ Can electronic memos–mail be sent between municipal departments, the municipality and citizens, and between the municipality and other organizations?

☐ Are there telecommunication systems for citizens services such as registering for educational and recreation programs, making payments, acquiring data, making inquiries, etc.?

- Be compliance-oriented (thus, checklists, not listings).
- Be for a third party (usually a subordinate).
- Provide indicators that the conditions are being met effectively and efficiently.

In effect, every human services manager should have a series of *monitor-compliance checklists* that are maintained in some form that can be readily referred to by specific dates (e.g., two weeks before initiation of a new program) or in terms of some generic time period (e.g., last week of every month). They can be kept in a series of folders with colored tabs or, with today's tech-

Table 9.4   Checklist: Monitoring Compliance

Items Checked No Indicate Need for Immediate Follow-Up!

Support services

Yes   No

☐ ☐ Do we have in place a system to monitor productivity and response time (from request to completed work) for secretarial services?

☐ ☐ Is responsibility fixed for inspection of rest rooms hourly?

☐ ☐ Is there a report analyzing the level of use of copy machines to determine the point at which purchase is more economical than leasing?

☐ ☐ Did the latest analysis of agency telephone needs indicate a new system would be cost-effective?

Agency image

☐ ☐ Is responsibility fixed to sample agency response to external telephone calls in terms of timeliness and good telephone manners?

☐ ☐ Do we have a system for measuring client rating of agency services?

☐ ☐ Is there a way that physical and psychic barriers to agency accessibility can be identified and removed?

☐ ☐ Do we have criteria and mechanisms for evaluating the agency's public information and community relations program?

Fundamental management processes

☐ ☐ Is someone responsible for periodically checking the agency's internal control system?

☐ ☐ Have we corrected all defects in our internal control system identified by the latest independent audit?

☐ ☐ Do we periodically check the speed of personnel paperwork to be sure it meets minimum time standards?

☐ ☐ Has our EEO and employee development program been updated and evaluated for effectiveness within the past six months?

nology, be kept in electronic form. Table 9.4 is an example of a monitor-compliance checklist; items checked No indicate a need for immediate follow-up by the manager.

The first task of each day would be the review of pertinent compliance checklists; the second task of each workday should be follow-up on compliance not yet achieved.

There are those who aver that human services offices have a reputation of being poorly run, and that more businesslike methods need to be used. This is generally not the case. Most human services agencies are dedicated to the value of the inherent creative potential of human beings. That creativity can be tapped if the people in the human services organization—clients, staff, policymakers, and community—operate in a totally supportive environment:

- One in which basic necessities are present
- One in which there is no unnecessary expenditure of physical or psychic energy
- One in which there is a base of regularity and expectation in daily office functioning that conveys a message of concern not only for the human services organizational mission but also for each individual involved

From this perspective, order in the form of SOPs, checklists, and procedures manuals are not an expression of control. They are the basis for shaping a human services organization focused on clients, mission, and staff. For the dynamic, creative manager therefore, order is a cornerstone for human services management.

Organization and Management Paradigms

There are a number of paradigms (i.e., a set of basic assumptions, concepts, and propositions) that influence and shape the fundamental management processes in human services organizations. The most dominant is the **control paradigm**, generally held by those whose prime concern is fiscal management. Others include the **client paradigm**, held by direct-service professionals (e.g., caseworkers, nurses, and physical therapists); the **mission paradigm**, held, on the one hand, by clinicians (e.g., physicians, psychiatrists, and youth service counselors) and, on the other hand, by program leaders—interest groups concerned with the success of their programs; and the **staff-development paradigm** held generally by employee-centered leaders (e.g., professional development specialists and union leaders).

The human services manager needs to be aware of all these paradigms in order to recognize their significance and weigh their relative strengths.

The Control Paradigm

Most human services organizations are set within a larger structure in which the chief executive and policymakers have organizational units available to control all suborganizations. Thus, control is necessary to shape overall organizational policies and strategies. For example, as with any federal agency, some of the controls the Department of Health and Human Services is subjected to would include the following:

Executive Branch

- Office of the president (various advisors)
- Office of Management and Budgeting (budget and finance)

- Office of Personnel Management (personnel)
- General Services Administration (purchasing, space, computers)
- Attorney general (legal)

Congress

- Government Accounting Office (fiscal and performance audits)
- Congressional committees (oversight)

These types of external controls on a federal human services agency can be found also in every state, county, and municipal government. They are present in every nonprofit and commercial human services organization. For example, there is no health or mental health organization that is not subject to some type of external control related to finances (e.g., rates), personnel (e.g., affirmative action), or standards (e.g., professional licensing, accreditation, and safety codes).

Although the courts have always been a source of control over organizational management, increasingly they are becoming more dominant by either mandating services or restricting them. It is even possible for the courts to take over and manage some human services organizations. Case 6.1 ("Dealing with the Kinetic World of Human Services Systems"), on page 150, is an illustration of how the management of an entire state mental retardation department was essentially being directed by monitors appointed by the courts to control the department's compliance with the decree of the court relative to deinstitutionalization.

Either because of external controls or in addition to them, most human services organizations institute internal controls: special units devoted to accounting, budgeting, personnel, central services, data processing, legal services, purchasing—all with their multiple sets of regulations designed to control clerical, technical, professional, and administrative employees who carry out human services programs. As you will recall from the discussion in Chapter 4, in the classic organization fostered by administrative management theorists, there were three types of organizational units: line, staff, and housekeeping. Theoretically, the latter were to provide support to line units, helping them carry out their mission. It is a fact, though, that housekeeping units often become centers of control over the line organizations.

In large organizations, departmental housekeeping control units are outposts for the central control units; thus, a human services department's personnel, budgeting, legal, or accounting unit will often have more loyalty to their central control counterpart (e.g., department of personnel, budget office, attorney general, etc.) than to their own department.

In the tension between freedom and order, these housekeeping control units impose the order necessary to any organization. Taken to the extreme they can create a control orientation that overwhelms and dominates the necessary expression of the other paradigms.

The Mission Paradigm

Peter Drucker (1974), one of the leading management writers in the United States, emphasizes that mission effectiveness is the purpose of a services institution (i.e., public or nonprofit organizations). He expresses the primary paradigm held by human services program managers: concern for effectiveness of program outcomes. Rino Patti and his associates (1987) eloquently plead the same case for human services management.

As human services entitlements have expanded in the second half of this century, many community organizations and nationwide associations have pressed for a strengthening of the mission paradigm. Essentially, those who foster this paradigm are concerned with more resources, more programs, and more clients of particular entitlement groups. Additionally, there is a concern for organizational structure: the existence of a program-management office at the federal, state, and county levels—interrelated and linked. As the reader can recognize, this paradigm clashed with the Reagan administration's control paradigm that pressed for a sharp cutback of entitlement human services programs.

An important element of the mission paradigm is its aggregate orientation: the client-aggregate value—a major concern for the effectiveness and quality of the program for clients as a collective group. Service professionals (who foster a client paradigm) have concern for individual clients and cases. Program management (see Chapter 10) is an expression of the mission paradigm; it emphasizes

- Organizational performance: Achievement of program objectives in terms of aggregate numbers of programs and clients
- Program achievement: Effectiveness in improving the client groups' quality of life; reducing or eliminating the problem for which the program was fashioned

The mission paradigm is client-centered, but in macro-terms. Many policy planners view the total human services system and devise programs for improving the quality of life of large aggregates of clients. Whether the macro-perspective is for the community or the entire nation, the focus is improving the life of a group of clients such as the frail elderly, the abused, the disabled, and single-parent families headed by women in poverty. Paradoxically the mission paradigm may include at one time human services planners, community organizers, program leaders, and managers. It is common for this group to seek ties with groups or associations in the community and with political forces (e.g., legislators and their staff; interest groups).

Although the mission paradigm can include some who are parochial in perspective (e.g., concerned only with the achievement of one organization's mission or the survival of one categorical program during the budget process), it also includes many who are concerned with increasing the overall level of societal resources to aggregate groups of human services programs and clients.

The tension of the mission paradigm evolves from having to prove the cost–benefit or cost-effectiveness of a program to those who foster the control paradigm, while being responsive to those who foster a client paradigm. Balancing this tension is often more an art than a science.

The Client Paradigm

As has been stated many times, the purpose of a human services organization is to create an environment that is responsive and supportive to clients who use the widest possible variety of available human services opportunities. The daily task of many human services professionals—particularly direct-service professionals such as caseworkers, group workers, clinicians, teachers, community workers, and recreationists—is the actual provision of services to specific, individual clients. Indeed, the human services system in totality does and should expend its greatest amount of energy and resources on the one-to-one contact with a client: in the client's home, a solo practitioner's office, a clinic, or an institution. Thus, for many human services workers, professional and clerical, whatever can be done for individual clients is the reason for a human services organization to exist. It is obvious that the client paradigm is necessary for a human services organization; how it is balanced with the other paradigms remains the manager's problem.

With the client paradigm, societal institutions are important only insofar as they facilitate the quality of the client contact because the benefit of the human services provision is in that contact. To the client paradigm, the human services system is a collection of highly individualized, specific client situations. To speak in terms of aggregate groups of clients is foreign to the client paradigm; to speak in terms of effective functioning of the Smith, Brown, Haskins, and Jones families as a result of "my" efforts is the focus of the client paradigm. This paradigm, besides being fostered by individual human services professionals and staff employees, is also strongly supported by professional organizations such as the National Association of Social Workers, the National League of Nursing, the American Public Health Association, and the American Psychological Association.

The client paradigm, as we have noted, fosters the notion that the human services organization and its management should be benign, even invisible. One of the primary purposes of human services management is the creation of an organizational climate that is conducive and supportive of the direct-service professionals who maintain a responsive human services environment. However, this cannot be accomplished in a vacuum. Human services organizations exist in an environment of intraorganizational and interorganizational relationships. To the human services manager goes the task of managing these relationships in a way that buffers the direct-service professional from other paradigmatic forces.

The human services manager therefore can anticipate playing the role of

Table 9.5   The Agony of Resource-Allocation Choices

Societal Issue	Client-Specific	Client-Aggregate
Reduction of cardiac disease	Open-heart surgery for one patient	2000 participants in aerobic-exercise programs
Infant mortality	Neonatal care for one high-risk baby	350 pregnant teenagers in nutritional programs
Mental health	Long-term care in a sub-urban mental health clinic for one sex offender	Recreational programs for 500 inner-city youths with backgrounds of anti-social behavior

being a *link* between organizational units (intraorganizational) or a *boundary spanner* between societal institutions (interorganizational). If we postulate the client paradigm as the paradigm of human services, then it follows that someone must serve as a buffer to protect direct-service professionals and their client-service relationships. As we will explore in Chapter 15—managing change and transition—this can become a major constraint when attempting to redesign human services systems to more effectively impact on the quality of life of client groups with critical needs.

The tension of the client paradigm includes the agony-of-public-choice issue, the clash between client-specific and client-aggregate first discussed in Chapter 2. Which of the choices in Table 9.5 would you make if resources were only available for one option? In essence, the clash between the client paradigm and other paradigms ultimately is bedded in the value-tension of the universal versus the particular.

The Staff-Development Paradigm

Human services organizations function because of a wide variety of employees—clerical, technical, professional, administrative, and managerial. There are many who foster a paradigm that views the growth and development of these employees as the major focal point of the organization. This paradigm is formed and supported, in the first instance, by employee organizations. Because human services employees have become more unionized, this paradigm has also become politicized to the extent that nationwide networks are formed with appropriate mass-communication and pressure-group methods. Teachers were among the first to unionize, but they have been followed by nurses, long-term-care employees, social workers, nonprofessional hospital employees, and even many middle-management program leaders.

But unions and employee organizations are not the only centers of support for the staff-development paradigm. Human resource development professionals (e.g., personnel administrators and staff-training professionals) are very concerned about employee development—for personal growth and organizational improvement purposes. Whereas unions are generally more concerned with employees' tangible benefits, human resource development professionals are concerned with the growth and development of employee careers, individually and collectively. Because most professional management associations are vitally concerned with staff development, it is not unusual to find human services managers strongly in support of the staff-development paradigm.

The conception of the organization as a learning environment is one that grows out of John Dewey's notion that the ideal school is one in which teachers continue to grow and change, to innovate and create (Sarason 1971). The staff-development paradigm therefore is a major motivational force for the technology of organizations as learning systems and for organizational development—the management of change and transitions. Those supporting the concern for managing change have given broad legitimacy to the staff-development paradigm.

We have discussed each of the four paradigms separately, but it should be clear that they operate simultaneously, generally in competition with each other. Sarah Miller (1980), in an edifying analysis, studies a piece of *workfare* legislation—in which she identified in the legislation, the administrative regulations, and the administering state agency, the loci of power and expression of words—that illustrated two competing paradigms (control versus mission). What is interesting in her analysis is the formation by each paradigmatic group of formal and informal coalitions (networks) of legislators, professionals, administrators, organizational units, and pressure groups who joined together to foster one of the two paradigms.

As in any aspect of human services organizations, the manager is left to deal with the tensions between these paradigms: control, mission, client, and staff-development. The roles of these paradigms are vital elements in the dynamic of the human services organization. Thus, the human services manager must develop tactics to support all paradigms simultaneously or advocate for specific ones that otherwise would be overwhelmed by other paradigms forced on the human services organization by external dynamics. It might be possible to postulate a static balance of paradigms as an ideal for the human services organization, but this would be in theory only, because in reality paradigmatic conflict is the norm.

Regulations and Administrative Law: The Foundation

The foundation of fundamental management processes rests on an additional cornerstone: regulations and administrative law. This is true for every human services organization: public, nonprofit, and commercial. As we examined in Chapter 2, federal, state, and local laws and regulations set the framework and boundaries for human services management and operations. It is an inescapable reality for everyone involved in the human services—policymakers, clerical, professional staff, managers, and clients. Without tracing the political, social, and economic evolution of our complex society that is so tied to administrative laws and regulations, it is important here to stress one point: *A solid understanding of the laws and regulations that create and bind a human services organization is the first order of business for everyone involved in human services management.* It is the starting point for productive and effective dispatch of the agency's mission and fundamental management processes.

It is not only necessary for a newly appointed human services manager to spend her first few days on the job studying carefully the laws and regulations that specify the mandatory and discretionary powers of the agency as well as its constraints, but she must also be careful to continually refer to the laws and regulations when there are questions of options and responsibilities. The source for a more refined definition of agency missions is in laws and regulations.

Although regulations and administrative law are the foundation of human services management, they differ depending on the legal basis of the agency. Public organizations have laws, statutes, and ordinances (depending on whether federal, state, county, or municipal) that specify in great detail obligations and constraints. These can be multiple in nature. A municipal human services agency, for example, may be guided by the local municipal charter and ordinances, as well as by state statutes (municipalities are creatures of state government). These are continually being changed and amended.

All human services organizations are subject to government regulations. Some may be function specific (e.g., cost control-related regulations that govern hospital rates); others may be general (e.g., affirmative action regulations that govern recruitment and hiring practices). All are continually being shaped by the courts—all the way to the Supreme Court—whose decisions become part of administrative law. Besides acquiring their own knowledge on this subject, wise human services managers soon learn to develop good communications with the agency's legal specialists.

As we explored in the introduction to Chapter 2 (Figure 2.1 on page 30), the human services manager is bound, among other things, by legal doctrines. Thus, administrative laws and regulations become vehicles for the control paradigm. The issue can be reduced to one's view of laws and regulations as constraints or as opportunities. They actually represent both. If viewed as constraints, the control paradigm will be dominant; if viewed as opportunities, the other paradigms will grow stronger. The solution is in recognizing the tensions that continually pull on the human services manager, and that should result in a blend of different, equally viable, and necessary values and pressures that shape the human services. Seeking a balance in the constraints and opportunities of administrative law and regulations is a major source of the tensions of human services that the reader can anticipate.

Summary

Every human services organization has some fundamental processes that relate to the management of programs, finances, people, data, and workplace—the environment in which all these processes take place. Even the management of the images that the organization projects to the community is a fundamental process for the human services manager. For all these processes, the human services manager must establish order: it is the foundation for a positive organizational environment that promotes a responsive, supportive human services agency. Difficult as it may be to appreciate administrative regulations, standard operating procedures, and checklists—the vehicles for establishing order in an institution—collectively these techniques are the basis for the creative management of a human services organization.

The creative manager also faces a number of forces that shape the fundamental processes of an organization. These forces carry with them a set of assumptions and propositions (e.g., a paradigm) that help or hinder the manager's attempts to shape the human services in ways that will creatively meet the dynamic requirements of the environment and the situation. At all times, at least four paradigms—control, client, mission, and staff-development—are competing for a dominant role in the shaping of a human services organization. Properly balanced these paradigms can lead to the productive use of fundamental management processes, in a way that guarantees the effectiveness of services to clients. When imbalanced the paradigms are not only barriers for effective and efficient delivery of human services but also severely limit the potential impact that such services can have on clients and community. The skillful use of the fundamental processes for institutional management is dependent on the manager's understanding of the dynamics of each of the paradigms, and appreciation of the way in which each can help or hinder dynamic, creative human services management.

10

Managing Programs

Program Planning and Implementation
The Techniques of Program Management

Strategy Formation
Basic Process
Policy Development and Management
Strategic Planning and Strategic Management
Management by Objectives
Strategic Roles
Strategic Goals and Policies

Program Planning and Budgeting
Program Planning and Implementation: Connecting Intent to Action
Program Development
Quantifying Program Performance and Impacts
Budgeting

Work–Resource Scheduling
A Model Work–Resource Schedule

Work–Resource Assigning
A Model Work–Resource Assignment

Program Planning and Implementation

The environment of the human services organization is highly dynamic. On a day-to-day basis, the human services manager is beset with a host of problems and activities that are multivaried and challenging. The organizational life of the human services manager is hectic, having to deal with major and minor issues, switching from one to the other very quickly. Achieving the agency's mission is carried out by (1) repetitive activities that operate on a daily, weekly, or monthly cycle and (2) specific programs or projects. In either case, the process is exciting and challenging. It is the means by which managers help shape society in terms of human services values.

For both the repetitive activities and specific programs of an agency, there is a process by which goals are defined, strategies and tactics selected, resource-allocation plans devised, and progress and results monitored in terms of effectiveness and productivity. This fundamental management process, classically known as **program planning and implementation**, is a set of administrative tools and techniques designed to manage human services programs.

The creative human services manager soon discovers that administrative tools and techniques do not operate separately, one at a time; instead, they are continually being assembled and reassembled (i.e., management repertoires) to meet the dynamically changing situation. Moreover, they are being assembled for a specific purpose. Increasingly, that purpose is to hold the human services organization responsible and accountable for carrying out the organization's mission *effectively,* as the first order of business, and *efficiently,* as the second order. Program planning and implementation must operate therefore from the starting point of (1) clearly setting the goals of the human services organization and (2) controlling the implementation of programs to ensure maximum performance for goal achievement and client impacts.

As Anthony and Young (1988) and K. Ramanthan (1982) note, program management has evolved from the confluence of three sets of management techniques, which have received a great deal of attention during the past several decades:

- Strategic planning: The process of setting long-range, future goals of the organization and developing major policies and plans for achieving these goals
- Management by objectives: A comprehensive integrated approach of management for results (goal achievement)
- Management-control systems: The collection, processing, retrieving, and dissemination of data in a dynamic fashion with automatic feedback loops and alerting mechanisms to indicate when the achievement of goals and objectives is deviating from predetermined milestones

The Techniques of Program Management

Briefly, the elements of program planning and implementation include the following sets of administrative techniques (see Figure 10.1); they have been integrated in a fashion that is conducive to self-management by each program team or by each program leader:

- Strategy formation
- Programming, planning, and budgeting
- Work–resource scheduling and assigning
- Work reporting, measuring, and monitoring
- Program and performance evaluation

Once the student–practitioner of human services management understands the rhythm of program management, it becomes a natural way of interrelating comprehensive sets of administrative techniques to improve both *performance* (effectiveness of services provided to clients) and *accountability* (efficient and economical use of community resources). This is important for managing creatively in a dynamic environment because feedback on results and performance is continual, permitting evaluation directed toward change and improvement to meet the needs of a changing environment.

Program planning and implementation is a modern, comprehensive use of POSDCORB (Planning, Organizing, Staffing, Directing, COordinating, Reporting, and Budgeting)—the basic administrative functions discussed in an earlier chapter. Under the influence of a systems (holistic) perspective, all these functions are now interrelated to constitute an integrated totality. It is an iterative, cyclical process that continues to operate smoothly once the process is tuned, much as the parts of a car engine need tuning in order to function smoothly.

Figure 10.1   Program Management

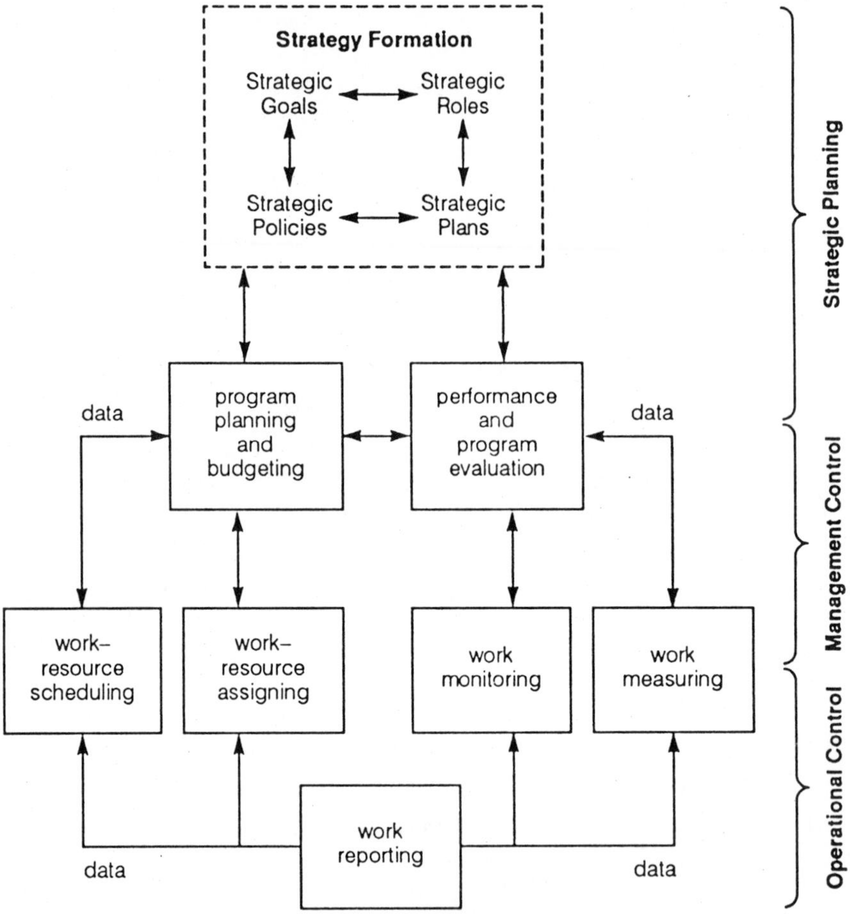

Underlying Principles.   Program planning and implementation is the application of cybernetic management, the dynamics that fashion a self-regulating, self-managing organization. It uses two very important management principles:

- **Management by exception**: Alerting managers to deviations from objectives or milestones in order to deal with exceptions from the routine
- **Management by anticipation**: Designing cybernetic systems so that all levels in an organization understand *in advance* the action that can be taken independently if performance deviates from predetermined milestones within a preset deviation range

There are two techniques and technologies that implement these two principles; they are feedback–feedforward and information systems:

Table 10.1   Levels of Organization and Management

Level	Primary Focus
Strategic planning	Setting the goals for the jurisdiction and developing major policies and plans for achieving these goals
Management control	Dividing the strategic plans into logical subdivisions and assigning responsibilities
	Being concerned with effective and efficient allocation of resources and interrelationships of programs
Operational performance and control	Carrying out the operations
	Determining and assigning specific people, machines, and materials needed to accomplish programs
	Measuring results
	Being concerned for day-to-day, week-to-week scheduling of tasks to be performed and assigning resources to each daily task
	Assessing results and reporting on the degree of success periodically for each program's accomplishments

- **Feedback–feedforward**: With the rise in popularity of cybernetics, feedback–feedforward has become a popular term. Technically, it relates to an automatic process. For example, as the heat rises in a room, the temperature rise *feeds back* to the thermostat, which turns off the furnace. When objectives of a program are set, program milestones are *fed forward* as targets for those responsible for the implementation of the program.

- **Information systems**: It is important to note from Figure 10.1 the flow of the total, classic, program-management process *and* the way in which each of the different elements are integrated as a comprehensive process. Data flows (popularly called a **management-information system [MIS]**) tie together the elements of classic program management using the technique of feedback–feedforward. This provides the basic data that report on work accomplished and measures, monitors, and evaluates results achieved. In modern times, an MIS is driven by an automated, integrated computer-based system that prepares a series of management-oriented reports.

Program planning and implementation is also based on a new perspective regarding the levels of organization and management. Traditionally, three terms have been used to categorize these levels: *top management, middle management* and *supervisory management*. In the mid-1960s, a new perspective was proposed and has become generally accepted today: strategic planning, management control, and operational performance and control (see Table 10.1).

The concepts of strategic planning, management control, and operational performance and control are essential elements of program management (see Figure 10.1). Although each person in a human services organization operates on one particular level of organization and management, all can and do participate in each level. For example, it is natural for a program leader to be called away from work dealing with day-to-day operational performance to a meeting that discusses the progress of a program (management control) and then move on to another meeting that evaluates the program in terms of what should be new, long-range goals for the agency (strategic planning).

Having discussed the underlying principles of program planning and implementation, we proceed to describing in detail each of its elements. For purposes of understanding the subject, we divide the total process into elements and discuss each separately, using a set of programs dealing with treatment of alcohol abuse (see Figure 10.4 on page 249) to illustrate the generic nature and potential of program management. Our framework, however, is always the integrated total process.

Strategy Formation

In the Chapter 8 discussion of the strategic-integrated approach to management, several definitions pertinent to strategy formation were provided. These are the bases for what follows, and the reader may wish to review them to set the scene for what happens next. The strategy formation process involves the following steps:

Basic Process

Step 1: Environmental Scanning. Compare the actual state with the ideal state. Identify and isolate the elements that differentiate the two. Determine what might be changed to achieve the desired state.

Step 2: Evaluation of Potential Strategic Roles. Determine the organizational roles that can be used to help achieve the strategic goals or enhance the organization's mission.

Step 3: Selection of Strategic Goals and Strategic Roles. Define and prioritize the goals and organizational roles that are most appropriate for achieving the future desired state in a way that is sufficiently clear and concise.

Step 4: Preparation of a Policy Statement. Present the organization's mission and intent in a strong and clear-cut fashion.

Most of the present approaches to strategy formation stress the interaction between the organization and the environment and the need to scan the environment to compare *what is* with *what should be*. In modern times, Alfred Chandler (1962) was the first to articulate the essential nature of strategies and strategy formation in managing organizations. He also stressed the organizational-environmental interaction, which uses systems, cybernetics, and information technologies.

On closer examination of the steps in the strategy-formation process, there are several additional critical elements and issues that need to be discussed and described.

Policy Development and Management

The conception of *administration* as "the execution of organizational policies," presented by Woodrow Wilson over 100 years ago (1887), continues to present our profession with a theoretical dilemma: To what extent do human services managers participate in the policy-development process of their agencies? In social work, for example, there are some who would argue that policy development is the province of planners, and the execution of the policies and plans developed by these planners would be the province of administrators.

Human services managers are neither spectators nor dictators in the formulation of organizational policies, nor should they be cast in the role of human robots who carry out the dictates of the power establishment of that society. Rather, their primary role is to manage the policy-development function, ensuring that there is in place a comprehensive, highly participatory process for the formulation of policies that are the end result of the strategy-formation process.

Managing the policy-development process can create an atmosphere of challenge and excitement for all human services organizations, particularly those in public jurisdictions where legislation and budgets are the source of all policies and programs. These are fashioned from the interaction of politically elected legislators, interest groups, and the professionals in the different government human services agencies. Any legislation, particularly that which is national in scope, must take into account the needs and interests of a broad spectrum of different groups of people, from different geographic areas, who have a variety of social, economic, and political values and philosophies.

Policy development is *iterative* (repetitive) in nature. It is a process that goes back and forth between different agents: policymakers, managers, planners, community organizers, clients, interest groups, and so on. The process can begin with the legislature, with interest groups, or with "the bureaucracy." If the latter, it is not uncommon for a group of clinicians in a large human services agency to suggest a new policy and program to the manager, who turns it over to the planning staff to refine.

The plan for the policy and program developed would then be sent to the chief executive's budget office for consideration and then sent informally to the agency's advisory body, made up of groups representing the interests of the agency's clients. It would continue on to a committee in the legislature for discussion and consideration. In each step of the process, the policy and program plan would most probably be sent back for revision and refinement. After several iterations, the plan would be sufficiently formalized to be approved by executive managers of the agency and, with the approval of the chief executive of the jurisdiction (e.g., president, governor, or mayor), presented to the legislature. At that point, another set of iterations begin as the process is focused on public involvement in the policy–program formation.

As we discuss further in this chapter, the iterative process of policy development is both within one element of program management (in this case, within strategy formation) and between other elements (e.g., strategy formation, program planning, resource–work scheduling, and program-performance evaluation).

Strategic Planning and Strategic Management

Although the idea of strategic planning and management is not new to the field, it has become increasingly popular in recent decades. This is particularly true because the strategic approach to management by Japanese organizations has been touted as the most effective in the world; therefore, attempts have been made to copy their success in the United States. One of those attempts has focused on **strategic planning**—concern for *long-term* goals and strategies.

Besides Chapter 8's definition, strategic planning can be described as the process of setting the long-range, future goals of the organization and developing major policies and plans for achieving these goals. It usually begins with *strategic thinking,* which is a way of approaching issues that is sensitive to

- The "big picture."
- The long-term implication of actions.
- The basic mission of an organization.
- A comprehensive view of societal trends.
- Basic changes in the environment.
- Maximization of benefits from available resources.
- The interrelationships among different activities.

Strategic thinking provides a framework for what many call *environmental scanning* or *opportunistic surveillance,* as James Thompson refers to it: "monitoring behavior which scans the environment for opportunities . . . which anticipates institutional trends" (1967, 151).

The emphasis on strategic planning in recent years has placed an equal emphasis on **strategic management**, administering organizations and systems from a strategic perspective. As we have stressed throughout the text, human services managers need proficiency in both institutional (organizational) management and systemic (strategic) management. It is a reflection of a perspective in the field first articulated by Thompson and quoted previously:

> Thus, in our view, the central function of administration is to keep the organization at the nexus of several necessary streams of action; and because the several streams are variable and moving, the nexus is not only moving but sometimes quite difficult to fathom.

The configuration necessary for survival comes neither from yielding to any and all pressures nor from manipulating all variables, but from finding the **strategic** variables. (1967, 147–48)

Management by Objectives

Management by objectives (MBOs) has been defined narrowly as the initial element of a goal-oriented approach to managing and broadly as a total integrated system of management for results (goal achievement). It can be either. Peter Drucker (1954) first articulated the centrality of the idea of MBOs. His concept was developed into a comprehensive system that is described by George Odiorne, one of the leading MBO proponents as

A process whereby the superior and the subordinate managements of an enterprise jointly identify the common goals, define each individual's major areas of responsibility in terms of the results expected of him, and use these measures as guides for operating the unit and assessing the contribution of each of its members. (1965, 104)

When objectives are defined in terms of the results to be achieved, generally one can anticipate what must occur in the organization or system. MBOs thus involve the following:

1. An employee writes objectives of what is to be accomplished in the next time frame, specifying the results that can be measured.
2. The employee meets with her subordinates to review the objectives and their contributions to the achievement of organizational goals.
3. From this review comes a set of objectives that subordinates will be committed to achieve within the time period.
4. Evaluation of employee performance is carried out in terms of the agreed-on objectives.

There are a number of benefits that accrue from MBOs. First, employees participate in the goal-setting process of the organization. Second, clear statements of what is to be accomplished and how that performance will be measured reduces ambiguity and employee anxiety. Last, it encourages mutual respect between the employee and her superior. Although there are criticisms of MBOs, the approach remains popular in many organizations.

Strategic Roles

Contrary to general thinking, selection of organizational roles is as important as selecting goals. Thus, it is necessary to define the **strategic role(s)** that an organization intends to play in the human services system during the strategy-formation process. A classic example of the critical importance of strategic-

Table 10.2   Strategic-Role Options: Welfare Payments

Strategic Role	Sets of Available Goal Options
Money funneler	Guards public funds. Keeps departmental regulations. Acts as surrogate parent. Provides doles.
Family supporter	Strengthens family functioning. Fosters self-sufficiency. Redistributes national wealth. Reestablishes meaningful life. Provides minimum quality of life.

Table 10.3   Strategic-Role Selection: Industrial Social Work

Role	Duties
Clinician	Under contract, provides direct counseling for the Employee Assistance Program (EAP) of local business corporations.
Community organizer	Works with community business corporations in helping them develop and establish their own EAP.

role selection is the federal government's selection of mortgage guarantor and tax-policy shaper to stimulate the rapid expansion of home building (e.g., to guarantee bank mortgages to young, potential homeowners with no credit ratings and to provide IRS tax deductions for homeowners). Compared with the strategic-role option of public-housing builder, the former strategic role creates the minimum of bureaucracy and uses the natural forces of the economy.

When selecting strategic roles for a human services organization, one encounters some interesting variables, foremost of which is values (see Table 10.2). As the reader will note, in the area of transfer payments, even when the income-maintenance human services manager attempts to have the agency adopt a family-supporter strategic role, legislators, taxpayers, and even some employees will view the department of income maintenance's role from a different value-base—as that of money funneler.

Selection of strategic roles is critical and must be undertaken with care. It should *not* begin with the concept that services provision is the only or even the initial option; preferably, it should be the option of last resort. For example, in Table 10.3, which strategic role would have a greater impact on a larger number of people? Even at the risk of repetition, but because of their importance, Figure 10.2 provides a listing of a number of different strategic roles available to the human services manager, classified in terms of classic strategies.

Figure 10.2   Potential Strategic Roles
for Human Services Organizations

Educate–Persuade

advocate
advisor
program demonstrator
public information provider
information and referral provider
interagency liason
community organizer
technical assistant
networking coodinator

Regulate

regulator
deregulator
standards creator
tax-policy changer
tax-incentives provider

---

dependent
(provide services)

↑

↓

interdependent
(stimulate services
acquisition)

Deliver Services

mutual-help groups promoter
monitor and evaluator
administrative reformer
deinstitutionalization supporter
loan guarantor
private-sector collaborator
financier (grants and loans)
contractor
direct purchaser
service provider (examples):
custodian, child developer,
skill developer, family supporter,
surrogate parent, mentor, and
clinician

Strategic Goals and Policies

What is a goal? Simply stated, a goal is something to strive for and work toward. It can be expressed in terms of *achieving* desirable outcomes (e.g., improve health) or in terms of *avoiding* undesirable outcomes (e.g., reduce or eliminate illness). In both cases, **a goal expresses some future desired state**, which, for the administrator, needs to be stated in specific terms.

The exact wording of a goal generally creates a clearer insight into the organizational mission and broadens the options for strategic roles. In addressing the example of excessive "welfare payments" (e.g., too great a dependence on AFDC [Aid for Families with Dependent Children]) in Table 10.4, an *achievement*-oriented goal statement would be *"Increased* economic self-sufficiency for a large number of families currently receiving AFDC"; while an *avoidance*-oriented goal statement would be *"Reduce* the number of families dependent on AFDC." It is important to note that when articulating goals that are to be communicated to the public, the tone of the wording sometimes acquires a life of its own. Also important to the decision on wording is the ultimate need for evaluation: Can one way of defining the problem be more readily assessed than another?

Although the wording of a strategic goal may seem insignificant, the reader will note that the strategy-formation process is designed to orient the human services organization toward altering the future, toward achieving some desired change in the environment. Thus, it is critical to think about the future and attempt to describe what it ought to be. This becomes the benchmark for evaluating the organization's success or failure in achieving the future desired situation, in terms of its effectiveness of improving the quality of life for those people targeted for the desired change.

Goal Ambiguity.   We live in a complex society, a complex world. So it is not surprising that the processes of human services organizations and systems are also complex and that the policies resulting from the strategy-formation process are often ambiguous. This is not because the participants in the process are not clear thinkers; it is quite the opposite. The ambiguity occurs because in our form of democracy, for every value in society, there are countervalues; for every interest, there are multiple counterinterests of various shades. Thus, to secure the necessary support for policies and funding of human services endeavors, consensus and compromise are generally necessary.

The result is that policies have to be stated in terms so broad and general that they are ambiguous. This means that human services managers must be both focused and creative in implementing programs to carry out agency missions and to achieve strategic roles and goals.

Case 10.1 illustrates goal ambiguity in day care for families on AFDC. To the many people who view "welfare" in negative terms, the only reason for additional public day-care funds for the families they view as a burden to society is to implement the strategic role of *babysitter:* supervise the chil-

Table 10.4   Strategic-Goal Statements

Issue 1: Too great a dependence on AFDC	Issue 2: High incidence of teenage alcohol abuse

	Future Desired State	
Process-Oriented (input)	Results-Oriented (output)	Effectiveness-Oriented (impact)
1. To provide AFDC and service support	Increased economic self-sufficiency	Improved quality of long-term, independent family functioning
2. To develop a teen-age alcoholism program	Reduced incidence of teenage alcohol abuse	Increased positive self-image and functioning of teenagers among family, peers, school, and community

dren during working hours so welfare mothers can be employed and get off AFDC rolls. But to other interest groups and to many human services professionals, day care for AFDC mothers presents an opportunity to implement the strategic role of *child developer:* provide support in improving the physical, mental, and emotional development of disadvantaged children so that they can eventually participate in the American dream. Case 10.1 suggests that the human services manager is faced with the need to carry out a multiple set of strategic roles. Experience indicates that for strategic-role definition, creativity and devotion to human services values are critical characteristics for human services management.

Case 10.1

Day Care: Child Development or Babysitting?

Despite her generally cool composure, Candi Saunders felt increasingly flustered as the meeting progressed. As director of the Mission Bay Day-Care Center, she had prepared a detailed, statistically based report of the progress of the center's children in terms of their educational, physical, and personality development. Initially, the board of directors had been pleased with the report and proud of their achievement in the three years since opening with a grant from the state's Department of Education.

But Len Downing, who was conducting the audit for the state, paid very little attention to the report other than to criticize it for containing insufficient fiscal-oriented data related to the impact of day care on the parents' incomes, reduction in their state welfare payments, average fees paid by parents, continued day-care eligibility of parents, and so on. What bothered Candi was that her board members were afraid that they might lose the Department of

Education grant; thus, they were siding with Len and insisting that Candi prepare the additional data for the audit.

"What about the data documenting each child's educational development? Surely the Department of Education would want the day-care center to be effective in its educational efforts!" Candi protested.

"You'd better reread the federal day-care law and regulations," Len answered. "It specifically states that the purpose of the funding is for reducing dependency on AFDC by freeing parents from child care so that they can become employed. In theory, the department agrees with you; but legally we are responsible to audit your conformity with the law."

Juanita Brown, the only parent on the board, tried to come to Candi's defense. "Candi and the other teachers devote hours and hours of unpaid time in helping our children grow and develop, which in the long run will even reduce the department's special education budget. Requiring additional time devoted to data collection, analysis, and reporting will only take time away from the educational, health, nutritional, and recreational programs for our children. Besides, you might as well be from the finance department of the state; you don't seem at all interested in the achievement of educational objectives!"

"I'm only the auditor, Mrs. Brown," Len replied. "I know our department is scrutinized closely by the feds and it would embarrass the governor if we lost day-care funding for failure to enforce their regulations. It would obviously also affect Mission Bay Day-Care Center's ability to operate. I'm only insisting that you keep fiscal-impact data. The law is the law."

Example. An application of strategy formation as it relates to alcohol abuse is presented as a strategic plan in Table 10.5.

Program Planning and Budgeting

Before examining the complex techniques that make up this element in classic program management, it is helpful to step back and view where it fits into the total process. Essentially, program planning and budgeting is a process in which

- Programs are developed.
- Effectiveness criteria are set.
- Objectives and performance milestones are set.
- Budgets are formulated.

Of necessity, this element of classic program management feeds back (is based on) strategy formation and feeds forward (sets the conditions for) work–

Table 10.5   Strategic Plan: Alcohol Abuse–Treatment Agency

Strategic Role	Strategic Goals	Program–Objective	Time Frame (1–3 yr)	(4–6 yr)
Custodian	Increased capacity for acute treatment	De-tox services: Increase capacity of de-tox services from 150 to 375 clients per year.	XXXXX	
		Crisis intervention: Provide 1500 hours of crisis intervention services to 250 clients.	XXXXX	
Therapist	Expanded treatment services	Community mental health clinics: Provide treatment to 1000 alcohol abusers annually in three clinics.	XXXXX	
	Increased employment Decreased alcohol dependency	Substance-abuse therapy: Establish therapeutic environment that offers mutual-help and individual counseling therapy annually to 525 clients.	XXXXX	
	Strengthened family stability	Family therapy: Create a family-therapy program that provides support to families of 210 clients.	XXXXX	
Community organizer	Increased level of available treatment services Reduced incidence of alcohol abuse	EAPs: Work with community business and industry to establish employee assistance programs for 30 percent of the community work force.		XXXXX
	Increased community concern for alcohol abuse Reduced incidence of drunken driving	Community awareness: In cooperation with community public relations agencies, develop an alcohol abuse– awareness program for industry and schools, with particular emphasis on drunken driving.		XXXXX

resource scheduling and assigning, work reporting, measuring and monitoring, and program-performance evaluation.

Because budgeting is such an essential element of financial management, it is treated in depth in Chapter 11 and only is included in the examples and illustrations in this chapter.

Program Planning and Implementation: Connecting Intent to Action

The observant reader might well be concerned that strategic roles, goals, and policies seem to be set without thinking about a crucial issue: Can they be achieved? This raises a more basic question: Which comes first—strategy formation (strategic planning) or program planning? It is almost a "chicken-or-egg" question: both must be undertaken in tandem, with close interaction. One cannot be completed without the other. Although we discuss each separately, the reader must never forget that classic program management is an *integrated process.*

Implementation has been called the Achilles' heel of management. Critics maintain that there is a tendency to spend too much time on strategic planning—*what* should be done—and insufficient time on program planning—*how* it should be accomplished. Unfortunately, in an environment where acquisition of resources is such an agonizing process, there is often a tendency to first formulate plans that "sell" the policy and to prepare detailed program-implementation plans only after resources have been received (e.g., the grant awarded or the budget increased).

Programs are the tactics by which strategic goals and policies will be achieved. Experienced human services managers try hard not to embark on the implementation of programs until careful and detailed program planning has been completed to ensure with reasonable certainty that what the agency is held accountable for can indeed be achieved effectively with given resources. Commitment to strategies, goals, policies, and programs should not be made until managers have undertaken detailed program planning—and, for that matter, work scheduling—to be assured that implementation is feasible.

The Basic Program-Planning Process.   The basic program-planning process (Figure 10.3) essentially includes the following steps:

1. Involve agency employees in determining a range of programs that can be used as tactics for achieving the specified strategic goal(s) and as a vehicle for carrying out the strategic role(s) selected during the policy-formation process.
2. Based on several analyses (e.g., cost–benefit, cost–effectiveness, and opportunity cost), assign weights to the various programs and prioritize them in terms of which can be most effective in helping achieve or reinforce strategic goals.
3. Select a proposed set of programs.
4. Define the objective of each program—desired quantifiable results that can be achieved within a specified period of time.
5. Develop performance milestones—quantitative measures of the anticipated achievement of a portion of the objective that will be reached by specific dates during the calendar year (referred to as targets).

Figure 10.3   Program-Planning Process

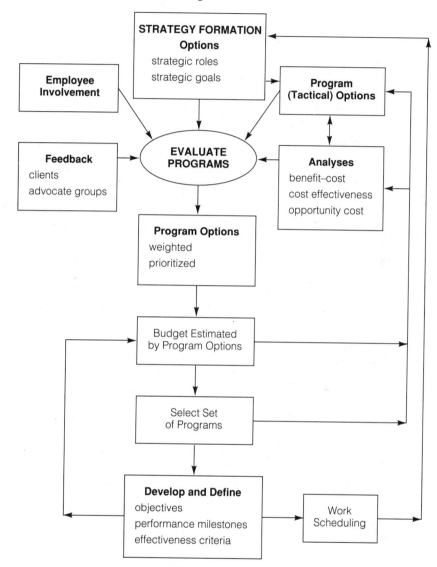

6. Develop impact criteria—quantitative and qualitative measures of the outcomes and impacts of programs on clients in terms of improving the quality of their lives.
7. Develop a budget for each program.
8. Reanalyze the articulated strategic goal(s) and role(s) in terms of program plans to determine whether they need modification to balance what is intended to be accomplished with estimates of what can be achieved.

9. Undertake an educational effort designed to enlighten agency employees.
10. Communicate with key groups of employees and various interest groups to enlist their support in securing approval of the programs.

The Relationship Between Strategy Formation and Program Planning.
Even though the two are closely interrelated, strategic planning can be distinguished from program planning in that it is policy-oriented, is cross-programmatic, deals with causes, is intergovernmental and interjurisdictional, and is impact-oriented. Strategic planning also has a multiyear time-period perspective to help the agency make long-term, future-oriented decisions.

Program planning is just the opposite. Its perspective is short-term, results-oriented, *intra*jurisdictional, and *intra*organizational in nature. It focuses on specific tactics that can achieve a selected goal in the most productive, effective manner. It assumes that quantifiable criteria can be developed to measure the performance of individuals and groups of employees.

As has been noted, both types of planning are undertaken in tandem, as an integrated and iterative process. Articulation of strategic goals, roles, and policies initiates program planning, which in turn indicates that the strategic goals and policies may have to be modified for the given resource level. This iterative (repetitive) cycle may occur several times during the lengthy planning process and, where appropriate, during the lengthy budgetary-legislative review process—until both are sufficiently balanced and implementation can be initiated.

In addition, strategic planning and program planning should not be completed until resource–work scheduling has been undertaken sufficiently for both policymakers and managers to be assured that the goals, policies, programs, and objectives are realistic and achievable. This process represents a tension between rational planning and incremental planning. The former is an informed, long-range, thoughtful consideration of complex sets of future choices; the latter is an evaluation of a few short-term options to select the one most likely to succeed.

The human services manager attempts to balance rational planning and incremental planning, taking advantage of opportunities as they present themselves, while holding to a rational plan within which incremental steps make sense.

Program Development

Figure 10.4 provides an illustration of program management that will be used for the remainder of this chapter. It will help concretize the following discussion of program development and the discussion of all other elements of classic program management discussed in the chapter. The illustration uses our example of alcohol abuse and is based on the strategy formation contained in Table 10.5 on page 245.

Figure 10.4 Program Management: Alcohol Abuse–Treatment Services

STRATEGY FORMATION

Role: Therapist and community organizer
Goal: Increased employment of alcohol-abusing adults through expanded use of larger number of treatment modalities

PROGRAM PLANNING AND BUDGETING

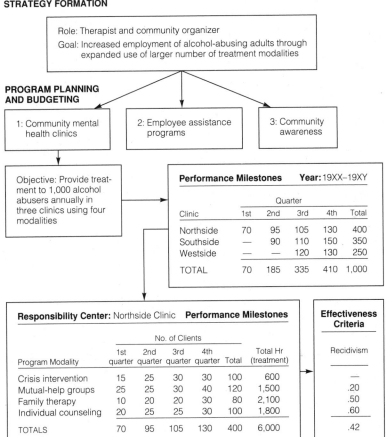

1: Community mental health clinics

2: Employee assistance programs

3: Community awareness

Objective: Provide treatment to 1,000 alcohol abusers annually in three clinics using four modalities

Performance Milestones   Year: 19XX–19XY

Clinic	Quarter				
	1st	2nd	3rd	4th	Total
Northside	70	95	105	130	400
Southside	—	90	110	150	350
Westside	—	—	120	130	250
TOTAL	70	185	335	410	1,000

Responsibility Center: Northside Clinic   **Performance Milestones**

Program Modality	No. of Clients					Total Hr (treatment)
	1st quarter	2nd quarter	3rd quarter	4th quarter	Total	
Crisis intervention	15	25	30	30	100	600
Mutual-help groups	25	25	30	40	120	1,500
Family therapy	10	20	20	30	80	2,100
Individual counseling	20	25	25	30	100	1,800
TOTALS	70	95	105	130	400	6,000

Effectiveness Criteria

Recidivism
—
.20
.50
.60
.42

Program Budget: 19XX–19XY

Program Modality	Personnel	Contractual	Commodities	Total
Crisis intervention	$ 18,000	$19,500	$10,500	$ 48,000
Mutual-help groups	45,000	21,000	15,000	81,000
Family therapy	63,000	16,500	7,500	87,000
Individual counseling	54,000	18,000	12,000	84,000
TOTALS	$180,000	$75,000	$45,000	$300,000

Unit Costs

Per Hr	Per Client
$80	$ 480
54	675
42	1,088
47	840
$50	$ 750

Figure 10.4 (continued)

WORK–RESOURCE SCHEDULE

Program Modality: Mutual-Help Groups
Responsibility Center: Northside Clinic

19XX–19XY

	1st Quarter		2nd Quarter		3rd Quarter		4th Quarter	
	Period	YTD	Period	YTD	Period	YTD	Period	YTD
Critical resources								
Group workers (hrs)	210	210	215	425	245	670	350	1,020
Psychologist (hrs)	100	100	100	200	130	330	150	480
Milestones								
No. of clients	25	25	25	50	30	80	40	120
No. of treatment hrs	310	310	315	625	375	1,000	500	1,500
Effectiveness								
Recidivism rate	.35	.35	.25	.30	.20	.25	.18	.20

WORK–RESOURCE ASSIGNMENT

Program Modality: Mutual-Help Groups **Period:** 3rd Quarter (Jan.–March 19XY)
Responsibility Center: Northside Clinic

		Required Resource Investment (hrs worked)	Quarterly Targets	
Critical Resource	Identification		Clients	Total Treatment Hr
Group workers	Pamela Daly	145	18	
	Michael Makovic	100	12	
Psychologist	Harold Stenback	130	30	
				375

WORK REPORTING

Program Modality: Mutual-Help Groups **Period:** 3rd Quarter (Jan.–March 19XY)
Report: Operational
Responsibility Center: Northside Clinic

		Treatment Hours			
		Period		YTD	
Critical Resource	Identification	Actual	Target	Actual	Target
Group workers	Pamela Daly	147	145	565	570
	Michael Makovic	104	100	104	100
Psychologist	Harold Stenback	132	130	340	330
TOTALS		383	375	1,009	1,000
Performance milestone					
No. of clients		31	30	83	80
Effectiveness criteria					
Recidivism rate		.21	.20	.23	.25

Figure 10.4 (*continued*)

WORK MONITORING–MEASURING

Program Modality: Mutual-Help Groups   **Period:** 3rd Quarter (Jan.–March 19XY)
Report: Management Control
Responsibility Center: Northside Clinic

Critical Resource	Resources Invested		Performance (YTD)		Effectiveness
	Period	YTD	No. of clients	No. of treatment hr	Recidivism (YTD)
Group workers					
Pamela Daly	1.01	0.99	1.01	0.99	1.03
Michael Makovic	1.04	1.04	1.08	1.04	0.96
Psychologist					
Harold Stenback	1.02	1.03	1.03	1.03	1.03
TOTALS	1.02	1.01	1.03	1.04	1.03

Report: Strategic   **Period:** 3rd Quarter (Jan.–March 19XY)
Cost Center: Mutual-Help Groups   **Policy Issue:** Alcohol Abuse

Responsibility Center	Resources Invested		Performance (YTD)		Effectiveness
	Period	YTD	No. of clients	No. of treatment hr	Recidivism (YTD)
Northside Clinic	1.02	1.01	1.03	1.04	1.03
Southside Clinic					
Westside Clinic					

Report: Strategic   **Period:** 3rd Quarter (Jan.–March 19XY)
Responsibility Center: Northside Clinic   **Policy Issue:** Alcohol Abuse

Program Modality	Resources Invested		Performance (YTD)		Effectiveness
	Period	YTD	No. of clients	No. of treatment hr	Recidivism (YTD)
Crisis intervention					
Mutual-help groups	1.02	1.01	1.03	1.04	1.03
Family therapy					
Individual counseling					

EVALUATION

Responsibility Center: Mutual-Help Groups   **Period:** (July 19XX–March 19XY)
   Policy Issue: Alcohol Abuse

Performance

Deviation from program plan: Objectives–milestones   1.03 (3% ahead of plan)
   Resources   1.01 (1% ahead of plan)
   Effectiveness criteria   1.03 (3% ahead of plan)

Program

Need additional data at end of year in terms of increased days of employment attributed to reduced alcohol abuse; reduced cases of driving while intoxicated; increased family stability of clients who have participated in mutual-help groups.

The Process.   To begin the discussion of the program-development process, it is important to define a number of terms that have been or will be used during this discussion of program planning and budgeting:

- **Program**: The vehicle (means) for reaching a strategic goal.
- **Objective**: The intended results *and* impacts of a program that can be quantified within a given period of time.
- **Performance milestone**: A quantitative measure of the anticipated achievement of a defined portion of the objective that is to be reached by specific dates during the time period (also referred to as *targets*).
- **Effectiveness criteria**: Quantitative and qualitative measures of the anticipated impact that the program is intended to achieve for individual or groups of clients and for the community.
- **Cost–benefit**: The amount of benefit produced by a given investment (sometimes referred to as ROI, return on investment.) The cost–benefit ratio (rate of return) is expressed as Investment/Net Benefit.
- **Cost–effectiveness**: A comparison of outcomes from different programs or program modalities from a given amount of investment.
- **Unit costs**: Relating investments (expenditures) to results using the formula Investment/Output.
- **Cost center**: An aggregation of expense.
- **Responsibility center**: Self-managing work groups responsible and accountable for implementing a program or program element.

The human services manager's key test during program planning is straightforward: Has this or will this program be the most effective way possible to reach the stated strategic goal? Is it appropriate for the strategic role(s) chosen by the agency? For example, work incentives, day care, and manpower training are appropriate programs for an income-maintenance agency that adopts a family-supporter strategic role; they are inappropriate for the agency that adopts the strategic role of money funneler.

There are several factors that influence the exact mix of programs that will be selected for detailed planning. They include research, the experience of other human services agencies, the availability of funds, employee support and ownership, the results of cost–benefit and cost–effectiveness analyses, the relative contribution of the program to the agency's strategic plans, and the interpersonal communications and negotiations within the agency. Consider, for example, nutritional programs for elderly people. Suppose someone presented the thesis that providing meals would reduce malnutrition among the elderly poor. A program of "congregate feeding" is mounted. In time, supported by detailed research, such a program was found to be successful in reducing poor nutrition among the elderly, and the program was funded by a federal agency on a widespread basis. Eventually, more detailed research data are accumulated to establish the degree to which congregate feeding reduces malnutrition more

Figure 10.5   Program-Development Process

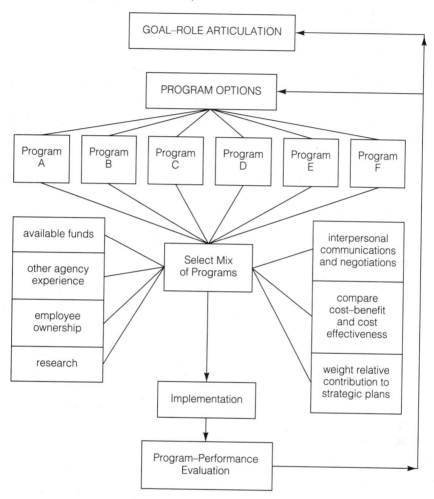

significantly than do alternative programs. Based on this research, we continue the congregate feeding until more research indicates that another program is more effective. The process can be seen in Figure 10.5.

The Program-Development Cycle.   There are several phases in the development of a human services program. Generally, they are design, implementation, and stabilization. During the design phase, the program is identified, objectives and other quantitative measures are developed, resources are aggregated, and a process developed by which agencies will be selected to implement the programs. In large government agencies or in large foundations, the latter sometimes involves the development of a request for proposal (RFP). An RFP is a document that seeks proposals from interested human services organizations and sets forth the specifications. Interested agencies prepare proposals and compete to be selected as one of the sites in which the new program will be implemented.

During the next phase, the program is implemented. Where an RFP is involved, contracts are entered into with the agencies selected on the basis of their proposal-response to the RFP. During the early years of a program, there is often a good deal of trial and error until the program is fine-tuned. The program is monitored closely, and design revisions are made to improve its impact. Agencies initially selected work hard to receive continued funding for the program. Where funding is not continued, the human services manager often becomes very creative in finding ways to continue the program through other sources.

In the stabilization phase, the program has been implemented with sufficient success that attempts are made to replicate the program in a larger number of human services agencies even nationwide, where possible. Those who are responsible for overall program management then seek to institutionalize the program politically in ways that ongoing funding will be assured. Human services agencies who are managing these programs become an interest group in themselves, working hard to preserve funding—for both altruistic and self-serving reasons.

Quantifying Program Performance and Impacts

From one perspective, program management can be viewed as applied research, as it requires a great deal of analysis and statistical calculation, much of which is concentrated on interrelating the two separate streams of data in an organization: *financial data* and *program data*. These analyses and computations measure and monitor the performance and impacts of programs, and are key to financial management, particularly budget preparation and execution, as covered in Chapter 11. However, they are presented again here because of their critical role in classic program management.

Objectives.   Objectives state the results and impacts that a program intends to accomplish within a given time period. The five criteria for well-defined objectives are

- The objectives are program-specific.
- Desired results are stated in clear, succinct terms.
- Desired results are quantifiable, if at all possible.
- Desired impacts on clients are stated in qualitative and, if possible, in quantitative terms.
- Time periods for accomplishing results and impacts are indicated.

In the following statement of an objective for parent effectiveness training (PET), we *underline* the desired results, place *circles* around that which can be quantified, place a *square* around the time period, and use **bold type** for the program impacts:

- Within a ⬚6⬚-month period, <u>provide Ⓘ10 sessions of parent effectiveness train-ing</u> to 100 families in order **to improve their child development and parenting skills**.

Program impacts are usually difficult to quantify. For the PET example above, any of the following impacts could be specified for parents who complete the PET program:

- Improved communication skills with their children
- More realistic view of their own aspirations for their children
- Increased ability to determine realistic goals for their children
- More effective in finding ways to help their children reach goals
- Stronger family functioning in a positive fashion (e.g., be able to deal with family problems more intelligently and more confidently)
- Openness and trust between parents and children

From another perspective, the PET also has impacts–outcomes for the children of the parents who complete the training. These most likely can be quantified in terms of parent, peer, school, and community relations (e.g., completed high school successfully, continued on to advanced technical schools or to college, began employment in work that has growth potential, did not abuse substances, did not become involved with the criminal justice system).

Table 10.6 presents several examples of objectives. Properly written objectives are the key to effective and productive managing of human services organizations and systems. They are also the basis for fashioning two critical sets of criteria for program management: performance milestones and effectiveness.

Performance Milestones.   Performance milestones measure the anticipated achievement of a portion of the objective that is to be reached by a specific date during the time period. Performance milestones, sometimes referred to as targets, are used to measure organizational and employee performance and productivity. In the alcohol abuse–treatment program illustration (Figure 10.4) several different performance milestones were used:

- Organizational: The community mental health clinics will treat 1000 clients during each of four quarters of the program year.
- Responsibility center: Of the 1000 clients to be treated by the program, 400 will receive 6000 hours of treatment in the Northside Clinic, broken down by each quarter of the program year.
- Program modality: Of the total of 400 clients to be treated by the Northside

Table 10.6   Writing Objectives

Program	Objective	Client Impact
Crisis intervention	*Open a center:* Provide crisis counseling to assist 900 people, provide emergency shelter for 250 people, and develop follow-up groups for 100 people in a year.	Provide 75 percent of clients the ability to deal with issues in their lives in a noncrisis climate.
Foster parent recruitment	*Foster parent training program:* Within one year, provide intensive, multifaceted training for 200 foster parents consisting of 85 training hours per parent.	Ninety-five percent of graduates become foster parents for minimum of three years.
Alcoholic ambulatory care	*Outpatient services:* Intervention, assessment, and treatment of alcoholism, for a total of 3640 counseling hours to 540 different persons during a year.	For at least a two-year period, 80 percent of clients no longer need alcohol abuse–treatment services.
Community mental health	*Transitional living program:* Provide supervised, full-time apartment living facilities for 25 people with support services, during a one-year period.	In-hospital treatment required by clients does not exceed one occurrence annually for a period of care less than fifteen days.
Abused women	*Emergency shelter program:* Provide an emergency shelter on a twenty-four-hour basis for a minimum of 180 abused women and their children during the next year.	Eighty-five percent of women and children reacquire ability for self-management of family life.
Disabled protection and advocacy	*Citizen advocacy programs:* Initiate five consumer task forces of at least 4 persons each who will target recipients and achieve 504 compliance in four locations within a period of five months.	Seventy-five percent of locations achieve compliance.
Positive youth development	*Teen service program:* Set up a program in which teens provide service to public and nonprofit organizations in the community.	Seventy percent of the teens commit themselves for permanent service tasks on a regular basis.

Clinic, 120 will receive 1500 hours of treatment in the mutual-help group modality.

- Employee: Eighteen clients will be treated by group worker Pamela Daly during the third quarter of the Northside Clinic's mutual-help group program modality.

All of the above set the conditions (feedfoward) for performance evaluation: we will be able to measure in quantitative terms what the program, responsibility center, and employee actually accomplished (outputs) compared to what they set out to achieve. Work reporting, measuring, and monitoring elements of classic program management will feed back to these performance milestones in order to compare *actual* results with *intended* results.

Effectiveness Criteria.   Effectiveness criteria are quantitative and qualitative measures of the anticipated impact that the program is intended to achieve for individual or groups of clients and for the community. Although there are many measures for the "success" of a human services organization, for human services managers, one measure should always be primary: *Has the action of the organization improved the quality of life of clients in quantitative and qualitative terms?* Effectiveness is the symbol for this measure.

In the alcohol abuse–treatment program illustration (Figure 10.4 on page 249), one criterion for effectiveness was used consistently: *recidivism rate.* Recall that the strategic goal of the alcohol abuse–treatment program is "increased employment of alcohol-abusing adults." If a recovering alcoholic can return to work and maintain a positive, wholesome functioning of self and family for the rest of her life, the effectiveness of the program is 100 percent. Not only has the quality of life for the client and those in the family, employment site, and community been improved, but each also can be measured in quantitative terms. Can you quantify some of these direct benefits? There are sufficient statistics to provide data to make such computations. If one of those clients were the man who drove into a bus full of children, thirty-seven of whom who died, the quantitative and qualitative benefits would soar. Because DWI (driving while intoxicated) has become a very sensitive societal issue, recidivism rate of alcoholics has a very direct relationship to quantitative and qualitative impacts of treatment on clients.

Benefit–Cost.   Benefit–cost, as it is referred to in human services terminology, or cost–benefit, as it is more commonly called, is the amount of benefit produced by a given investment; it sometimes is also referred to as return on investment (ROI). Computing the benefits from a program or set of services to clients is by far the most difficult statistical analysis for classic program management and human services management. Some benefits are difficult to quantify. They should nevertheless be identified without any dollar value placed on them. For example, reducing waiting time of unemployed clients at an employment service office from sixty minutes to fifteen minutes will reduce their stress and respect their dignity even though it might not bring any increased economic benefit to society.

Benefits can be computed in terms of *achievement* or *avoidance.* In our illustration of program management in this chapter (Figure 10.4) a client whose alcohol abuse–treatment services resulted in return to daily activities of home and work, without relapse into alcohol abuse, benefits could be computed in both of the following ways:

- Achievement: Increased material benefit (economic gain) to the client or to society. EXAMPLE: The additional salary earned over a lifetime

- Avoidance: Decreased cost to an individual or society. EXAMPLE: Avoidance of cost of treatment, institutionalization, and family subsidies

Whether computed in terms of achievement or avoidance, the benefits in the above example can be quantified in dollars and cents.

As can be anticipated, nonmaterial, nonquantifiable benefits can, of course, also be desirable outcomes to be achieved (e.g., strengthening family stability or increased self-esteem) or undesirable impacts to be avoided (e.g., family disintegration).

When computing benefits, it is important to recognize that they can have multiple effects. For example, successful day care for an AFDC parent can bring about a ripple effect that goes beyond safe child supervision, and includes:

For the Parents

- Steady income from a job; reduction in the need for a transfer payment (welfare); improved standard of living
- Increased self-esteem; personal growth
- Reduced family stress; improvement in quality of family life

For the Children

- Improved physical development through improved health and nutritional care; reduced present and future health problems
- Educational development; better preparation for success in school
- Improved emotional development; a better functioning child

Data for a good benefit analysis come from the literature, research reports, demographic data sources, and from other human services organizations that make their cost analyses available. Table 10.7 provides the benefit–cost ratio formula, the general approach to computing benefits, and an example drawn from an in-hospital rehabilitation program. In essence, benefit–cost analyses for some of the human services (the health services foremost) boils down to the cost of extending life, in varying degrees of quality (e.g., from being fully independent to being totally dependent). The phrase used for this measure is **QALY** (Quality-Adjusted Life Years); it refers to the premium a person is willing to pay to extend life or the minimum sum a person is prepared to pay in exchange for longer life—the value each of us place on our lives.

Placing a monetary value on human life is difficult and controversial. Many professionals reject the notion that human services even have to be valued in terms of human life. Others feel that computing the value of human life simply can't be done. It is possible to compute the potential earnings of individuals based on the educational level completed (e.g., high school diploma, college degree, graduate degree), but there is no other commonly agreed upon method of placing value on life. Although human services planners and thinkers agonize over this issue, the lawyers, judges, and courts of our society make just such computations every day in liability cases. The issue, then, is one of values

Table 10.7 Benefit–cost analysis

Formula: Benefit–cost ratio $= \dfrac{\text{Net benefits (total benefits} - \text{investment)}}{\text{Investment}}$

General approach to computing benefits

Benefits

Quantitative	Increased personal income over lifetime
	Increase to gross national product
	Increased economic development
	Maintain current level–condition (e.g., housing stock: rehabilitation vs. demolish and rebuild, and move and rent)
	Increased ability to cope–operate independently
	Provide jobs (increase employment)
	Increased tax payments
	Increased productivity

Decrease costs of services (for X years)

Decreased costs of institutionalization or hospitalization

Decreased losses from arson, destruction, robberies, riots, etc.

Decreased subsidies–support

Decreased recidivism (cost of continued services)

Prevent deterioration or destruction

Prevent occurrences of conditions (malnutrition, hypothermia, etc.) and event (fire; entry into institution)

Nonquantitative Increased psyche (sense of self-worth, personal achievement)

Increased family stability

Increased skills: lifetime, employability, physical development, and psychological development

Extended life by degrees of quality (from bedridden, totally dependent to ambulatory and independent)

Decreased feelings of alienation–loneliness

Decreased family disintegration

Decreased feeling of insecurity–anxiety

Prevent or delay personal deterioration

Example: Benefit–cost for self-care program: head–neck cancer in-hospital rehabilitation

Impacts	Reduced Hospital Stay	Reduced Nursing Home Stay	Eliminate Emergency Room Admissions	Total
Cost per case	$800	$2,400	$100	
Number of cases	750	425	500	
Total benefit	600,000	1,020,000	50,000	$1,670,000
Program costs				300,000
Net benefits				$1,370,000

Narrative:
The benefit–cost matrix is based on the first year's operation and three project program impacts: reduced hospital stays, reducing nursing home discharges, and eliminating emergency room admissions. It is based on a yearly milestone caseload of 1000 patients. The figures are calculated on the following:

1. Hospital stay will be reduced on the average of four days. If daily average cost is $200, then cost per case is $800. Because the hospital stay will be reduced for 75 percent of the 1000 patients, the hospital reduction will be for 750 patients.
2. Nursing costs average $800 per month. If the average nursing home stay is three months, then the cost per case is $2400. Because 500 patients were discharged to nursing homes, it is projected that 85 percent (425) of these patients will not need nursing home care.
3. The cost of an emergency room admission is $100 per patient. If 50 percent of the patients previously returned to the emergency room, the benefit is estimated for 500 cases.

rather than one of mechanics. Consistently in this text, we indicate that human service clinicians and managers place a higher value on human beings than they do on things. This is not, however, the dominant value in our "bottom-line" "money-culture" society, and this acute value-tension is an ever-present element when doing a benefit–cost analysis.

There are also a number of technical issues related to benefit–cost analysis. We will briefly review a few:

1. *Opportunity Cost:* Grover Starling (1979, 698) defines opportunity cost as: "The true cost of choosing one alternative rather than another. Opportunity cost, also called alternative cost, represents the implicit cost to an individual of the highest foregone alternative." In essence, computing opportunity costs approaches comparing different programs and projects not in terms of their immediate cost, but in terms of their net economic benefits. If program A costs $175,000 and returns an economic benefit of $400,000, whereas program B costs $125,000 and returns a benefit of $250,000, then the opportunity cost for selecting the less expensive program B is $100,000.

2. *Benefit–Cost Versus Cost–Effectiveness:* When benefits are computed and associated with investments to arrive at what is the greatest benefit to society for a given amount of resource, the analysis is oriented toward benefit–cost or return on investment.

    However, when a decision is made to invest in a *specific* set of benefits (e.g., reducing alcohol abuse), the analysis of benefits and investments is oriented toward the most effective tactic (program) to reach the strategic goal. In our illustration (Figure 10.4), the investment of $300,000 in four program modalities was considered the most effective use of that resource in terms of the greatest impact (benefits) that can accrue to individual clients and to society. This type of analysis is known as cost–effectiveness analysis.

    Benefit–cost analyses are generally associated with strategy formation and strategic planning; cost–effectiveness analyses are considered an integral element of program planning.

3. *Discounting:* Because investments and benefits extend over a period of time for most programs, it is important that dollars spent in the future and benefits accrued in the future are discounted to the present in order to express all dollar amounts in the same terms. Technically, it is necessary to apply a discount rate for all computations of benefits and investments. The discount rate is usually a rate that approximates the average rate of return on private-sector investments.

4. *Unit Costs:* With the heightened concern for modern management of human services organizations, there has come pressure to relate financial data with program data. The result is unit costs. For example, the illustration for alcohol abuse–treatment programs (Figure 10.4) indicates the following unit costs:

Northside Clinic	*Per Hour*	*Per Client*
▪ Crisis intervention	$80	$480
▪ Mutual-help groups	54	675
▪ Family therapy	42	1088
▪ Individual counseling	47	840

Is this data of any value? As a policymaker, what questions would you ask? Are these costs in line with the unit costs of the other two clinics? How can the hourly cost of family therapy be the lowest while the client unit cost is the highest? As a human services manager, what questions would you ask: Why is the unit costs of some modalities higher than the others? Can we decrease the per-client cost of individual counseling from $1085 to $990 without a reduction in effectiveness?

Unit costs are vital; they can be compared in terms of time (last year, this year, next year), in terms of a standard (e.g., a national standard), or market prices (e.g., the purchase price in a contract with a private human services agency).

Budgeting

As the human services manager soon discovers, the budget is a multi-faceted administrative concept and technique. Although it is vital to program management, it is obviously one of the cornerstones of financial management. For that reason, we cover budgeting in great detail in Chapter 11.

Budgets come in different formats, but it is important to emphasize here that to be a program management tool, the budget must be *program-oriented*. As can be noted from Figure 10.4, the recommended budget is formatted as a matrix. This permits use of a line-item budget, while allowing for tracking of investments and expenditures in terms of different programs, program modalities, responsibility centers, and cost centers.

Work–Resource Scheduling

Detailed planning for program implementation is undertaken during the work–resource scheduling process. In essence, it is an attempt to determine critical resource requirements for the achievement of the objectives of the program(s), spread over the life of the effort. The key question is: Do we have enough *critical resources* to achieve that for which we will be held accountable? If the answer is no, then the human services manager has only two options: obtain increased resources or reduce the goals and objectives to be achieved.

As noted earlier, the process of strategy formation, program planning and budgeting, and work–resource scheduling is interrelated and iterative. As the decisions are being made during strategic planning and program planning, the detailed planning of work–resource scheduling must be a part of the policy-decision deliberations and is the joint responsibility of human services managers and program leaders, along with top executives and policymakers. In effect, *strategy formation and program planning and budgeting cannot be completed until work–resource scheduling is also complete.*

Work–resource scheduling is a critical pivotal element in classic program management. As Figure 10.3 indicates, scheduling of work and resources ties back to (feed backs to) strategy formation (the setting of roles, strategies, goals, and policies) and then to program planning and budgeting (the delineation of programs with their objectives, performance milestones, and effectiveness criteria). In addition, it sets the conditions for feedforward by designating for each time period the investment of critical resources and performance targets required to achieve the program and responsibility center's objectives. These are set for each time period, as well as for the cumulative year to date.

Work–resource schedules specify the *critical resources* required to achieve program objectives. Whereas a budget identifies (and controls) all resources, in a work–resource schedule, only those resources on which program achievement depends are identified.

A Model Work–Resource Schedule

Figure 10.4 illustrates a model work–resource schedule. As with all of the remaining elements of classic program management, the work–resource schedule includes the following important features:

1. The program or program modality is identified.
2. Responsibility centers are designated and identified.
3. Critical resources are specified.
4. Time periods (generally in terms of weeks, months, or quarters) are specified.
5. Year-to-date figures are given.
6. Level of resource requirements is specified.
7. Performance milestones are given for each responsibility center for each time period, for each responsiblity center for year to date, and for the program modality for time period and year to date.
8. Effectiveness criteria are given for each time period and year to date.

Several of these features need additional discussion.

Responsibility Centers.   Responsibility centers fix responsibility and accountability, and set the framework for independent self-management. Ideally organizational units or groups of employees should manage themselves along some mutually agreed-on plan (schedule), primarily so that everyone can feel invested in the mission (goals and objectives) of the organization.

Critical Resources.　Human services managers need to ask of each program: What are the most critical resources without which the program cannot meet the designated objectives? In Figure 10.4, the schedule indicates that for the Northside Clinic's Mutual-Help Group Program modality, 915 hours of group workers and 460 hours of a psychologist are required, otherwise the performance milestones of 120 clients and 1500 treatment-hours cannot be achieved during the year.

The program budget indicates all resources required; they include a large number of personnel, contractual, and commodity investments. But to accomplish the modality of mutual-help groups, the program administrator designates the group workers and psychologist as most critical for program achievement. In essence, the choice of what represents the critical resource for a schedule is up to each program leader. We should keep in mind that a schedule sets up a series of indicators that will help everyone in the organization keep track of program achievement. As long as selected critical resources are closely tied to achievement of objectives, they can serve as the focal point for a schedule.

The work–resource schedule must indicate the level of resource required to achieve the work to be accomplished. Usually, this is expressed in terms of work-hours: How many hours of effort are required to accomplish what we set out to achieve for each time period?

Year to Date.　Besides developing schedules for each period, it is important to indicate the cumulative totals. The reason is obvious. Looking ahead to management reporting, one may fall behind, for example, in either resource utilization or in achieving a milestone for the third quarter, but be ahead in the year-to-date targets. The reverse is also true. For program management and management control, administrators need to know not only if they are meeting each time period's targets, but more important, if they are also on schedule from the beginning of the program to date.

Work–Resource Assigning

Work–resource assigning builds on the predecessor elements of classic program management (strategy formation, program planning and budgeting, and work–resource scheduling) and lays the foundation for subsequent elements (work reporting, measuring, monitoring, and program-performance evaluation). Assignment can be merged with a schedule if (1) the program is so small and staff is so fixed that staff assignments stay the same all year and (2) the organization or agency is such that a staff person is only assigned to one program, full-time, all year. But when one person can devote work-hours to several programs, or when staff changes are made often, then assignments are separated from the schedules and are only made up shortly before the beginning of each time period.

A Model Work–Resource Assignment

Using Figure 10.4 as a model work–resource assignment, note several features in the assigning process. The work–resource assignment is the vehicle by which specific resources (people and equipment) are assigned to specific programs, for each time period. For example, in the model schedule, 245 treatment-hours were required for group workers during the third quarter. Now this is specifically assigned to the following:

Group Worker	Work-Hours	Clients
▪ Pamela Daly	145	18
▪ Michael Makovic	100	12

Like the schedule, the work–resource assignment contains the following features:

1. The program or program modality is identified.
2. Responsibility centers are designated and identified.
3. Critical resources category and level are specified.
4. The specific time period (generally in terms of weeks, months, or quarters [thirteen weeks]) is indicated.
5. Level of resource requirements is indicated for each critical resource for the specific time period and for the program modality for the time period.
6. Performance milestones are indicated for the specific program modality for the specific time period, for each employee for the specific time period, and for the program modality for the time period.

Several of these features need further discussion.

Assignments for Each Time Period.   Assignments are made for the same time intervals as the schedule. Our example program uses quarters (three months, thirteen weeks), and the model is an assignment for the third quarter (Jan.–March 19XY). When the system is geared toward quarters, the actual assignment would most probably be made one month prior to the initiation of the quarter. If a monthly or weekly time period is used, the actual detailed assignment will take place with sufficient lead time so that all affected will be clear on their upcoming assignment.

Identify Individual Resources and Indicate Level of Effort.   Clear designation is essential. Each person should be identified by name. Where equipment is the critical resource, the description and identification number of the equipment should be used. The level of effort, usually in work-hours, should be indicated for each of the identified specific resources.

All assigned resources, in total, should tie back to the schedule. As noted, in the model schedule, the total treatment-hours required of group workers during the third period was 245. The assignment provides further details by indicating Pamela Daly's level of 145 and Michael Makovic's 100 hours.

Performance Contributions.   A model assignment needs to show the contribution of all elements to the program's performance milestones, thus tying the system to the program's objectives. Obviously, the milestones indicated on a work–resource assignment should be the same as those on the work–resource schedule.

Work Reporting

Upon completion of the work–resource assigning element of program management, the stage is set for program implementation. The system has gone from *intention*—goals, policies, programs, objectives, budgets, plans, and schedules; to *implementation*—assignment of resources; to eventual *accomplishment*—reporting, measuring, monitoring, and evaluating.

Work reporting is a vital instrument for comparing what actually resulted from program implementation with what the intended results were supposed to be. It not only ties together the previous elements of program management, work reporting provides the basic data for the remaining elements: measuring, monitoring, and evaluating. Together these elements are known popularly as a management-information system (MIS).

Human services organizations have always made use of the MIS; but until the advent of computers, they were difficult to maintain because of the large quantities of data to process. As can be appreciated from the discussion thus far, classic program management requires the processing of large volumes of data. The methodical design of an integrated computer-based MIS provides the means by which this data processing can be automated. Such a design automatically meets each of the different types of management reporting needs, namely:

- Strategic planning: Are goals being achieved?
- Management control: Are programs on schedule? Achieving objectives? Within costs?
- Operational control: Are resources available when needed? Are resources used efficiently? Effectively?

Because the key to a successful MIS is the skillful design of computer-based, management-oriented reports, Chapter 13 discusses in greater detail the way in which computer technologies can be used for MIS purposes.

For classic program management, there are three types of management-oriented reports required, namely:

- Work reporting: The reporting of data pertinent to management
- Work measuring: The statistical manipulation of data
- Work monitoring: The use of data and statistics to evaluate program progress and performance

Each uses a selected number of data variables that are of sufficient importance to indicate to managers the degree of success of a program or operation. This notion has been discussed by Tom Peters (1988), one of the current, leading, popular management writers. In the technical MIS literature, these variables are called critical success factors.

Let us discuss the three types of management-oriented reports that are integral elements of classic program management.

A Model Work Report

Figure 10.4 provides a model for an **operational performance management report**. It contains the following features:

1. The responsibility center and program modality are identified.
2. Management level of the report and time period are designated.
3. Critical resources are specified.
4. Target resource investment is compared to actual resources invested.
5. Target performance milestones are compared with actual performance milestones reached.
6. Target effectiveness criteria are compared with actual effectiveness rates achieved.
7. Each of the data comparisons for features 4–6 above are made for the time period being reported, for year to date, for each specific critical resources (e.g., individual employee), and for the responsibility center.

The model illustrated in Figure 10.4 on page 249 ties the work report to the Northside Clinic's mutual-help group program modality for the third quarter (Jan.– March) of 19XY and for the group worker and psychologist critical resources assigned to Pamela Daly, Michael Makovic, and Harold Stenback, respectively. The only new data being reported are the *actual* data; all target data were implanted in the system by the other elements of classic program management. In essence, feedforward and feedback are both automatic with this type of report.

This model operational performance work report illustrates a basic work report. It lays the foundation for two additional elements of classic program management: work measuring and work monitoring.

Work Measuring and Work Monitoring

Management-Control Reports

A well-designed operational management report sets the stage for work measuring and monitoring, and becomes the basis for all subsequent program management operations, as shown in Figure 10.1 on page 234. Well-designed and well-executed reports provide all the necessary data to support the two important functions of management by exception and management by anticipation, as discussed in this chapter's section on program management techniques. Operational managers use such reports to control day-to-day performance. Program managers also use them to measure and monitor the progress toward achievement of program objectives (i.e., performance milestones and effectiveness criteria), and to identify quickly programs that need attention because they are behind schedule, utilizing more resources than allocated, or not achieving results. Well-designed work reports, therefore, are the foundation for measuring and monitoring program performance.

Work measuring is the analysis of quantified data, calculated usually for a comparison basis. In our model (Figure 10.4), this includes measurement of resources invested (hours worked), performance (clients treated), and effectiveness (recidivism rates).

Work measuring is the foundation of **work monitoring**, which is a systematic means of keeping track of performance progress. The reader will note from our model that work monitoring indicates the progress of the program: Is it on, ahead, or behind schedule?

There are three basic methods of displaying work measurement and monitoring data:

1. **Tables of data**. Display of data in tabular form encourages comparison of the data. For example, the data for Pamela Daly (Figure 10.4) are:

	Target	Actual
▪ Resource (work-hours)	145	147
▪ Performance (number of clients)	18	19
▪ Effectiveness (recidivism rate)	25	27

2. **Indices**. To reduce the number of columns of data and to provide a format that automatically compares actual and target, an index is formed by dividing the actual by the target. Thus, 1.00 (100 percent) means that the actual was exactly the same as the target; 0.90 means that the actual was 10 percent below the target; 1.10 means that the actual was 10 percent higher than the target. To compare the actual and target data for Pamela Daly:

- ▪ Resource (work-hours) $147 \div 145 = 1.01$ (1 percent over)
- ▪ Performance (number of clients) $19 \div 18 = 1.06$ (6 percent over)
- ▪ Effectiveness (recidivism rate) $.82 \div .80 = 1.03$ (3 percent over)

3. **Graphic displays**. On the theory that a picture is worth a thousand words, data can be shown best in graphic form. This is particularly true in the age of user-friendly desktop computers (see Chapter 13). The most popular graphic forms are *graphs*—using the x and y coordinates of a plane to show trends over time—and *bar charts*—using parallel bars, color-coded, or shaded symbols indicating time periods of data variables. The rapid expansion of computer-based, color graphic display capabilities is making this option very popular, particularly when reports have to be presented to a meeting of program managers or grant funders.

When monitoring work, a key concept is the **extent of deviation**: Was the difference between the actual and the target significant? The degree of deviation fluctuates for different programs. In some cases, a 1-percent deviation can be critical; in others, because target milestones are estimates, a 5-percent deviation can be considered acceptable. For example, the data for Pamela Daly yield the following:

YTD Work-Hours		YTD Clients Treated		YTD Recidivism Rate	
(target)	*(actual)*	*(target)*	*(actual)*	*(target)*	*(actual)*
570	565	68	69	.25	.27
0.99		1.01		1.03	
− 1 percent		+ 1 percent		+ 3 percent	

The fact that Pamela worked 1 percent less than anticipated, yet treated 1 percent more clients than expected would be considered very good, but not necessarily significant. For this type of program modality, to have a 3-percent cure rate greater than targeted could be significant.

Strategic-Planning Reports

The reader will note that, as we move from operational and management-control reports to strategic-planning reports, the data become less specific toward individual resources (employees or equipment) and become more general, focusing on responsibility and cost centers and on entire programs. Drawing on the other reports, the strategic-planning reports focus on the discernment of patterns. Developed primarily for policymaking groups, these reports attempt to view programs in macro-terms: What is the progress of the program in terms of achieving the strategic goal? Are there differences between the achievements of different programs, program modalities, and responsibility centers, such that some are more effective than others? Should we shift resources from one cost center to another to more effectively achieve our goals?

In our program-management model (Figure 10.4), two types of strategic-planning reports are presented:

- One focuses on comparing the different program modalities within the same responsibility center.

- The other focuses on comparing the same program modality among the different responsibility centers.

Both are concerned with the results of the time period being reported (third quarter [Jan.–March 19XY]) *and* on the year-to-date progress.

Neither of the strategic-planning reports focuses on the types of critical resources used or identifies the specific resource. These data can be presented to a policy board when a problem arises and additional data are requested. This highlights the principle that all types of management-oriented reports draw on the same data; they differ in their focus on different levels of organizational issues, which are repeated for purposes of emphasis:

- Strategic planning: Are goals being achieved?

- Management control: Are programs well managed? On schedule? Within costs? Achieving milestones and effectiveness criteria?

- Operational performance and control: Are resources in place to implement the day-to-day scheduled work?

Performance and Program Evaluation

The final component of classic program management is evaluation, which has two perspectives:

- Feedback: Did we do what we set out to accomplish?
- Feedforward: What should we do next?

The work reporting, measuring, and monitoring elements provide some of the data for evaluation—specifically, performance data that compare intended results with actual results, as shown in Figure 10.6.

The literature on evaluation is quite extensive, because there is widespread recognition of its importance to the human services and the subject is very complex. There is specific terminology, and one needs to devote time to acquiring this element of the system. Edward Suchman (1968) suggests the types of program-evaluation measurements listed in Table 10.8.

Performance evaluation is a skill most human services managers master quite readily. Program evaluation is more complex and is a highly technical field, one that requires extensive study. The human services manager needs to remain current with developments in this aspect of the field, while developing a professional in the organization who will be a specialist in program evaluation.

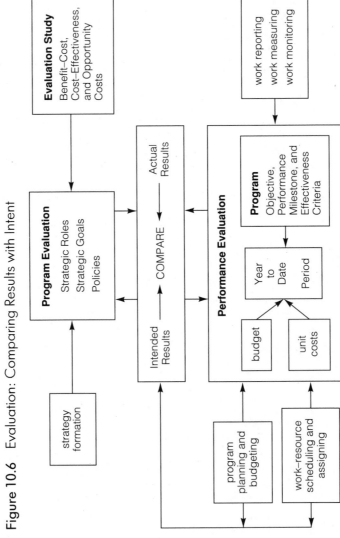

Figure 10.6 Evaluation: Comparing Results with Intent

Table 10.8   Program-Evaluation Measurements

Type	Method of Measuring	Example
Efficiency	Output/Input	4.8 client-contact hours per group worker treatment-hour.
Adequacy	Output/Need	Twelve percent of adult alcohol abusers received treatment.
Performance	Output	83 clients participated in mutual-help groups in Northside Clinic.
Effort	Input	1009 treatment-hours by group workers and psychologist.
Process	Output = A Function of Effort	If the professional treatment-hours could be doubled, the number of clients in mutual-help groups could be doubled.

Differentiating Program from Performance Evaluation

The two types of evaluations differentiate in the manner indicated in Table 10.9. In our model (Figure 10.4), both types of evaluation were illustrated for our alcohol abuse–treatment program. From this perspective, program and performance evaluation serve two different purposes:

- Program Evaluation. *Organization's missions:* Are goals being achieved effectively?
  Policy management: Are we properly guiding the agency?
- Performance Evaluation. *Control:* Are we meeting schedules? Achieving results?
  Quality: Is the work up to standard? Up to the workers' potential?

In essence, although both performance and program evaluations are inherent elements of program management, the former can be generated automatically whereas the latter require an additional, more difficult, and more specialized effort.

But regardless of which type of evaluation, both are necessary as the starting and restarting point for program planning and implementation. They place the community, policymakers, managers, and clinicians in a position to decide:

- Should we now continue, expand, contract, or revise programs?
- Should we abolish the program and take another tactic toward reaching the same goal?
- Should we pursue new goals?

The key question is, What new strategies are called for now that we have viewed the results of our effort on this issue? In effect, evaluation (program or

Table 10.9 Program and Performance Evaluation:
Alcohol Abuse–Treatment Services

Program Evaluation	Performance Evaluation		
1. Have the goals been achieved? a. Decreased alcohol dependence b. Increased use of services c. Increased employment	1. Have the program objectives been achieved?		
		Target	*Actual*
	No. of clients	400	398
	Unit costs/client	$750	$783
2. How do we measure decreased dependence on alcohol? a. Reduction in lost workdays b. Reduction in people-abuse cases c. Reduction in DWI cases	Recidivism	42%	18%
	2. How did responsibility center perform? *Mutual-Help Group:*		
3. What period of time is required to measure reduced alcohol dependence?	No. of clients	120	122
	Unit costs	$675	$645
4. How do we know if mental health clinics' services affected reduced alcohol dependence?	Recidivism	20%	15%
	Level of Resources:		
5. Which treatment modality is most effective in reducing alcohol dependence?	Group workers	915	890
	Psychologist	460	475

performance) can be viewed as *either* closing the program-management process *or* as its starting point. Both views are equally valid.

Summary

One of the most important fundamental management processes for the human services manager is a comprehensive, integrated set of administrative tools and techniques known as program management. It provides a uniform, methodical process for program planning and implementation: setting the goals of the agency and controlling the implementation of programs to ensure maximum performance. In time, it becomes the natural way for a human services manager to deal creatively and innovatively with a turbulent, changing environment.

Program management includes several sets of complex administrative techniques that are integrated to be conducive to effective management: strategy formation; program planning and budgeting; work–resource scheduling and assigning; work reporting, measuring, and monitoring; and program-performance evaluation. Program management stresses constant feedback and feedforward, continually comparing actual results with intended results, for the purpose of adaptation, change, and improvement. Collectively, the technologies of program management are the means by which the human services organization can be responsible and accountable for carrying out its mission effectively and efficiently.

11

Managing Finances

Mobilizing Resources

Effective Budgeting
Grant Acquisition
Contracting
Fund-Raising
Volunteer Management

Creative Financial Management

Summary

Good financial management skills are a necessity for human services managers. Although this is obvious during periods of decremental management, the need for good fiscal acumen in the creative management of human services programs should also be appreciated. It is important therefore at the outset of a discussion of the fundamental processes of financial management in human services organizations to stress two points: (1) All elements of financial management should be interrelated and integrated, both for good control and minimizing paperwork; (2) financial management should be interrelated with program management (discussed in Chapter 10). The latter point needs further discussion. Although financial management should be designed and carried out to support and aid program management, too often this is not true. Particularly in times of cutback management with its emphasis on "accountability," the pressure on human services managers is to exercise good fiscal management for control purposes only, to which program management is subordinated. Nothing could be more detrimental to excellence in human services management.

There is a symbiotic relationship between program management and financial management, the creative management of an agency's mission in a time of resource cutback. This should be appreciated by all involved in human services organizations. The two should not operate independent of each other or antagonistic to one another. There should not be two separate processing systems—one for financial data and the other for program data; they should be integrated into one data-processing system.

This requires compromise by both sets of professions in the agency: finance staff should orient their processes in a way that will help forecast the most effective achievement of program goals; human services professionals should provide data that orient financial data in program terms. To the human services manager goes the difficult task of setting the climate where both financial and program professionals recognize that they are mutual, sharing members of the same team. In an era of cutback management, such a task will be a gargantuan challenge for the reader—student and practitioner.

Following a discussion of the ways in which finance administration differs for public and nonprofit organizations, we turn our attention to the elements of financial management: accounting and bookkeeping, budget preparation and execution, financial statements and fiscal reporting, controls, fund-raising and managing finances. The latter is of extreme importance for it focuses on strategies that human services organizations need to explore and exploit to survive during a period in our society when major resource adjustments are being made among the different sectors of the economy, while still finding more effective means of carrying out organizational missions.

Case 11.1

Part 2: River City, Inc.*

Nan Rogers had just about finished her orientation for Betty McDermott, River City's director of a new entity—Young Family Support Centers. "For us, Betty, financial management follows three simple guidelines: who's the client; who's paying; what's the service."

"Come on, Nan," Betty responded, "it must be more complicated than that. When I was with the state Department of Children and Youth, River City had a great reputation. Accurate and reliable accounting reports, cost and productivity reports broken down by cost center, responsibility centers, clients, and geographic area. We used the budget estimates, performance and productivity analyses you submitted in your proposals as a guideline for negotiating with other agencies. What's your secret, a good accounting system?"

"That, of course," Nan responded, "and a finance director who is gentle but firm. But I would say that the key is comprehensive financial and programmatic data that are collected from two forms and then maintained in a computer system that has great flexibility for data analysis."

"What are the two forms?" Betty asked.

Nan smiled. "How did you know I was about to get around to that part of your orientation? These two forms are a must and will be among your first tasks: making sure that they are filled out religiously and accurately. The first is straightforward: a registration form for new clients, which on one piece of paper provides us with the necessary demographic data. It also provides all financial data we need—source of payment, responsible payor, employer where appropriate—plus authorization for release of data to third-party payers when necessary."

"The second form," Nan continued, "that's the key one. It's completed by each clinician every day. Here, look at the data it requires."

- Client: Number and name
- Program Data: Service code, program–team code, diagnosis code, units of service, and number seen

- Financial Data: Third party to be billed, charge for visit, and source of payment
- Logistics: time and location code

"By the way, Betty, this is an *exception document:* data are entered only if there is a change from the basic data in the computer. So completing this daily transaction register is simpler than most people think."

"You're telling me, all accounting and program data come from these two forms," Betty asked with a slight puzzled look.

Nan smiled. "It's amazing. We do have a great reputation for quick, accurate, and comprehensive financial and program reports. In addition, our cost and productivity analyses are our hallmark. Our funds come from four state agencies (mental health, health, social services, and education), from the city, from the United Way, from two foundations, from the school district, from several corporations in the area, and, of course, from third-party payers. All of them have great confidence in the reliability of our financial data."

Betty frowned. "This is not nice to ask, Nan, but we've known each other for a long time. Is River City a business or a community services agency?"

"I felt that way when I first came, Betty. But now I know that the two not only can be compatible, but also set a tone, for all of us who work for River City. That projects itself to our clients and to our community. Sure these data put us in a position to respond quickly to opportunities in the community. A year from now, let's take a look at this. See if you come to the same conclusion I've reached. But don't ask me why—having a reputation for being good in managing finances translates into having a good reputation in delivering services. Most important of all, our clients feel good about coming to River City."

"I have to admit, Nan," Betty commented, "part of the reason why I accepted your offer to come here was because of your great reputation in the community. If the secret of that reputation are these two forms, maybe you ought to patent them!"

"No," Nan responded, "if anything, we should share them with other agencies."

*Parts 1 and 3 of the River City case can be found in Chapters 8 and 16, respectively.

Perhaps the best way to begin the discussion is to use River City, Inc., once again as a case to illustrate the critical nature of sound financial management for creative human services management. It illustrates an important point. When a human services agency is perceived to have excellent financial management, it is assumed that the agency's ability to manage services is also effective. The human services manager strives therefore to achieve excellence in financial management as a foundation for service effectiveness.

Peculiarities of Public and Nonprofit Organizational Finances

Not only are there important differences between financial management for commercial organizations and that of public–nonprofit organizations, their fiscal environments are very different. In all governments, financial management systems are set by other units: budget systems, accounting–bookkeeping systems, fiscal reporting, internal control, external control—all are preset. When a human services manager takes a job in federal, state, or local government, one of the first areas of attention must be to become familiar with the detailed standard operating procedures (SOPs) for financial management of that government.

Increasingly, these are based on GAAFR (government accounting, auditing, and fiscal reporting) statements, which are becoming required accounting guidelines for all government jurisdictions in the United States (see National Council on Government Accounting, 1979). Without that specific knowledge, there will be continual problems—from the most insignificant to the most critical. The human services manager most likely will have to draw on the knowledge and talents of someone experienced in that government, who knows the detailed regulations and, more important, knows the key actors in the financial management organizational units. In addition, to provide the data necessary to support program management needed for human services environments (ergo, the mission and client paradigms), it may be necessary to create an additional financial management system because most central government financial systems do not support program management (i.e., they are oriented largely toward the control paradigm).

Most human services managers in large governments may not be able to live up to performance criteria of good financial management. If efficient payment of bills in seven calendar days is an ideal SOP, what do you do when two months is the existing time period for invoice payments in your government? Even recognition that the untrusting public insists on multiple checks and balances by four different agencies, which results in the two-month processing period, does not help the human services manager. He is encumbered in trying to develop a basic administrative approach that creates an environment conducive to efficiency and effectiveness.

In addition, in large public organizations, human service managers may have very limited roles to play in the financial management system: cash management or invoice processing most likely will be the responsibility of a separate government unit. Although this relieves the human services manager from some of the burden of financial management, it also creates problems. Fiscal reporting and cost accounting, both critical for program management, may become headaches. The central government's SOPs may retard, not aid, a human services agency in maintaining its own cost accounts because central financial reports may be four to eight weeks out of date by the time they are received.

But perhaps the greatest difference between public–nonprofit organizational financial management and that found in commercial organizations is the lack of ability to measure profit or loss and the incentives surrounding this fact. But even without the profit incentive, an approach to efficient and productive financial management is as valid in the world of government and nonprofit organizations as it is in commercial organizations. This can, and should be, an ideal for human services managers.

Accounting and Bookkeeping

As already noted, developing a quality accounting system for a human services organization may not be in the hands of the administrator—it may be in existence when she accepts the position. But where possible, a wise human services manager will seek expert help, from board member–staff–consultant, in setting up and improving the accounting system. It is a complex, dynamic field that needs the expertise of a specialist.

Figure 11.1 provides an overview of the elements of an accounting system—the starting point for our discussion of financial management.

The reader notes that at the heart of the system is the equation:

$$\text{Assets} = \text{Liabilities} + \text{Fund Balance}$$
$$(\text{Owned}) = (\text{Owed}) + (\text{Worth–Equity})$$

This equation should be a model for human services management; it sets the conditions for good account record keeping, and even more important, good control. Discussing bookkeeping systems will help clarify the point.

Bookkeeping Systems

Bookkeeping systems can proceed from the most simple manual to the most complex computerized system. In general, they can be categorized as follows.

Accounting Bases. **Cash accounting** indicates the recording of a financial transaction when it is in the form of cash only. An **accrual system** records the transaction when it occurs: money is due or owed even though no cash is involved. Table 11.1 illustrates the difference. In effect, the cash basis of bookkeeping records transactions only when cash passes to or from the agency regardless of when the transaction actually takes place.

The accrual basis of bookkeeping is real time: Record the transaction (cash in or cash out) at the moment when the transaction takes place. When this actually occurs is the issue; for example, should a $500 typewriter expenditure be recorded as an expense when (1) The requisition was submitted to the purchasing officer? (2) The order was placed with the manufacturer? (3) The type-

Figure 11.1   Accounting System

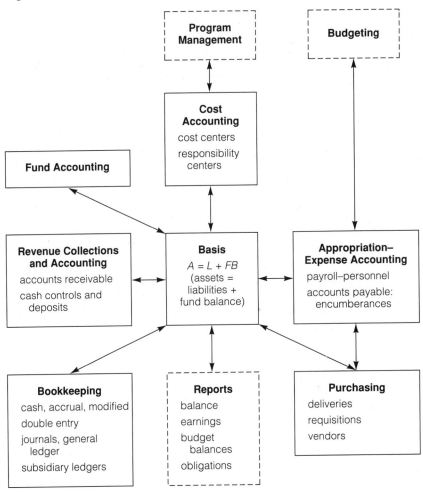

writer was actually received? (4) The manufacturer's invoice was received? Some accrual systems record the expenditure as an *accounts payable* when the order is placed; in a cash system, the order creates an encumbrance until the payment is made; for example, if a human services manager has $1000 in an office equipment account, in a cash system, what remains to be spent is calculated thus:

- Budget $1000
- Minus expenditure —
- Minus encumbrance 500
- Balance available $ 500

Table 11.1 Cash Versus Accrual

		Cash System	Accrual System
Example 1: J. Jones visits the family clinic and receives $50 worth of services.			
Situation (a):	Mr. Jones pays the $50 before leaving the clinic.		
	(a) Add to *Revenues*	$50	$50
Situation (b):	Mr. Jones does not pay, but receives a bill for $50.		
	(b) Add to *Revenues*	—	$50
Example 2: The family health clinic purchases a $500 typewriter.			
Situation (c):	Typewriter delivered; invoice is enclosed.		
	(c) Add to *Office Expenses*	—	$500
Situation (d):	Check for $500 is mailed to the typewriter company.		
	(d) Add to *Office Expenses*	$500	$500

In the accrual system, the accounts payable achieves the same result by immediately reducing the available balance for the office equipment account.

The modified accrual or modified cash basis of bookkeeping is used by a large number of public–nonprofit human service organizations. It records for revenues—only on a cash basis (the cash system); for expenditures—when committed (the accrual system). In our example in Table 11.1, the modified accrual basis would record Mr. Jones's $50 only when the cash was received, but would record the expenditure for the typewriter when it was ordered. Note that this is a very conservative bookkeeping system; depending on the situation, it is also a sound approach to financial management.

Cash versus accrual has many implications, too numerous to discuss. Let us indicate just two issues:

1. An accurate picture of the agency's finances: the accrual system reflects the real financial status of an agency.
2. Cash management: money makes money; thus, knowledge of your cash position is critical. To some, financial management is the ability to maintain use of available cash for optimum program achievement. This means, make money with your money. If a check is written today, it will not be cashed for three to seven days; why not keep the cash invested for that period of time to earn interest for your agency, rather than deducting it from your bookkeeping system's balance when the check is written? Otherwise, you make banks rich because they earn the interest of your agency's money.

Because each human services organization is different, it is best to start conservatively and use a modified accrual basis for your bookkeeping system until the expertise is available for a more aggressive financial management approach.

Figure 11.2   Double-Entry Bookkeeping System: (a) Before
Payment—Opening Balances; (b) Transaction—the
Payment; (c) After Payment—Closing Balances

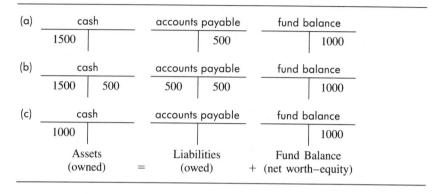

Method of Recording Financial Transactions.   The simplest bookkeeping system is a checkbook, with which the reader is quite familiar; in effect, this is a **single-entry system**, which provides a chronological recording of financial transactions and reflects the current available cash in your agency. But if you want to summarize the total expenses of one type of budget item (i.e., salaries), you have to go through your checkbook stubs, categorize check payments, and add up subtotals.

Double-entry bookkeeping is a method of recording financial transactions that goes back to the central formula of Figure 11.1:

$$\text{Assets} = \text{Liabilities} + \text{Fund Balance}$$

Each bookkeeping entry is made in a way that keeps both sides of the equation in balance in a way of knowing if your bookkeeping system is in balance.

Under the double-entry system, each account is a **T account** (because graphically it looks like a *T*). A typical T account for cash can be seen in Figure 11.2. A **debit** and a **credit** reflect the two sides of the transaction, with the debit recorded on the left side of the T account and the credit recorded on the right side.

Let us look at an example of double-entry bookkeeping using T accounts, using the following transactions:

Opening Balances

- Cash $1500
- Accounts payable $500
- Fund balance $1000

Transaction

- We pay the $500 (currently encumbered in our accounts payable) we owe the manufacturer for the typewriter they sent us when we ordered it.

Closing Balances

- Cash $1000
- Fund balance $1000

Figure 11.2 records the double-entry bookkeeping entries for the above transaction. Note that the system is in balance because at all times both sides of the equation are equal.

Bookkeeping and accounting may seem confusing initially, but with a little effort, a working familiarity of the subject can be acquired. A minimum knowledge is vital in order to explore financial management issues and not to be continually at a disadvantage with accounting specialists. The human services manager therefore should devote energy to acquiring basic knowledge and skills in bookkeeping and accounting.

Types of Records.   The last subject necessary for any discussion of bookkeeping systems is the nature of the different records. These can be journals, books, and ledgers. **Journals** are usually consecutive recordings of bookkeeping transactions. They indicate the date of the transaction, an explanation of the transaction, its amount, and the individual accounts affected. **Books** are used to provide an up-to-date analysis of transactions. The **cash receipts** and **cash disbursement** books are good examples. Use of these two books represents a more elaborate bookkeeping system than does the checkbook. Books are used with either single-entry or double-entry systems. In effect, a book lists chronologically, indicating the date and total amount, and then records the transaction under separate columns, with each column headed with a different category of transaction. (For example, a cash receipts book for a church would have columns for each of the following: plate collections, envelopes and pledges, special gifts, nursery school, and miscellaneous. The reader probably can understand why bookkeepers use multicolumn paper.) When a page is completed in a book, all columns are totaled and balanced. Usually transactions are kept for the month and totals transferred to the beginning of the following month. **Ledgers** are individual accounts. They are either general or detailed (subsidiary).

Types of Accounts.   There are several major types of accounts that are generally found in public and nonprofit human services organizations, namely: funds, revenues, expenditures, and appropriations.

- *Fund Accounting.* The basis of most human services organizational accounting is fund accounting, which Malvern Gross and William Warshauer define as "a system of accounting in which separate records are kept for assets restricted . . . to certain specific purposes or uses" (1979, 26). In

Table 11.2 Accounting Code Structure

Expenditure Classification Scheme	Code	Example
000 Fund	001	General
0 Function	1	General government
00 Department–program	07	Finance
00 Division–service–activity–program	07	Purchasing
00 Performance cost center	02	Procurement
00 Job, task, project, etc.	02	Bid solicitation
0 Statutory analysis	1	Salaries and wages
00 Resources	01	Work time

An example of the application of the classification scheme to a division of the finance department is presented at the right-hand side of the exhibit.

Source: City of Cambridge Budget Manual.

essence, fund accounting is a system in which all financial transactions for revenues and expenditures are separated by their source: taxes, grants, subsidies, fees, gifts, endowments, and so forth. For government agencies, the revenues and expenditures related to the basic budget are usually called the **general fund**. For federal agencies, the general fund is usually based on income taxes; for state governments it is usually a combination of sales tax–corporate tax–income tax; for local government, it is usually property taxes. For nonprofit organizations, the general fund is usually based on fees, fund raising, or United Way subsidies.

The vast majority of human services organizations have separate sources of funding for which they must keep separate accounting for the in flow and out flow for each source. It is not atypical to find a nonprofit or public agency with several human services programs, each of which can have two or more sources of funding. Most human services organizations have several different sources of funds for which they are required to maintain separate accounting systems. Usually, each fund has an identical accounting system, but each is kept separately, one from the other. This task is simplified by requiring all financial transactions to be coded; the first category in the accounting code structure is fund. Table 11.2 shows an example of a municipal accounting code structure; note how fund is the first code group for expenditures.

- *Revenue Accounting.* Because resources of a human services organization are so critical, an accounting system is developed to keep order and control in the recording of their receipt. For public agencies, usually the revenue accounting system is predetermined and maintained by a separate tax (revenue) department. Even so, large public human services departments and institutions have financial directors or chief fiscal officers who either keep the original revenue accounting records or receive data from a central financial department that permits them to maintain revenue accounts. Tax collections are usually the responsibility of a separate government agency (i.e., tax collector, revenue departments). But the receipt of funds from clients or other organizations (e.g., fees charges, third-party payments, grants, gifts) are collected by human services organizations in an accounting control system that keeps revenue accounts both in the agency and in the central revenue collection department.

Nonprofit, private human services organizations have peculiar needs for their revenue accounting. For example, where fund-raising is a major source of revenue, the system must be set up to track the collection of payments on pledges. Thus, detailed accounts receivable for pledges must be maintained for each donor. In addition, where the agency depends on third-party payments, the revenue accounts must be monitored to ensure that reimbursement billings are presented to the third-party payor and ultimately received.

Revenue accounting systems relate to issues of depositing funds in a bank and to cash management and cash flow. Each of these topics will be discussed briefly later in the chapter.

■ *Expenditure or Appropriation Accounting.* Before discussing these types of accounts, it is important to point out that some authors (Lehan 1980) use the word *investment* rather than *expenditure* on the theory that a public or nonprofit organization makes an investment for the purpose of returning to society a specific benefit. This has already been presented in Chapter 10 in the discussion of cost–benefit and ROI (return on investment).

The expenditure (investment) accounting systems for public and nonprofit agencies are usually based on budgets—how much was appropriated to each agency. Appropriation accounting reports show total appropriations broken down into a system of accounts that controls each item of investment (e.g., salaries by department). The level of detail in an appropriation accounting system is usually uniform for the total government jurisdiction, and the human services agency usually has to conform. The level of detail in the expenditure (investment) accounting is tied to the level of detail of the budget appropriation. For example, the amount of photocopying the public nurses are permitted in the agency can be limited by the photocopy line item appropriation in their budget. If they expend this amount with two months left in the fiscal year, they must find other sources (charge photocopying to a nonbudgeted fund or request a transfer of a surplus from another appropriation account).

Generally, the two major elements of an appropriation or investment (expenditure) accounting system are payroll (personnel costs usually add up to 60 percent or more of an agency's budget) and the purchase of goods and services. In most government units, this is called the **accounts payable** component in the accounting system: for each commodity or service purchased or contracted for, the amount due is posted for each vendor and invoice payment initiated. The accounts are twofold: one for each vendor–contractor; the other for the type of investment (e.g., rent, utilities, office supplies, consulting, etc.). As already noted, in some human services organizations an encumbrance is made to the investment (expenditure) accounting system when an intent to purchase becomes official (e.g., a purchase order is issued). This restricts the remaining amount of the unexpended funds in the impacted records.

Basic Accounting System Elements

Are there common elements to be found in every accounting system? Yes . . . three: the fiscal year, the accounting code structure, and a standard chart of accounts.

Fiscal Year. Every organization has a fiscal year. In state or local governments, this is usually July 1 of this year to June 30 of next year. In the federal government, it is October 1 of this year to September 30 of next year. Nonprofit organizations select their own fiscal year. It could coincide with the calendar year (January 1 through December 31 of the same year).

A fiscal year can be a twelve-month period beginning the first of any month. Usually the fiscal year selected is related to the calendar of the policy group (Congress or a state legislature) or to the articles of incorporation of the nonprofit organization.

Accounting Code Structure. It is generally accepted that every accounting system should have a common account-numbering system that is used for all accounting transactions. For the public human services agency, this may be predetermined and applied to all government departments in the jurisdiction. Nonprofit human services organizations usually develop their own, although some are probably influenced by funders, such as the United Way.

Table 11.2 presents an example of an accounting code structure for expenditures. One can note that it is composed of several levels to provide sufficient data for accounting (the control paradigm) and program management (the mission paradigm). If a system were totally client-paradigm oriented, it would attempt to develop a system in which accounting data is organized for each client or each group of clients. This would necessitate adding a client code category to the account code structure.

Note in Table 11.2 that the first code group in the structure is fund. This relates to our discussion that indicates that the basis of public and nonprofit organizational accounting is fund accounting.

Chart of Accounts. All human services organizations will have an accounting system that uses a common chart of accounts. It is a classification of all revenue and expenditure accounts with a sequenced set of account-coding numbers. Each agency sets up their own chart of accounts; but in some cases, the chart of accounts is imposed by the association, federation, funder, or government with whom the agency relates. For example, a United Way agency of an area would require all human services organizations it funds to use the same account code structure for supplies, rent, utilities, and other expenses.

A government account code structure would be more complex. For example, a municipality would have account code groupings: 30(N) general operations, 31(N) professional-technical services, 32(N) plant operation, 33(N) plant maintenance, and so on. Each of the above then is further subdivided; plant operation (32[N]), for example, would be detail coded as follows: 320 fuel, 321 power, 322 cleaning supplies–services, 323 security services, 324 rent, 325 insurance, 326 extermination supplies–services, 327 snow removal, and 328 depreciation. The human services manager can anticipate using a chart of accounts for the organization, one that will tie into the larger jurisdiction or to other human services organizations.

Cost Accounting

In most human services organizations, accounting data and program data flow in two unrelated information streams. Unless these separate systems are interrelated, effective program management is impossible because unit costs cannot be developed for cost centers or responsibility centers. As you recall from our Chapter 10 discussion, both are essential for classic program management.

The two separate streams of data (accounting and program) can be interrelated by reporting *every* employee's time and effort by programs, services, and clients. The key technical issue is reporting (i.e., charging) staff time appropriately. As Table 11.2 indicates, the account code structure is the key integrating device because it provides sufficient details so that costs can be aggregated by any level of investment (expenditure) classification needed. When accounting records—for personnel wages and salaries, commodities, contracts, and so on—are maintained in detailed coded fashion, the organization is maintaining cost accounting.

To arrive at unit costs, it is necessary to arrive at a method of allocating fixed costs to different cost centers (e.g., programs, responsibility centers). **Fixed costs** are considered the overhead of an agency (e.g., rent, heat, electricity); **variable costs** (e.g., wages, supplies) increase or decrease with the volume of clients. Accountants and budget analysts have experience in allocating fixed costs. Edward Lehan (1981) explores this issue because the allocation method selected has significant implications for the human services manager concerned with an accounting system that is sufficiently dynamic to permit creative management.

Cost accounting is vital for human services management; it provides the opportunity ultimately to permit each client to be a cost center. This becomes the basis for integrated, individualized services delivery, an important building block for transorganizational human services systems, which will be explored in detail in Part V of this text (systemic management). In recent years, health systems have shifted over to a cost-accounting system that makes each patient a cost center. The technique used was the DRG (diagnostic-related groups) that classify 383 types of cases encountered in the hospital acute-care setting; each DRG represents a class of patients requiring similar hospital services. The development of the DRGs was primarily a move toward health-cost containment. It nevertheless provides the basis for permitting each patient to be a cost center.

The ability to permit each patient in a hospital, each pupil in a school, each client of a social services agency, or each participant in a recreation program to become a cost center provides the opportunity to fashion human services systems infinitely more effective. For the creative, dynamic human services manager, cost accounting therefore is a necessary prerequisite to shaping human services systems that respond in a more dynamic fashion to the rapidly changing needs of people and community.

However, implementing cost accounting in a human services agency is not a technical issue primarily. In most agencies, it meets with resistance: "It is too much work" is argued both by accountants–bookkeepers and by program leaders. More important, it is resisted by human services professionals who react strongly against the notion that they should complete time reports that ultimately place a cost on client services and on human lives. They view cost accounting as a system imposed by managers for control purposes; they fail to recognize a client-paradigm and mission-paradigm value that is the focus of a Michael Jackson hit song: "If you want to change the world, start with the person in your mirror!"

The issue is not control-oriented; rather it is client-oriented. Improving the impact of human services systems on clients is a shared goal for everyone in the human services. Knowing whether or not improvements have been achieved requires some degree of measurement, not only in aggregate terms but also in terms of each client. This is the purpose of cost accounting in a human services agency.

Purchasing and Procurement

In most human services organizations, the procurement of commodities and contractual services is centralized under the financial unit. For public and many nonprofit agencies, standardized procedures are put into place to cover the total purchasing process from initial requisition to delivery of the item or service purchased.

Depending on the dollar amount of the procurement, public announcement is required, setting forth the specifications of the commodities of services sought. Bids are solicited through public announcements or from a list of vendors who apply in advance for certification of reliability. The bids are opened in a public meeting. They are prioritized according to the extent of meeting the required specifications and lowest dollar amount, and selection is made according to both the lowest dollar amount of the bid and effectiveness for meeting the "specs." A purchase order is issued and receipt of the commodities or services is verified, following which payment is initiated on the vendor's invoice.

For items that will cost below a minimum amount, the human services manager may solicit three bids and submit them to the central purchasing unit, which then makes a selection based on the data presented. The same procedures are permissible in emergencies or where time is critical (e.g., purchasing a vital part for one of the agency's cars).

Initially, purchasing was centralized to avoid favoritism or nepotism. It was an attempt to guarantee *equal access* by any vendor, giving them equal opportunity to sell their commodities or services to the agency. With the thrust of professional human services management, *economy* became the second rationale for central purchasing—finding the least expensive commodity or services that meets minimum specifications. Economy can also be achieved by aggregating all agency purchasing requirements and securing lower prices because of bulk purchases.

Equal access and economy are inherent management values in centralized purchasing. This coincides with fundamental human services values. However, the trade-off is time and paperwork. The paperwork procedures for centralized purchasing generally has a built-in time interval of several weeks between the request for the commodity–service and its delivery. In addition, the time between receipt of the item and payment to the vendor can also take weeks, with all of the necessary checks and balances of internal control. The amount of paper (i.e., red tape) is significant, regardless of the dollar amount of the purchase.

The human services manager attempts to find the means for balancing the values of equal access and economy with the overall efficiency and paperwork burden of the agency, giving program leaders the flexibility to implement with dispatch. This is usually achieved by planning major purchases well in advance of their need in program implementation. In addition, purchasing regulations and procedures are analyzed to balance central control with program-management flexibility, and different arrangements are developed. For instance, an annual bidding process and selection of a vendor results in an *open contract,* permitting agency employees to procure items during the year from the agreed-upon price list (e.g., for office supplies). In recent times, purchasing cooperatives, or consortia, have been developed by a number of human services agencies to secure the advantage of bulk purchasing.

Recently, centralized purchasing has been used as a policy vehicle: Human services policymakers and managers use the purchasing power of the agency to help minority or female-owned businesses, to support vendors based in the community, or to refuse to purchase from vendors whose companies do not have an affirmative action program. Although this is controversial, it does recognize the baseline human services commitment of the agency.

When used in an efficient and balanced fashion, centralized purchasing and procurement of commodities and services for human services organizations is an important element of effective management of finances.

Budgeting

As the student and practitioner in human services management soon discovers, the budget is a many-splendored administrative tool. As a general-purpose mechanism, budgeting is essential to such subjects as strategic management, program management, self-management, team management, and human services policy development and planning. But whatever else it might be, budgeting is a fundamental management process, one of the most essential. Thus, its mastery is vital for every human services manager.

There are two equally important elements of budgeting: preparation and execution. Both are critical for human services management. Budget preparation includes a series of activities that result in the final adoption of the organization's annual budget. Ideally, it involves all employees of an organization (e.g., clerical, professional, program leaders, and managers), policymakers of the organization (e.g., the board or politically elected legislative body), and members of the community, both individuals and groups.

Budget execution involves an additional set of activities that use the organization's adopted budget. Although the budget is viewed differently by different groups related to a human services organization, budget execution is the vehicle by which things get done, services get delivered, and the human services environment is shaped. Budget execution is also the brake that keeps human services managers under control—either by the chief executive, the policy group, the client group, or the community itself. It is even the means by which the human services manager exercises self-control. These subjects are discussed next.

The Nature of Budget Preparation

A Political Process. Whether it is for political forces and pressure groups in a government, or interest groups representing client groups that attempt to influence the board of directors of private, nonprofit agencies, the budget is the focal point of the resource-allocation process. Thus, budget preparation is a highly political process in which decisions are made on policy issues: level of services in the community, extent to which public funds will leverage private investments in services, and so on.

During periods of decremental management, reducing or abolishing services are the two major fiscal strategies. But there are two other critical strategies necessary for budget preparation:

- **Goal Displacement**. Increased investment, for example, in elderly services is more important (provides a greater societal return–benefit) than
  continued investment in public school education, so our increased program
  needs can be funded at the expense of decreasing public school education
  needs (e.g., decreased school population compared to increasing elderly
  population).

- **Means Substitution**. For example, using a more productive means of
  achieving the same goal—that is, public school education is still important—we can develop a more efficient system of education by reducing the
  number of schools and the days needed for school while increasing instruction through the community cable TV system.

Whichever the rationale, each human services organization function
and program is competing for the same resources and must convince policymakers of its relative worth. Thus, in times of decremental, as well as incremental, management, the above strategies are important. Viewed as a
political process, the rationality and logic of budget preparation may have
to be balanced with the ability of human services officials and administrators to exert political influence, either directly or through interest groups.
(The reader should note that the term *goal displacement* is used here specifically from a budget perspective; from an operational perspective, the
term customarily refers to situations where means becomes ends, and thus
displace the goals of an agency.)

Many policies in public and nonprofit organizations are never stated as
such. Instead, they find expression in a budget that therefore becomes a
political statement setting forth the organization's (or jurisdiction's) policies. As a political document, the budget essentially defines strategic roles
for the organization; sets service levels; adjusts the economy, shifting resources from one sector to the other and/or adding value to the economy;
and defines the parameters for the execution of programs.

A Program-Planning Process.   The budget and its preparation are also a process for planning the agency's programs. It requires detailed description of
goals, objectives, program milestones, effectiveness criteria, and resource requirements. It also requires advance estimates of the likelihood that the resources to be budgeted are adequate for the end results expected. If administrators and agencies are to be held accountable, they need to set forth that which
can be expected for a given level of resources.

When the budget is considered a program-planning document, concern
shifts to linking results to resources. This shifts the focus to preparing sufficiently detailed plans for program implementation that gives everyone—
clients, professionals, administrators, and policymakers—the assurance that
what the human services organization commits itself to do can indeed be
accomplished.

A Management Process.   The budget-preparation process is used by human services managers to review annually each unit in the organization—its programs, processes, and procedures. It is an opportunity for "show and tell"— to describe accomplishments and to provide the rationale for future needs. A prime concern of human services management is program implementation. The **budget** therefore is a program-management document that focuses on cost and responsibility centers and the degree to which performance milestones and effectiveness criteria have been met.

As a management process, budget preparation is tied to other administration functions, all of which are focused on achieving program service and cost objectives.

An Accounting Process.   The results of the budget-preparation process become the benchmarks for the accounting system. To control the flow of funds— into and out of an agency—accountants need revenue and investment (expenditure) account names, identification numbers, and amounts in each account. The budget-preparation process provides these, and they become the basis for the initiation of the annual appropriation (budget) accounting system.

From an accounting control perspective, budgeting is dominated by accountants and bookkeepers who approve or disapprove financial transactions. Human services managers and direct-service professionals are concerned with what is the result of agency-resource investments (expenditures)—for example, the effectiveness of programs and services to clients. Financial officials and accountants rarely think in these terms. Using the budget document as their authority, they focus on the resource itself:

- Is it available?
- Is it being expended in accordance with the proper budget account?
- Is the budget account in jeopardy of being overexpended?

The management ability of human services administrators will be judged on the basis of their accounting control of the budget. It is an important corollary to effective program management.

A Human Process.   One often forgets that the budget process is a human process that pits one human being (or a group of human beings) against another in a competitive stance. The budget-preparation process ultimately has a large impact on humans: first, on clients; second, on the people who will implement the budget—the staff of a human services agency, for example—and on the people in the community who stand to gain or lose. The human services administrator therefore needs skills in relating to and communicating with other people if the budget-preparation process is to be successful from the vantage point of his agency and society.

A Process for Altering the Future.   Perhaps the most important aspect of budget preparation for human services management is that it is a process by which the future can be altered. Because a budget expresses (1) where the organization will be by the end of the next fiscal year (which in terms of the budget preparation calendar can be eighteen to twenty-four months in the future) and (2) what should be done to see that the future point is reached, the human services manager can take the results of human services planning and use the budget-preparation process as a vital mechanism for trying to change the future, albeit in incremental steps. When part of a multiyear effort, as a means of altering the future, budgeting preparation is thus critical for human services management.

Budget-Preparation Mechanisms

There are several important mechanisms that the human services manager can use for preparing a budget: the budget format, the program memorandum, the schedule, data accumulation, meetings–hearings–presentations, staff utilization, and follow-up. Each is briefly discussed.

The Budget Format.   Remember: "Formats are important! People tend to think about what is put before them." With that statement, Lehan (1981) focuses on what he considers probably the most critical element of the budgeting process—the format. The basic budget format is one that is oriented toward expressing expenditures (investments) in terms of objects (i.e., personal services, contractual services, commodities, etc.). It is called the **line-item budget** (LIB). In the thirty-year period following World War II (1945–1975), several new budget formats were developed to express new approaches to budgeting. Table 11.3 summarizes these.

Each approach is based on a different budget format. That the format is critical can be seen from the three examples of the identical budget, used for the Alcohol Abuse–Treatment Services illustration in Chapter 10. Table 11.4 is the traditional line-item budget (LIB); Table 11.5 is a performance budget (PerB); and Table 11.6 is a program budget (ProB). The LIB tells little about the programs of the agency beyond its total resource-investment requirement. The PerB provides performance, effective criteria, and unit-cost data that focus on a number of accountability, performance, client-impact, and productivity issues. Only the ProB begins to format the data that can be used to consider issues of cost–benefit and ROI. Format, and thus the budget approach, is a critical consideration for human services management.

LIBs (or historical budgets) focus on increments: What is the incremental increase of next year's request over this year's budget? Is it greater than the inflation rate? If so, why? But other budget formats focus on a number of

Table 11.3   Overview of Different Formats
and Approaches to Budgeting

Type of Budget	Emphasis	Distinguishing Features	Whose Budget?
Line item–historical (LIB)	Cost for people, commodity, and contractual investments	Accounting reports comparing previous years' expenses to budget requests broken down by expense item and account number code (expense objects)	Accountants
Performance (PerB)	Relates investments to units of work performed or accomplished	Time reports; performance reports; cost criteria; accounting reports by objects, performance, and unit costs	Managers
Program-oriented (ProB) (PPBS)	Total costs of programs–services Contribution of investments to goals and objectives Comparative worth of alternative programs	Issue paper (program memorandum): goal statement, milestones, performance criteria, alternatives Cross classification of investments cost–benefit analyses Time and performance reporting Budgeting reports by objects, programs, services, or cost centers	Economists, planners
Zero-base (ZBB)	Comparative service output levels related to different investment levels Prioritized service, program activities of organization Reassess programs and services de novo	Program structure Service decision packages (with levels of investment service outcomes) Priority lists Performance reporting Time reporting	Taxpayers, consumers

NOTE: The acronyms are adapted from Lehan (1981) who differentiates a program budget (ProB) from a program-planning budgeting system (PPBS).

issues that permit use of a number of several administrative techniques and tools that lead to more sophisticated and creative human services management. In these newer formats, Lehan (1981) lists eleven elements of a model budget (Table 11.7).

Table 11.4 Line-Item Budget (LIB)

Expenditure Classification	1990–1991 Budget	1991–1992 Proposed	1991–1992 Approved
Personnel			
110 Professional	$104,300	$122,800	$120,450
120 Administrative	44,200	56,275	52,200
130 Benefits	31,500	40,925	37,850
100 TOTAL Personnel	$180,000	$220,000	$210,500
Contractual			
210 Occupancy	$36,800	$41,650	$39,950
220 Maintenance	11,200	17,950	14,250
230 Telephone	16,650	19,850	18,125
240 Printing	10,350	16,750	14,950
200 TOTAL Contractual	$75,000	$96,200	$87,275
Commodities			
310 Supplies	$14,750	$17,150	$16,350
320 Postage and shipping	11,225	14,400	13,575
330 Professional development	10,750	12,350	11,125
340 Travel	6,325	8,400	7,950
350 Dues	1,950	2,350	2,050
300 TOTAL Commodities	$45,000	$54,650	$51,050
TOTAL EXPENDITURES	$300,000	$370,850	$348,825

Table 11.5 Performance Budget (PerB)

Expenditures	1990–1991 Budget	1991–1992 Proposed
Personnel	$180,000	$220,000
Contractual	75,000	96,200
Commodities	45,000	54,650
TOTAL EXPENDITURES	$300,000	$370,850
Performance Data		
Milestones:		
Clients	400	525
Treatment-hours	6,000	8,050
Effectiveness criteria:		
Recidivism rate	.42	.38
Unit costs:		
Per client	$750	$706
Per hour	$50	$46

Table 11.6   Program Budget (ProB)

Program Modality	1990–1991			
	Personnel	Contractual	Commodities	TOTAL
Crisis intervention	$ 18,000	$19,500	$10,500	$ 48,000
Mutual-help groups	45,000	21,000	15,000	81,000
Family therapy	63,000	16,500	7,500	87,000
Individual counseling	54,000	18,000	12,000	84,000
TOTALS	$180,000	$75,000	$45,000	$300,000

Table 11.7   Elements of a Model Budget: Health Home Care

① *Investments:*   1991–1992
    Administrative support $ 15,000
    Home care services   55,000
                                                                          $ 70,000

② *Financing plan:*
    Private grant $ 7,000
    Service charges   61,600
    Property taxes   1,400
                                                                          $ 70,000

③ *Estimated benefits:*
    Unneeded institutional care $200,000
    Unneeded nursing care   24,000
    Patient productivity   25,000
                                                                        $249,000

④ *Plans for 1991–1992:* Started last year as an efficient, less costly alternative to institutionalized care, a home-care team on contract from the ABC Rehab Center, can be expected to deliver coordinated therapeutic services to an estimated 220 persons in the next fiscal year, up 20 when compared with the current-year estimate.

⑤ *Performance data:*

	Cases	Unit Cost ⑦
Present year	200	$325
Budget year 1	220	318
Future year 2	240	313
Future year 3	260	308

Cross classification: The following exhibit classifies the home-care service by three impact categories:

Impacts	Reducing Personal Dependence	Reducing Economic Dependence	General Welfare
⑥ *Investments:*			
Number of cases	70	60	90
Case cost	$22,275	19,090	28,635
Benefits:			
Unneeded institutional care	$60,000	50,000	90,000
Unneeded nurse care	24,000		
Patient productivity		25,000	
	$84,000	75,000	90,000

Table 11.7   (continued)

⑧ *Net benefits:* Total benefits are expected to exceed costs by $179,000.

⑨ *Return on investments:*

Investment (current)	$70,000
Total benefit (current)	$249,000
Net benefit	$179,000
Return on investment	256%

For every $1 invested in this program, $2.56 was returned to the community. This was derived from

Eliminating 600 hospital days	($100/day)
Eliminating 600 nursing days	($ 40/day)
Eliminating 500 days of institutional care	($100/day)
Decreasing sick pay 500 days	($ 50/day)

⑩ *Forecast:* As originally specified, we are attempting to reduce the high cost of institutionalizing stroke and fracture victims and the chronically ill by providing therapeutic services in the home, where support costs are at a minimum. The program has grown rapidly from 0 to 200 cases in the first two years.

⑪ It will grow marginally in the next five years, responding to population growth and a projected effort to coordinate more closely with doctors and hospitals to further reduce the hospitalization time of stroke and accident victims.

Key:

① Cost centers (summarizing subsidiary cost centers and variable, fixed, object of expenditure identifiers)
② Financing plan (including revenue offset to taxes)
③ Estimated benefits (including benefits known to be positive, but of unknown value)
④ Goal statement
⑤ Performance data comparison
⑥ Cross classification (isolating costs for marginal analysis)
⑦ Unit-cost calculations (illustrating cost variances)
⑧ Commentary on estimated benefits
⑨ Return on investments
⑩ Commentary on current year experience
⑪ Projections

Source: Adapted with permission from Edward A. Lehan, *Simplified Governmental Budgeting* (Chicago: Government Finance Officers Association, 1981).

Program Memorandum.   As part of the annual budget-preparation process, it is often necessary to present a **program memorandum**, or **issue paper**. This sets forth the arguments for initiating a new program that will meet a recognized community need and/or that will further the organization's mission. A program memorandum includes the following elements:

- Problem definition and goal(s)
- Financing plan
- Target population

- Performance criteria
- Impacts and benefits
- Multiyear projections
- Rejected alternatives

To develop program memoranda, human services managers need to create a series of folders on different community issues and needs. During the year, data (newspaper and magazine articles, conversations, interviews, thoughts) are accumulated in the appropriate folder, and at budget-preparation time, a program memorandum is prepared for the budget-formulation process.

Lehan provides an illustration of a program memo for a home care program and for recreation programs (1980 45, 51).

Schedule. Budget preparation usually adheres to a rigid calendar. Because most administrators must prepare their budgets for their subunits and then assemble them into a total budget for their department's presentation to a higher organizational level, the process is quite lengthy. The process starts within the human services agency and involves all levels of the organization. It then moves to the finance–budget office and eventually to the chief executive. In a large government bureaucracy, the budget process will then involve the central budget unit, the budget director, the mayor–city manager, governor, or perhaps even the president of the United States. Then the process begins to involve policymakers (Congress, state legislatures, or city councils) of the jurisdiction. Public hearings are generally held. Eventually, the budget is adopted, usually on or before a legislatively mandated calendar date. Robert Anthony and Regina Herzlinger note (1980) that for a federal agency this can involve fifteen months.

Data Accumulation. The quality of budget preparation depends on the quality of data that are accumulated and manipulated. Generally, quantity of data is not as important as the creative way data are presented. It is at this point that it becomes critical to interrelate program data with financial data.

It is also important to note that the accumulation of data for the initial budget presentation must be matched with an ability to further manipulate that data or to add new data that can be helpful in presenting new insights into the budget process at every step in the schedule cycle.

Meetings–Hearings–Presentations. Budget preparation can be viewed as a process of a series of meetings in between which data must be prepared, analyzed, revised, and proposed once again. Sometimes these meetings are closed and internal. At other times, they are public and open. Thus, the human services manager could think of these meetings as opportunities for marketing programs. Use of good public information and graphic techniques in all media goes a long way helping administrators and program leaders "sell" their budget (ergo, their programs and services) to all levels of the organization, to policy-makers, and to the public.

Staff Utilization.   Large human services agencies will have full-time budget analysts, but most human services managers will be their own budget analysts. The entire organization should identify with the budget-preparation process and be willing to work actively in it. Because the level and quality of agency ser-vices is dependent on the budget, it obviously needs everyone's attention. Ad-ministrators have to combat the general feeling of employees—professionals and clerical—that the budget-preparation process has been turned over to one person—the human services manager. It is important to sensitize everyone involved in a human services organization that collective, not singular, re-sponsibility for budget preparation is the best guarantee of achieving the agency's missions.

Follow-Up.   Many service professionals who are program leaders assume that their role in the budget-preparation process is completed at the time when the department budget is finalized and forwarded to the human services manager and on to the policy-making body. Everyone concerned with a human services program—clerical, professional, administrative, and managerial employees—needs to remain alert through the total budget-schedule cycle, closely following the progress of their portion of the budget—making sure cuts are minimal and, where possible, acquiring additional funds. It is a delicate process because at every organizational level subordinates may be in conflict with their superiors. Consensus should be achieved where possible; where conflict is apparent, open and honest differences preserve future working relationships.

This raises an important issue: To what extent can a human services man-ager lobby, through a community-support group, for restoration of a budget cut made by her superior? Is open lobbying unprofessional or organizationally un-wise because disloyalty is never cherished? These are difficult questions to an-swer because overt conflict with one's administrative superiors can be viewed negatively. George Brager and Stephen Holloway (1978), although discussing issues of direct services and not budget, refer to the ethical and professional tensions in overt or covert activities that are in conflict with a superior's mana-gerial decision.

Generally, community (pressure) groups are welcomed by agency admin-istrators. They are viewed as important resources for communications to politi-cal leaders, particularly in reference to client needs. The professional has a responsibility to honestly and objectively present resource requirements to meet community needs. The political community—formal and informal—must then make the difficult choices in community-resource allocations. Thus, where human services managers recognize the need for year-round client-group–community-group support, energizing them for the budget-support process is a natural process.

The Nature of Budget Execution

The execution of a budget consists of processes and mechanisms by which program activities are undertaken under fiscal controls tied to the adopted budget. These mechanisms are discussed later in this chapter. It is important first to describe briefly the several different aspects of this control process that are important for the human services manager. These processes consist of a mix of controls (most of which are inherent techniques of the control paradigm discussed in the introduction to Part IV): accounting; program management; personnel management; productivity; and management style. All may not be exercised in any one human services organization, but their potentiality for application exists.

Budget Execution as Accounting Control. Order is necessary in every organization, and the accounting and bookkeeping staffs are the cornerstone for maintaining order. They do so through the budget-execution process, because the flow of resources through an organization is highly controlled by financial–accounting processes and procedures that are tied to specific budget accounts. To the accountant or bookkeeper, the key questions are: Does your program or organization unit have an authorized budget account for the specific expenditure you intend to make? If so, do you have sufficient funds remaining in the account? In some human services organizations, mechanisms are in place that permit additional accounting control questions such as, Are you expending funds within the approved *rate* of expenditure? Although there are other accounting procedures that create control over an agency's finances, the budget is one of the most fundamental accounting control mechanisms. It is a wise human services manager who clears in advance with his accounting staff any intended new or unusual program activity.

Budget Execution as Program-Management Control. A well-planned and well-designed program management–control system contains several program-management mechanisms. These include unit and aggregated costs, performance milestones, and amount of scheduled resources for each program for each program period and year to date. The execution of the budget needs to be related to program and performance data systems to permit the staff of a human services organization and/or program—clerical, professional, and administrative—to maintain control over the effectiveness and productivity of their programs. Used positively, these controls can actually enhance the mission paradigm.

Budget Execution as Personnel-Management Control. The management of human resources includes the need to maintain control over the number of people employed in each category, the amount of pay each receives, and changes in their remuneration. Personnel-management controls are necessary and desirable for each organizational unit and its programs. Because a great number of human services organizations are funded by different sources, each of which have restrictions or regulations related to personnel, the execution of the budget is an important process for control over program expenditures for human resources. This can be used positively by a human services manager to enhance the staff development paradigm (e.g., provide incentives, provide approval for changes in pay status); it also can be a negative process (e.g., "cop out" to pressures for higher remuneration by pleading inability to circumvent the restrictions placed by the approved budget).

Budget Execution as Productivity–Economy Control.   As noted above, the budget can be a statement of the level of services in a community and can be used by public or nonprofit organizations to leverage service provision as an element of the community's economy. In the process of executing the budget, the human services manager should also be concerned with the strategic planning function and the client paradigm—checking the extent to which the agency's or program's activities are influencing the economy of a geographic area and helping specific client groups. There are computer modeling systems that are available to assist an administrator in measuring the fiscal impact of different program expenditures.

Budget Execution as a Vehicle for Controlling Managerial Style.   Mechanisms in the budget-execution process influence the management system and managerial leadership styles of an organization. These both affect a human services manager or provides her with an opportunity to set a style. For example, the *level of aggregation* refers to the level of detail versus summary account data that appears in a budget. Budgeting and accounting provide an opportunity for extreme details in record keeping. For example, the salary of one physical therapist—John Barenz—can appear in a budget and the amount he receives each pay period can be used for account control purposes. On the other hand, this amount of detail can be summarized or aggregated to the total salaries of all the physical therapists. It is even possible to summarize or aggregate further by showing only the total budgeted amount for professional salaries. This process is known as *aggregation* and in preparing–executing the budget, the level at which account data are aggregated has important implications.

The level of aggregation can be uniform for all human services programs, or it can be up to each program leader, thus giving each program leader opportunity to exercise an individual style of management. The level of aggregation is a major influence over the level of independence by which responsibility centers have freedom for program management—an important device for the staff development and mission paradigms. Table 11.8 illustrates this. There is an obvious difference between permitting a program leader the freedom to control at the program level (Example 1 in Table 11.8) than exercising control through line-item details (Example 4 in Table 11.8).

Table 11.8 Levels of Budget Aggregation (Program:
Alcohol Abuse Treatment)

Example 1	Program	Mutual-help groups	$202,500
Example 2	Responsibility center	Northside Clinic	81,000
		Southside Clinic	70,875
		Westside Clinic	50,625
Example 3	Line-item totals	Northside Clinic:	
		Personnel	45,000
		Commodities	21,000
		Contractual	15,000
Example 4	Line-item details	Northside Clinic personnel:	
		Director	9,220
		Group workers	18,300
		Psychologist	17,480

The transactional-analysis relationship (to refer to interpersonal dynamics) between supervisor and supervisee is quite different between these two extremes in levels of aggregation that serve as control over program leaders. The former (aggregation at the program level) controls on the basis of results and gives the program leader the opportunity for self-management. Controlling by detailed line-item aggregation is accounting control and exercises strong direction over the program leader's administration of the programs.

From an accounting point of view, aggregation at the program level or at the organizational level simplifies the accounting process by reducing significantly the need to process budget account changes; because a budget is a forecast made several months in advance of the date a transaction occurs, the more detailed the prediction, the less likely it will be accurate.

Budget-Execution Mechanisms

Many mechanisms are available for guiding and controlling the execution of the budget. We discuss five: quarterly allotments, prior approvals, recisions, monthly appropriation reports, and account transfers. Although these mechanisms are most often found in large public agencies, understanding each will give the human services manager insights into the budget-execution process; used creatively, budget mechanisms can be aids in managing change and improvements rather than just means for maintaining the status quo.

Quarterly Allotments.   When a budget is approved, an administrator or program leader immediately has a vision of available resources that can be used. Such is not the case. Financially oriented administrators attempt to portion out budget funds slowly. Their rationale is both natural (e.g., they are the maintainers of the control paradigm in the organization) and necessary (e.g., revenues flow during the course of the year becoming available only when received). Good cash management necessitates relating agency outflow with its resource inflow.

Thus, budget offices sometimes require quarterly allotments—a detailed plan whereby for each account the manager must indicate how much of the total budgeted amount will be required in each of the year's quarters.

Once agreed on, the manager and program leaders have available only the amount of the budget resources alloted to the thirteen-week period. If services are provided at an even pace throughout the year, each quarterly allotment would be 25 percent of the total budgeted amount. Generally, the flow of agency resources are uneven amounts for different times during the year.

Prior Approvals. As if to add insult to injury, even when amounts of the budget are released for the agency's use, prior approval is necessary in many organizations for both personnel issues (e.g., new employees to be hired or changes in level of expenditures for current staff) and in purchasing issues (commodities and contracts). By slowing its response to agency requests for prior approvals, the financial office gains a surplus—the ultimate in good financial management viewed from the control-paradigm perspective. For example, if a vacancy occurs in an agency, it takes X days to find a replacement. If X is stretched out to sixty workdays, that is 17 percent of the salary of the person being replaced. The agency never will see that amount unless it is successful in arguing with the chief executive that, if there is a surplus toward the end of the budget year, this sum should be available for program purposes to support and enhance the client and mission paradigms.

Prior approval therefore is an important budget-execution mechanism. It is the chief means for keeping an administrator or program leader within the limits of their budget accounts.

Recision of Funds. Where the jurisdiction or agency is unsure of the flow of revenues (e.g., a grant may not be approved or projected revenues may not be received) or when there is a specific policy of cutback, recisions will be instituted. For example, even though $200,000 was made available for Program A during a previous budget-preparation period, X percent may be "frozen" and not made available for use. Sometimes the recision is only temporary, waiting to see if anticipated revenues materialize. On other occasions, recisions may be final, in a decremental management move. Sound financial management from the control-paradigm perspective here conflicts with the agency's sound program management, which flows out of the service/mission–effectiveness paradigm.

In many situations, a good human services manager can successfully win the fight for full or partial restoration of the frozen funds by convincing finance-oriented officials of their agency's accountability and fiscal responsibility.

Monthly Appropriation Accounting Reports. As already noted above, a typical appropriation accounting report shows how much, by each account, has been spent and how much remains (e.g., is unexpended and unencumbered).

This type of report is critical for keeping track of available resources for program-management purposes. Where a modern computer system is in place, this type of accounting data is "on line" (e.g., available at any time) by means of a video terminal. The human services manager or program leader can immediately ascertain those budget accounts that may be overexpended and those that can be used, or transferred, to help in the effort to achieve service objectives. Because reports are always after the fact (usually not available until days or weeks following the end of the reporting period), the use of an on-line computer system for appropriation accounting is important for dynamic program management and for the mission paradigm. As microcomputers become more readily available, this will be true for small, as well as large, human services organizations.

Transfers.   At a particular time in the year, usually toward the end of a budget period, the appropriation accounting report begins to show certain accounts with credit (overexpended) balances and others with surpluses. The human services manager appreciates the fact that budget are projections made one or two years before the actual period of program management. Thus, the need to transfer funds from an underexpended budget account to one that is overexpended is a necessity. It is also an indication of either the manager's and program leader's projection abilities or, more important, the level of aggregation. The greater the level of budget account details, the greater the need for transfer between accounts.

Requests for transfers require the approval of managers, chief executives, and, depending on the organizational level and dollar level, approval of the policy group itself. In other words, transfers of small amounts of the budget may be within the discretion of the financial officer or the chief executive. Larger amounts need the approval, for example, of the board of directors or the city council.

Predicting the future or—as in the case of the human services manager as a change agent—altering the future, is difficult. Thus, a human services manager or program leader must carefully argue for and execute transfers between budget accounts.

There are no incentives for surpluses in program-budget accounts; if anything they are disincentives because amounts unexpected may lead to decreased budget amounts in the following year. Usually, unexpended budget amounts are transferred to the chief executive's general fund; if this ends in a surplus, it is considered a sign of his financial management acumen. Depending on the managerial style of the chief executive, this can also evoke an image that the human services managers and program leaders also display excellent financial management skills. Because of the disincentive for a surplus, managers have a goal of using 99.9 percent of their budgets; thus, transfers become a critical budget-execution mechanism, particularly in a fund-accounting system.

Financial Statements and Fiscal Reporting

A good financial system needs several well-designed reports for a variety of purposes: Are funds being spent for their proper purpose? Is cash flow being managed such that money does not have to be borrowed and excess cash can be invested? Is each separate fund solvent? Has the agency's net worth increased or decreased?

Each agency must develop a system of fiscal reports to meet its own needs. For a public human services agency (e.g., federal, state, county, municipal), these may be prescribed by the financial director of the jurisdiction or an outside accountant–auditor. The same may be true for private nonprofit agencies; upon taking a new position with a private agency, the human services manager may find that the financial reports have been designed and initiated by prior accounting–auditing firms. Changes therefore must be made slowly and most probably with prior approval of the board.

Tables 11.9 and 11.10 illustrate the most common financial reports for a private human services agency.

	Table Number
■ Statement of income and expenditures	11.9
■ Balance sheet	11.10
■ Changes in fund balance (net worth)	11.9, 11.10

These reports also illustrate essential elements of financial reports for human services agencies: separation of different funds to indicate clearly their separate status and comparison between two different years.

Note that Table 11.9 comes close to indicating the profit and loss from operations during a period of time; Table 11.10 illustrates a balance sheet, the financial status of the agency; and both figures also indicate the change of fund balance (net worth) of the agency.

In public human services agencies, the appropriation accounting report is the major financial report; this has already been described above. This report is augmented with reports on the status of revenue collections compared to estimates of revenues anticipated. As already noted, because the basis of public and nonprofit organization financial accounting is fund accounting, all reports are prepared in a fashion that segregates financial data for each fund.

Table 11.9   Winfield Family Services: Statement
of Income and Expenditures

	1989 Unrestricted Funds	1989 Restricted Funds	1989 Combined Totals	1988 Combined Totals
Support, Net				
Department of Mental Health	$3,598,211	—	$3,598,211	$2,498,775
Department of Youth Services	1,012,381	—	1,012,381	854,238
Department of Social Services	1,002,566	—	1,002,566	986,328
Other	409,601	—	409,601	289,597
	6,022,759	—	6,022,759	4,628,938
Revenues				
Retail sales	33,070	—	33,070	—
Donations	13,919	17,159	31,078	22,660
Membership fees	—	—	—	1,895
Annual meeting	1,650	—	1,650	1,678
Insurance–repair reimbursements	12,956	4,375	17,331	121,403
Interest	9,269	—	9,269	9,955
Miscellaneous	27,652	650	28,302	34,640
	98,516	22,184	120,700	192,231
TOTAL SUPPORT AND REVENUE	6,121,275	22,184	6,143,459	4,821,169
Expenses				
Programmatic expenses	5,481,007	16,411	5,497,418	4,059,914
Administrative and general expenses	571,785	—	571,785	483,831
	6,052,792	16,411	6,069,203	4,543,745
EXCESS OF SUPPORT AND REVENUE OVER EXPENSES	$ 68,483	$ 5,773	$ 74,256	$ 277,424

Auditing and Control

It is far too easy for financial professionals to confuse the necessity for tight controls over finances in our form of body politic with the control paradigm of management—the need to autocratically direct all organizational activities in a highly centralized fashion. Besides discussing this issue, we review generally accepted control practices, both internal and external.

Table 11.10 Winfield Family Services: Balance Sheet

Assets	1989	1988
Current Assets		
Cash	$ 126,102	$ 107,309
Accounts receivable	641,809	481,062
Prepaid expenses	31,022	14,120
	798,933	602,491
	444,653	509,220
Real-Estate and Equipment—at Cost, Net Other Assets		
Restricted equipment	222,660	161,827
Security deposits	16,383	14,036
	239,043	175,863
TOTAL ASSETS	$1,482,629	$1,287,574

Liabilities and Fund Balance	1989	1988
Current Liabilities		
Notes payable—current portion	$ 15,914	$ 16,586
Mortgages payable—current portion	5,806	5,641
Accounts payable	228,037	177,952
Deferred income	24,148	7,176
Accrued expenses payable	95,587	36,628
	369,492	243,983
Long-Term Liabilities		
Notes payable—noncurrent portion	42,357	37,883
Mortgages payable—noncurrent portion	185,785	255,802
	228,142	293,685
Fund Balance		
General operating	488,395	419,912
Restricted	396,600	329,994
	884,995	749,906
TOTAL LIABILITIES AND FUND BALANCE	$1,482,629	$1,287,574

Control Bases. In the form of democracy fashioned in the United States, the political form of society is founded on the distrust of excessive power. This has always been very clear in government agencies, but there are signs that society's distrust of power is spreading to nonprofit organizations and even commercial organizations (e.g., increased public regulation of business; union leaders or consumer advocates sitting on the boards of major corporations).

Rather than entering into a philosophical-political discussion of why a system based on distrust of power is desirable or necessary, let us focus on its implications for good financial management of human services organizations.

It means that there will be several checks and balances within an organization to ensure that uses of financial resources are not abused by any one person or group of people—for personal or organizational self-interest. Although some checks and balances may be excessive in terms of efficiency and marginal for control purposes (e.g., the practice that a board, as a group, approves *all* checks for payment), checks and balances are important for two major reasons:

1. Even a suspicion of abuse of funds would do irreparable damage to an agency's image as being an effective human services organization. In fact and in image, controls are necessary to maintain the integrity of the agency in the community, particularly for its clients.
2. Like it or not, if one has an image of being a poor or sloppy financial manager, it is automatically assumed that she is a poor human services program manager.

Human services professionals are particularly dedicated to a society in which all individuals retain power over their own lives. When it is necessary to form societal institutions for the betterment of members of society, it is necessary in such formation to give power to individuals and groups of persons. Such power is a trust. Although the vast majority of people can maintain that power trust, a few people might abuse that power. To protect future generations, controls are imposed to prescribe and circumscribe the power we give others over our clients' lives. Financial controls are a natural part of guarding against the abuse of power.

A number of managers confuse the inherent good financial management need to institute controls to limit power abuse with an organizational management style characterized as autocratic, centralized control over the total organization. They view organization with a control paradigm. In terms of finances, they signal: "We at the center of the organization, close to the chief executive, keep close control over what you spend. We have little interest in helping you accomplish your specified mission." As Lehan noted (1978), financial professionals have a mental set toward "organizational arithmetic" (e.g., control over organizational expenditures) rather than a set toward "community arithmetic" (e.g., planning the way in which organizational resources can leverage the greatest good for human services program—mission achievement—the mission paradigm).

Whatever the bases, financial controls are necessary and must be developed by each human services manager (e.g., internal controls); at the same time, the policy board (political legislature, council, or board of directors) must hire an independent auditor to exercise external controls.

Internal Controls.   Internal controls are procedures and mechanisms that are put into operation in a public agency to continuously check the fiscal integrity of the financial management of the agency. They are designed primarily for two purposes: to prevent the possibility of any fiscal abuse in the agency and to

Table 11.11 Examples of Different Internal-Control Items or Issues

Payroll

1. Are initial rates of pay authorized in writing?
2. Are test checks made of time-card recording and processing?
3. Are overtime amounts reviewed?
4. Are payroll checks distributed by someone other than the person who prepares them or by the employees' immediate supervisor?
5. Are payroll checks distributed in person from one central location once a year?

Revenue Collections

1. Are prenumbered, multicopy forms used when cash is received?
2. Do cash registers have an automatic sequence number that is also stamped on the taxpayer's receipt?
3. Is the person making the deposit different and unrelated from the person preparing the revenue collections for bank depositing?
4. Are receivables verified directly with taxpayers annually?
5. Are employees who handle cash bonded?

Purchasing

1. Is purchasing independent of accounting or receivables?
2. Are purchase orders prenumbered and checked for sequence?
3. Are competitive quotations solicited from different suppliers?
4. Are lists of vendors who are approved maintained?
5. Is a copy of each purchase order sent directly to the accounting unit?

Receiving

1. Is there a central receiving point?
2. Are receiving reports prenumbered and checked for sequence?
3. Does accounting get a copy of receiving reports?
4. Is there periodic verification that receiving reports are accurate?
5. Is there a process by which goods received meet the "specs"?

develop a self-regulating process by which the financial systems can automatically check on and control their own integrity and reliability.

It is the responsibility of the human services manager to be sure that (1) internal-control checklists, such as that illustrated in Table 11.11, are in place in the agency; (2) that they are followed meticulously; and (3) that they are continually improved to strengthen fiscal integrity.

Internal-control checklists are usually developed by the agency's accounting staff, the jurisdiction's central financial unit, the external auditors of the agency, or CPA firms hired as consultants to develop modern internal-control processes and procedures. The internal-control procedures are developed for all aspects of the financial management system: revenue collections, cash receipting and depositing, disbursement of cash, accounts receivable, accounts payable, payroll, inventory, fixed assets, and purchasing.

Large human services organizations often have dedicated internal control and auditing units operating within the central financial unit or under the chief executive. Their duties are to monitor the internal-control mechanisms to be sure that they are being followed by agency employees and to identify areas in which internal controls should be improved and strengthened. As many of the financial management systems become computerized, internal auditors have had to acquire the ability to install their own computer-based internal-control procedures.

External Controls.   All organizations—commercial, nonprofit, and public— are subject to an annual audit by an independent accountant–auditor selected by the policy-making group. The auditor's report is given to the policy-making group but must be made public. Thus, it is a very important source of negative incentives to manage finances soundly. In extreme cases, external auditors discover fraud or embezzlement; in other situations, they discover areas of poor financial management that if not corrected can lead to suspicion of fraud or embezzlement.

External audits are mandated legally for all human services organizations. They may be required also by financial institutions that are providing financial support to the organization.

Increasingly, human services organizations are subject to another type of external audit—**the funder's audit**. Because grants, contracts, and third-party payments have become such a major part of human services organizational resources, the providers of the resources insist on auditing that segment of the agency's finances related to each funder's interest. The Government Accounting Office (GAO) of the federal government (or their state government counterpart) thus may be part of most human services manager's lives.

Because fund accounting is the basis of all human services organizational financial accounting, on the surface, an audit of each fund should be relatively simple. What complicates it is that different or peculiar accounting requirements may be imposed by each funder. And where funds for different sources are mixed to support one program or one employee's salary, record keeping to trace the flow of the funder's resources is difficult.

In short, to meet the needs of all external-control agents—the independent auditor of the agency's policy group or the auditor of the funders—a great amount of financial record keeping is required. An external audit checklist would include the following:

- Are the audit trials for all financial transactions adequate?
- Did a sampling of financial transactions prove 100 percent adherence to internal-control procedures?

- Can the payroll records be validated with actual staff employed?
- Can account balances be verified?

The independent, external audit is primarily prepared for the policy-making body of the human services organization. But because audit reports are made public generally and scanned closely by the media, they become an important stimulus to strive for effective financial management in the agency. Human services managers recognize that independent audits help identify areas of improvement necessary in agency fiscal systems. At the same time, managers must be prepared to quickly inform the public, through the media if necessary, that not only has the agency made all the corrections recommended by the independent auditors, but that, in many cases, the vast majority of agency funds are being managed with complete integrity and the audit report deals with comparatively minor problems.

As noted several times, even the slightest hint of fiscal impropriety tarnishes the public's image of the human services agency's ability to manage efficiently and effectively. Thus, all findings of the independent audit must be dealt with to the satisfaction of the auditors. At the same time, these findings need to be placed in perspective: for most agencies, the vast majority of funds are managed with fiscal accuracy. But because managers are expected to manage with 100 percent accuracy, there is little tolerance for even minor flaws in the organization's fiscal systems.

In the past few decades, there have been two new developments in external audits. The first is the funder's audit. Because many human services agencies now receive funds from a number of different sources (e.g., grants, contracts, transfer payments), the providers of the resources conduct their own audits. Thus, most human services institutions have several external audits conducted over and above the legislatively mandated independent audit.

The second development concerns the fact that external audits have begun to go beyond fiscal audits, to include *management audits, efficiency audits,* and/or *performance audits.* Oriented toward improving organizational accountability, such audits focus on the productivity and effectiveness of government agencies in carrying out their mandates and their missions. The Comptroller General of the United States reported several examples of these new types of audits:

- Compliance with applicable laws and regulations. EXAMPLES: Grant funds, adherence to affirmative action regulations, and adherence to contract requirements.
- Efficiency and economy in using resources. EXAMPLES: Ineffective procedures or more costly than justified, duplication of effort, inefficient or uneconomical use of equipment, overstaffing, and faulty buying practices.
- Effectiveness in achieving program results. EXAMPLES: Validity of criteria used to judge program effectiveness, accuracy of data accumulated, and reliability of results obtained.

For human services managers concerned with a mission- or client-paradigm perspective, such audits are very helpful.

Managing Money

When the human services manager considers that a large number of people make their livelihood solely by buying and selling money (in all its forms— cash, bonds, certificate of deposits [CDs], stocks, property, metals, and etc.), then it is wise to become at least sufficiently informed to know what type of advice is needed and where such advice can be obtained to the best advantage of the agency. Often, in exchange for your agency's business, a bank will pro- vide the service. When an agency has a good endowment base in property and stocks, investment companies will want your agency's business. Because it is such a dynamic, even international field, the money market does require a level of expertise that probably warrants hiring an expert, either as a consultant to the agency or, if the agency is large enough, as the financial director of the agency. In the case of the latter, rather than seeking someone who is more expert in accounting and bookkeeping, it may be wiser to employ as the agency's financial director someone whose experience is more in managing finances, leaving to the agency's auditors the task of creating an accounting system to ensure maximum accounting controls.

Increasingly, for all sectors of the economy, managers of human services agencies need to increase their knowledge of managing money. Two elements of this skill base include cash-flow management and debt management, both of which will be briefly discussed.

Cash-Flow Management

Every human services organization needs to have cash available today for its cash needs today. Having too much or too little cash—either case—will result in a loss of financial resources for the agency. In the former, too much cash not being invested results in lost interest that the agency could have gained. Too little cash availability means that the agency has to borrow on a short-term basis to pay bills and thus has to incur the expense of interest on the funds borrowed.

Cash-flow management is the process of planning for the smooth flow of the cash of a human services agency—maximizing the cash on hand and mini- mizing the need to use (and pay interest on) somebody else's cash. It requires planning—predicting and projecting revenues and expenditures for each week of agency operations during a year's period. Many human services managers develop an annual cash-flow analysis that is kept current; it projects estimated receipts and payments for each period. From this, the net cash gain–loss is computed to arrive at the level of cumulative loans required during a six- or twelve-month period if a desired cash level is to be maintained.

Essentially, good cash-flow management works on two principles: accelerate inflow; decelerate outflows. The former can range from personally picking up grant checks at their sources to billing for third-party payments the same day clients receive services. The latter, slowing the outflow of cash, can range from making payments at the very last moment (to take advantage of purchase discounts) to using the cash float for the few days it takes your agency's check to clear the bank (i.e., the time between when your agency writes the check and when it clears the payee's bank account). Obviously, good bookkeeping procedures are critical to this process, plus someone who is responsible to devote time and effort to the process.

For many human services agencies—particularly private, nonprofit agencies—cash management also involves the expert use of its endowment funds. As noted under fund-raising, an essential part of financial management is increasing the resource bases of an agency through convincing people to leave funds or property to the agency for general or special purposes. If an agency is successful in this aspect of fund-raising, then it must also be successful in the management of endowment funds and property received. Because most of this will be initially received, or subsequently acquired, in the form of corporate stocks and bonds or government bonds, it requires the expertise of an investment specialist. For most agencies, the assistance of experts in this process must be sought outside the agency, usually by turning to a bank or investment company, for a fee. It would be ideal to have in-house capability through the agency's financial director or through a retiree who, as a member of the agency's board of directors, contributes time and expertise to this function. Regardless of the approach, agency investments and property need the time and effort of an expert. It is a requirement of sound management of finances.

Debt Management

Using debt wisely is as important as good cash management. Although many agencies try to avoid debt, most human services managers try to understand the wise use of short-term and long-term debt. This is true for commercial, nonprofit, and public human services organizations.

All organizations, the human services included, need to plan carefully for capital improvements. It is vital to have a capital budget for the agency, one that projects the capital fund needs of the agency over the next five- to ten-year period. Each year, as the capital budget plan is updated, the current need is part of the current-year operating budget, both in terms of debt service (the amount of operating funds required to retire debt or to pay the interest on debt) and in terms of operating funds needed for capital improvement. Purchasing a motor vehicle for the agency requires a capital expenditure; it takes sound planning to purchase (over a three- to five-year period) a new vehicle rather than continue to spend money on repairing the existing vehicle. The human services manager must have data that indicate the proper time to purchase new instead of continuing to repair old equipment.

Debt management for the manager of a public human services organization is different but still requires knowledge and skills on the subject. Because large public organizations turn the problem of debt management over to the separate financial department, this is not a day-to-day concern of the human services manager. But understanding the debt position of the public jurisdiction is important for timing the requests for capital improvements. For example, if the department of mental health of a state government needs a new community clinic built, one that will necessitate the borrowing of several millions of dollars, it is best to submit such a request to the state's capital budget office during the year when the state's outstanding debt is at its lowest or when the bond market is advantageous for the state to borrow. Thus knowledge of this subject, and sensitivity to its mechanics in your public jurisdiction, is important for all public human services managers.

But is long-term debt the only aspect of debt management important for the human services manager? No, more than likely, most managers of private, nonprofit agencies and commercial human services organizations will be engaged in short-term debt management—borrowing money for brief periods just to have available cash to cover critical expenses such as paychecks for agency employees. Although there will be many times in managers' careers when they will have to borrow on a short-term basis to cover operating expenses, the reader can recognize that such a practice should be kept to a minimum and undertaken, if possible, when money is cheap. But because most human service organizations are dependent on their resources from another organization (i.e., a government agency or a third-party payment agency), the control over inflow is difficult. All too often, inflow of monies due from other organizations is erratic, and the human services manager has no choice but to borrow on a short-term basis. Many grants are paid in the form of reimbursing the agency for actual expenses; negotiating for payment of grant funds on a scheduled basis (i.e., so much each quarter), with the last quarter's payment based on a final accounting, can provide improved stability in cash flow and reduce the pressure for short-term borrowing.

Because the cost of money (debt) changes, the human services manager may need to refinance a loan to decrease the cost of the debt. Because this is also a complex area of finance, it would be advisable to acquire an expert advisor, either someone on the agency's board or a paid expert in this field. Because it is highly related to legal and accounting–tax issues, debt management requires someone knowledgeable in the intricacies and complexities of the subject. Knowing where to acquire such expert advice and how to evaluate the continued use of this expertise may be among the chief skills of the human services manager in this aspect of managing finances.

Mobilizing Resources

Mobilizing the resources for the organization is about the best example of creative, dynamic human services management. It becomes a focal point for integrating a number of managerial skills. Let's go back and reread Case 11.1. See if you can detect all the critical building blocks for Nan Rogers's style of creative management that draws on both institutional and systemic management skills, some that we have discussed already, others that we will soon cover. See if you can analyze graphically the repertoire of management skills she used; compare your analysis with the one I have developed at the beginning of Chapter 16. It's a good example of the manifold skills of the creative, dynamic human services manager: skillful in every aspect of institutional and systemic management; skillful in blending the full range of managerial skills to shape a unique management repertoire, one that is highly dynamic and highly creative.

Nan Rogers is a good example of how the human services manager has to be a creative financial manager—both in *financial management* and in *managing finances*. These two terms are not just a play on words. In the former, Nan had to be creative in the way she scanned the environment looking for new opportunities and then developed transorganizational arrangements that would generate resources. She then had to put into place fundamental financial management processes that assured everyone—funders, clients, staff, board, and community—that she could manage finances (resources) efficiently, productively, and effectively. Some agencies are good at mobilizing resources; others at managing the resources once acquired. While each is necessary, by themselves they are not sufficient. They are a living example of the value-tension between freedom and order. To be creative in financial management, the rigor of processes and procedures for managing finances must be in place. Nan understood and dealt with this value-tension. It was important for her success. For if anything, she had to be dynamic (e.g., ready to move quickly as the environment changed rapidly) and creative (e.g., be innovative, developing new ways of meeting client and community needs).

Nothing illustrates creativity more than the task of generating resources and revenues. Every human services manager faces that task, whether operating in a government, proprietary, or nonprofit, private agency. The ways of being creative are different for each. But to carry out organizational and professional human services missions in the dynamic environment that the 1990s represents, creative resource mobilization is not only vital but also a necessity for the human services manager.

There are a number of ways to generate revenues, some very traditional, others entrepreneurial in nature they are so new. Referring to the River City case and Case 11.2 will help the reader in the following discussion of the different approaches to resource mobilization.

Case 11.2

Professional Fund-Raising

The United Fund Board of Columbia sat around their conference table, contemplating Director Michael Mitchell's annual report. Besides reporting on the results of their campaign this year, Mike provided an overview of human services fund-raising in the United States during the past twenty years and recommended a strategic plan for the board's consideration.

"Pretty sobering, Mike," commented the board chair Beth Baker. "You're forcing us to think in terms of professional fund-raising, and I'm having a hard time shaking my past history of volunteering for community services by working for the United Fund."

"It's hard, Beth," Mike responded, "but I suggest that the fund-raising scene is changing so fast that we have no choice. We have to begin thinking like professional fund-raisers. Nationwide, the United Fund is losing part of their market share, though charitable contributions are increasing slightly in our nation. My using the term *market share* indicates my mind has been captured by the marketing, PR, advertising mentality of the United States today."

"But our contributors and volunteers have remained pretty loyal to us this past decade," Beth noted.

Mike quickly answered, "Trouble is, the past is no predictor for the future. One of our largest companies, True Value Foods, has just been bought out by a larger corporation who has linked their products to Little League with a multimillion TV blitz. It's a lose-lose situation for us either way: Either we start giving to the Little League of Columbia or anticipate that True Value will reduce the level of their contribution to our campaign."

"Trouble is, Mike," Rich McCory, one of the board members commented, "it's going to take money to make money, isn't it?"

"Yep," Mike answered, "can't get away from it. Among my recommendations are increased efforts with small companies and direct mailing to area residents. The administrative cost for the former is five to ten percent of everything raised; for the latter it's twenty-five percent. Those are high compared to our usual cost of one to two percent administrative costs where the majority of our contributors are payroll-deducted."

"Well, that in a way is front money; we should be able to recapture our administrative costs," Rich responded. "But what is this fund-raising strategy called *government-linked value added*?"

"Well, the state of Ohio allocated funds for neighborhood assistance for certain geographic areas in which they wanted to stimulate community development—physical and social. Where we can link a company's contribution to one of these neighborhoods, that company can take a fifty percent credit on their state business tax. It would be well worth it for us to invest in another staff member to devote full time to this strategy. It's complex, but the return is worth the investment."

"That's a far cry from what United Funds are supposed to do, Mike," Beth commented.

"Well, Beth," Mike noted, "we keep telling our human services agencies that they have to be very creative in the way they mobilize resources in today's turbulent environment. Shouldn't we display a little of that creativity also?"

"What do you say, Beth?" Rich challenged. "You're an executive in the human resources department of Ohio State. Think we can stage a TV telethon weekend organized and managed by the students? It will have multiple pay-offs: cement 'town–gown' relations; give the students an opportunity for community service; give the faculty work-experience opportunities; condition students to becoming contributors in the future; give some of our neighborhood residents a chance for direct contact with some of their idols—don't forget we have a few all-American football players at the university. We'd be dealing with two potential markets: the residents of Columbia and the residents of the university. Although we generally don't think in those terms, the latter represents a multimillion dollar market."

"Must admit, Rich," Mike commented, "though I'm enthusiastic about the telethon effort, it scares me. It will take a lot of effort to get it off the ground. The best thing going for it—if we can get it off the ground—it can become an annual that will have its own momentum."

Rich smiled, "I move that we adopt Mike's plan and that we phase it in over the next three years. Better now than later."

Effective Budgeting

What constitutes effective budgeting? The discussion of budget preparation and execution earlier was quite extensive and gave several clues as to the different criteria one could use to answer this question. But to most human services managers, the answer is simple: Did I receive the resources I initially requested in my budget?

For human services managers operating in government jurisdictions, resource mobilization is largely through the budget-preparation process. This means that being actively involved in every phase of this process is critical. As noted in our earlier discussion, it will be necessary to work closely with client-advocate and interest groups when the process shifts its focus to the legislature. Direct lobbying with policymakers is generally not permitted without approval of top executives.

Increasingly, public human services managers—particularly at the state and federal government levels—are finding themselves increasing their time and effort in two roles: providing grants and contracting. The grantee and the contractee generally are community agencies—municipalities, private non-profit agencies, and some proprietary agencies. Thus, during the resource-mobilization period (e.g., the public agency's budget is being reviewed by the legislature), the key advocates lobbying for the public human services manager's budget are the grantees, contractees, and client-interest groups. The latter are playing out their human services management role of creative financing for community agencies (see below). They are working closely with the former (the public human services manager) as he plays out the role of being an effective resource mobilizer through the public budgeting process.

The shift in strategic roles of public human services organizations—*from* service provider *to* grantor–contractor can be traced to the populus tax-reduction movements of the 1970s (e.g., California's Proposition 13; Massachusetts' Proposition 2½). Not only did it permit greater flexibility for government human services managers, it also shifted their focus in financial management *from* organizational arithmetic (e.g., how can we divide up the pie within our organization) *to* community arithmetic (e.g., how can we leverage our limited resources to stimulate resources that could be generated from the community). The latter role in turn required government human services managers to maintain their institutional management skills and blend them with increased skill in systemic management, interorganizational relations, and community organizing. If you were a government human services manager with a large budget for providing grants and contracts to community agencies, who do you think would be the primary lobbyists for your budget in the legislature? Don't need to answer that question, do I?

Either as an institutional manager or as a systemic manager, the key to generating revenues for government human services managers is being effective in the budget process.

Grant Acquisition

A major source for generating revenues for community human services agencies, primarily nonprofit–private agencies and proprietary agencies, is acquiring grants. There is a fairly standard process, namely:

- For the grantor, preparing an RFP (request for proposal)
- For the grantee, preparing a grant proposal

There are times when an unsolicited grant is prepared by a human services agency and presented to a foundation or to a state or federal government agency. Whether solicited or unsolicited, the preparation of a grant is a major skill for a human services manager. An even greater skill is working with a potential funder and convincing them to accept your grant proposal.

Requests for Proposals (RFP).   There are several fairly standard steps that are followed in preparing an RFP. They include the following:

1. The granting agency develops specifications for
   - Program design.
   - Funding parameters.
   - Time frame.
   - Monitoring process.
   - Selection criteria.
   - Selection procedure.
2. The RFP document is prepared. It sets forth
   - Grant and program specifications.
   - Requirements for proposals to be submitted.
   - Selection criteria and procedure.
3. The RFP document is issued to prospective grantees, with a deadline.
4. Proposals are received from potential grantees by the deadline.
5. Initial evaluation phase selects the finalists.
6. Finalists are interviewed.
7. Grantees are selected.

Grant Proposals.   On the one hand, preparing a proposal in response to an RFP is not difficult. A well-written RFP document provides all the guidelines required. In preparing grants that are eventually selected for funding, the human services manager who is an effective resource mobilizer needs three capabilities:

1. The logistical support within the agency to respond quickly with a quality grant-proposal document.
2. The ability to design an approach to program design that meets the RFP specifications in a creative and innovative fashion.
3. The ability to think strategically: How can a talented team, within our agency and together with other community resources, be organized in a way that will enhance the probability of the grant proposal being successful?

This is not the place to set forth the detail of *grantsmanship*. It is both an art and a science. There are both materials and skill-acquisition opportunities that are available to the human services manager. This is the place, however, to emphasize that the effective human services manager is an effective grantsperson. It is a fact of life for human services resource mobilization.

Contracting

Increasingly, a large number of human services organizations are finding themselves in the contracting business—either as contractor or contractee. Either way it requires skills for the human services manager.

Selling Services.   There are a large number of financial-legal details required for contracting—both in the process and in the document. Initially, the knowledge and skills of lawyers and certified accountants will be required. Once developed, they can be drawn up on a pro forma basis.

What is equally, if not more, important are the human services-delivery and program-management requirements that are the core of the contract *and* the requirements that the contractee must meet, both in terms of programmatic and financial outcomes and results. Increasingly, the focus in contracting has shifted to **contract management**, for both the contractor and contractee, and to **quality-assured purchases of services**.

The latter has become of particular importance as the human services have become increasingly *privatized* (i.e., services delivered by for-profit human services agencies). There is a great deal of concern that the quality of human services will be degraded as they are delivered by proprietary companies interested primarily in delivering services for profit. A municipal visiting nurse can deliver home care, for example, or such services can be contracted to the XYZ National Home Care Corporation. The cost per visit of the latter can be less expensive than the former. For the same amount of budget resources, more home visits can be made with the private corporation. But do the two result in a different level and quality of service? If so, how can this difference in quality be measured? Conversely, what qualitatively measurable criteria can be used to assure that quality of the less-expensive service meets the contract requirements? The issue of quality assurance is critical for both human services contractor and contractee. It is particularly difficult for the former, who must set forth such criteria in the initial contract and then monitor the results.

Buying Services.   For the human services manager who acquires a number of different contracts—some from the same contractor, others from different contractors—being a contractee is very demanding. There must be in place the rigor of fundamental institutional management—for managing program, finances, people, and information. All techniques, technologies, concepts, and approaches set forth in Part IV are vital, as well as their artful blending.

For example, the fundamental building block for Nan Rogers (Case 11.1, page 275) was her "Transaction Register," which each clinician filled out daily. It represented an automated system: the one-time single input of all the necessary programmatic and financial data that could be used for the full range of institutional management—managing programs, finances, people, information, and image. With these data in hand, not only could clients, community, and contractors measure with hard data both the effectiveness and productivity of services, but it also served to create the image of excellence in human services management that permitted Nan to broaden the base of her agency. Her image of excellence as a major human services agency in the community was enhanced by her image of excellence as a human services organizational manager. She and the other executives in her agency always had at their fingertips all data necessary to take advantage of new human services opportunities in the community.

The case of River City, Inc., also provides an example of another trend in financial management. Human services managers play *both* roles in contracting, sometimes even for the same set of client programs: at times they are contractees; at other times, they are contractors themselves. River City, Inc., sometimes uses contracts, sometimes *affiliation agreements*. The latter set forth the following between two human services agencies: scope of work, fee schedule, time period, and total cost of services. Such agreements are generally more flexible than contracts.

As with grantsmanship, this is not the place to set forth the details of *contracting*. It also is an art and a science. There are materials and skill-acquisition opportunities that are available to the human services manager. This is the place, however, to emphasize that the effective human services manager is an effective contractor, contractee, or both. It is a fact of life for human services resource mobilization.

Fund-Raising

Fund-raising, the direct solicitation of funds from individuals and corporations, has been the traditional approach to revenue generation for human services organizations, particularly nonprofit, private agencies. But as Case 11.2 (page 315) illustrates, even this has changed significantly and has become more sophisticated, opening up a new range of concepts, approaches, and techniques. Before reviewing some traditional aspects of fund-raising, a few comments are needed on the dynamic nature of fund-raising during the current decade.

Public human services organizations mobilize resources through the budget process. In essence the source of the funds are taxes. In some situations, short-term loans or long-term bonds are used to fund the activities, tasks, functions, and programs of government human services agencies.

Commercial human services organizations are heavily dependent on client fees and third-party payments, usually insurance plans or employee-benefit programs. In some situations, additional resources are mobilized through government contracts. It is also not unusual for commercial human services organizations to mobilize resources from financial institutions, such as investment banks directly, or from investors.

Private, nonprofit human services agencies historically have resorted to fund-raising. Over 80 percent of all funds are donated by individuals. The majority of funds raised in the United States are by and for religious institutions; the next largest amount of funds are raised for health and educational purposes. Universities, for example, have consistently been very active in direct fund-raising, traditionally from their alumni.

In the United States, most communities approach fund-raising for human services agencies as a cooperative effort. These combined fund-raising efforts are largely by the United Way, followed by the Combined Health Appeal, and International Service Agencies campaigns. Besides communitywide campaigns, private social services agencies generate an equal amount of revenues from their own fund-raising efforts.

During the current decade, major structural changes have occurred in fund-raising. Given patterns of revenue generation no longer can be taken for granted. TV telethons for a specific human service (e.g., a specific children's disease) have been undertaken under the leadership of TV and movie stars. Televised concerts by groups of leading rock groups have raised funds worldwide for specific causes. Cause-related marketing in which commercial organizations link the sale of their products to a specific human service is commonplace. Value-received sales (e.g., selling candy bars, T shirts, or even food for home viewing of the Superbowl) is also commonplace. Public institutions such as universities or institutions for the disabled create foundations or nonprofit support groups with the purpose of raising millions from their alumni and from the general community. With the reduction in government funding of human services, nonprofit agencies have been put in the position of having to compete with each other for the disposable income of the general population. This has spawned a variety of creative approaches to fund-raising that continues to expand.

More than ever before, human services managers today have had to become very creative and dynamic in generating necessary revenues. As you review the following discussion of different approaches to resource generation and mobilization, you also need to be aware that these dynamic changes have also heightened the universal versus particular value-tension. Should a human services manager work cooperatively with colleagues and other community or jurisdiction human services agencies to create a larger pie for everyone or be concerned with self-interest and survival of one's own agency?

Direct Fund-Raising. In some situations, an agency solicits individuals or commercial companies for contributions—either in actual cash or pledges to pay cash. Such fund-raising is organized as an annual event or a schedule of annual events that usually includes fund-raising/food-oriented meetings for which only donors of certain amounts can attend. Usually some method of solicitation is undertaken, often with volunteers organized into teams and trained to cover specific donors. Direct fund-raising can be specific—that is, the name of each donor is known in advance, and a direct contact made. But direct fund-raising can also be general—volunteers knocking on doors in each geographic area of a community.

Records are maintained so that billings can be automatic and payments processed; with sufficient volume, computer-based data processing may be used. The record keeping of payments from year to year is vital for future fund-raising efforts because a goal of direct fund-raising is to have donors increase what they gave the previous year.

Volunteers can be organized into teams, then trained and stimulated to meet quotas that represent increased fund-raising goals of the drive. Many means of public relations are energized to motivate the potential donor—using every conceivable emotion and tactic: pride, guilt, conformity, tax avoidance, fame, and public notoriety. The ethical and professional issues raised by these tactics are part of the tension of human services management.

Depending on the magnitude of the task, a human services agency may opt to turn fund-raising over to a consulting or special fund-raising organization. If this approach is used, care should be exercised that the percentage of costs for the raising effort is not excessive—if possible, less than 10 percent. The public is becoming wary of organizations that spend more on fund-raising than they do on the purpose for which the funds are being raised.

In many cases, most of the funds donated come from a small percentage of the donors. Thus, care must be exercised in personal treatment of such donors. Donors may be individuals, families, or trust funds set up by families or corporations of all sizes. Although most direct fund-raising is for providing services to clients and some operating expenses, construction efforts are undertaken periodically. In these cases, large donors are often encouraged to give or pledge a large sum to underwrite all of the new building or a portion of the building, which will then bear their name in perpetuity.

Indirect Fund-Raising.   There is no shortage of ideas for indirect fund-raising—from holding dances in railroad stations, telethons with TV entertainment from Las Vegas, raffles of all types, thrift shops, cake sales, candy sales, and so on. One variation is to specialize—that is, sell fruit cakes each year during the December holiday season. For more ideas, the human services manager can turn to experts, volunteers, and the literature.

But indirect funds can come from other sources: money, stocks and bonds, or property left in a will; property while a donor is still alive; an insurance policy in which the human services agency is the beneficiary. Some human services organizations solicit items from famous personalities and then auction them to raise funds. Church members often hold a supper or perform a musical—all to raise funds. Church members are accustomed to the notion of tithing (i.e., biblical mandate to give 10 percent for the needy) and in many cases make pledges paid annually for several years.

The creative ways of raising funds—direct and indirect—seem to know no bounds. To a human services manager concerned with provision of client services, fund-raising may seem tangential, often distasteful. But when it is a necessity of organizational life, it can become an integral part of the agency.

Volunteer Management

When it comes to mobilizing resources, religious institutions long ago realized that a significant portion of their resources (15 to 20 percent) were in the form of volunteers. Too often we get trapped in our own thinking: The only way to provide services is to hire a staff. If two people are working in your agency side-by-side, one is paid a salary out of the agency's budget and the other is a volunteer, which of the two represent an agency resource that can be quantified in a comprehensive budget? *Both,* obviously.

In many public jurisdictions, there is a concept of *expenditure budgets.* A good example of this would be in San Francisco, where a city ordinance was passed indicating that to develop and construct an office-building complex in the city, the developer had to agree in advance that in exchange for a reduction of property taxes for the first five years after construction, the developer had to create and maintain day care for those who eventually work in the building. The annual cost of that day care represented a human services resource, even though it cannot be found in any budget of one of the departments of the city of San Francisco.

A complete analysis of the resources of a human services organization must include the equivalent dollar figure for volunteers who give their time and effort to the agency. On the other side of that coin, an effective human services manager devotes time and energy to making volunteers an integral part of the people-management process. For an organization such as the Red Cross, because the majority of their personnel are volunteers, people management (human resources management) equals volunteer management. Most hospitals also devote a great deal of attention to this aspect of people management.

This is not the place for detailed descriptions of techniques for volunteer management. But as with other aspects of managing finances, this is the place to emphasize that the significant use of volunteers as resources for a human services organization is another sign of effective financial management.

Creative Financial Management

As several of the cases in this text illustrate, particularly the River City, Inc., and the Family Development Center cases, effective financial management in the human services today requires creative financing. This essentially involves successfully blending creative management:

- Image management: Being viewed as an effective, productive manager of services, programs, finances, people, and systems.
- Program management: Using classic program-management protocols and processes to be effective and productive.
- Financial management: Maintaining detailed program and cost accounts that meet auditing standards and that permit optimum use of resources.
- People management: Staffing with highly motivated and skilled professionals who are highly committed to clients, community, and agency.
- Data management: Maintaining a modern computer–telecommunication system that provides data necessary for ultimate rigor and ultimate flexibility.

- Strategic management: Succeeding in opportunistic surveillance—scanning the environment to look for opportunities that will mobilize additional resources to enhance the quality of clients' lives.

- Systemic management: Fashioning and managing systems that cut across a number of organizations in a way that the human services environment of clients and community grow, develop, and expand.

An analysis of most human services organizations illustrates the fact that most draw their resources from a number of sources and in a number of different ways: budgets, fees, third-party payments, fund-raising, contracts, grants, and volunteers. The hallmark of creative financial management is the art of blending (1) all these resources in a way that they mutually enhance each other and (2) all the different elements of management so that they are integrated and synergistic.

Summary

As with any of the fundamental management processes, the key issue will be finding a good balance between the need to be proficient in the details of financial management and the desire to maintain perspective over all of the complex aspects of the subject and their relationships. Because the theme of Part IV is that the human services manager must be sure that necessary, fundamental management processes are in place and being carried out effectively and efficiently, the challenge to the human services management student and practitioner is to acquire sufficient knowledge and skills in financial management to recognize that the required order in this fundamental area is indeed in place in the agency and is also being monitored daily. Once achieved, such order provides vital support for the creative management of the human services organization and for a balanced blending of the different paradigms that ultimately shape a human services organization.

12

Managing People

The Issue: From Personnel Administration to Human Resources Development

The essence of human services management is a group process: tapping the combined knowledge, experience, and energy of a group of people and channeling it to create an environment responsive to and supportive of the human needs of society. The centrality of people to the organization and operations of the human services means that one of the human services manager's chief functions is the management of the people who staff the agency.

As a **people manager**, the human services administrator is faced with developing mechanisms, processes, and dynamics that will (1) channel the best possible human talent and energy to achieving the missions of human services institutions and (2) provide the means by which human services employees can meet a significant number of their material and psychic needs, individually and collectively, from their employment in human services institutions. This has proven to be a complex and often difficult task.

In recent years, there has been a refocusing of the people-managing processes *from* traditional personnel administration *to* human resources development, a shift that emphasizes people as the primary resource and asset of any organization. At one level, this task is relatively simple because of the inherent satisfaction that can be derived from working jointly with other people to accomplish desirable and meaningful improvements in society. But at another level, the task is fraught with all of the complexity and frailty of human beings interacting with each other.

Frequently, the environment of human services organizations is such that the control paradigm is dominant. This often means dealing with human beings as objects, appendages of an organizational machine whose motivation is primarily economic. But fortunately many other human services organizations are perceived as vehicles for the expression of the innate human potential that exists in all of us. It is the latter, who foster a staff-development paradigm, who are working to move traditional personnel administration to a new definition, one of human resources development.

The roots of modern personnel administration for public and nonprofit organizations can be traced to 1883, when the passage of the Pendleton Act for federal government employment created a personnel system based on *merit*. Entrance and promotion in a merit system was founded on a process of open competition, consisting of the following principal elements: adequate publicity, opportunity to apply, realistic standards, absence of discrimination, ranking on the basis of ability, and knowledge of results.

The merit system was a creature of an "antispoils-system" movement. Thus, a control model was developed bent on keeping the scoundrels out—the "scoundrels" being the political hacks who were part of every incoming political machine as it swept to power. In time the control paradigm became such a major element of professional personnel administration that it became almost an end unto itself, constraining the development of public, nonprofit organizations that were oriented toward the mission paradigm and/or the staff-development paradigm.

Many human services organizations are still dominated by the control paradigm. This is particularly true during an era of limited human services resources, when a major control over the flow of funds is through the personnel function. The people-management function presents the human services administrator with a major challenge: To what extent can a human services organization operate in a climate focused on human resources development with a staff-development paradigm, despite the extreme pressure exercised by the control of traditional personnel systems? For the reader, it may turn out to be a lifetime challenge.

Fortunately, three forces support attempts to replace traditional personnel management with human resources development, namely:

- Minority-group mainstreaming

- The women's movement

- Advocates of the staff-development paradigm

In Chapter 7, we examined the dynamics of the first two forces because they are emerging as the primary employment resource for most human services organizations. The latter force is relatively new. It has grown out of a recognition of the new demographics of the worker in the United States. During the next two decades, it will be reinforced as we move into a period of labor shortage. This latter force supports the principle set forth by the seer of American management, Peter Drucker (1954): It is the function of the manager to see that each person is encouraged to develop her own potential to the limits of her ability and desire.

The movement of the people-management function from a control paradigm to a staff-development paradigm is still in the process of unfolding. The human services manager has the opportunity to participate in this process.

The Basic People Management Skills

The primary talent for managing people in human services organizations is skill in *blending* and *linking* organizational goals with personal-professional goals. In its most simplified form, such skill includes:

1. Establishing organizational performance goals and then communicating them clearly to all employees.
2. Continually ascertaining employee's personal and professional goals.
3. Blending and linking these two sets of goals.

Figure 12.1   Blending: The Critical People-Management Skill

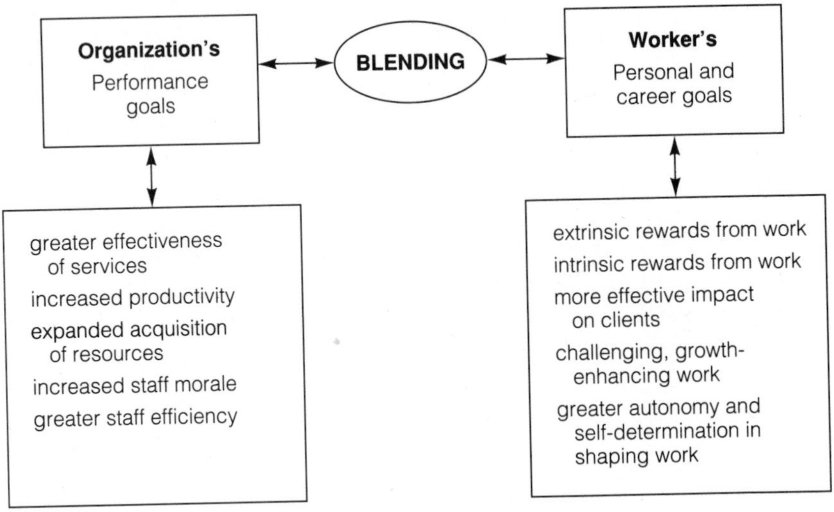

Source: Adapted from Myron E. Weiner, "Managing People for Enhanced Performance" in *Managing for Service Effectiveness in Social Welfare Organizations,* edited by Rino J. Patti, et al. (New York: Haworth, 1988).

As Figure 12.1 indicates, the criteria for measuring organizational goals and personal-professional goals are quite different, but they both emanate from the same source: the job. The starting point of people management skills is the fact that the job links the individual and the organization. As Chester Barnard (1938), James March and Herbert Simon (1958), and James Thompson (1967) conceptualized, the job is the basis for what they labeled the **inducements–contributions theory**. This theory asserts that the individual–organization linkage is based on a formal or informal contract that expresses the inducements an organization offers to an employee in exchange for his willingness to make contributions to the organization (Table 12.1). The inducements–contributions contract lays the foundation for the design of people-management processes and systems in human services organizations. Its goal is seeking congruence and convergence between the individual employee's career goals and the organization's mission.

Traditional Personnel Management Functions

Whatever the paradigm, control or staff-development, there are some practical functions of personnel management that are fundamental to every human services organization. It is necessary therefore that a human services manager master them and be sure that they are in place, working smoothly. To be effec-

Table 12.1   The Inducements–Contributions Contract

The Individual	The Organization
▪ The job links the individual to a career and a status–role in a social system and thus helps meet personal needs and aspirations.	▪ The job provides qualified human resources (energy and skills) necessary for the achievement of organizational missions.
▪ Limits are placed on the behavior that the individual can exhibit in the organization.	▪ Receives limited array of individual's total possible behavior.
▪ Quid pro quo: Defines what jobs the individual is expected to do and defines appropriate rewards.	▪ Quid pro quo: Defines the jobs the individual is expected to do and defines rewards for performance.
▪ Provides opportunities, constraints, and "sphere of action" for career building.	▪ Means for exchanging today's efforts for today's inducements; opportunity for skills acquisition and visibility.

tive and efficient, the organization requires fundamental personnel processes that work in such an orderly manner that they can be expected and anticipated. Figure 12.2 portrays these fundamental people-management functions, which we will briefly review.

Classification

The cornerstone of the personnel system in a human services organization is a schema in which all jobs in the organization have been classified by **positions**. Each position is analyzed, evaluated, rated, and ranked according to location in the organizational hierarchy; the specific tasks, duties, and responsibilities required; and the skills needed. Each position has a title, the grouping or class it belongs to, its location in the pay plan, its organizational authority, and the number of other positions (people) supervised, if any.

A position classification schema is generally developed by a specialist, either by a consulting firm or by a staff member of the agency's personnel department. Development of such a schema involves the following steps:

1. **Job analysis**: Analyzing the tasks of a job (i.e., activities performed, tools required, working conditions, skills required) and preparing job descriptions. The latter indicate the tasks to be performed and the extent to which the work will be performed under supervision or the requirement of independent judgment, knowledge, and experience.
2. **Classification**: Grouping the positions, based on their similarities, into classes. A class is considered a group of positions sufficiently alike in respect to tasks, duties, and responsibilities that they are treated as a group for common treatment in personnel matters.

Figure 12.2   Overview of Traditional
              Personnel Management Functions

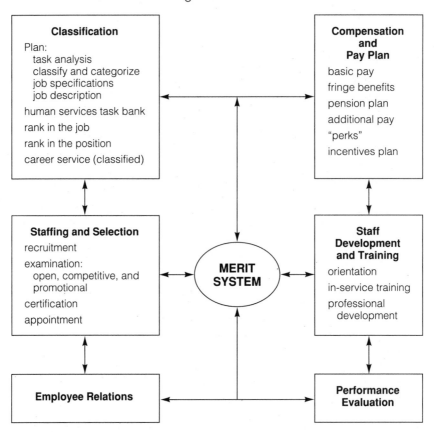

3. **Job description**: Preparing specifications and performance criteria for each class (Figure 12.3).
4. **Categorization**: Allocating individual positions to each of the classes defined and described. These become the basis of a position classification plan for the agency (Table 12.2).

Peter Pecora and Michael Austin (1987) suggest that a comprehensive, computerized task bank should be used in modern human services personnel management systems. The task bank that they have developed consists of 447 different task statements that cover the vast majority of human services clinical and administrative tasks and the major, special human services program areas: adoptions and foster care, protective services, day–residential–group care, legal services–court work, and education and hospital. An example of a task statement in this bank would be the following:

Table 12.2   Position Classification Plan

Classified Class Code	Position Title	Pay Grade	Pay Range
1937	Director of protective services	MG 19	$53,820–66,604
1948	Regional director of childrens' and protective services	MP 19	47,508–56,539
	Program supervisor:	MP 15	41,727–49,284
6584	Social worker		
6363	Public assistance		
6620	Psychiatric social worker associate	SG 22	35,620–42,886
7760	Social work supervisor	SG 21	31,395–36,706
	Social worker:	NC 18	27,033–32,089
7713	General		
7744	Spanish-speaking		
	Case worker:	NC 15	23,001–28,818
1495	General		
1518	Spanish-speaking		
	Social worker trainee:	SG 13	21,786–24,496
7746	General		
7747	Spanish-speaking		

(22) Develop intermediate treatment objectives for a client during a convalescent period in order to enhance client functioning.

The position classification plans for most human services organizations in the United States are developed using the **rank-in-the-job approach**, that is, emphasizing specific requirements for each position. Another approach, popular in other countries, is **rank-in-the-person**, which emphasizes different levels of abilities and experience (e.g., associate professor in a university; colonel in the army). Although the latter is more difficult to develop for large, complex human services organizations that involve a variety of different disciplines, it provides more flexibility for more effective human services functioning.

Staffing and Selection

The position classification plan is the basis for selecting the most qualified person to fill the positions in a human services agency. The staffing process consists of four steps: (1) recruitment; (2) examination; (3) certification; and (4) appointment.

Figure 12.3   Job Description:
Regional Director of Children's and Protective Services

Classified   MP 19
Class Code: 1948   Effective date
                                                April 20 1990

Summary of Class
In a region of the Department of Children and Youth Services; plans,
organizes, directs, and controls the administration of assigned programs.

Supervision Received
Works under the direction of the Director of the Division of Children's
and Protective Services or other administrative official of a higher
grade.

Supervision Exercised
Supervises assigned professional and technical staff and may assist in
the supervision, administration, and coordination of activities of other
personnel under contract with the department.

Examples of Duties
Administers assigned children and youth child welfare programs within
the region for children and youth as required; identifies needs of children in the region for the purpose of determining available community
resources and for gathering data to facilitate overall planning of the department; recommends changes in policy for better service or more efficient administration; identifies and evaluates need for personnel, budget, space, allocation of equipment, vehicles, and supplies; makes
evaluations and prepares reports detailing regional activities, program
operational status, and client statistics; performs evaluations and makes
recommendations for staffing levels; cooperates with and shares appropriate information with the Regional Advisory Committee; supervises
and coordinates purchase-of-service agreements with personnel agencies
and/or facilities as assigned; represents the commissioner in community and public relations activities within the region as assigned; speaks
before lay and professional groups presenting to the public the department's views on children's needs and issues as assigned; meets regularly
with supervisory staff to discuss problem areas, program effectiveness,
and procedures; reviews and evaluates work performance and atten-
dance of assigned staff; applies progressive discipline when necessary;
performs related duties as required.

Minimum Qualifications Required: Knowledge, Skill, and Ability
Considerable knowledge of the principles of social service management, coordination, and operational administration; considerable knowledge of programs dealing with delinquent, neglected, abused, dependent, mentally ill, or emotionally disturbed children; knowledge of the
legal aspects of guardianship, custodial care, and confidentiality of
records; considerable ability to analyze all aspects of child welfare administration and to recommend and implement change; considerable

Figure 12.3   (continued)

administrative ability; considerable ability in written and/or oral communication and instruction; ability to deal effectively with others.

Experience and Training
General: A master's degree in social work and four years employment in child welfare administration.

Special Experience: Two years of the general experience *must* be in a supervisory capacity at or above the level of program supervisor.

Substitutions Allowed
- The ten years employment in child welfare administration may be substituted for the entire general experience. Candidates must still possess the special experience.
- A combination of undergraduate college education and employment in child care administration totaling ten years may be substituted for the entire general experience. Candidates must still possess the special experience.

Special Requirements
A current motor vehicle operator's license may be required during employment in this class.

There are essentially two categories of selection: open-competitive and promotional. The latter is limited only to employees currently working for the agency making the appointment. In either category, although the criteria and mechanisms may be different, the same four steps are followed. Before briefly describing each of the four steps in the selection process, it should be noted that for public human services organizations, the process only applies to competitive career service positions. In every position classification plan, there are certain unclassified positions that are exempted from the selection process: elected officials, top executives and their personal assistants, positions considered confidential in nature, temporary or part-time positions, and some laborers. The question of which positions should properly be exempted from the competitive career service can be a subject for considerable debate.

As the reader would anticipate, human services organizations aggressively use equal opportunity and affirmative action guidelines for all of the following selection and staffing steps.

Recruitment. Widest possible media use should publicize a vacancy in a human services organization so that qualified candidates have the opportunity to compete for the opening. Posting announcements in appropriate locations that describe the vacancy and the qualifications is a popular method. Other methods include the following:

- Publishing notices in local, statewide, and nationwide newspapers.
- Advertising in professional newsletters.
- Listing the vacancy in job-availability listings of professional associations.
- Mailing announcements to individuals who have expressed interest in such positions.

Most of these methods are passive in nature. The intent is to circulate information about the vacancies as widely as possible, leaving it to qualified candidates to learn about the opening and apply on their own initiative.

In recent years, because of criticism that the standard recruitment methods excluded women and minorities, recruitment has become more aggressive. Representatives of the human services agency make personal visits to college campuses, professional association meetings, community groups, and the like for the purpose of identifying candidates and encouraging them to apply for the openings. For critical top-level vacancies, personnel departments use the popular private-business recruitment method of hiring a "headhunter" (i.e., a private personnel search firm) to seek out top candidates.

Recruitment is often limited by the imposition of certain criteria like the requirement that qualified candidates be residents of the jurisdiction or be currently employed by the agency. Such criteria may be the result of emotional negotiations between employees and the personnel department, and the human services manager may find herself awkwardly on both sides of such issues.

Examination.   The examination process is primarily concerned with objectivity, validity, and reliability. On the surface, this may seem easy to achieve; in practice, it is difficult. The standard examination methods are:

- Written tests
- Oral-technical panels
- Performance tests
- Personal interviews

Written tests and performance tests are easy to administer and score, and the results can easily be ranked. But the content of these tests can be controversial, either because they are skewed to favor certain groups (e.g., those with experience compared with those with greater education and training) or because they contain material not job-related in order to eliminate those groups that traditionally have not had equal opportunity in certain jobs (e.g., jobs that mainly go to white men).

It has been noted in recent years that certain very qualified candidates are *test phobic:* they "freeze" under the tension of a competitive written test. Other candidates have acquired the skill of passing written examinations even though in terms of practical ability they may not be very proficient. This contrasts with other candidates who may do poorly on written tests but perform the job effectively and productively.

Oral-technical examinations are time-consuming and thus are usually used only to select candidates for certain positions. A panel of three to five experts in the area for which a candidate is being sought conduct a group interview of the top qualifying candidates. The panel then rates these candidates, using criteria provided by the personnel department.

Interviews are usually used only for special, top executive positions. A panel of experts reviews the applications of all eligible candidates, ranking them in accordance with criteria developed by the personnel department. The human services manager making the appointment then personally interviews the top candidates. The personal interview is also one of the primary examination methods used by private agencies.

In recent years, another examination method used for top positions is the **management-assessment process**. This calls for the top candidates to undertake, individually or collectively, a series of experiential exercises and self-evaluation tests that attempts to identify their strengths and weaknesses. (See "Career Development" later in the chapter.)

One of the most difficult and controversial areas of the examination process begins even before the examinations are conducted: the systematic screening of all applications to eliminate those who are ineligible—that is, those who do not meet the minimum qualifications required for the position. In most cases, this screening–evaluation is almost automatic: the candidate does or does not meet the minimum qualifying criteria. But in other cases, the issue of eligibility is subject to debate. Generally, when there is some question of meeting minimum qualifications, evaluation by several different personnel department examiners will ensure the objectivity of this screening process.

Imperfect as they may seem at times, examinations are vital to the personnel selection process. For human services managers, the challenge is to continually make improvements in examination mechanisms, either adapting those currently in use or developing new selection techniques.

Certification.   Whichever means of examination is used, a list is prepared certifying those candidates who are determined eligible for appointment, ranking them in order of their scores. The list of certified candidates usually remains in effect for a certain period of time. Thus, those candidates not appointed to the originally announced vacancy continue to be eligible for appointment as other vacancies occur, without having to repeat the examination.

Somewhere in the process, it is important to check the references of applicants. Generally, it is too time-consuming to undertake this task until the final list of candidates is drawn up, prior to certifying them on a list of those eligible for appointment. Experience has proven that there are preferred approaches to checking candidate references to acquire clear and reliable data about candidates' prior experience.

Certification is generally initiated when the human services agency with the vacancy requisitions the personnel unit for candidates eligible for appointment. The requisition results in a limited eligibility list of certified candidates, which is forwarded to the appointing officer.

Appointment.   Certification by the personnel unit is limited only in terms of the numbers of names on the list. Usually, the appointing official receives the three to five names at the top of the list of eligible candidates. If there is more than one vacancy to be filled, the number of names will be expanded.

The appointing officer then contacts the candidates on the certified list to ascertain whether or not they are still available for employment and still interested in being appointed. In some cases, the candidate is provided an opportunity to waive appointment: pass up the immediate vacancy but remain in the present sequence on the certified eligible register. In either case, the appointing officer may request additional names of candidates to permit a choice from the top three or five certified candidates.

At this point, personal interviews with each of the certified candidates are generally conducted by the appointing officer. Follow-up interviews are possible. There are guidelines for such interviews, both in terms of following the correct affirmative action guidelines and in terms of eliciting sufficient information on which to make a judgment.

Eventually, the appointing officer makes a choice and informs the personnel department of the appointment. Eligible candidates who were not appointed remain on the register for consideration for future vacancies. The rank-order list is adjusted, taking into account the removal of the candidate who has been appointed.

As we noted in our Chapter 7 discussion of women and minorities in human services management, in the final appointment process there may be suspicion of discrimination because of such factors as age, sex, color, or race. There might even have been political pressure exerted during the final selection process. A human services manager must be sensitive to the possibility that such factors can influence the final choice. It is critical therefore that an administrator use enlightened objectivity as the ultimate criterion for the final selection of the most qualified candidate.

It sometimes happens that a human services manager may wish to appoint someone who has a known track record of outstanding performance in the particular skills and experience being sought. At the same time, the manager is faced with a selection process that certifies less-qualified candidates. This can create an interesting problem.

Although every attempt should be made to perfect and improve the personnel system–selection process, this area will be a likely source of value-tensions for the human services manager.

Compensation and Pay Plans

As the inducements–contributions contract suggests, workers expect incentives and rewards for contributing their energy and effort to the effective and efficient achievement of the agency's goals. These rewards are both material and psychic. The rewards-and-incentive system for personnel management must meet several criteria, including some of the following:

- Reward level: A level of rewards high enough to meet basic needs of the employees
- Equity: *External*—equal to or greater than those in other agencies; *internal*—fair distribution among all employees
- Individuality: Rewards that fit the needs of individuals
- Performance: Relating rewards to individual and group performance
- Structure: Distributing rewards to fit the management style and the organization's hierarchy

Basic Pay Plan.   For each position classification schema, a basic pay plan is developed and adopted. Based on the concept of "equal pay for equal work," each class of positions is analyzed and placed within the pay plan so that positions of comparable knowledge, skill, and responsibility receive comparable pay. Each position has a minimum and a maximum pay; there are a specific number of annual increments of equal amounts that an employee receives until the maximum is reached. Because the position classification plan deals with sets of related positions (e.g., social worker trainee, caseworker, social worker II, social work supervisor), the minimum-maximum pay increases for each position as the level of knowledge, skill, and responsibilities increases (see Table 12.2 on page 331).

The basic pay plan has to take into account the labor market of the jurisdiction. For example, if there is a shortage of nurses, they will receive higher salaries because their supply is limited. Most human services agency pay plans, however, are more sensitive to available resources than to offering compensation levels that will attract the most talented and experienced people to the organization. For large, public human services organizations, the basic pay plan applies to every agency in the jurisdiction. This may limit the ability to offer incentives needed to recruit exceptional candidates, although it is sometimes possible to appoint someone to a position above the minimum pay level, if a strong case can be made.

The basic pay plan can be a source of frustration for the human services manager who recognizes that improved productivity and effectiveness is related to reward and increased compensation. The basic pay plan generally can only be changed in one of three ways:

- A percentage increase for all employees in a jurisdiction, either recommended by management during the budget process or negotiated by the employee organization (e.g., labor union) representing the employees

- An upgrade of a set of positions to a higher-pay category, brought about by pressure from employees in that group or by labor-market pressures
- The installation of a new comprehensive basic pay plan that has been recommended by an outside consultant

While the additional compensation mechanisms are more limited in public and nonprofit human services organization than in proprietary agencies, there are still a number of supplemental pay opportunities: overtime, longevity, incentives, and fringe benefits.

Overtime Pay.   Many human services employees receive *overtime pay* for working off-hours, on weekends, or on holidays (sometimes for one-and-one-half or two times their basic pay rate). As unions became stronger, overtime compensation is specified in the pay plan, working conditions, or union contracts. For managers or professionals in human services organizations, overtime is rare; instead, there is a practice of providing *comp time*—compensatory time off from work, with pay, on a day that is convenient for the agency and the professional.

Longevity Pay.   Some human services organizations have a compensation plan that includes longevity pay, additional pay to employees who have been with the agency for over ten, fifteen, twenty, even twenty-five years. This type of compensation is for the purpose of retention—encouraging good employees to remain with the same agency. The amount of the longevity pay increases for employees the longer they remain in the agency.

Incentive Plans.   Traditionally, the incentive pay or bonus mechanisms have not been an integral element of compensation plans of public and nonprofit human services organizations. But in recent years, there has been a trend toward two types of such plans:

- Performance contracts: Management incentive plans whereby different levels of performance objectives are set annually, with pay increases based on levels of actual achievement
- Performance–merit awards: Lump-sum bonuses or pay increases for outstanding achievements or performance

Incentive plans in human services organizations are still more an ideal than a reality; for the human services manager, they remain an opportunity for employee motivation that has yet to be fully explored.

Fringe Benefits.   It is estimated that fringe benefits account for 30 to 35 percent of the compensation of many human services employees. They generally include the following:

- Paid holidays: From six to eleven days per year
- Paid vacations: One to three weeks, depending on the length of employee service
- Sick leave: Up to fifteen days per year; when not taken, they can accumulate to a maximum (e.g., up to ninety days)
- Personal leave: For major illness or death in the family
- Parenting leave: Increasingly available for pregnant employees or for mothers of newborn or newly adopted children; also available for fathers of newborn children in some organizations
- Group insurance: Hospital, surgical, medical, dental, major medical, income protection, or life insurance coverage
- Pension and retirement: Payments to supplement employees' contributions
- Services: Day care; respite care; employees assistance programs (EAPs)

Fringe benefits have become a major building block in the provision of human services for the workers of most modern welfare states.

Traditionally, one of the reasons that the base pay of public human services employees was lower than that of comparable employees in private agencies was the government *pension systems* that provided greater security for retirement. In recent years, as public pay plans became more competitive in the job market, as the number of public employees grew, and as retired public employees began to practice "double-dipping" (e.g., retired military personnel working for federal-state government and eventually receiving two pensions plus Social Security) the pension and retirement practices of governments were subjected to critical analysis and are in a period of reassessment and revision.

Staff Development and Training

Traditionally, personnel managers have administered the organizations's staff-development and training program. Those who took this function seriously provided professional and technical training programs (e.g., courses, seminars, and workshops) conducted on the premises of the organization or arranged for employees to visit off-site locations (e.g., local universities, distant universities, and training centers). Some larger organizations have hired trainers with specialized skills as staff employees of the personnel department. A large, state government welfare department may have a team of several trainers who concentrate on upgrading technical knowledge and skills (e.g., interviewing skills and complying with latest federal regulations, procedures, and record-keeping methods). These trainers most probably would also conduct supervisory training. For more complex management training, special seminars and workshops may be arranged with trainers from outside the organization and it is not uncommon to find public and nonprofit organizations contracting with nearby universities to conduct a comprehensive set of specialized educational offerings for operational, professional, and managerial employees. In addition, employees may be encouraged through stipends to continue their formal education and acquire bachelor's or master's degrees in human services fields.

Staff development can be subdivided into in-service training and professional development. **In-service training** is undertaken for a large number of purposes:

- Orientation
- Improved performance
- Broadening skill base of employees
- Training trainers—providing supervisors with training skills so that they can train those they supervise
- Management development

Of these, *orientation* is the most critical and should not be neglected; indeed, it should be undertaken annually, even for employees who have been working in the agency for several years. Although the orientation for the new appointee is a form of introduction to the work environment of the agency, orientation for the veteran employee serves a broad number of purposes, not the least of which is the opportunity to create a renewal of employees' feelings of mutuality and sharing of the responsibility for the productive and effective achievement of agency missions.

In many organizations the focus of training programs has been skill and knowledge acquisition to improve organizational productivity. Other organizations emphasize *professional development*, to help the employee develop her potential (the staff-development paradigm). Although there may be organizational payoff with both approaches, the latter embodies a genuine desire to see people develop their full potentialities.

In recent years, many enlightened staff-development and -training programs have been based on Malcolm Knowles's (1978) theory of **androgogy**—adult learning (in contrast to *pedagogy,* child learning theory). The essentials of androgogy are that adults are:

- Motivated to learn as they experience needs.
- Oriented to life and problem situations for learning.
- Rich in experience as a learning resource.
- In strong need of self-directness.
- Individually unique in style, pace, and media of learning.

To Knowles, the learning climate must include a psychological environment characterized by mutuality, respectfulness, collaboration, and informality. Most professional trainers have come to adopt Knowles's theory of androgogy as the foundation of organization and staff development and training.

Performance Evaluations

Ascertaining and recording the performance of employees is a traditional element of fundamental people management. It is the basis not only for improving an employee's abilities, training, pay increases, promotions, and issues of discipline but it also validates the selection processes of the agency. Performance evaluations usually are prepared by the immediate supervisor; the employee has the right to review it and, where necessary, record a difference of opinion about the evaluation.

There are several different types of performance-evaluation approaches. Pecora and Austin (1987) and George Milkovich and John Boudreau (1988), for example, identify the following different types:

- Graphic rating scales
- Work standards
- Essays
- Management by objectives/results (MBO/MOR)
- Adjective checklist
- Behaviorally anchored ratings scales (BARS)
- Ranking
- Forced choice
- Critical incident
- Assessment center

Whereas MBO/MOR focuses on the results of an employee's performance, the BARS approach concentrates on specific work behaviors. The latter is an attempt to make the evaluation method less subjective. Pecora and Austin (1987) recommend an approach that combines MBO/MOR with the BARS methodology.

Effective employee evaluation through performance appraisals remain a challenge for many human services organizations. Too often such evaluation is inadequate because it is difficult to perform, or is undertaken in a perfunctory manner. Although there are usually established criteria, many of the ratings are essentially subjective in nature. In addition, the process is sometimes viewed cynically because pay increases tend to be automatic, and, in a merit system career service, it is quite difficult to fire an employee after the initial probationary period. The challenge for the human services manager is to instill in both employee and supervisor the notion that performance evaluations should relate to the employee's personal and professional development, rather than to issues of reward or punishment. Relating performance evaluation to career development is a new human resources development trend, which we discuss later.

Employee Relations

For years every organization has had formal and informal means of improving the organization's relationships with employees. The former methods have included monthly publications, periodic socials (e.g, holiday parties and picnics), an employee cafeteria, and an employee recreation program. Informally, the organization may encourage the formation of credit unions, vacation clubs, sports teams, and so forth. Employee relations also include

- Recognition of achievement.
- Procedures for handling poor performance.
- Food–children–transportation services.
- Employee communications (e.g., informal newsletters, bulletin boards).
- Safety management.
- Medical programs.

There has been an increasing trend toward the formation of employees' unions or associations that negotiate formally with the human services agency for employee-working conditions. Some unions have become militant and exercise their right to strike. Where union contracts exist, the employee/employer relationship becomes very formalized, placing the requirement on each human services manager to study carefully the mandatory and discretionary requirements of the contract. In general, a human services manager needs knowledge and skills in all aspects of dealing with employee organizations, union or non-union. In certain aspects of this field, expert assistance and advice from outside the organization is wise; for example, contract negotiations may require expertise and experience that should be called on when needed.

Human Resources Development: Some Recent Trends

Thus far we have considered a cluster of processes that are the core of traditional personnel mangement. There are, however, a number of newer concepts, processes, and skills that have resulted from trends in people management during recent decades (Figure 12.4). These constitute what is now being termed **human resources development**.

Affirmative Action

Dennis Gilbert and Joseph Kahl (1987: 75–6) indicate that both minorities and women have made significant progress in the work force of the United States. Women were only 28 percent of the work force in 1950; by 1990 this had passed 40 percent with the prediction that they would comprise about half the

Figure 12.4   Human Resources Development: Some Recent Trends

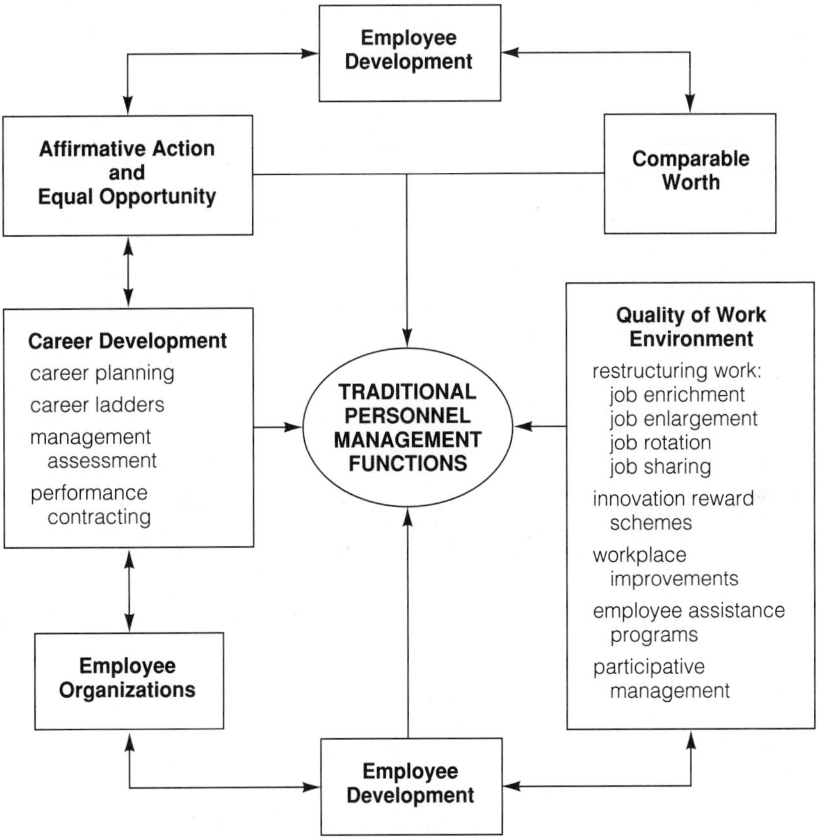

labor force by the turn of the century. Blacks also made significant progress. In 1940 the vast majority of blacks were in the lowest occupational categories (e.g., laborers and service workers); by 1980 70 percent were in the upper six categories of the occupation structure of the labor force.

But women and blacks are still underrepresented in upper-management positions and many of the professions—dentistry and engineering, for example. Women are crowded into a small number of pink-collar occupations (e.g., secretaries, cashiers, and hairdressers), which offer lower pay and prestige than other positions that require the same level of education and training. While affirmative action has been a catalyst for the progress made by women and minorities during the past several decades, the need for it is still very apparent.

Affirmative action and equal opportunity are both concepts and legal necessities. One of the catalysts for a reconceptualization of traditional personnel management was the push for equal opportunity and affirmative action that

Table 12.3   Federal Employment Discrimination Laws
               and Executive Orders

Enactment	Entitlement
Title VII, 1964 Civil Rights Act	Prohibits discrimination based on race, religion, sex, and national origin.
Executive Orders 11246 and 11375 (1965)	Shifts focus of equal opportunity to affirmative action.
Equal Pay Act of 1963	Prohibits sex difference in pay for substantially equal work.
1967 Age Discrimination in Employment Act	Prohibits discrimination against those between ages of forty and seventy.
Executive Order 11478	Prohibits discrimination also based on marital status, political affiliation, physical disability.
Rehabilitation Act of 1973; Executive Order 11914	Prohibits discrimination based on physical or mental disability and shifts focus to affirmative action.
1974 Veterans Readjustment Act	Prohibits discrimination against disabled veterans and shifts focus to affirmative action for Vietnam-era veterans.

grew out of the civil rights movement of the 1960s, when minority groups pushed for greater representation in the staffing patterns of organizations. Their basic thesis was that the standard mechanisms for personnel administration (e.g., position classification plans, recruitment and selection, and pay plans) discriminated against minority groups, a view strongly supported with the rise of the women's movement.

Affirmative action focuses on actions and decisions of employers that enhance employment, upgrading, and retention of groups previously discriminated against such as women, minorities, the disabled, the elderly, and veterans. It is a more vigorous and proactive stance than **equal opportunity**, which essentially restrains practices that discriminate. Legislation and regulations now require the preparation of affirmative action plans, setting forth exactly how the organization will ensure equal opportunity for all—regardless of race, religion, sex, color, age, disability, sexual preference, or marital status. In many large human services organizations, the manager works with an affirmative action officer who scrutinizes personnel actions to ensure that the plan is being followed, and there is a good deal of debate on which definition of equal opportunity to apply.

There are many federal, state, and municipal laws and regulations concerning discrimination and equal opportunity in employment. In the federal government, for example, they include those listed in Table 12.3.

One of the human services administrator's people-management responsibilities is to ensure that every employee moves as far as she can or wants to in an organization, without any artificial constraints. Equal opportunity and affirmative action are important elements of the staff-development paradigm. Although one must become familiar with the legal necessities of affirmative action, more important is the need to focus creatively on the maximum development of an organization's human resources—primarily from the perspective of each employee and ultimately from the perspective of the agency.

Comparable Worth

Equal pay for equal work has been one of the cornerstones of personnel systems. In recent years, the concept of *equal pay for work of equal value,* or more simply **comparable worth**, has added an important new dimension to people management founded on human resources development. Studies have indicated that jobs populated by women and minorities receive significantly less (approximately 40 percent less) pay than jobs held primarily by men, even for the same work. They also show that while men and women may be performing identical work in an organization, they are assigned different titles and pay grades, with the net result that women earn less than men for the same work. In such situations, personnel systems must be corrected to ensure equal pay for equal work.

But the focus of comparable worth is to analyze all jobs in an organization to arrive at a basis for determining if different work is actually comparable in terms of education and experience requirements, level of responsibility and skills required, and value of contribution to the organization's performance. There is no lack of techniques and approaches to ensure comparable worth— the real issue is priority, values, and perceptions.

With the increasing percentage of women and minorities in human services organizations, the struggle for comparable worth became a major issue of the 1970s and 1980s; its solution remains a challenge for the 1990s. A human services manager committed to the staff-development paradigm for the management of human resources must continually be sensitive to the issue of comparable worth and develop new, creative mechanisms in the organization that will make it a reality. For human services organizations dedicated to human development—and largely staffed by women and members of minority groups— comparable worth is clearly a fundamental operating management principle.

Employee Organizations

Even though the decade of the 1980s was not one of rapid expansion of unions, most human services administrators have to deal with formal employee organizations. This places a requirement on the manager to acquire the necessary knowledge and skills. It has become an area of specialization that not only has its own body of literature but also may lead to the formal appointment of a professional within the human services organization dedicated to dealing with unions and employee organizations. In its most comprehensive perspective, this specialty is known as **labor relations**.

The field of labor relations includes such areas as aspects of unionization (e.g., a union shop, closed shop, preferential shop, and right to work), collective bargaining, grievances, arbitration, and conflict resolution (strikes, unfair labor practices, picketing, and lockouts). In many cases, human services managers may have to draw on the expertise of consulting specialists to assist with some or all of the above problems. For example, if the union has national affiliation with the AFL–CIO AFSCME (American Federation of State, County, and Municipal Employees), the union will be represented by the federation's full-time expert in labor relations. To enter into collective bargaining with a specialist may place the human services manager at a disadvantage unless there is also a specialist on the management team involved in the collective bargaining.

Essentially, the two primary aspects of labor relations are contract negotiations and contract implementation. The negotiations process can take a long time; its aim is an agreement that both management (managers and policymakers) and the union (employees) can accept. In the event of an impasse (e.g., nonagreement), the parties have several alternatives, namely:

- Mediation: A third party (e.g., a neutral labor relations specialist) sits down with representatives of the union and management and tries to encourage them to work out their differences.

- Fact finding: A third-party labor relations expert investigates the issues that separate the two parties and submits a report identifying the areas of difference, with the hope that the report will help the union and management work out their differences.

- Arbitration: A mutually agreed-on arbitrator investigates the situation and is given the authority to impose a settlement. This is called *binding arbitration*. Other forms of arbitration include *advisory arbitration* and *final-offer arbitration*. In the latter, each party provides the arbitrator with their final offer, and the arbitrator selects the best of the two.

If all the conflict-resolution processes do not work, the union may call a strike to place pressure on the policymakers and managers of the organization. Even though some states prohibit public and nonprofit organization employees from striking, it is not unusual to find *walkouts* or *slowdowns* (e.g., employees calling in sick), which have the same effect as strikes.

When negotiations result in a contract, it generally has to be approved by the employees themselves and by the policy-making body of the organization or jurisdiction. Once approved, the contract must be implemented by both parties. A contract will include such items as

- Union and employee security.
- Grievance and arbitration procedures.

- Health and safety provisions.
- Disciplinary procedures.
- Working conditions.
- Compensation and benefits.
- Seniority provisions.
- Contract expiration date.

Generally, the union will elect or appoint union stewards for each of the sub-units in the agency, who will monitor all aspects of the contract's implementation. Human services managers at all levels of the agency need to become familiar with the details of the contract to ensure that it is being carried out correctly.

Dealing with unions through negotiations and contract implementation may require a change in attitude from management's traditional views, which may be adversarial. Labor unions are a fact of life for many human services organizations. They tend to keep managers "on their toes," and can be an effective focal point for the implementing aspects of the staff-development paradigm throughout the organization. Contract provisions can be the impetus for improving the working environment of employees. When viewed from this perspective, an employee organization can be a constructive and vital element of human services management founded on the staff-development paradigm.

Career Development

The human services manager is dedicated to creating an environment in which workers continue to grow personally and professionally. From this perspective, staff development and training becomes a subset of career development, which itself is a subset of the human-development paradigm. Michael Austin (1981) emphasizes that the starting point of this process is recognition of the difference among workers, as they pass through four stages in their career: exploration, establishment, maintenance, and decline. John Van Maanen and Edgar Schein (1977) suggest that a worker's career is dependent on the interaction between three stages of development for the employee: self-development, career development, and family development. An understanding of the different stages in career development is important for the human services manager who places a high priority on the career development of the agency's workers.

Career Planning. Lynne Moore Healy, Catherine Havens, and Alice Chin (1989) stress the importance of career planning, particularly for women and minorities interested in human services careers. **Career planning** involves the initiation of formal and informal activities that help a worker develop a career plan. This plan sets forth the goals of the career, the type of work and position one aspires to over time, the career ladder to that ideal position, and the professional development effort the employee needs to undertake to achieve these career goals. Career planning activities include the following:

Employee	*Human Services Manager*
▪ Assess abilities and interests	▪ Help initiate career planning
▪ Analyze career options	▪ Provide career-planning resources
▪ Ascertain career objectives	▪ Counsel and advise employees
▪ Develop a career action–plan	▪ Provide training
▪ Implement the career action–plan	▪ Support implementation of action–plans

Career planning is moving toward interactive computer-based programs that help workers develop career plans.

Career Ladders.   Closely related to career planning is the development of career ladders for individual employees. Most position classification systems have built-in **career ladders**—clear-cut opportunities for employees to advance from positions of lower to higher levels of ability, responsibility, and authority. But with the rise of the women's movement in recent years, position classification systems have been subjected to the criticism that they serve to dead-end too many employees, particularly those in the lower echelons of the organization. The issue primarily focuses on the problem of developing a transition from one set of positions (e.g., clerical and secretarial in nature) to another set of positions (e.g., junior management) to enable continued advancement. This can be accomplished through an aggressive training and staff-development program (see Figure 12.5). Career ladders can be opened up by examining the position classification system in detail to work out transition arrangements between families of positions.

The real importance of affirmative action and equal opportunity compliance to the agency are the payoffs derived from tapping an employee's knowledge and skill capabilities, through personal and professional development.

Management Assessment.   As a starting point for individualized management-development efforts, modern human services personnel systems have begun to use the **management-assessment process** to help managers at all levels identify their strengths and weaknesses, under the guidance of trained assessors.

The management-assessment process includes a series of individualized and group tests and exercises (see Figure 12.6) that measures the individual's current and potential managerial capabilities. Working with career counselors and trainers, the data can be used by workers to build on their strengths and identify bodies of knowledge and skills that can be acquired through the additional investment of time and effort. Management assessment is an important methodology for career development; its use is also an indication that the human

Figure 12.5 Clerical and Secretarial
Employee Advancement Program (CSEAP)

The CSEAP was established in 1979 by agreement between the State of New York and the Administrative Services Unit (ASU) of the Civil Services Employees Association (CSEA). The state–CSEA goal in joining forces for this effort is reflected in the program's name: clerical and secretarial advancement.

CSEAP serves the more than 37,000 New York State employees in the Administrative Services bargaining unit and over fifty-five state departments and agencies. The program seeks to improve morale, mobility, and productivity by providing training, development, and advancement opportunities.

CSEAP has opened career and salary doors for clerical and secretarial employees in three broad areas:

- *Clerical and Secretarial Careers:* CSEAP has expanded career opportunities in the clerical and secretarial field. New titles such as Information Processing Specialist, Library Clerk, and Treatment Unit Clerk allow agencies and employees to redefine careers in keeping with changes in technology and office management.

- *Paraprofessional Careers:* CSEAP has helped expand paraprofessional career opportunities in both technical and administrative fields. Over 400 ASU employees have moved to such paraprofessional titles as Legal Assistant Trainee, Health Program Aide, and Investigative Aide.

- *Professional Careers:* CSEAP has helped build bridges to professional careers in recognition of the joint labor–management benefits of eliminating artificial barriers. Former clerical and secretarial employees are now in professional personnel, budgeting, counselor, investment officer, and administrative positions, to name only a few.

The Department of Civil Service administers CSEAP in cooperation with the governor's Office of Employee Relations (OER) and the Civil Services Employees Association.

The Employee Advancement Section of the Department of Civil Service works with New York State agencies and other units of the department to implement the program. The section provides technical assistance to agencies, coordinates transition examinations, training, and other services directed to helping ASU employees realize their full potential in public service. CSEAP is funded by New York State with funds allocated through state–CSEA negotiations and approved by the New York State legislature.

Figure 12.6   Management-Assessment Center: General Information

What is an assessment center?

An assessment center is a procedure (not a place) that uses multiple assessment techniques to evaluate candidates for promotion. These assessment techniques are job simulations based on a specific job analysis of the position for which the candidates are being assessed.

The assessment techniques are a series of exercises and group activities in which the candidates are observed by trained assessors. The candidates are then evaluated based on the knowledges, skills, abilities, and personal characteristics needed to perform the particular job for which they are candidates. The exercises and group activities are specially designed to measure these knowledges, skills, abilities, and personal characteristics. In some instances, they are close replications of the actual work a person will perform in the job.

Examples of the exercises and what they assess:

Dimensions Assessed	*In-Basket*	*Oral Interview*	*Group Exercise*	*Problem Analysis*
Oral communication	X	X	X	X
Written communication	X	X		
Decision making	X			X
Problem analysis	X	X	X	X
Stress tolerance	X	X	X	
Leadership	X	X	X	
Sensitivity	X	X	X	
Planning and organization	X	X		X
Delegation	X	X		
Judgment	X	X	X	X
Organizational sensitivity	X		X	X
Decisiveness		X	X	
Adaptability		X	X	
Initiative			X	
Integrity			X	

How will candidates benefit from the Assessment Center should they not be chosen for the position?

Each candidate can have an interview with one of the assessors in order to go over the strengths and weaknesses observed during the assessment center. This provides the candidates with the opportunity to make professional development plans directed specifically toward strengthening those areas that need to be strengthened.

Source: Adapted from the Assessment Center of the Institute of Public Service, University of Connecticut; Director: M. Jane Cleare

services organization is moving toward a conception of people management founded in human resources development.

Performance Contracting.   The confluence of two movements has resulted in a new trend in human resources management that is known as **performance contracting**. The first is the thrust toward greater results, accountability, and greater productivity improvements. The second is the human development movement that has stressed the need for managers committed to John Gardner's concept of self-renewal:

> Exploration of the full range of his own potentialities is not something that the self-renewing man leaves to the chances of life. It is something he pursues systematically, or at least avidly, to the end of his days. . . . And by potentialities I mean not just skills, but the full range of his capabilities for sensing, wondering, learning, understanding, loving and aspiring. (1964, 11–12)

One of the results has been a trend in management toward performance contracting, either imposed from a higher level of management or self-imposed. When developed by top management, it relates achievement of program-performance measures with pay increments; for example:

Achievement of Performance Measures	*Pay Increases*
▪ Exceeded	14 percent
▪ Achieved	7 percent
▪ Did not achieve	0 percent

As each manager submits detailed annual plans for program management, the process is formalized through a contract that sets down anticipated performance measures to be achieved by the year's end, and relates pay increases to the evaluation of the performance.

In organizations that have shifted to a staff-development paradigm, the emphasis in performance contracting is on self-assessment and self-improvement. In essence each employee assesses his own strengths and weaknesses. During the year, courses and workshops are taken at the employee's own initiative to overcome identified weaknesses. Performance contracts may or may not lead to higher pay at the end of the year. More important, the contract is a self-contract—"I will monitor my own improvement combining both quantifiable and qualitative measures."

From this perspective, the self-improvement performance contract is important as a fundamental management methodology in support of the human resources development philosophy of people management. Self-renewal and human development are desirable individual and group goals in their own rights, with valuable benefits for the organization.

Performance contracts have thus far been mainly applied to managers; although they can be used effectively for individual workers. Each employee develops her own annual contract to improve her performance, with the criterion being the degree to which each employee contributes to more effective client outcomes while achieving intrinsic and extrinsic rewards. It is an expression of Tom Peters's (1987) concept of value added: a process of innovations in which services continually bring some new additional value to clients.

Quality of the Work Environment

During the past two decades, there has been growing concern over a number of problems at the work place that negatively affect the productivity of workers in the United States. These include: boredom and alienation; high absenteeism; lower-quality products and services; work-related stress; lack of concern, pride, and interest in work; and alcohol and drug abuse on the job. The symbol for this trend has been QWL—quality of work life.

The QWL movement is worldwide; in the United States, it has concentrated on four activities (Milkovich and Glueck 1985):

- Participative and self-management: Quality circles, team building, and self-managing work groups
- Restructuring work: Work redesign, job enrichment, job enlargement, flex-hours, four-day workweek, job rotation, and job sharing.
- Workplace improvements: Improved physical work conditions, and wellness programs and facilities
- Innovative reward schemes: Flex-benefits, gain-sharing, and employee assistance programs (EAPs)

Let us briefly review some of these.

Restructuring Work. The work of Richard Hackman and G. R. Oldham (1980) proposes that, rather than adapting people to jobs, optimizing worker–work relationships also requires adapting jobs to people. In their ideal job-characteristics model, they indicated the relationships listed in Table 12.4.

Classification schema that assign titles, duties, and responsibilities to all employees in an organization are a traditional personnel management process. They create the order necessary for efficient achievement of employee performance objectives and organizational outcomes. But when applied as rigid straightjackets they restrict the freedom necessary for creative human services management to provide the opportunity for the development of each person's full potential.

In recent years, the field has moved in the direction of combining tasks into a general set of tasks and duties. This move has been called **job enrichment** and **job enlargement**. It attempts to provide each employee more freedom to participate in a broader range of more interesting facets of work. Other tech-

Table 12.4   Job-Characteristics Model

Core Job Characteristics	Critical Psychological States	Outcomes
■ Skill variety ■ Task identity ■ Task significance ■ Autonomy ■ Feedback from job	■ Meaningfulness of the work ■ Responsibility for work outcomes ■ Knowledge of actual results of work	■ High internal work motivation ■ High growth satisfaction ■ High general job satisfaction ■ High work effectiveness

niques used to help workers find work more stimulating include **job rotation** and **job sharing**. These techniques have been defined as the following:

- Job enrichment: Incorporating different tasks in the same job (including tasks performed by others)

- Job enlargement: Increased discretion or decision making so that employees can take on some duties of the superior

- Job rotation: Employees take turns performing several different related jobs

- Job sharing: A special type of part-time work in which a single full-time job is divided between two workers

Participative and Self-Management.   Peters (1987) stresses the critical importance of self-managing work groups. He joins with a worldwide movement that starts from the premise that employees know best how to manage themselves. This thesis represents the culmination of the staff-development paradigm—that any and all employees in an organization can be involved in both organizational direction and self-management. Employees can participate in decisions relative to both the direction of the organization (e.g., mission, goals, and objects) as well as the means for achieving them (e.g., deciding on specific work tasks for each employee). This idea flows from Stafford Beer's (1979) cybernetic management conception of organizations being self-managed and self-regulated.

Self-management, an ideal toward which human services managers should strive, implies specific techniques and work systems designs. Models for self-managing work groups have been developed (e.g., see Hackman and Oldham 1980). As Chapter 10 indicates, a classic program-management system that uses responsibility centers designed for management by anticipation and exception is one set of technologies for self-management. Although some questions have been raised as to their effective transferability from Japan to human services systems in the United States, **quality circles** (QCs) have also become a popular self-management technique. QCs are small problem-solving groups of line employees who meet to make improvements in the operations and management of work.

Another facet of participative and self-management concerns a redefinition of client and clinician roles in human services organizations. Anthony Maluccio (1979), for example, calls for a redefinition of clients in terms of resources rather than carriers of pathology. This represents another facet of participative and self-management. When clients are viewed as partners in the helping process, a **client-outcome monitoring system** becomes an important self-management process. It places high priority on client feedback as a means of helping employees monitor the effectiveness of their own performance in terms of outcomes or impacts on clients.

Innovative Reward Schemes. An increasingly acceptable people-management practice is **flexible-benefits systems** for employees. In this cafeteria-style approach to benefits, workers can select the specific benefits they wish to have, depending on their specific needs at any one time (e.g., day-care support for workers with infants, and long-term care support for employees with older parents who need care).

This marks the beginning of an approach to people management that ultimately will see personnel systems individualized for each employee. It is not unlike efforts to provide individualized services packages for clients; they both are based on the flexible-systems approach to the production of goods and services. With the rapid spread of computer technologies, we have the ability to individualize people-management systems.

As we noted in the Chapter 7 discussion of the growing role of women and minorities in the work force of the 1990s, the demographics of workers has changed significantly. Faced with a shortage of labor, organizations will realize that retention is the dominant factor in people management. Family-oriented benefits and rewards will be offered in return for employee loyalty to their employer. Annual turnover rates of the average organization in the United States is 14 percent; the cost of losing a worker and retraining a successor has been shown to be one-and-one-half times the employee's salary. The pressure to reduce annual turnover rates to 5 percent, to lower absenteeism, and to recruit knowledgeable and experienced workers in a world of labor shortages will increase the importance of reward and incentive systems that focus on family benefits. Not only will the "cafeteria" of benefits broaden to include paid parental leaves, job sharing, respite care, and flex-hours, but organizations are also creating flexible-spending accounts by subtracting from the employee's pretax gross income and using the funds to pay for child care for the employee's offspring.

The concern for improved rewards and benefits for workers has initiated the development of **Employee Assistance Programs** (EAPs), many of which are contracted out to community human services agencies. In modern human resources development systems, an EAP is designed to provide twenty-four-hour services to the employee and his family, for the full range of human issues and services (e.g., services for employees with alcohol, marital, mental health, and adolescent problems and issues). Whether the issue is an employee's own problem, or that of a member of his family, investment in an EAP to deal with the issue and retain the employee is generally accepted as cost-effective for the organization. In many cases, the services can be funded from the health insurance plans of the employer. Although financing the services is important, the availability of an EAP to be responsive to employees' human services needs is of equal importance.

Workplace Improvements.   The last QWL activity focuses on improvements in physical aspects of the workplace. These start with design improvements that emphasize the aesthetic and ergonomic aspects of offices, with colorful, functional, and attractive office furnishings and facilities. They can also include major investment in facilities that foster employee wellness, such as indoor and outdoor jogging tracks, gymnasiums, physical fitness rooms, swimming pools, saunas, and a variety of other wellness and organizational recreation programs.

Summary

Traditional personnel management concentrated its focus primarily on the functions of job analysis, position classification, staffing and selection, pay plans, performance evaluation, and employee relations. Increasingly, there has been a trend to augment traditional personnel management with additional activities that redirect the focus to issues of human resources development. These include affirmative action, comparable worth, employee organizations, career development, and quality of the work environment. For both traditional personnel management and human resource development functions, the critical people management skill is the blending of workers' personal and career goals with the organization's performance goals.

Although the obvious emphasis of human resources development is on the staff-development paradigm, the mission and client paradigms are direct beneficiaries. Highly motivated, dedicated employees of a human services organization lead to greater effectiveness of services for individual clients as well as greater productivity for programs. In effect, creative human services management is the blending of paradigms that achieves synergy through the balancing of the different impacts a human services organization can have on a community.

13

Managing Information and Computers

Our Evolving Electronic Environment

From a Mechanical to an Electronic Environment
Multiple Perceptions of the Computer-Electronic Technologies

What the Computer Can and Cannot Do

History
The Basics of Electronics
Basic Functions of Computers
The Hardware Revolution
The Genie's Marvelous Microchip
The Software Revolution

Using the Computer and Electronic Technologies

The Past Thirty Years
Can Clients Use Computers?
Computers for Clinicians: Friend or Foe?
Administrative Uses of Computers

Managing Computer-Based Information

Options for Acquiring Computer Capability
Steps for Designing a System and Acquiring Computers

The Decades Ahead

Summary

Managing information is a fundamental process for every organization, and the processing of this information is largely based on the rapid growth of the computer–electronic technologies. For the human services manager, the computer offers the opportunity for making major improvements in agency operations and management. It can be used almost instantly, off-the-shelf so to speak, for the agency as it exists and functions. Or it can be the foundation for a major redesign of the organization, an effort that may take years of careful planning and implementation. The cases in this and previous chapters illustrate a variety of computer applications applied to human services organizations as they exist. The case of the new Automated Eligibility Management System presented in this and other chapters (Chapters 4 and 15) illustrates, by contrast, a four-year period of concentrated planning and implementation of a complex, fundamental new approach to information management, based on the potential offered by computer technology.

There are no human services managers who couldn't use computers, for both the agency's and their personal benefit. However, because of their relative newness and because some people may be wary of computers, they are sometimes avoided as seeming too complex and technical. It should be remembered that automobiles, telephones, and TVs are also complex and highly technical. Yet most of us use them with little formal training and quickly integrate them into our lives.

As a student or practitioner of human services management, you may want to take a course to start you off in computer use, or you may just want to begin using computers. Either way, you can immediately be introduced to what seems like the modern-day version of the Genie of Aladdin's lamp. (Remember? You rub the lamp, and out pops a Genie, ready to do anything you ask.) Today's Genie is the microchip—electronic circuits, invisible to the naked eye, that harness the energy of the electron as it speeds along at 186,000 miles per second (i.e., about seven-and-one-half times around the earth at the equator in the space of time between two snaps of your fingers). That's pretty fast.

The Genie of the microchip can be a miracle worker. But beware! The Magic Genie can also become a demon who challenges the human services manager as to who is really the "master." To exploit Genie's full potential, the human services manager needs to understand what this Genie can and cannot do. The problem is that the Genie is learning to do more every day—another reason why human services management is so dynamic in nature, a constant theme in this text.

The marvelous Genie of the microchip emerged at the right time. In an industrialized, complex society with increasing population, the *interrelationships* of people, things, institutions, and events increase at a geometric rate. Therefore, we are faced with

A Problem

- Increasingly, the minds of human services employees are having difficulty in handling all the interrelationships of people, things, institutions, and events that continuously bombard a human services organization in each of the 3600 seconds of every hour of every day.

A Possible Direction

- For centuries we have surrounded ourselves with extensions of ourselves to help us get through the day. Telephones, wireless radios, motor vehicles, and electricity are just a few of the latest technological extensions of human beings.

A Hopeful Solution

- Like these other technologies, the computer is an extension of ourselves that can help us deal with and shape our environment as we strive toward a society of unparalleled material and human prosperity. The marvelous Genie of the microchip came along fortuitously to rescue us from being inundated by the bombardment of environmental stimuli. The beneficiaries are more than the operating, professional, and administrative staff of human services organizations. Our clients and the community are the primary beneficiaries. That's what this chapter is all about.

Our Evolving Electronic Environment

From a Mechanical to an Electronic Environment

We used the word *computer* throughout the above discussion; actually, a more precise term would be *electronic technologies*. After all, the versatile microchip

- Computes and reports
- Draws pictures
- Composes and plays music
- Designs airplanes

- Prints newspapers
- Sends us gorgeous colored pictures of the rings of Saturn
- Talks to someone who is sight-impaired
- Communicates with someone who is hearing-impaired
- Shows us the movement of clouds during the daily TV weather report
- Changes the beat of our heart as we jog (if our heart needs the help of an electronic pacemaker)

and performs wondrously in hundreds of other ways. Clearly, the word *computer* doesn't begin to cover its multiplicity of functions.

It is therefore inaccurate to call today's electronics explosion merely a computer revolution. Human services managers need to recognize that we are currently experiencing the merger and marriage of several electronic technologies that heretofore have been viewed as separate and distinct. The more common uses include the following:

- Computing
- Word and text processing
- Telecommunications
- Sound processing
- Image processing

All these functions are being merged as our home and work environments become increasingly electronic. The marvelous microchip captures the power and speed of the electron and turns it into various tools for our use.

What is really happening? After 500 years of using paper as our primary medium for retaining the memory of society and after 200 years of using mechanical devices to provide the energy and tools for societal processes, *we are shifting to the electron as the source of societal energy and the medium for societal memory.* From one perspective, it's an exciting time to be a manager of a human services organization because you are in the middle of dramatic, fundamental, and dynamic changes. From another perspective, these changes will be so rapid that keeping up with them will be most challenging. Each day will bring something new. Look at the new, but by now commonplace items that we have acquired in just the past few years:

- Electronic typewriters
- Electronic mail
- Electronic drafting machines
- Electronic telephones
- Electronic filing cabinets
- Electronic bank tellers

Figure 13.1 A Modern-Day Office

- Electronic desktop publishing
- Electronic data-statistical analysis

Look at Figure 13.1, a modern-day office; try to picture it without these wonderful electronic devices.

It can be said that the current electronic revolution is a marriage of two sets of technologies:

- **Automation**: The processing of data in digital symbols (e.g., name and birthdate taken from a birth certificate and entered into a computer)
- **Photomation**: The processing of data in a whole-image form (e.g., the birth certificate itself is stored in a video compact disc)

Micrographic systems, holography, and compact (laser) discs are used to store symbolic, whole-image, and audio data in three-dimensional patterns for quick retrieval and display on paper, on a screen, or through a speaker.

Multiple Perceptions of the Computer-Electronic Technologies

The starting point for human services managers who want to exploit the full range of the electronic technologies is to understand the different perceptions of these technologies and to approach technology use with a blend of these perceptions. At this point in the evolution of electronic technologies, eight per-

Figure 13.2 Multiple Perceptions of
Computer–Electronic Technologies

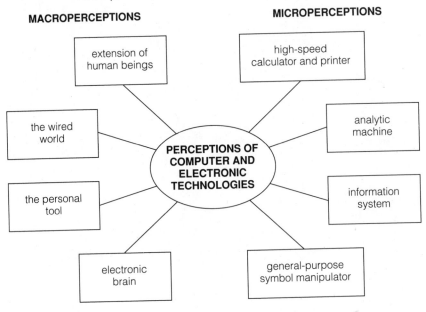

MACROPERCEPTIONS

MICROPERCEPTIONS

extension of
human beings

high-speed
calculator and printer

the wired
world

analytic
machine

PERCEPTIONS OF
COMPUTER AND
ELECTRONIC
TECHNOLOGIES

the personal
tool

information
system

electronic
brain

general-purpose
symbol manipulator

ceptions have been identified. Four of these can be categorized as **macroper-spectives** (overarching, all-encompassing) and four as **microperspectives** (specific, bounded) (Figure 13.2).

Macroperspectives.

- *Extensions of humans:* Every technology is an extension of humans; the automobile, telephone, airplane, and wireless radio are all good examples. They permit us to do more, have contact with more people, and keep track of more things than we could without such devices.

- *The wired world:* Whether with actual wires (telephone lines, fiber optics, or cable) or electronic frequencies (microwaves and communication satellites), we are quickly becoming wired cities, a wired nation, a wired world. Our dwelling units and our community institutions are being linked electronically. As reported in "Computers for Social Work Practitioners" (Winter 1983 *NASW Practice Digest*), several social work agencies already provide their clinicians with computer access to electronic libraries (e.g., National Library of Medicine and National Institute of Mental Health). Having wired up their agencies with the world to benefit the staff, the next logical step for human services managers will be to let clients have direct use of the benefits of the electronic human services system.

- *The personal tool:* Sooner or later, through the reduced costs of mass production, every technology passes a cost threshold that makes it widely available for day-to-day use. It then becomes a common way of helping people improve the amount, speed, and quality of their accomplishment of work and home chores. We are almost at this point with desktop computers. Increasingly, the day-to-day personal productivity of human services managers, and that of their clinical-clerical staff, can be increased significantly with microcomputers. We surround ourselves, at work and at home, with artifacts to help us do more during the day. The computer has become another artifact that everyone can now use to be more effective in what they set out to accomplish.

- *The electronic brain:* From the very beginning, computers had the reputation of being electronic brains. Nothing could have been further from the truth; they are *dumb machines* with electronic components programmed by humans to do specific tasks. Initially, the field of **artificial intelligence** (AI) was limited to university research, but increasingly, a form of AI called an *expert system* is being used and is even considered by social services agencies (see the bibliography for this chapter) for a variety of applications. Data are symbols that, when related to referents in human minds, become information. Today's computers have data bases organized in information systems. Tomorrow's expert systems will have knowledge bases, with the computer inferring the meaning of several related data items to mimic the human brain. When perfected, the concept of a computer as an electronic brain may be applied to improve the effectiveness of human services organizations.

Microperspectives.

- *High-speed calculator and printer:* One of the major uses of the computer has been as a high-speed machine capable of taking in data, performing complex calculations, maintaining records and accounts, and printing large volumes of documents such as reports and payments, all based on the original data.

- *Analytic machine:* Historically, one of the first computer programmers in the world was a woman, by the delightful name of Lady Ada Lovelace, who programmed Charles Babbage's analytic machine, a mechanical device that could perform calculations. From the outset, the computer was viewed similarly as an analytic machine capable of the statistical and mathematical computation of large volumes of data in seconds. In many universities and research centers this is still the dominant perception and use of the computer-related technologies.

- *Information system:* From the very beginning, the computer technologies were viewed as information technologies. This represents a bias on the part of theorists who view the organization as a decision machine. Decisions require data that in turn require data processing and systems for data flows (e.g., information systems). Thus, one of the primary perceptions of the computer-related technologies, with emphasis on *management-information systems* (MIS), has emerged. This perception has led naturally to the need for organizations to view information as a resource and manage it appropriately. Some large organizations have a chief information officer (CIO) who is responsible for information resource management (IRM). In all human services organizations and systems, a well-designed information system has become a prerequisite for effective management.

- *General-purpose symbol manipulator:* Essentially, the computer manipulates symbols. To the technology, they are devoid of meaning. The whole English language can be reduced to only twenty-six alphabetic symbols, which may be used to form tens of thousands of words. This perception of the computer technologies has a great deal of potential. While established organizational structures may be virtually inflexible, data symbols can be very flexible. Because the environment of human services organizations is interdisciplinary and interorganizational, using computers to support the formation and structuring of adhocracies, temporary organizations, is now a reality. The concept of flexible-systems production, covered in Chapter 8, could come about only because of the computer. Computers are the vehicle for integrating, for serving every single client, and for providing the range of services available from a variety of different human services organizations. In terms of systemic and strategic management, this perception of computers is vital for effective, modern human services management (see Chapter 16).

What the Computer Can and Cannot Do

There is no mystery in the electronic technologies. They operate out of a basic scientific principle some of us learned in high school science: Electrons flow at the speed of light (approximately 186,000 miles per second). But what we really need to recognize is something we learned in social studies: Our society has inherited and is dealing with the last phase of the Industrial Revolution. Previous phases harnessed the power of mechanical devices to supplement the muscles of human beings; the present phase is harnessing the power of the electron to supplement the mental processes.

There is no mystery in how the computer and other electronic technologies function. To put you in a better position to understand what these technologies can and cannot do, we review briefly, for those who may not be familiar with them, a few fundamentals including (1) the history of this technology; (2) some basics of electronics; (3) the essential elements of a computer system; (4) the revolution in hardware—how Genie's marvelous microchip came into being; and (5) the revolution in software—how the microchip has become user-friendly, ready, and available to serve anyone who is interested.

History

The evolution of the computer and telecommunications technologies can be traced over a period of centuries to theorists and scientists working the fields of mathematics, logic, electronics, communications, and production control. The first commercial application of computers was a huge UNIVAC computer installed in 1954 in a General Electric plant in Louisville, Kentucky. It occupied a large, highly climate-controlled room. The rapid development of transistors, followed by NASA's push to land a person on the moon before 1970, became the catalyst for microminiaturization of electronic circuits, which led to the rapid spread of ever smaller computers. You may be wearing on your wrist a device with greater capacity than existed in that first computer room.

When looking at a computer, it is hard to believe that they exist primarily because of two theories–concepts:

- **Cybernetics:** Self-regulation through feedback. By inspecting an operation and comparing it against a preset standard, machines can attain self-regulation, similar to the processes in a human.

- **Two-valued logic:** The logical notion of 1 (substance) and 0 (nothing). Two-valued logic is the basis of the binary system of numbers and the alphabet: by developing codes made up of *1s* and *0s,* the computer can differentiate a 2 from a 7, as well as a *G* from an *L.*

These two theoretical concepts serve as the foundation for the creation of a computer system. Cybernetics permits computers to be self-regulating, self-controlling. Two-valued logic is the basis for translating the alphabet and numbers into electronic symbols that can be processed and communicated within and between computers.

The Basics of Electronics

All electronic devices are made up of a combination of four basic elements:

- **Pulses** of electrons that come in a series so fast that you think you see a steady stream (e.g., a light bulb).

- **A path** for the electron that is in the form of electric wires, telephone wires, cables, fiber optics, and so on. Paths for pulses do not need wires; they can be beamed through the air (e.g., radio or television frequencies, microwave and communication satellites).

- **Pulse changing, receiving**, or **amplifying** devices, such as a telephone, change your voice into a pulse, send the pulse through a path, and then turn the pulse back into a voice. The speaker in your radio is also a device that changes pulses back into voice or music. Radio and television take a pulse from a distant station and strengthen (amplify) it.

- **Pulse retaining** devices such as tape recorders, compact audio discs, video cassettes, magnetic computer disks. Each stores the pulse by magnetizing a surface, which can be "read" or played back at some future time.

In general terms, every electronic device you use (computers, word processors, TV or radio, compact disc player, and microwave oven) are all combinations of these four basic electronic elements. The real genius in these four components is in the technology. Fortunately, one does not have to understand in any detail the complexity of circuitry that makes up the computer and other electronic devices.

Basic Functions of Computers

The computer is a group of interconnected machines that have five primary functions (identify each in the photograph of Figure 13.1):

- **Input**: Converts symbols (e.g., the client's name and address) into electronically coded pulses that can be manipulated by machines (e.g., holes in a punch card or pulses initiated by typing on the keyboard of a video display terminal).
- **Arithmetic–Logic**: Add, subtract, multiply, and divide and compare symbols for typical logic processes (e.g., greater than, less than, equal to).
- **Control**: Integrates and coordinates all the interconnected system components. There are two forms of control: *permanent control*—circuitry built into the machine by the manufacturer (e.g., the symbol 98 opens circuits necessary to multiply two numbers) and *temporary control*—the set of instructions prepared by a programmer using the permanent control symbols (e.g., programs for maintaining client records, word processing, or spreadsheet programs).
- **Storage (memory)**: Retains electronic pulses either inside the machine (inside its memory) or in devices that maintain your data (e.g., floppy [flexible] or hard [rigid and fixed] disks).
- **Output**: Converts electronic or magnetic pulses into symbols or characters that humans can understand (e.g., printed reports, displays on video terminals).

The control component in the system is the one on which we particularly need to focus. It provides the ability to program, creating software that guides the application (utilization) of the electronic technologies according to our needs. We discuss the software revolution shortly.

The Hardware Revolution

In computer jargon, **hardware** refers to the electronic device itself. Since 1954 we have seen a revolution in the hardware of the computer-related technologies. We have gone through several generations of hardware by using different electronic technologies (e.g., vacuum tubes, transistors, chips, and, finally, the microchip [technically known as VLSI—Very Large-Scale Integrated Circuits]).

In every generation, there was a revolution as size was reduced radically and capacity increased. We are now at the point where a desktop computer, which costs under $3000, is ten times more powerful than the computer of twenty years ago that filled a large room and cost $3 million. The three categories of computers are becoming increasingly hard to distinguish. Generally though, they can be defined as follows:

- **Maxicomputers** or **mainframe** computers consist of a large number of interconnected electronic devices and require a large staff to program, operate, and manage. They are usually housed in a large, air-conditioned room with access limited to people in the agency with security clearance. The maxicomputer is managed by a data-processing or information-systems unit.

  Maxi-mainframe computers have the capability of controlling the simultaneous operation of a large number of terminals, printers, and other-size computers. These are interconnected by a telecommunication system, which can be national or international in scope.

  Most large human services organizations in federal and state government departments, hospitals, universities, and large municipalities have a maxi-mainframe computer. Our case study of the state of Connecticut Eligibility Management System (EMS) is an example of such a system. In terms of outright purchase, such computers usually cost several million dollars, or they may be leased for varying amounts.

- **Minicomputers** are essentially smaller versions of a large maxicomputer. They are smaller in size, and are less complicated to operate. They can function as a centrally controlled mainframe computer or as a decentralized computer for a small subunit within a larger human services organization. Many private, nonprofit human services agencies, which are usually smaller, use a minicomputer, which also can control the simultaneous operation of several terminals tied together with a telecommunications system.

  In terms of outright purchase, a minicomputer ranges in costs from $25,000 to several hundreds of thousands of dollars.

- **Microcomputers** have many names: PCs (personal computers); home computers; desktop computers; end-user computers. Technically, they are known as microprocessors. Compared to maxicomputers and minicomputers, which are heavy and large and require a trained staff to operate, microcomputers are light and can be assembled by anyone willing to learn. They have been developed much like stereo music systems: buy different components and assemble them yourself, at home or on your desk in your office. They are considered user-friendly: you can begin to use them as soon as you have them out of the box and connected, with a minimum of technical expertise required. The cost of a micro is also more user-friendly, running a range from several hundred to several thousand dollars.

Microcomputers are "intelligent." You can use them for clinical or administrative tasks. On the other hand, terminals connected to a mainframe (whether maxi or mini) are considered "dumb." They can only do what the central mainframe computer wlll let them do. A microprocessor is the best of both worlds. They can be used as an intelligent computer and, when desired, connected to a mainframe computer to become a dumb terminal. (These terms have nothing to do with IQ, and their implications will be discussed further along.) Because of the microcomputer, practically all human services organizations can now exploit the marvels of the microchip.

Actually, we are surrounded by another generation of computers, which are almost invisible. The Genie of the microchip performs your commands just about everywhere: in microwave ovens at home, in the toys and dolls of our children, in greeting cards that provide music when opened, in pacemakers for people with heart problems, in our automobiles, on our wrists in multifunction watches; on and on. Why? The marvelous microchip (in actuality, microprocessor) is so small that many can be held in the palm of your hand and can be programmed for an almost infinite variety of functions.

The Genie's Marvelous Microchip

In the early 1960s, NASA and the Defense Department, each for their own obvious purposes, invested heavily in microelectronics. To get very large computers into a very small space, a process of microminiaturization of electronic circuits was undertaken. It is not a difficult process to understand:

1. Draw a complicated electronic circuit on a large piece of paper.
2. Photograph it.
3. Reduce the photograph to microfilm size.
4. "Burn" the picture (make a print of it) on silicon that has been treated with a chemical.

The result: Genie's marvelous microchip—a very complicated circuit printed on silicon (a semiconductor) in a size so small that the naked eye cannot see all of the details.

The Software Revolution

You will recall that **software** is a set of instructions fed into a computer system that takes *control* of that system temporarily. During the past thirty years, we have also seen a revolution in software. Initially, programmers had to write computer instructions in the language of the computer, which generally meant a series of numbers and symbols. Many programmers still write in machine language.

To simplify the life of programmers, a number of programs were written so that some English-type code words could be used for programming. The most popular were

- FORTRAN (*FOR*mula *TRAN*slator) for statistical-type applications
- BASIC (*B*eginner's *A*ll-Purpose *S*ymbolic *I*nstruction *C*ode), a common, easily learned programming language for nonprofessional programmers
- COBOL (*CO*mmon *B*usiness-*O*riented *L*anguage) for business-type applications

But the greatest revolution in software has been the development of many commercially available **user-friendly software** programs that do not require any user programming, just the ability to follow the directions in the program manual—usually a simple skill to master.

With this latest revolution, the human services manager need only know a minimum about the hardware or software to exploit them for a number of uses: filing data, keeping a calendar electronically, writing letters or reports, sending mail electronically, preparing and publishing a newsletter electronically, and so on. Table 13.1 briefly describes the most popular user-friendly software programs available for microcomputers (desktop and home computers.) They are all priced from about $50 to $600. If you were to hire a programmer to write such software, each would cost several thousands of dollars. User-friendly software represents not only the widespread availability of the latest technology worldwide, but it also represents significant savings in cost of software for the human services agency.

As marvelous as Genie's microchip is, its powers pale when compared to the human brain. As the science-fiction literature illustrates, the day may come when we have computers that become the electronic brains of robots. Many of you have already seen such examples at the movies or on Saturday morning TV programs for children.

As noted earlier, we are making major progress in the field of AI, expert systems, and in robotics. In the bibliography to this chapter, you can see that this subject is already being discussed for the human services—clinicians as well as managers. The day may come when a human services manager has an expert system that can monitor the agency during the evenings and on weekends. At that point, the first item of business when starting to work will be to ask the computer: What are my priority tasks for today? This may seem threat-

Table 13.1 User-Friendly Software

- Word processing prepares written materials and reports; turns the computer into electronic typewriter.
- Filer (data management) structures data for storage, manipulation, and retrieval; turns the computer into an electronic filing cabinet.
- Electronic spreadsheets are matrix-like grids to store data and/or values that can be interrelated for making projections; turns the computer into a forecasting and a "what-if" machine.
- Graphics prepare bar, line, or pie charts of data or draws pictures that can be seen on a video terminal or printed for inclusion in reports; turns the computer into a graphic arts machine.
- Statistics analyze quantitative data; turns the computer into an analytic machine.
- Accounting creates and maintains financial records; turns computer into an accounting machine.
- Communications sends electronic messages (mail and memos) to other agencies; turns the computer into a telephone–teletype machine.
- Scheduling lists work activities–events, schedules and monitors them, and allocates resources; turns the computer into a PERT machine.
- Education is for self-instructional purposes; turns the computer into a learning and staff-development machine.

ening, but remember, *your* expert system is only "controlling" you in the fashion *you* taught it to do in the first place. Computers only control what they are allowed to control.

At the present state of the art, computers and electronic devices are only a collection of circuits and electronic components. They have no intelligence, science-fiction films to the contrary notwithstanding. They can only carry out, usually accurately and continuously, that which they have been instructed to do through software. They can also pull together and organize a lot of data for you that will be helpful for clinical and administrative purposes. When you realize that most of the employees of a human services organization, operational, clinical and adminstrative, spend much of their time doing a lot of machinelike tasks, the ability to free humans to do that which only humans can do is sufficient reason to exploit the potential of this technology.

Using the Computer and Electronic Technologies

As students and practitioners in human services management, it is appropriate to ask at this point: What are the ways in which these technologies have been and can be used? How can the computer benefit clients, clinicians, and administrators? A good starting point is to look briefly at the past thirty years of computers and the human services.

The Past Thirty Years

Most people in the human services probably do not realize that over and above the Defense Department and NASA, the prime movers in the development of the computer-related technologies were actually the human services. From the inception of technology use, the U.S. Department of Health, Education, and Welfare (now the Department of Health and Human Services) has been a major user of computers and a catalyst for electronic technology transfer to public, commercial, and nonprofit human services organizations. The extent of pioneering of these technologies at every stage of their evolution can be measured in two ways.

Volume of Hardware–Software Utilization: Geographic and Institutional Spread. HEW's (HHS) direct utilization of the technology, and its function as a catalyst of computer technology use through research, demonstration, and funding, resulted in one of the largest volume operations of computer-based data processing in the world. Probably the largest nonmilitary computer installation has been that which maintains the Social Security records and processes Social Security payments. Computer use has been intensive and extensive in the following human services functions for several decades:

- Income maintenance
- Health
- Mental health
- Public school education
- Libraries
- Social Security

- Social services
- Hospitals
- Health insurance
- Universities
- Travel and leisure
- Employment–unemployment

Thus, all human services related to these operations have played a pivotal role in transfer of these technologies and have accounted for a significant portion of the burgeoning electronic technology industry in the United States.

Although their target human services organizations were primarily public, most large voluntary human services agencies and even many business organizations (e.g., insurance companies under contract to administer Medicare payments) use computers in part because of HEW (HHS) funding. The eligibility management system (EMS) in our case study can be found in several state governments, funded largely by HHS.

Beyond making investments in technology transfer into the organizations that were the primary human services providers (e.g., health, public health, welfare, education, mental health, mental retardation, elderly services, and youth services), HEW (HHS) also participated in research and development efforts that involved computer use in municipalities and counties and in many nonprofit organizations, thus disseminating them far and wide throughout the United States.

Extent of Technology Application. Although the initial thrust of HEW (HHS) utilization and sponsorship of computer use was organizational in nature (e.g., transaction processing, data base maintenance, planning, and management), the department's commitment to other forms of the technology has been equally strong. For example, the rapid growth of medical technology in hospitals can still be traced to HEW (HHS) initial funding. Practically all of today's diagnostic equipment uses some form of the microchip. Although this equipment is very expensive and has contributed to medical-cost inflation, it has also resulted in significantly improved health care delivery, which both increases quality of life and, in some ways, offsets the increased costs.

Another example of HEW (HHS) investment is the research and operation of several national and international health–medical telecommunications systems whose functions range all the way from pure research and diagnostics to actual health-care delivery. For communities in remote areas who use them for help with difficult cases, this signifies a major improvement in health care.

There is probably no area of human services that has not been touched by computers. Because the technology keeps improving and the costs keep getting lower, there is a new wave of computer use in the human services, with rapid spread of microcomputers to small agencies and increasingly to the desktops of employees in large organizations. The latter represents a new dimension in technology use. The major rationale for computer use in the past thirty years has been **organizational productivity**, that is, improving the effectiveness and efficiency of the human services organization. In the next two decades, the focus will be on **personal productivity**, that is, improving the effectiveness and productivity of each operational, clinical, and administrative employee in a human services organization.

For the human services manager, the question is no longer just how can these technologies be used to improve the organization. The question is also, How can each employee do more and better by using the technology? As a matter of fact, we are now at the point where the real question can be asked, What can Genie's marvelous microchip do for each of our clients, directly as well as indirectly?

Can Clients Use Computers?

The first priority users of human services agency computers should be, and eventually will be, the clients, citizens, and institutions of a community. Table 13.2 gives some clues as to what this direct computer-use can include.

Direct client–computer interaction is consistent with human services values—strengthening a client's ability to manage his own life, keeping in mind that a professional worker has designed the program of the computer, and is monitoring all of the transactions.

Table 13.2   Direct Use of Human Services Agency Computers by Clients, Citizens, and Institutions in a Community

Each client, citizen, group, or institution in society should have the capability to use the computer system of public and nonprofit organizations in appropriate ways. One rarely thinks of such computer systems being available to the public user, except perhaps in libraries, which are probably the pioneers of this concept. The primary design of such systems should be to provide direct access to citizens and community organizations. In general terms, such applications would include the following:

- Tickler: Giving reminders to clients or citizens
- Instructor: Providing cradle-to-grave education
- Searcher: Putting information at the fingertips of people
- Resource: Helping pinpoint potential, available resources
- Scheduler: Making appointments directly
- Transactor: Processing paperwork
- Dispatcher: Arranging for normal or emergency help

Specifically, direct use of computers by the public is designed to answer such directives as

- Where can I get home care?
- What is the earliest appointment I can get at the clinic?
- What's holding up my paperwork? What can I do to resolve the problem?
- I would like to register; please handle all the recordkeeping.
- Is there space on the minibus today so I can get to the seniors' noontime nutritional and social program?

Examples for social services include the following:

- Application processing
- Job vacancies tickler
- Day-care registration
- Arrange temporary home care
- Schedule a minibus
- Health–nutrition advisory
- Arrange appointments

- Eligibility determination
- Housing vacancies tickler
- Job-training registration
- Emergency assistance
- Emergency dispatching
- Home management
- Arrange payments

There are three different possible system designs that are client-focused:

- Level 1: Agency stand-alone system
- Level 2: Agency system tied into a computerized system of all community social services agencies
- Level 3: Computerized community social services system, with the ability for clients to dial up from homes and use directly

The specifications for all three of these systems are described more fully in Chapter 14. We are currently in a period where the most common are Level 1 and 2 systems; they are designed for indirect use by clients and citizens. Our case study of the EMS is an excellent example of a sophisticated state-of-the-art Level 2 system. Within the next two decades, we will begin to see Level 3 human services systems, which will provide people with an ability to use the benefits of the system directly.

The following are some useful guidelines for creating a client-friendly agency computer system:

- All paperwork is simplified and minimized; within the agency; between the agency, client, and third parties; on clinical issues; and on financial matters.

- Appointments with clinicians are simplified so that appointments are easy to make, waiting for workers is minimized, reminders of appointments are sent, and changes are quickly communicated.

- Services are individualized and integrated so that assessments are transdisciplinary, services packages are multidisciplinary, one worker coordinates all services, services packages are personalized, services delivery is monitored, and backup worker is available if necessary.

- Status and progress of services is clear and apparent in that anticipated outcomes are clear in advance and progress is communicated regularly.

- Client's records are accurate, comprehensive, complete, timely, confidential, and protected.

Our discussion thus far has focused on the direct use of human services computer systems by clients and community. There is another aspect of computer–client interaction that continues to make advances in providing enabling technology for blind and deaf users and cognitive rehabilitation for the traumatic brain injured (TBI), among others. There is even some significant experimentation in bionics, the use of electronic components for body and brain functioning. This is an exciting area of direct computer use for people that will probably have startling breakthroughs during the coming decade.

Computers for Clinicians: Friend or Foe?

Some human services clinicians have a negative attitude toward computers for a variety of reasons, not the least of which is to protect what they perceive as the core of the agency: human-to-human interactions. At the same time, most clinicians realize the potential of the microchip and are interested in harnessing that potential. One way of making the move to computerization is with a turnkey system. In computer jargon, a **turnkey system** is a complete and comprehensive computer system that has been specially designed for a particular set of applications and is available for immediate use. For a fee, the turnkey company will install the equipment, train your staff, and start things up—all within a short time period. They will even send staff to come in to support you during the first few days you start up with the system.

Computer technologies have been applied to the needs of mental health agencies for a long time. Dr. Marc Schwartz (1984) documents the continued rapid growth of applications in the following aspects of this field:

- Mental health information systems
- Community mental health centers
- Mental retardation
- Prediction and consultation
- Psychological testing
- Screening and histories
- Behavior therapy–Biofeedback
- Problem-oriented medical record and treatment planning

- Alcohol programs
- Drug abuse programs
- Automated nursing notes
- Diagnosis
- Case status
- Psychotherapy
- Program evaluation
- Quality assurance
- Treatment monitoring

More as an experiment than as a serious treatment modality, a program called ELIZA was written and popularized for microcomputers many years ago. It mimicked the responses of a psychotherapist and allowed the patient to interact with the program with surprisingly successful results. Today, computer-aided therapy is being taken more seriously, with the primary work being undertaken by those interested in AI and expert systems. There is even indication that, in some areas of therapy (e.g., with sexual abusers), clients may be more ready to interact with computer systems than with a human therapist. This aspect of computer use elicits strong reactions from some clinicians. Only time and more work in this area will tell whether it will be a useful tool to the profession.

There is a small "caveat" (warning). Words like *computerphobia* (Is the computer going to eat up all the vital data if it's touched the wrong way?), *cyberphobia* (the shivers, vertigo, stomach aches, and cold sweats sometimes experienced by employees when a computer appears on their desk), and *computerphilia* (I love my computer; it can solve all the world's problems) have entered the vocabularies of organizational management, as they and their staffs encounter computers for the first time. To some extent, these are real concerns and require sensitivity and awareness of human services managers. There really are many people who are uncomfortable with machines and who need special help to reach a level where they can operate them with ease.

Social workers, in all sizes of private, commercial, and public agencies, have begun integrating the computer-related technologies into their practice. The following items appear on a sample identified by William H. Butterfield (1985) as computer applications for practitioners:

- Intake and diagnosis
- Maintaining client data base
- Client accounting
- Word processing
- Fund-raising
- Decision support—researching relevant cases
- Client demographics
- Worker productivity
- Client tracking
- Computer-aided tutoring

- Working with hi-tech clients
- Bioengineering
- Behavioral analysis and evaluation
- Monitoring client progress
- Clinical social work practice— treatment process files: client data, assessment and goals, intervention, treatment evaluation—supplementary files: practice notes, practice accounts, community resources, practice information

Further, the application of AI to the field of social work is already being researched. Thus far there has not been significant impact, but there are sufficient indications that the human services manager will indeed be faced, over the next decade, with issues related to expert systems in human services organizations. This too will require knowledge, sensitivity, and understanding.

Administrative Uses of Computers

Practically every human services agency has used computers for administrative purposes or soon will be. The human services manager wears two hats in this process: (1) how to best apply and use the computer; (2) how to manage computer use in the organization most beneficially. Let us deal first with the former.

The world of organizational management traditionally divides computer systems into three categories: information systems, computer-based quantitative analysis, and office automation. This is an unfortunate and unwarranted division because human services managers are really dealing with one central task that encompasses all three categories, namely: how to harness the energy of the electron for organizational processes and institutional memory. Because we are dealing with an emerging electronic environment within the agency, in the community, and in society, it behooves the dynamic administrator to maintain a broad, open, and opportunistic perspective. For administration of a human services organization, the electron can be harnessed to

- Process transactions.
- Automate the work environment.
- Manage data flow.
- Enhance sociotechnical systems.

- Analyze data.
- Improve the manager's own work.

Let us look at each of these briefly.

The Transaction Processor.   Transactions in human services organizations and systems are a continuous flow that goes on twenty-four hours a day, seven days a week. A transaction can be simple—the client mails in a check to pay the agency for services; or complex—multisource diagnostic data on a client trigger a number of agency processes. A human services transaction triggers flows of data that ultimately impact clinical and administrative employees in that and other agencies. These triggers can be *episodic,* occurring randomly, or *periodic,* that is, on schedule (a client's file must be updated and sent to a social worker twenty-four hours prior to a scheduled appointment). Think about the number of episodic and periodic transactions that bombard you daily or weekly and you can see the utility of the computer as a *reliable, rapid transaction processor.*

Workstations: Automating the Work Environment.   Humans have always surrounded themselves—at work or play—with tools and devices to ease their lives. Observe the artifacts on any desk: staplers, mail trays, calculators, telephones, message pads, typewriters, dictating machines, containers for clips– pencils–pens, clocks, and lamps. All help people perform their work and be more efficient; in effect a *workstation* is the base for performing daily tasks.

As we move from a manual to an electronic environment, with the emergence of different types of electronic devices at the work place, we are moving ultimately toward two types of electronic workstations (Table 13.3).

Information Systems.   From the beginnings of computer use, the focus has been on information systems. This flows out of a perspective of organizations as decision systems (recall the discussions in Part II). One of the first books on computer use in human services (Schoech 1982) focused on two primary applications for human services management:

- MIS: Management information systems provide information to automate programmed management decisions.
- DSS: Decision support systems provide data-analytic ability to support managers in their decisions–actions.

Not only do other scholars agree with this perception, but they go further: The computer-based MIS and DSS of a human services organization alter the bases of power and decision-making authority as they currently exist in such organizations (Caputo 1988).

Most discussions of MIS or DSS need to begin by differentiating between *data* and *information.* The former is meaning-free; the latter is data to which

Table 13.3   Functions of Workstations in an Electronic
Work Environment

General-Purpose Workstations	Special-Purpose Workstations
Electronic transaction processor	Computer-aided therapy
Electronic filing	Computer-aided mapping
Electronic mail	Electronic funds transfer
Electronic calendars	Voice recognition–response
Electronic scheduler	Remote sensing
Desktop publishing	Teleconferencing: video, voice, documents, data
Electronic spreadsheets	
Desktop statistical analysis	Computer-aided learning
Word processing	Process control
Nationwide data retrieval and document retrieval	
Electronic communications: voice, data, text, whole image	
Graphic analysis	

humans apply a referent to provide a meaning. For example, what is the meaning of the following word? *Collections.* If you are a public sanitarian, it means picking up garbage. If you are a priest, it means church donations, a bill collector, chasing after people who owe money, and for those who like stamps, it is what they keep in their albums.

Differentiating data from information leads to a very important conclusion: Computers can only process data; human beings must take data and convert it into information. In effect each of us is our own information system. When talking about a manager's use of computers, the term *management-information system* should really be changed to *management-oriented reporting.*

Technology is neutral; technology application is not. The human services manager needs to have an awareness of the way in which her underlying values influence the way in which systems are designed for data flows, data processing, data bases, and management-oriented reports. Even further, the design of computer systems in human services organizations should be the result of a process that involves as many different people with as many different perspectives and values as is possible. Note in our case study of the EMS that the system's planning process was not only founded on the principle of involving department employees of all levels, but also actually created a process for such an approach. As I have noted repeatedly, this process is one developed by Kurt Lewin and Margaret Mead; it is called *action research* (see Marrow 1969). It is based on a simple but powerful premise: *Change is best managed by those most affected by the change.* Every tool and technique used by human services organizations is applied with a set of value-biases. The best a manager can do is be aware that this is happening and create a process that attempts to broaden the value-biases.

As Figure 10.4 (page 249) illustrated in our chapter on program management, the majority of day-to-day data required for operational management and management control of programs and services can be embedded in automated, integrated computer systems, called the agency's MIS. Data required for strategic planning and management usually cannot be automated, at least not until expert systems are designed for this purpose. These processes are dependent on the human manager, who can use the power of the computer to support his decisions and actions. The latter can be considered the agency's DSS, but the manager recognizes that the decisions and actions flow out of perceptions and values, not out of the technology itself.

Sociotechnical Systems.   Another way of looking at a dominant administrative use of computer technologies in human services organizations is that they are complex sociotechnical systems. A *sociotechnical system* consists of people, computer-related hardware and software, automated data bases, and organizational procedures, all interacting in a prescribed pattern.

The interaction of human beings and technology must be designed with care, with an attempt to balance a broad set of concerns, needs, and values. As we learned from our Chapter 4 discussion of systems theories, all elements of a system interact and influence each other. These interactions are sensitive and complex; they need fine-tuning. In our case of the EMS, even the colors used on the computer terminal for different types of data were chosen carefully to be user-friendly to the eye of the employees who will interact with the system.

Practically every major human services system in the United States is a complex, sophisticated sociotechnical system. Whether we are talking about education, health, social services, mental health, income transfers (be they student loans, veterans benefits, or Social Security), health insurance, or recreation, the computer-related technologies have been used as an integral element of the sociotechnical systems necessary to administer the human services institutions and systems in the United States. Figure 13.3 illustrates the sociotechnical system of the EMS described in Case 13.1. Being large and complex, it requires a large centralized computer with a telecommunications system that is statewide and even communicates to agencies outside of the state. It typifies a countless number of statewide and nationwide human services systems that require large computers and sophisticated telecommunications systems.

Because it covers a large geographic area, the EMS is an example of a **wide-area network** (WAN) telecommunication system. A WAN is typically found in very large organizations such as state and federal government human services departments. Increasingly, however, small agencies are also affected by carefully designed sociotechnical systems in which computers and telecommunications are the critical technologies for what is called a **local-area network** (LAN). This type of system is contained within a small geographic area.

It is part of a much larger telecommunications network system in which several small agencies manage their own data and also share some data with each other. All workstations in a LAN are user-friendly microprocessors, tied together by another larger microprocessor. The software is all user-friendly, and each workstation has a telecommunications capability to other computer systems within and outside the jurisdiction.

Case 13.1

Part 2:* Eligibility Management System

As noted in Part 1 of this case, EMS is a complex and sophisticated sociotechnical system that uses state-of-the-art computer and telecommunications technologies (see Figure 13.3). The design and planning process itself was organized and orchestrated very carefully to make sure that EMS was an integral part of the department's overall efforts to improve program management, combat abuses, and improve services to eligible clients. The department had two overall goals: provide critical assistance to Connecticut's low-income population while improving administration of the programs that provide assistance. The direction of the planning and design effort was placed in the hands of department program professionals. They in turn were supported by the data-processing staff and by a vendor selected after a comprehensive RFP process. Under contract the vendor had to design and implement the system, turning it over to the state once it had operated successfully in accordance to specifications. EMS was operationalized on a very large on-line computer operated by the Connecticut Department of Administrative Service Data Center.

Each of the subsystems of the EMS has different components:

Client Certification

- Screening
- Eligibility
- Scheduling
- Home visits
- EPSDT

- Intake
- Case maintenance
- Address inquiry
- Fair hearings
- Resources

- Alerts
- Promptness tracking
- Letter and notice generation
- Job connection

Financial Information and Control

- Issuances
- Benefit history
- Overpayments–Recoupments

- Expenditure accounting
- Bank reconciliation
- Financial reporting

Management Information and Control

- Quality control
- Management reporting

- Ad hoc reporting

Figure 13.3 Overview of an EMS

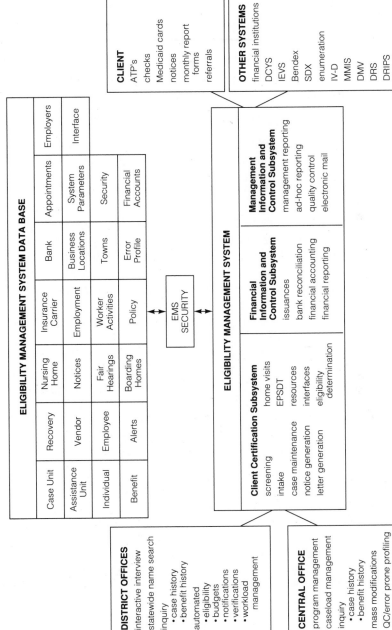

ELIGIBILITY MANAGEMENT SYSTEM DATA BASE

Case Unit	Recovery	Nursing Home	Insurance Carrier	Bank	Appointments	Employers
Assistance Unit	Vendor	Notices	Employment	Business Locations	System Parameters	Interface
Individual	Employee	Fair Hearings	Worker Activities	Towns	Security	
Benefit	Alerts	Boarding Homes	Policy	Error Profile	Financial Accounts	

EMS SECURITY

ELIGIBILITY MANAGEMENT SYSTEM

Client Certification Subsystem
screening
intake
case maintenance
notice generation
letter generation
home visits
EPSDT
resources
interfaces
eligibility determination

Financial Information and Control Subsystem
issuances
bank reconciliation
financial accounting
financial reporting

Management Information and Control Subsystem
management reporting
ad-hoc reporting
quality control
electronic mail

DISTRICT OFFICES
interactive interview
statewide name search
inquiry
 • case history
 • benefit history
automated
 • eligibility
 • budgets
 • notifications
 • verifications
 • workload management

CENTRAL OFFICE
program management
caseload management
inquiry
 • case history
 • benefit history
mass modifications
QC/error prone profiling
benefit recovery

CLIENT
ATP's
checks
Medicaid cards
notices
monthly report forms
referrals

OTHER SYSTEMS
financial institutions
DCYS
IEVS
Bendex
SDX
enumeration
IV-D
MMIS
DMV
DRS
DRIPS
DHS

EMS is an integrated system; each subsystem is automated and integrated. The system permits two types of automation:

- Human–machine: Electronic devices manipulate data and provide the human with data that become the basis for decisions and actions.
- Decision-rule: Besides processing data, the electronic-based system makes the decision (client is eligible for payment) and takes action (prepares the check), all in accordance with decision-rules set by professional staff.

Even though employees will use EMS through dumb terminals, the system has been designed to be user-friendly. A series of menus leads the employees through the different components of the subsystems; at any time, the system can switch automatically to other menus, as needed. Even help menus are available. Everything has been automated, even overnight, automated confirmation of client data with area and nationwide data bases. EMS is truly a transorganizational (interorganizational) system in that procedurally and technologically it is linked to different state agencies (Departments of Children and Youth Services, Human Resources, Motor Vehicles, Revenues Services), to federal systems (BENDEX, SDX), and to private systems (bank match).

EMS is not only user-friendly but is also ergonomic in design (ergonomics is the science of human–technology interfaces). Seven different colors are used in the menus on the terminals. The specific color selected for each type of component and data was selected after a careful research study of eye strain in humans, what the eye considers pleasant to work with, and what will signal an important transaction.

The EMS planning committee is proud of the results of four years of planning and design. Building on the collective knowledge and experience of a countless number of department employees from all organizational strata, the expertise of in-house and consultants, and the experience of other states that have implemented an EMS, the state of Connecticut EMS represents one of the most complex, sophisticated, state-of-the-art systems that can be found in any organization in the United States, public or private.

*Parts 1 and 3 of this case appear in Chapters 4 and 15, respectively.

Data Analysis.   Another major administrative use of the computer-related technologies is *data analysis*. Statistical and quantitative analysis has a longer history of computer use than does the application of the technology to organizational purposes. The term *computer* carries with it the image and symbol of a machine that can compute and calculate enormous amounts of data at unbelievable speeds. As a result, the technology of computer-based data analysis is quite sophisticated—in terms of hardware, software, and available electronic data bases and data services. Everyone in a human services organization—operational personnel, clinicians and professional workers, technical staff, policy and program planners, and managers themselves—can and should be using these empowering resources. For the manager, it provides the means for a vastly enhanced DSS (decision-support system).

The four ingredients for computer-based data analysis readily exist for any human services managers. They include

- User-friendly quantitative analysis software.
- "Number-crunching" computers of all sizes.
- Electronic data bases that are ready sources of electronic, computerized data.
- Technological capabilities to communicate electronically to data bases anywhere in the United States.

The first user-friendly quantitative analysis software packages were SPSS and SAS. Initially, they were only available on large central computers at university and research centers but are now also available for desktop microcomputers. It is now possible to obtain a variety of inexpensive, user-friendly data analysis software packages for all the major desktop microcomputers. Even more exciting is the rapid growth of user-friendly desktop computer graphic software using colors to enhance the analysis, particularly for geographic data bases (e.g., geoprocessing demographic data related to the mapping of a community—streets, blocks, census tracts).

There has been a rapid growth in the number of electronic data bases specifically related to the human services. Not only libraries but also many human services agencies are using these data bases. They can be accessed by dialing a local telephone number that connects the agency's computer to a nationwide telecommunications system. Examples of these electronic data bases would include the National Institute of Mental Health, Psychological Abstracts, Exceptional Child Education Resources, MEDLARS (the National Library of Medicine), Career and Guidance Information System, and many more.

Data has always been vital for the effective and productive functioning of human services organizations. Because most agencies are modernizing and automating their information-dissemination systems, for clients, staff, and other agencies in the community, data once contained only in a library are now being made available electronically. In many communities, services such as *information and referral* (I&R) are now being automated and tied together in a statewide network. Professional associations are creating *bulletin boards* just for their members, as a rapid means of exchanging information, data, and technical reports or to send electronic memos asking for solutions to general problems. The more sophisticated agencies have human services planners who develop and track models, looking for indicators as to the organization's impact on their client group (e.g., tracking the factors affecting poverty rates in a community; tracking infant mortality, birth weight of babies and pregnancy health services).

The Human Services Manager's Personal Use of Computers.   The desktop computer in the office of the human services manager is commonplace, a fairly recent phenomenon. Although (sometimes) it interacts with agencywide computer systems, it is primarily being used to enhance the function of managing the agency. Off-the-shelf user-friendly software packages are available for a human services manager for the following types of applications:

- Electronic spreadsheet
- Word processing
- Data base management
- Desktop publishing
- Telecommunications
- Calendar–scheduler
- Computer graphics
- Project management
- Visual presentations
- Data analysis

User-friendly software packages for each of the above continue to be developed at a fast rate. The best way to become aware of which software to use is by networking with colleagues, visiting computer stores that provide tutorials, or perusing a number of relevant magazines. Often large human services departments will standardize the particular software packages their managers are to use to enhance transferability of data and know-how.

Large human services organizations also are developing management workstations that have a system that combines most of the above software applications with the data base systems of the agencies. These workstations are then part of what is being called an executive information system (EIS).

Managing Computer-Based Information

Thus far this chapter has focused on *how* the computer-related technologies can be used to improve the human services organization's effectiveness and productivity. We need now to shift our focus to *managing* that use.

During the past decade, the term *information-resource management* (IRM) has become popular. Correctly, it views information as a major resource for an organization, which needs to be managed in the same way that people, finances, and programs are managed. Let us deal briefly with a number of issues related to managing computer-based information.

Options for Acquiring Computer Capability

There are a number of options for acquiring the capability of the computer-related technologies. They include the following:

- *Purchase:* Purchasing equipment and software from a computer company; this is for large systems, requiring employment of a staff of technicians.
- *Rent/lease:* Renting or leasing of equipment and possibly the software, by an agency employing a staff of computer specialists/technicians.
- *Time-share:* Using terminals and a telecommunications system, interconnecting with a third party's large computer system (hardware–software).
- *Service center:* Contracting with another organization to do all of your agency's data processing.
- *Turnkey:* Purchasing a system from a company that specializes in packaging computer hardware and software specifically designed for your agency; after training the agency's staff, this company turns over the package to your agency.

The best option for a specific human services agency depends on its requirements, the operation and management strategies, the resources the agency is able to commit to technology use, and the policies of the jurisdiction in which the agency is located. All of these elements require careful consideration.

Steps for Designing a System and Acquiring Computers

There are a number of ways to approach the process of designing computer systems for an agency wishing to acquire computer capability. Because the subject is so complex and technical, a detailed discussion is not possible. In brief the system-design and computer-acquisition process involves the following steps:

1. Form a group to guide and steer the process.
2. Identify short-term and long-term goals.
3. Assess the data requirements of all levels of the organization: operations performance, management control, and strategic planning.
4. Conceptualize the required system.
5. Identify the technology-strategy options and selection of the optimal ones, given the available resources and constraints.
6. Develop a computer-technology master plan for the organization.
7. Define the systems specifications: hardware and software.
8. Prepare and issue an RFP.
9. Evaluate vendors' proposals.
10. Select the best system.
11. Implement the new system.

12. Orient and train employees.
13. Monitor and evaluate the new system.

An agency can hire consultants or outside companies to design systems and assist in the acquisition of computer-related technologies. Another approach, usually found in larger human services organizations, is to create a **data processing unit**, employing a director of data processing and a staff of systems analysts, programmers, computer operators, and data-entry employees. Many human services organizations use a combination of these approaches with in-house staff and outside consultants and contract specialists as needed.

Acquiring a computer system represents a major organizational change. Therefore, as indicated in Step 1 above, it is very important to create an in-house steering group to guide the design and computer-acquisition effort. This group is made up of employees in the human services agency, those most affected by the change, usually from a variety of different programs and organizational levels. The *immediate function* of this technology-steering group is to guide the process of designing the computer system, whereas the *long-term function* involves facilitating the transfer of electronic technologies into the operations and management of the agency. Both functions are critical because electronic technologies change so rapidly that a human services manager has to continually reassess what is the most cost-effective technology strategy at any given time. For example, whether to choose a large computer network with dumb terminals or a series of interconnected supermicrocomputer-based LANs is a complex design question involving such factors as management philosophy and culture, past history of computer use, amount of available resources, and involvement of employees in the organization at all levels, including top management. The availability of an indigenous, experienced, electronic technology–steering committee that understands the organization will prove very valuable for most human services managers.

Organizing for Modern-Information Management. In today's organizations, information is viewed as a resource that needs to be managed like any organizational asset. Large and even medium-size human services organizations generally have a special data-processing unit devoted to managing the computer operation. As the EMS case illustrates, the design of high-volume, organizationwide computer systems is very complex. It requires specialists with training and experience who know how to deal with very large computer systems with hundreds of terminals and connected by a telecommunications system covering a large geographic area. The complexity of such systems is further increased by having to interconnect with a large number of desktop (micro) computers. With the growing recognition that data and information represent a major resource for the organization, data-processing units increasingly are placed under a top executive, who carries one of the following titles: director of management-information systems, chief information officer, or director of information-resource management.

In small human services agencies, the technology tends to be smaller and more user-friendly. Agency employees—clerical, clinical, and administrative—operate the system themselves. Generally, these agencies do not need a full-time specialist on staff; instead, consultants are used to assist initially in the design and installation of the system. Initially, agency employees lean on consultants until they have acquired sufficient knowledge and skills capacity to operate the system by themselves.

Information Resource Management (IRM).   Beyond being concerned about properly organizing the management of information-processing systems in an agency, the human services manager must also organize the management of information as a resource. This has two primary emphases: technology transfer and information-system planning. As noted previously, both should be carried out under the guidance of a technology-steering group for the agency, a group that represents the diversity of the organization.

Facilitating the transfer and utilization of the electronic technologies into the agency and building the capacity of agency employees to manage the technology transfer themselves is the first IRM task of an agency. In large human services organizations, a special staff can be assigned this task; in smaller agencies, the services of consultants or institutions of higher learning can be utilized. The first general task is the education and training of agency employees to introduce them to the technology and to provide them with the necessary skills for using the wide variety of user-friendly software. It is then necessary to focus on helping employees acquire the appropriate hardware and software, such that they can exploit the full potential of the technology.

Information-systems planning requires a methodical process that rationalizes data and data flows in the organization. Information is viewed in its broadest form and in the widest possible array of media—digital, text, whole-image, and voice. Computer-electronic systems are then developed to exploit the full use of agency and environmental information for the efficient and effective achievement of client-service outcomes. Increasingly, this includes the daily on-line availability of the information that provides an up-to-date, comprehensive picture of the agency and its activities to all employees, for the full variety of their needs. In essence the goal of IRM is clear: managing information as a precious resource for the human services agency.

The Decades Ahead

Before attempting to discuss the decades ahead for computer-related technologies and human services, two points deserve consideration:

1. We are talking about a wide range of electronic technologies that goes far beyond just the computer. They interrelate to deal with data and symbols

in one of four forms: digital, voice, whole-image, and text. These technologies include telecommunications (cable, fiber optics, satellites, etc.), facsimile (FAX) processing, micrographics, high-altitude photogrammetry, reprographics, video graphics, voice recognition, and optical–laser processing (laser compact discs), to mention the more common ones, and new marvels are in the offing.

2. It is not hard to picture the future of the electronic technologies—especially if you read science fiction. Harder to predict is the timing and mix of technology transfer, depending, as it does, on marketing strategies, consumer attitudes, resource allocations, and other factors, most of which are not rational in nature.

Despite these observations, it is possible to risk a number of predictions about the next twenty-five years of human services use of the electronic technologies:

1. As the communications in a particular setting become increasingly electronic, a redefinition of services and services delivery will be required. Service-delivery options for a human services agency will range from dealing with clients in person to clients dealing directly, independently, and electronically with agencies.

2. Human services agencies' centralized mainframe systems will be integrated with end users' microcomputers. In turn both will be integrated with the systems of other human services organizations, particularly as they focus on specific client groups (e.g., at-risk youth, frail elderly, developmentally challenged, families in poverty) or focus on specific issues (e.g., child and youth development, career enhancement, leisure and health improvement).

3. We are already beginning to see the shift from data-based systems to knowledge-based systems in the human services. Literature on human services expert systems (a form of AI) is already surfacing (see Wallace Gingerich 1988). We can anticipate the presence of AI robots as assistants in the operations, planning, and management of human services agencies within the coming decade (although it is unlikely that they will look like characters from *Star Wars*).

4. The ideal design of a computer system (Figure 13.4) for human services organization will be achievable, and will focus on three major groupings of applications: direct use by citizens and community institutions, extending employees' decision–action capabilities, and organizational support. These are founded on the automated routines and integrated data processing in the agency, allowing professional staff to do the things they are uniquely qualified to do.

5. The ultimate impact of electronic technologies on any human services professional or organization will be to call into question, and thereby provide the opportunity to significantly alter, the traditional roles that such a person and institution have played in society thus far. The impact of this

Figure 13.4   A Model for the Effective Use of Computers
in Human Services Organizations

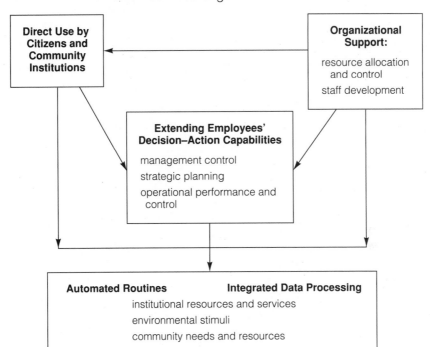

Source: Adapted from Myron E. Weiner, *Public Automation: 2001* (Storrs; CT: University of Connecticut, 1971).

will be not only major improvements of the productivity of our national economy but also, more important, of the effectiveness and the quality of services for individuals, families, and groups.

6. The ultimate purpose of a new technology is not only to improve what humans already do but also to add those things heretofore impossible. The new frontier of the computer-related technology therefore is not only superior data-processing systems that can be used by human services organizations and their clients. The new frontier is the use of the technology for example, for the disabled, to aid paraplegics with locomotion, mutes with speech, or deaf people with receiving normal communication. Such applications will be by far the most outstanding contribution of the electronic technologies to the human services.

7. While there are a number of points raised by the change to computer-based information management that require careful consideration (i.e., automation, jobs, ergonomics), one in particular has important implications that require discussion.

The literature on privacy and confidentiality in computer use is extensive. The abuse by some computer-based information systems has led to legislation directed toward protecting the rights of citizens. For most organizations, this has created a tension between freedom of information versus privacy–confidentiality. Human services agencies are particularly vulnerable in this area, and thus have an additional tension: client privacy and confidentiality versus effective human services delivery. For example, should an adoption file be opened to provide the adoptee with medical data about the birth parents? Should a substance abuse–treatment agency have access to physicians' and hospital medical records of a client? Should the identity of AIDS patients in hospitals be shared with other agencies? Should youth service agencies share data with public school pupil services and vice versa? Should IRS tax records be opened to assist a child-support enforcement agency in searching for a father required to provide financial support to his child?

While some may disagree, we would argue that a technology is neutral; it is how the human beings in an organization use computers that can impact on individuals and society. Thus, beyond nationwide regulations and constitutional protection, human services managers will need to create additional guidelines in this area that express their professional concerns. The best mechanism would be a **data-access control plan**, carefully developed on a communitywide basis by human services agencies and client-advocacy groups that see the need for a consensual set of guidelines to deal with this issue. Finding the difficult balance between improving the comprehensive nature of services delivery for a client and protecting the privacy of that client is a challenge that each community should work out in its own way.

There are a large number of technical and organizational means available of protecting the confidentiality of human services data, though none are foolproof. There are experts in the field who specialize in technologies to protect the confidentiality and safety of computer systems; there are also a number of people who by design or by mischief compromise the confidentiality of data. The issue is one that will require constant vigilance of the human services manager.

Summary

Managing information and computers has become one of the most crucial and fundamental processes for human services management. In this chapter we dealt with an overview of the technology itself; discussed the nature of the evolving electronic environment and the multiple perceptions that one can have of this phenomenon; indicated some of the things computers can and cannot do; provided examples and models of technology applications for client, clinician, clerical employees, and managers themselves; pointed out directions and different options for managing computer-based information now and for the next decades; and discussed some implications of computer use for the human services.

Managing computer-based information is fraught with tensions between opposing and equally viable sets of values. Technology can be both a boon and a bane. The shaping of technology use is in the hands of those who become "computer literate," knowledgeable, and involved. Whatever the attitudes a human services manager may have on the subject, she probably has no choice but to participate. Nonparticipation will by default also shape technology use, and as a result, society itself; and more likely in ways less palatable.

This new technology is a valuable key to improving the productivity of the human services. We need the Magic Genie on our staff. But more important, it challenges the creative human services manager to use the full potentialities of these electronic technologies not only to increase effectiveness of client services and to improve the quality of the human services systemic environment but also to form those solutions that are much needed but will not exist unless a caring mind—perhaps yours—creates them.

PART

V

Systemic Management

I ncreasingly, human services organizations are finding themselves involved in a large number of transorganizational (interorganizational) systems, as networks of human services organizations join together to provide a more comprehensive set of unique services to individual clients. Part V, the last set of chapters in the book, deals with the knowledge and skills necessary for systemic management of transorganizational systems. It requires a strategic, as compared to a structural, approach to human services management.

Research is vital to all aspects of social work and human services practice. For managers, applied research includes a number of analytic technologies—the most critical of which is systems analysis applied to the human services. Chapter 14 provides guidelines, models, specifications, and criteria for the design or redesign of more effective human services transorganizational systems. A systems analyst's "tool kit" is included in this chapter because of its vital importance to the systemic management of the human services.

Often, attempts are made to manage a newly designed transorganizational system without thoughtful and careful planning of how the transition from the existing to the new system will be implemented. Experience has shown that this lack of advanced planning for change management can be a fatal mistake. Experience has also shown that the most effective way of managing the transition to a new transorganizational system is by having the change managed by those most affected by that change. These topics are the subject of Chapter 15.

Even though the techniques and technologies of systemic management are largely the same as those for institutional management, the former is quite distinct from the latter. The key difference is in the concept of management repertoire: The assembling of a particular set of techniques that when used in concert can exploit heretofore untapped potential in the standard management technologies and can effectively manage transorganizational systems. For example, the computer not only is used as a technology but it actually also represents a whole new form of systemic management. Using classic examples to illustrate systemic management, Chapter 16 illustrates how strategic management calls for a significantly different concept of management that can, and must, be mastered along with institutional management.

14

Analyzing and Designing Systems

Research in Human Services Management

General Purposes
The Research Rigor
Analytic Techniques

Transorganizational Systems: Some Examples

Level 1: Single-Agency Client with Individualized Case Management
Level 2: Multiple-Agency Client with Managed Services
Level 3: Integrated Community Human Services System
  with Client Self-Management

Transorganizational Systems: Common Specifications

Managed Care
Comprehensive, Unique Set of Client Services
Client-Managed Systems
Adaptive Organizations
Meta-System Management
Integrated Service–Delivery Technologies
Integrated Computer–Telecommunications Information Systems

Analysis of Transorganizational Systems
Underlying Perceptions
The Systems Analyst's Tool Kit

Summary

Systemic management starts with the ability to analyze and redesign human services systems that cross organizational boundaries. Picking up on trends first identified in Chapters 6 and 8, this chapter focuses on a number of important areas that improve the human services manager's skills in transorganizational systems analysis and design.

The manager is continually called on to apply the rigor and technology of research to the task of improving the management of human services organizations and systems. The analysis and design of systems are one of those major areas for applied research in human services management. Chapter 14 begins therefore with a brief discussion of research as it relates to human services management.

Research in Human Services Management

General Purposes

Research is an integral element of the human services, whether one fulfills the role of clinician, planner, community organizer, or administrator. For the latter, the use of research and analysis is a continual necessity for the management of human services organizations. The end result is not merely the effective performance of the agency, vital as that may be, but also the maintenance of a responsive peripheral environment that will support the agency's particular aggregate group of clients in their efforts to acquire human services offerings.

Analysis is the means by which managers use research perspectives and techniques for the improvement of the human services. The end results and purposes of good utilization of analytic techniques are several:

Effectiveness

- Impact–outcome   Achieving desired client outcomes
- Service quality   Accessibility, timeliness, proficiency
- Client satisfaction   Direct feedback, reapplications

Productivity

- Methodic   Organizational arithmetic: unit costs, caseloads, optimum staff utilization, simplified paper flow

- Systemic   Systems arithmetic: task-force management, network management, services integration

- Strategic   Community arithmetic: leverage public investments, promote mutual-help groups, advocacy, tax policies

Eudemony (Quality of Life)

- Achieve mission   Reach organization–systems goals

- Growth and stability   Human prosperity: happiness, enlightenment; long-term equilibrium with environment

- Public interest   Neutral competence to protect common good

Scholars differ as to which of the above are the most important purposes of research applied to human services management. Rino Patti and his colleagues (1987) stress service effectiveness as the only meaningful measure of human services organizations. Peter Drucker (1974) notes that service institutions are at a disadvantage because they do not have profit as their ultimate measure of effectiveness. Thus, although they need to be concerned about efficiency, "performance and results" are the primary measure of service institutions. *Effectiveness is the primary measure of human services organizations.*

But the human services manager must also use analytic (research) techniques to streamline operations and reduce unit costs, arriving at the increased levels of efficiency and productivity on which policymakers, even society, insist. Moreover, creative human services management concentrates on change, reform, systemic redesign, growth, and development in the way in which we shape our societal environment to be more responsive to and supportive of client-group efforts to take advantage of service opportunities. Systemic management is concerned about organizational strategic options available to organizations to maintain a more cost-effective, responsive human services environment. By analyzing a complex system more precisely, human services managers can arrive at several new alternative options to improve the effectiveness, as well as the productivity, of the human services.

Creative human services management is dedicated to fashioning, changing, and reforming the human services systems for purposes of improvement. Systemic management is the vehicle for carrying out this primary responsibility of the human services manager, and excellent research and analytic techniques are very important. A possible impediment to this effort is the classic tension between two values: systems maintenance and systems change. But change is the hallmark of the human services organizational environment, and the rigor of research blended with appropriate analytic techniques holds the key to change to a more responsive and a more supportive human services environment.

Table 14.1   Analytic Techniques for Improving
             Human Services Organizations

Type	Definition	Examples
Management	An objective analysis of structure and procedures of an organization	Methods and procedures, paperwork simplification, records management, work measurement
Operations	Use of higher mathematics for solving operational problems and to provide management with a more logical basis for making predictions and choices	Probability, waiting lines, sequencing, allocating scarce resources, routing, facility location
Systems	Continuous cycle of designing alternative systems to achieve organizational objectives and evaluating these alternatives in terms of effectiveness and cost	Systems initiation, definition, conceptualization, design, model simulation, development, testing, and implementation
Community	Comprehensive socioeconomic analysis of a geographic area, searching for interrelationships among the multifaceted processes of society and its institutions	Neighborhood profiles, demographic studies, needs assessment, input–output analysis
Policy	Complex, dynamic process oriented toward the utilization of the scientific method for solving problems of public importance	Econometrics, financial investment–divestment analysis, Delphi process, social indicators
Social	Identification and analysis of societal problems, exploring historical and structural relationships, with an orientation toward social justice and to promote responses by individuals and groups to current societal issues	Neighborhood profiles, societal issue studies, reality construction, hermeneutics

The Research Rigor

The scientific method demands rigor of any serious researcher—whether in the physical or the social sciences. This is equally true for the analysis and improvement of human services organizations and systems. Essentially, the analytic process requires the following operations, which are used in an iterative, interrelated fashion:

1. Issue–problem identification
2. Issue–problem definition
3. Thesis–hypothesis articulation
4. Objectives–constraints definition

5. Data collection
6. Data analysis
7. Formulation–evaluation of alternative solutions
8. Presentation and adoption
9. Testing and experimentation
10. Implementation

Precise identification of problems is an important element because too often programs are mounted and resources expended before the problem has been accurately defined. For example, what a community calls "the problem of teenage substance abuse" may actually be the result of derailed development, teenage alienation, a deficit of recreational opportunities, and lack of positive roles for young people living in a turbulent, changing society. All of these problems can be addressed, but first they must be clearly understood.

Analytic Techniques

Since the midtwentieth century, six analytic techniques necessary for modern human services management have emerged. These provide comprehensive and detailed analytic perspectives of human services issues, problems, organizations, and systems (Table 14.1). Use of research rigor and human services analytic techniques are important tools for the analysis and design of transorganizational systems, and the foundation for systemic management in human services organizations.

Transorganizational Systems: Some Examples

There are three types of transorganizational systems, each one operating at a different level. Before presenting the techniques and tests for analyzing such systems, some examples would be helpful.

- Level 1   A single-agency client with individualized case management
- Level 2   A multiple-agency client with managed services
- Level 3   An integrated community human services system with client self-management

Increasingly, human services administrators are having to manage in these types of transorganizational systems, of which Level 1 is most common. Each of the three levels are described briefly in a scenario, followed by a description of their respective systems specifications.

Level 1: Single-Agency Client with Individualized Case Management

These types of transorganizational systems (Figure 14.1) have become popular with state government mental retardation or mental health agencies, primarily for clients who have been deinstitutionalized. Systems have been developed in which an interdisciplinary team assesses a client's needs and develops a unique package of services. A case manager is assigned to work with the client, make arrangements with community agencies to provide services to the client, and monitor the delivery of those services. The client is transferred to some type of community-living arrangement or to live at home with other family members. The case manager generally operates out of one of the state agency's regional offices. See Chapter 4 for a case in managed care (Case 4.2, page 86) for a scenario that describes such a system. The specifications for this Level 1 transorganizational system are the following:

- Interdisciplinary team (IDT) assessment
- Criteria-driven outcome
- Unique service package
- Client-managed services
- Single-agency computer system with interconnectivity
- Case management
- Meta-system manager

Level 2: Multiple-Agency Client with Managed Services

Efforts to develop Level 2 transorganizational systems have been under way in some communities for years, but these types of systems are not yet commonplace. Recent interest in attempting to help welfare recipients to become employed has created the pressure for designing Level 2 systems. Several state agencies (income security, social services, children and youth services, labor) join together with community job-training and social service agencies to create a system by which, for example, a recipient of AFDC receives day care, transportation, and job training until permanent employment is secured. New pressures to deal with school dropouts are receiving increased attention in a large number of communities and result in Level 2 systems that interrelate, at the minimum, public school, health, police, job training, social services, youth services, and recreational agencies.

Most generally, the organizational mechanism for tying these agencies together is a team or task force. Here also a **case-management system** is usually put into place. Increasingly, Level 2 systems are using an integrated computer-information system as an integral element of the case-management system. Most clients in a Level 2 system are assigned a case manager who functions in three roles: client mentor, case monitor, and systems change agent. In Level 1

Figure 14.1   Single-Agency Client with Individualized
Case Management

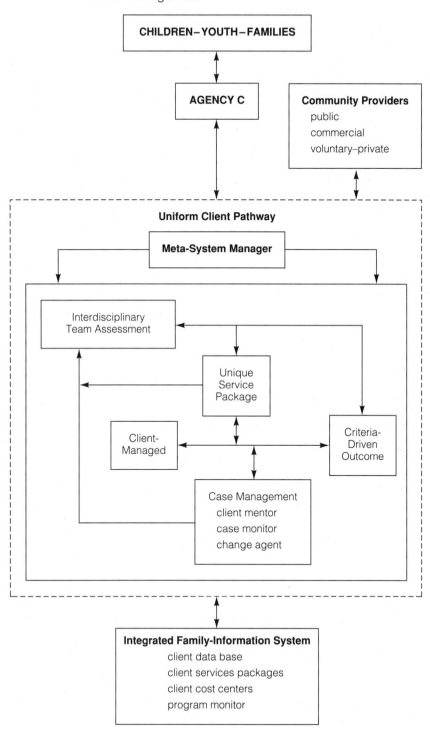

systems, the burden of spanning organizational boundaries was largely on the case manager. This is also true in Level 2 systems. However, the major burden of boundary spanning is on the team or task force being held accountable for effectively dealing with the problem.

Scenario.   Lydia Ortiz is a pregnant teenager in the city of Winfield, which has created a Youth Development Task Force. This task force includes professionals from Winfield's public school system, youth services bureau, health department, and police and recreational departments. In addition, membership on the task force includes social workers from several state government departments: children and youth, social services, income security, and mental health. The Regional Job–Partnership Training Council also participates in the task force, as does the Business and Industry Council of Winfield county. The task force developed an integrated youth services system (IYSS)—a Level 2 system.

Lydia's situation was brought to the attention of the task force by her foster parents. They were worried not only about her health during pregnancy but about the effect her becoming a teen mother would have on her future. For all intents and purposes, she has already dropped out of high school, where she was technically in tenth grade. She and her boyfriend, Conrado Nunez, talked about getting married, but they gave up on the idea. He had dropped out of school and could not find a permanent job. He had been charged with dealing drugs, but the Winfield police did not have sufficient evidence to prosecute. This, however, limited his employability.

When Lydia went to Winfield's Mother and Child Clinic for her sixth-month checkup, she was assigned to Barbara Reyes, a nurse at the clinic who was also a member of Winfield's Youth Development Task Force. Encouraged by Barbara, Lydia agreed to participate in the task force's IYSS. An integrated services package was developed using a computer terminal in the city's health department. It followed a uniform protocol developed by the system's IDT. The individualized services package developed for Lydia included a wide range of health, school, job-training, home-management, and recreational services; providers were selected, all of whom were members of IYSS.

Barbara Reyes agreed to be the case monitor but enlisted the help of Lydia's foster mother. Both were instructed on how to manage the service delivery themselves. The outcome criteria for Lydia were fairly clear: good medical attention during pregnancy and birth, child and day care, job training in a local company tied into her public school education, and home-management counseling. All data relative to Lydia's case were maintained in the IYSS integrated computer system. Barbara received automatic reports on situations where progress was being monitored according to preset performance criteria. Lydia's progress was sufficient to encourage her to involve Conrado as a client of IYSS also.

Members of the Youth Development Task Force initially had a difficult time managing the IYSS. It required a set of values and skills that were different

Figure 14.2   Multiple-Agency Client with Integrated-Services
            Management

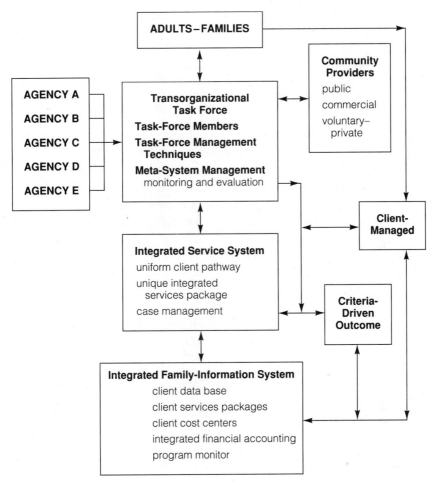

than what they had experienced in managing their departmental and agency programs. But they worked with an experienced trainer and facilitator, assigned to them by one of the local insurance companies, who helped them solidify their task force–management abilities.

Specifications.   A Level 2 system is described graphically in Figure 14.2. Its specifications include the following:

- Transorganizational team or task force
- Task force–management techniques

- Integrated-service system
- Uniform client pathway
- Unique, integrated service–package
- Outcome criteria
- Client self-management
- Integrated computer–telecommunications system
- Task force–team monitoring and evaluation

Level 3: Integrated Community Human Services System with Client Self-Management

Level 3 systems are essentially still on the human services systems designers' drawing boards because the different levels of transorganizational systems have a nesting quality. A Level 3 system can only be built on the experience and sophistication of managing the previous levels. It may therefore take another decade before Level 3 transorganizational systems are in use because the implementation of Level 2 systems is so recent and rare.

Essentially, a Level 3 system interrelates the vast majority of human services agencies in a community—public, private, and commercial. It is guided by a multidisciplinary team of professionals from different agencies formed to develop a number of transorganizational systems. The team undertakes comprehensive strategic planning, out of which develops a number of task forces, each one charged with developing Level 2 systems. Ultimately, people living in a community have available the widest possible range of options for service acquisition to deal with each client comprehensively and uniquely. Such systems could be energized directly from their dwelling using an integrated telecommunications system.

Technologically, the elements of a Level 3 system are still evolving. Although Level 1 and 2 systems are gradually becoming more commonplace because of pressures from the environment, this is not true for Level 3 systems. They may well not be fully developed until the twenty-first century. The following scenario (Case 14.1) illustrates a Level 3 transorganizational system. It is designed using the following specifications:

- Multidisciplinary, transorganizational human services team
- Transorganizational management techniques
- Automated catalog of resources
- Automated assessment of needs
- Response strategies
- Client self-managed, individualized services package
- Automation of backup-service options

- Integrated computer-telecommunications system
- Team evaluation and monitoring

Case 14.1

Scenario: Level 3 Transorganizational System

Sarah Martin put down the drink in her hand, sadly looked about, and realized she had reached a point of desperation. She was surrounded by boxes yet to be unpacked, in the living room of a tiny Scottstown apartment where she had just moved from her beloved suburban home. Her sparse divorce settlement did not leave sufficient funds to maintain the big house. Without skills or income, she felt hopelessly alone as she absent-mindedly opened an envelope that had arrived earlier in the mail. It was from the EAP office of her ex-husband's employer. The letter indicated that there were certain entitlements still available to her. A brochure published by the Scottstown Social Services Department was included with the letter. The brochure summarized several options for her and her family: (1) a list of community social services agencies she could contact directly; (2) how to contact the EAP office; (3) how to contact her municipal social services department; or (4) how to, through her cable TV system, dial into what was called "HELPMATE.3." The brochure went on to explain that this was an animated user-friendly system with which residents of the Long River region could interact electronically if they needed advice regarding available help from the various social services agencies in the region. "HELPMATE.3" seemed interesting and nonthreatening, so she went to the home of a friend who had cable TV. The friend was intrigued. Together they followed the instructions and soon were involved in a color animated film, which provided categories of situations. The brochure from the EAP office had indicated that Sarah might want to explore the category entitled "single-parent families," which she did. This spelled out a number of areas of service support: financial, insurance, day care, latch-key care, employment, housing, counseling, public schools, job training, youth services, elderly services, recreation, and so on.

"HELPMATE.3" then provided Sarah with another set of options: (1) use as an on-screen encyclopedia of social services for information gathering; (2) energize and package your own services from the available offerings; (3) contact an agency to serve as a professional diagnosis–service plan developer; (4) the same as option 3, only with the same agency serving as advocate–monitor. Sarah felt both interested and better informed but was still too depressed and overwhelmed to go it alone, so she chose option 3. Knowing that she needed professional guidance, she made an appointment with the Scottstown social services director for the following day.

At her meeting with Sarah, Edith Singer, the director of the city of Scottstown Social Services Department used the "HELPMATE.3" terminal on her desk to open a computer file for Sarah, entering the responses that described her situation, prompted by a series of computer questions. Edith then spent the rest of the time counseling Sarah and set up another appointment for two days later.

When Sarah came next time, Edith had a printout of the status of several of the items already being processed. Their meeting began by reviewing these:

1. Within forty-eight hours, Sarah would receive a general assistance check to tide her over until AFDC and food stamps began to arrive. These had been applied for through the computer system.
2. AFDC and food stamps would begin in three weeks and continue until Sarah's employment reached a level of self-support. This would be monitored through the computer system.
3. Several possible job openings suited to Sarah's limited skills were provided. A quick check through the system showed that one had been filled that morning but the others were still available.
4. There were several day-care options for Sarah's one-year-old daughter; a temporary reservation was made at the one with a vacancy nearest to Sarah's home, and an appointment made for Sarah's personal visit to the selected day-care site.

Following a review of these items, Edith and Sarah dealt with the issues of joining a "reemerging homemaker" support group, as well as exploring the possibility for a job-training program that would develop her natural potentials into marketable skills.

Both of these involved "HELPMATE.3" to identify possible programs and to allow Sarah to explore her options. Edith eventually helped her register in the programs of her choice and provided both of the agencies who administered these programs with the necessary information regarding Sarah's case. As time progressed, it would be possible for all agencies involved to exchange whatever information was appropriate through controlled access to Sarah's file as it was updated.

Sarah and Edith agreed to meet once a week for the next two months for direct counseling. Before leaving, Sarah expressed to Edith her great appreciation for her concern and for the speed and efficiency with which her seemingly insurmountable problems had been addressed. As she walked out, she turned her head and smiled, probably for the first time in days. The thought that had flashed through her head was, "How do I say thanks to that computer on Edith's desk?"

"HELPMATE.3" was designed, and is now managed, by a regionwide consortium of human services agencies (the Long River Region Human Services Council). As can be anticipated, there are a large number of different adaptive organizations created for policy development, day-to-day management, and quality-assurance monitoring of the communitywide regional system. Level 3 systems require a broader range of skills: strategic planning and policy formation (scanning the environment for new opportunities and new priorities [opportunistic surveillance]); energizing and initiating new systems using lobbying, negotiating, and boundary-spanning skills; systems analysis involving conceptualization, design, development, and implementation of both macrosystems and microsystems. For this much larger group of professionals, continuous orientation and professional development and training in acquiring the values and skills of transorganizational management were necessary.

Transorganizational Systems: Common Specifications

A review of all three levels of transorganizational systems and their specifications indicates a number of common specifications used currently in the design of transorganizational systems. These grow out of the trends in human services systems initially identified in Chapter 6.

Managed Care

Anne Stoline and Jonathan Weiner (1988) note that during the past two decades the health-care field has undergone a radical shift in systemic design. Traditionally, the system was dominated by fee for service (FFS). Under this system, the provider charged the client a fee for each separate service; payment was made to the provider after the service was provided, under some type of a reimbursement arrangement—directly to the provider by a third party (e.g., insurance company or government agency) or to the client, who paid the provider. Increasingly, the health-care field is being dominated by alternative-delivery systems, primarily a HMO (health maintenance organization) or by a PPO (preferred provider organization). In these new systems, health care is "managed." Managed care is used to describe a range of utilization controls that are applied to manage the practices of service providers.

The specification for managed care has grown out of the confluence of three trends in society, some specific to human services, some general to the design of societal service systems: flexible-production systems, services integration, and proscriptive pricing. As we examined in Chapter 8, there has been a shift away from mass production of goods and services and a move toward the systems that provide a unique product or set of services for individual customers and clients. It flows out of the premise that the design of **flexible-production systems** not only meets the unique need of each person in society but also is more economic and productive for the producer–provider.

On the thesis that there is a great deal of duplication and overlapping in the provision of services in society, the movement toward **services integration** has been a concern of human services planners and designers for two decades. The average user of services in society has to navigate a complicated, fragmented, complex, and often confusing "nonsystem" of separate, isolated agencies, each providing their own services from their own disciplinary perspective. The issue grows not only out of the concern for more productive use of limited human services resources but also the concern for redesigning services delivery in a interrelated fashion such that clients receive a set of services unique to their specific needs. The primary goal is greater effectiveness of services in terms of client impact and outcomes.

In recent years, as the costs of health care have escalated at a faster rate than the general cost of living, the federal government has implemented a new approach to reimbursement of payments for services. The FFS system was essentially a cost-plus approach to reimbursing the costs of services: the provider charged for the services and added a set percentage for their overhead. This system was an incentive for providers (solo providers [physicians] as well as institutions [hospitals]) to provide more services because the greater the amount of services, the larger the cost reimbursement. As an attempt to control health-care costs, the federal government adopted a **proscriptive-pricing** arrangement for in-hospital care: a set fee for a specific set of services. All possible in-hospital medical procedures were categorized into diagnostically related groups (DRGs) and a price was set for each DRG, based on detailed cost analysis.

Modern systems designers assume that both the productivity and the effectiveness of services delivery will be improved by using the specification of managed care in the design of human services systems. The recent popularity of case managers is a visible sign of the move toward systems with this specification.

Comprehensive, Unique Set of Client Services

The same forces that produced managed care have also brought about an increasing commitment to packaging a unique set of services for each client. Initially, this specification was built into transorganizational systems for clients requiring a range of health, mental health, physical disability, and developmental disability services. Efforts are currently underway to redesign systems that deal with child welfare, school dropouts, family services, and "welfare" (AFDC). In each of these system-redesign efforts, the specification for a comprehensive, unique set of client services is a requirement.

This specification is consistent with the latest thinking in modern management: design of transorganizational systems that use the principles of a flexible-production system of goods and services and of cybernetic management. The former was discussed in Chapter 8; cybernetic management will be discussed in Chapter 16. Both are necessary elements of strategic-systemic management of the human services.

Client-Managed Systems

The primary person responsible for managing a complex system of interacting sets of specialized elements is the client who is trying to exploit the variety built into the system such that the goods or services of the system will meet her *unique* set of needs. Transorganizational systems managers therefore strive to create and maintain an environment that is responsive to and supportive of people as they seek a set of services that meets their individualized needs in an optimal fashion (i.e., with the least expenditure of individual and collective physical and psychic energy and resources).

The widest possible variety of delivery modes, then, should be structured to provide choices for individuals, to encourage them, at times to assist them, and to acquire services in an independent fashion. At different ages and stages of life, people acquire services at differing levels of organizational dependency. Thus, some clients will need a temporary or permanent advocate, facilitator, or case manager, whether a relative, volunteer, or professional. The structuring of service-delivery options is redundant in nature such that backup options are always available if and when needed.

In both Level 1 and 2 transorganizational systems, the client receives assistance in managing the set of services packaged to meet his unique needs. Where necessary, a member of the family, a volunteer, or a social worker serves as client advocate to facilitate the service provision process. The degree to which others participate in this process depends on each client's level of functioning.

Adaptive Organizations

Experienced human services managers recognize the presence of one or more "temporary" organizational forms when dealing with a transorganizational system. Its role and function vary, depending on the level of such system. A required specification of many Level 1 systems is an IDT, a team of multidisciplinary professionals who provide their knowledge, skills, and experiences to bring about a comprehensive set of services that can meet the unique needs of a client.

Level 2 transorganizational systems generally are managed by a task force, made up of professionals from different public, private, and proprietary agencies, who are focused on the most critical issues faced by a community, such as school dropouts, for example. By themselves, none of these youth-oriented organizations could effectively cope with such a complex issue. By working together as a task force that functions across the boundaries of different human services organizations and systems, however, this temporary organizational form has the potential for more effective impact on at-risk youth. Other task forces involving social work administrators focus on the frail elderly, single-parent families in poverty, the homeless, child sexual abuse, and so forth. Members of a task force retain their bureaucratic positions while they play specific roles in the temporary organization.

Transorganizational management requires one or more types of organizational arrangements that are called adaptive, synthetic, adhocratic, or temporary. Focused on interrelating different structures, these organizational forms generally are fashioned as task forces, projects, teams, networks, interjurisdictional bodies, or matrix organizations. They involve the formal or informal connecting of different organizations for some collective undertaking.

In adaptive organizations, the functions of the managers include (1) the opportunistic surveillance of the environment, such that there is a coalignment in time and space of streams of institutionalized action, and staying at the nexus of several variables and moving streams of action that force the nexus itself to be dynamic; (2) assembling clusters of administrative techniques in dynamic configurations to form repertoires of creative responses to an environment that is characterized by complexity and turbulence; and (3) designing the maximum possible range of options in complex cybernetic systems of interacting organizational elements, to provide optimal responsiveness to the widest variety of individuals with unique needs.

Meta-System Management

The meta-system is a system over and above the basic system. It is a "higher-order system" capable of changing its component institutions as needed. The meta-system is also a monitoring system whose only product or function is to test the stability of the operational system, that is, providing goods or services in a way that regulates and manages itself to meet the unique needs of each client.

Transorganizational systems need managing at the meta-level to continuously monitor the degree to which the system is meeting all design specifications and to make necessary design revisions when the system's results fall below the outcome criteria (e.g., responsiveness, confidentiality, performance effectiveness). In a Level 1 situation, the meta-system manager is someone designated from within the single agency, usually the program manager at some state agency regional office; in Level 2 systems, the task force designates a member to serve in that capacity.

Integrated Service–Delivery Technologies

Technologies for integrating services delivery have been highly developed for almost two decades, growing steadily since the late 1960s and early 1970s when services integration was a focal point for human services change. It is not surprising that such technologies represent the core of Level 1 transorganizational systems:

- Interdisciplinary assessment and diagnosis of needs
- Development of a unique service package
- Development of outcome criteria
- Case management (mentoring, monitoring, and systems change)

Together with the specification of an integrated computer system, these technologies represent the fundamental service-delivery changes that were developed during that period. The same technologies are present in the Level 2 system case vignette, where the integrated service delivery was central to such a system.

Integrated service–delivery systems can also include the option for a **uniform client pathway** (see Figure 14.1). This process is followed uniformly by *each* provider agency. This assures clients that regardless of the point of entry into a system, each provider follows a uniform process for clients to enter and receive services from the system. This provides the designer of transorganizational systems with an optional design that might be more acceptable by service providers who are very protective of their turf. For example, a youth development task force could develop an integrated service–delivery system that sets up *one* Level 1 system housed in the public school system because their resources, power, and professional prestige generally gives them a dominance position among bureaucracies. Or the task force could decide that a client pathway should be developed by each provider such that clients are dealt with in a uniform fashion. In the case of the latter, if an at-risk youth were first detected by the health department, then the assessment and diagnosis would be by a health department–initiated IDT, but the unique services package would include all the services provided by the different member agencies of the task force.

In effect integrated services can be achieved by a large number of different mechanisms, technologies, and arrangements. This provides the planners of Level 2 transorganizational systems the necessary flexibility in their design efforts.

Integrated Computer–Telecommunications Information Systems

Harnessing the electron as both the energy source and medium for institutional-systemic processes and memory is a vital specification for transorganizational management. Over and above being exploited for information systems, office automation, and data bases, electronic technologies are also the means by which adaptive (temporary) organizations are interrelated, particularly for flexible-systems provision of individualized products and services.

In Chapter 13, we examined the concept that the primary use of human services computer systems should be clients and agencies in the community. At that time, three levels of client-focused systems were suggested, as well as specifications for an agency computer system that is client-friendly. When approaching the design of transorganizational human services systems, this concept becomes even more important and necessary.

An integrated computer–telecommunications system, available to all (clients, service providers, and human services managers), is the "glue" by which a transorganizational system is held together as an adaptive organization. Given today's electronic technologies, this can take one of several forms: a central computer with several terminals used in each of the agencies who are participating in the adaptive organization; or a telecommunication network of minicomputers or microcomputers (PCs), which can operate as stand-alone systems for individual agencies and as an interconnected telecommunications network. In general, this integrated system has at least three requirements: (1) a common and shared data set for each client's individualized service plan (ISP), complete with techniques for protecting privacy; (2) a dual-reporting system that aggregates data in terms of reporting needs for each employee or professional's bureaucratic agency *and* in terms of reporting needs for the adaptive organization itself; and (3) data-analysis feedback capabilities that include both internal and external data bases.

Level 1 and 2 transorganizational systems have identical integrated information–system specifications: client data base, client-services packages, client cost centers, and program monitors. Because a Level 2 system is multiple-agency in focus, which means that a client uses resources for services from several different sources, another specification is integrated financial accounting. Level 1 systems are operated generally by a single agency; for Level 2 systems, the separate computer systems of each service provider are tied together by a telecommunications network that adheres to identical computer standards and protocols. The specifications for a Level 3 system require "advanced" applications for its integrated-information system that include (1) an automated resource catalog, (2) automated needs assessment, (3) automated service responses, and (4) automated backup options.

As noted earlier, Level 3 systems will most likely take many years to fully evolve, because they can only be built on the experience and sophistication of transorganizational management at the other two levels.

Analysis of Transorganizational Systems

Underlying Perceptions

There are a number of important perceptions that serve as a foundation for the analysis of transorganizational systems. They include the following.

Shared-Interrelated Purpose.   Because all efforts can only be measured ultimately in terms of impact on human beings, all disciplines and societal organizations share the same purpose. Social services, education, public safety, health, economic development, environmental quality, and the myriad of societal institutions are all vested interests in the system of humans and environment. Just as people and their environment cannot be segmented, neither can the various organizational units acting on their behalf operate totally independently of each other, nor can they have exclusive credit for the well-being or life furthering of members of society.

Because all organizations work from a common base of human and societal needs, then it follows that organizational missions are highly interrelated. There are numerous ways, for example, that a recreational professional provides services that would also meet the goals of education, social services, health, mental health, youth services, economics, senior services, and public safety.

Multiple Organizational Foci.   A societal institution—public, nonprofit, or proprietary—has to be focused in three ways if it is to completely fulfill its responsibility to society:

- Primary: Carrying out the stated legal purposes of the organization
- Special purpose: Performing special, often temporary, missions that require multiprofessional talents and joint efforts
- Cross-community: Serving the ongoing needs of people—individually or collectively—whose satisfaction is the mutual responsibility of many institutions in a jurisdiction or community

As noted in Chapter 6, the primary functional focus is the concern largely of institutional management; while systemic management concerns itself with special-purpose and cross-community missions and needs. This picks up on a theme first noted in Chapter 6. To be fully effective, a human services organization (such as the municipal youth services bureau illustrated in Figure 6.1, page 137) relies on managing with two simultaneous and coexisting forms of management: institutional and systemic.

Systems as Networks of Relationships.   A human services system encompasses a set of people, processes, programs, or organizational entities that are linked together in a network of relationships for some type of common purpose. Each human services organization finds itself in a variety of systemic networks that can be classified as follows in Table 14.2. Each network can also be classified according to its organizational focus: primary, special purpose, or cross-community.

The Systems Analyst's Tool Kit

There is both an art and a science to being an effective systems analyst. The art refers to a particular quality of mind that operates as a "third eye," much like that of a skilled photographer, that can observe more than what the naked eye sees. The art of systems analysis is brought to the task by the human services manager. It is the science of systems analysis that is addressed in this chapter.

Table 14.2 Different Types of Systemic Networks

Focus	Type	Examples
Function	Intraorganizational	Mental health (MH)
	Interorganizational	Mental health
		Physical health
		Recreation
Organization	Intraorganizational	Divisions within a state department of mental health
	Interorganizational	MH district office
		Community MH clinic
		Nonprofit family agency
		Group home
Jurisdiction	Intraorganizational	Different agencies of state government
	Interorganizational	State, municipal, nonprofit, and proprietary agencies

Effective systems analysis is best achieved with groups of people, prefer-ably from different organizations and professional disciplines; this brings the broadest set of perspectives to the analysis process. Analysts collect data through direct observations, interviews, or collection of forms and reports. They use paper, preferably of newsprint size, sharp pencils, markers (prefer-ably of many colors), and plastic templates with a variety of symbols (e.g., squares, triangles, diamonds, rectangles, circles, lines of all types, arc arrows). Analysis results are reduced to paper in graphic or tabular form; it takes several drafts and much discussion until the final product is produced—a report that analyzes the existing system and recommends what would be an ideal system.

What are the tools and techniques that the systems analyst tends to find most helpful in this process? We will attempt to cover briefly those that are considered most helpful for the human services manager facing the task of analyzing and redesigning a transorganizational system.

The Basic Elements of a System.   As is generally understood, a system has four elements:

In effect, any system is a chain of interacting subsystems with its four elements. Feedback occurs not only within a subsystem but between each of the subsys-tems. Stafford Beer (1979), the leading theorist for cybernetic management of

Figure 14.3   Macroanalysis: Reducing Infant Mortality

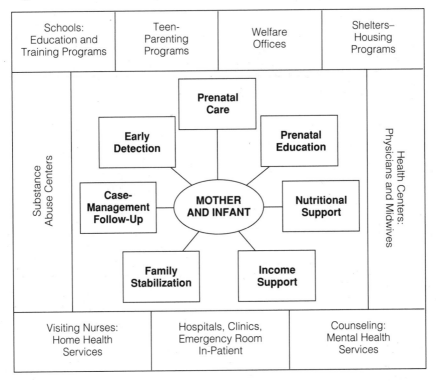

transorganizational systems, suggests that a good way to think of systems and subsystems is to view them as nesting wooden painted dolls, one set within (and affecting) the other.

Two Perspectives: Macroanalysis and Microanalysis.   The analysis of human services systems is the starting point for redesigning an existing system to improve its effectiveness. Generally, this is approached from two perspectives:

- **Macroanalysis**: The method of developing a universal pattern for the delivery system of each human services function (e.g., health, education, social services, mental health) or functional component. A pattern consists of a classification of service providers, a classification of services, and a network of client-referral paths connecting the classes of service providers. This pattern is independent of agencies and jurisdictions.

- **Microanalysis**: The process of identifying the individual service providers operating in a specific geographic area and the specific service each offers. This type of analysis then traces the network of linkages and types of interrelationships that connect the service providers.

Figure 14.4   Microanalysis: Neonatal-Care Response System

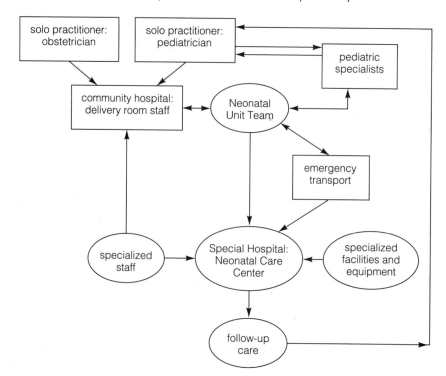

Figures 14.3 and 14.4 illustrate these two analytic approaches for the function of infant health care.

Vertical and Horizontal Systems.   The basic pattern of human services in the United States is strongly influenced by federal categorical programs vertically structured within an intergovernmental framework. Increasingly, there is a need to link and create a horizontal network of different, functionally based organizational systems, funded from a variety of categorical sources. These horizontal systems are transorganizational in nature and focus on clients with multiple problems or needing multiple services, generally living in a common geographic area.

Systems as Networks of Agencies Linked Together.   Another way of looking at transorganizational systems is to view them as linked networks of agencies. These networks can be multiple and complex. For example, four agencies can form a corporation to purchase apartments, which they refurbish and then make available to a community re-entry system. In the latter system, the same four agencies form another network to work with clients being moved from mental health institutions into the community. Each of the four agencies could lease an apartment and sublet it to a client who has been deinstitutionalized; arranging housing would be only one of the services each agency provides these clients.

In analyzing systems that are networks of different human services organizations, a key attribute to be classified is the linkage between the different agencies. The following are some of the different ways in which the linkages can be classified:

- Types of exchanges   Funds
  Staff
  Space
  Clients
  Data

- Nature   Cooperative-competitive
  Voluntary-mandatory
  Formal-informal
  Continuous-occasional
  Reciprocal-nonreciprocal exchange

- Level   Client
  Program
  Board
  Workers
  Management

- Mechanisms   Joint: planning, policy development, outreach, programming, use of staff, intake–assessment, and evaluation
  Co-location of offices
  Case management
  Contracting–subcontracting
  Reporting
  Program
  Financial

Integration–Coordination. In transorganizational systems, there are several levels of integration–coordination. There is the service-delivery level, where a functionary of the system works directly with clients in order to integrate and coordinate services. There is also the systems-management level in which, for example, a district office manages contracts with community agencies in order to coordinate and integrate the range of services available to the client. Increasingly, one form of integration–coordination is being called case management; the other is being called service system management or network management.

In the health services field, the terms *vertical integration* and *horizontal integration* are used:

- **Vertical integration**: One organization coordinates a group of agencies–facilities that collectively offer many levels of services (e.g., an HMO).
- **Horizontal integration**: One organization operates or coordinates a number of facilities–agencies that provides the same level of service (e.g., one agency operates a number of group homes for mental health clients re-entering the community).

Case management has become increasingly a specification of transorganizational systems. This has caused some confusion about the definitions, functions, and professional skills necessary for case management. For the purposes of understanding and analysis, let us view some of the variables of case management that the systems analyst must identify and use in system redesign:

- Level of professional training and experience required
- Range of duties: assess needs of clients; develop treatment plan; refer to treatment services; monitor client services, quality and quantity; advocacy; purchase services, core and supportive; monitor client progress; develop new client pathways; and develop new client services
- Frequency of client contact
- Authority and power
- Caseload
- Degree of mix: clinical services and case-management services
- Organizational placement: part of agency providing core services, separate case-management agency

Managed-Care Systems.   As already noted, many transorganizational human services systems are being classified as managed-care systems because they attempt to coordinate and integrate the delivery of services for the unique needs of each client. To the systems analyst, a number of attributes of managed-care systems are particularly important. They include the following:

- Service-delivery criteria   Comprehensive services
                                Continuity of services: interdisciplinary, longitudinal, and assigned worker
                                Accessibility of services: geographic, time flexibility, and financial
                                Client-driven
                                Unique service package
                                Least restrictive setting
                                Efficient and economic
                                Clear accountability: programmatic and financial
                                Culturally specific
                                Service-quality standards
                                Adequate liability coverage
                                Guaranteed client rights

Table 14.3   Strategies for Transorganizational
             Systemic Management

Strategy	Role or Duty
Educator	Leadership Advising Technical assistance Information and referral Facilitation
Regulator	Regulating Enforcing standards Evaluating Monitoring
Indirect provider	Entitlement (resource transfers) Guarantee loans Contracting (direct purchasing) Shape tax policies Administrative reform Financing: grants–loans Advocate Promote mutual-help groups Program demonstration and experimentation Technical assistance Tax incentives
Direct provider	Core Supportive Coordinative (case management)

- Management criteria   One lead agency
  Systems: financial and accounting, personnel,
  clinical records, information, program planning, and program evaluation
  Quality assurance: peer review, utilization review, and standards–criteria
  Monitoring: key performance indicators, site
  visits, and reporting

Strategies for Systemic Management.   The last attribute of transorganizational systems that needs to be included in the systems analyst's tool kit picks
up on the discussion in Chapter 8—different strategies for systemic management. Fundamentally there are three such strategies: educational, regulatory,
and service provision (direct and indirect). Table 14.3 concludes this chapter's
discussion of the analysis of transorganizational systems by listing the different strategies for managing such systems that are open to human services
managers.

Summary

Systemic management requires an ability to analyze and design human services systems, particularly those that span the boundaries of organizations and link together several human services agencies. It necessitates knowledge and skill in systems analysis, one of six analytic methodologies used to improve the effectiveness of human services organizations and systems. Each of these analytic methodologies must be applied with the same scientific rigor as any serious research endeavor.

There are several different types of transorganizational systems: those that are designed for a single agency, for multiple agencies tied together for the purpose of managed care, or for an integrated communitywide approach to services. All these systems generally use a common set of specifications that include managed care, a unique set of client services, client-managed systems, adaptive organizations, meta-system management, and integrated approaches to service-delivery technologies and information systems.

There is both an art and a science to being an effective systems analyst. The knowledge and skill in the science of transorganizational systems analysis and design can be acquired; there are a number of analytic tools and techniques generally used for this process. Although the art of systems analysis is important during the analytic phase of the effort, it becomes crucial in the process of conceptualizing how a transorganizational system can be designed or redesigned. Effective systems analysis is best achieved therefore when groups of professionals from different organizations and disciplines join to perform the analysis and design. This assures the widest possible range of different perspectives necessary to analyze and reconstruct a complex system in which human beings interact with each other and their environment.

15

Managing the Transition to New Systems

Managing Change: An Overview

Change and Transition: Some Issues

An Approach to Change and Transition

Summary

Case 15.1 _____

Part 3:* Eligibility Management System

To the surprise of many, Naomi Birch, a senior policy analyst for the Department of Income Security, was appointed director of the department's EMS. With her several years of experience in the department and with an M.S.W. in policy planning, Naomi's appointment signalled the intention of the top management of the department to have the new system shaped by program professionals and not by data-processing specialists. Although Naomi had no formal background in computers, as a top policy planner she understood intimately the program and processing environment of the department. As director of EMS, she reported to the department's newly appointed director of program policy.

Naomi's first task was to organize the planning-and-design process. She recognized quickly that this process would be one of managing major change and transition for everyone in the department, as well as for the clients and a large number of other agencies. Her background in social work led her to choose an open, involving process—the action research approach, which is based on the premise that change is best managed by those most affected by the change. To achieve maximum user involvement, Naomi put in place a number of key participants:

- The executive committee: The top department executives, including the director of data processing and the director of field operations

- The planning committee: Twelve key administrators in the department, including the directors of finance, personnel, program policy, training, eligibility services, and data processing

- The working committees: A cross section of headquarters and field employees from all levels of the organization, committees formed were current operations, training, technical, applications, future district organization, reporting requirements, and readiness

To ensure thorough communications, minutes of each committee meeting were circulated and made available to all key administrators and professionals in the department, and a monthly *EMS Update* newsletter was circulated to all employees.

Naomi contracted for a systems consultant to serve as the technical advisor for her staff from the beginning of the operation. Prior to implementation, one of the supervisors in a district office was assigned to coordinate the implementation of EMS in the various district offices. Every district office employee received thirty-five hours of orientation and training. The department's training unit did the planning for this large undertaking and district workers were trained to run the sophisticated computer system by using an equally sophisticated computer-assisted training system. Moreover, key eligibility workers in each district office who were trained then had the responsibility for training other workers in their district offices (this approach is known as "training of trainers").

At the last meeting of the executive committee, the deputy commissioner for administration commented, "I must admit that, at first, the decision to put the management of EMS planning under the program deputy put my nose out of joint. But in hindsight, it was the right decision."

"Why do you say that now, Bill?" Naomi asked.

"Well," Bill continued, "there is no question that the eligibility workers in the district offices now feel a strong ownership of EMS. That's critical. In addition, we tapped the creativity of the best and the brightest in each district. They could see that this was more than just a new computer system. This was a whole new departmental approach to our clients and our mission."

"What's more," chimed in Marian Grant, the deputy commissioner for programs, "this involvement gave everyone a chance to share ideas from the commissioner to the eligibility workers. We even got the feds to buy into our system, rather than just keep criticizing that we weren't following their EMS-design guidelines. It may take more time, but managing such a major transition with all this involvement certainly does pay off in the long run!"

*Parts 1 and 2 of the EMS case appear in Chapters 4 and 13, respectively.

Part 3 of Case 15.1 is a good starting point for a chapter devoted to managing the transition to a new or redesigned system. It illustrates a number of critical issues:

1. The most perfect analysis and redesign of a transorganizational human services system is of no value unless properly implemented.
2. The implementation of a new or redesigned transorganizational system is a major change for everyone involved in the current system.
3. The transition from an existing system to a newly redesigned system must be carefully planned.
4. The change to a new system must be managed with great skill.
5. In all of the above, the key ingredient is to have those most affected by the change involved in managing the change.
6. Management of a newly redesigned transorganizational system cannot begin until steps 1–5 have been successfully accomplished.
7. This change and transition process is guided by the classic ROI (return-on-investment) principle: The quantitative and qualitative benefits from a new or redesigned transorganizational human services system can only be accrued when there is an appropriate investment in resources, time, and energy.

The department executives in our case study recognized that to manage the analysis, design, and transition to the new EMS, would require a process lasting a four-to-five-year period, and would involve hundreds of employees in the department. Even though a knowledge and understanding of high-level computer technology was a prerequisite, the executives recognized that the heart of the project was managing the change and transition to the new system. They therefore searched for someone in the department who had the talent to manage the transition. Naomi Birch, whose background was in human services planning, was chosen. Although initially Naomi had minimal knowledge and experience in modern computer technologies, department executives correctly judged that over the four years Naomi would acquire expert-level knowledge and skills in computer-systems design. What was needed most was her ability to manage change.

To be an effective systems manager, the human services administrator must acquire the necessary knowledge and skills to manage change and transition. Thus, before addressing the subject of management of transorganizational systems, it is necessary to deal with the subject of this chapter: change management.

Managing Change: An Overview

Strategies for Managing Change and Transitions

The process of organizational change captured the attention of writers during the post-World War II era. These researchers recognized that institutional change would remain a high-priority societal issue for the remainder of the twentieth century. They were correct; this issue remains one of the most important areas of focus for management thinkers.

Warren Bennis, one of the first to devote his research and writing on managing organizational change, and Burt Nanus, note that change must permeate the whole organization. It is the manager's role to create larger visions for the organization and then engage employees' imaginations in pursuit of them. An essential factor in leadership therefore is "the capacity to influence and organize meaning for the members of the organization" (1985, 33).

In *The Change Masters* (1983), an extensive study of managers who were leaders of change and innovation in their organizations, Rosabeth Moss Kanter identified two opposing approaches to management: integrative action versus segmentalism. The former views problems as an integrated whole, challenging established practices; the latter isolates and compartmentalizes problems, dealing with them as narrowly as possible. Organizations with segmentalist approaches to management have a difficult time dealing with change and innovation. The opposite is true of those who have an integrative approach to organizational issues. Kanter (1983) found five forces that serve as the building blocks to productive organizational change: (1) ability to depart from tradition; (2) presence of an external force, such as a crisis or a galvanizing event; (3) carefully developed strategic decisions by organizational managers;

(4) presence of an individual who becomes the prime mover of the change; and (5) a number of "action vehicles" that permit employees to carry out the change. One such action vehicle is the concept of the *parallel organization* (see Chapter 4)—organizations that use hierarchy oriented toward maintenance of routine operations and participative adhocracies focused on problem solving and change (Kanter 1983).

To the popular management writer Tom Peters, "loving change, tumult, even chaos is a pre-requisite for survival, let alone success." To Peters, the world is changing at such an accelerating pace that a fast-changing society demands that we learn to love change—we have no choice. In the face of everything being placed on the agenda for change, we are meeting the challenge with inflexibility: "inflexible systems, inflexible front-line people—and worst of all, inflexible managers" (1987, 55–56). Does Peters have any suggestions for how to manage change and innovation? First, he stresses the need to dramatically increase the organization's capacity for continuous flux. There should be a constant search for new ideas and "creative swiping": copying from others those changes and innovations that have been successful. In fact, Peters suggests that managers create "learning organizations" that become copycats, adapters, and enhancers of successful innovations of other agencies (1987, 278–83; 560–66). He argues that change must become the norm for an organization and that the primary role of managers is to make things better and different—incrementally and dramatically—day-by-day. The most common question, one asked several times each day, should be: What exactly have you changed today?

The discussion of change-management literature in Chapter 5 noted several different perspectives on this subject. One of the most important for our purposes in this chapter was grouping the planned-change strategies, as listed in Table 15.1.

For a long time, managers have understood that change is generally achieved by one of two methods, commonly known as the "carrot or stick" approach.

1. The change techniques that can be derived from the empirical-rational strategy represent use of the carrot—material or intrinsic rewards that provide the necessary incentive to change because people have a natural concern for their self-interest.
2. Change methods that flow out of the power-coercive strategy represent use of the stick—some form of power that forces people to accept the change.

But are these the only two approaches to the management of change and transition? Some modern administrators, particularly those in the human services management field, have been dissatisfied with both the carrot and stick change strategies. While admittedly both do result in change, both also have negative by-products. In public and nonprofit human services organizations, there are insufficient rewards to provide powerful carrots (incentives) for change, so the stick is generally used. The results are twofold: (1) In many situations, the

Table 15.1 Change Strategies

Category	Definition
Empirical-rational	Humans will follow their rational self-interest.
Normative-reeducative	Change will occur as the people involved change their attitudes, values, relationships, and skills.
Power-coercive	Humans will change mainly because of the application of some form of power.

change is superficial and temporary, thus limiting the full potential that could be derived from the new system were it properly implemented; and (2) the resistance to change is so deep that the new system is sabotaged in minor and major ways. More important, workers' morale is diminished significantly, with adverse effects on the quality and quantity of services to clients. In effect, too often the potential benefits of the new system are offset by the reduction in productivity and quality of services provision that results from lowered employee morale because coercion was used to implement the new system.

The second change strategy—normative-reeducative—has become very popular and has great potential. Many modern management writers search for factors that have made Japanese management more effective than management in the United States during the past two decades. Among other things, they note that in the United States, we tend to introduce changes too rapidly without sufficient discussion by those affected. Without proper preparation, the implementation of changes can be difficult, time-consuming, and often aborted. The opposite is true in Japan. Having spent what seems like an inordinate amount of time forming the plans and preparing the participants, the implementation is smooth because all parties affected know what to expect and have "ownership."

Although the carrot and the stick still remain the major strategies for managing change in some organizations, a large number of modern management professionals are dedicated to the normative-reeducative strategy. They believe in and use a body of thought and techniques known as organizational development (OD). Because of its importance to the modern approach to managing change and transitions, this subject will be reviewed briefly.

Organizational Development

Management is essentially a form of group work—working with a group of humans as they pull together for a common purpose. This insight, noted by several organizational writers and researchers in human relations, organizational psychology, sociotechnical systems, group dynamics, interorganizational relations, planned change, role theory, and social exchange, serves as the antecedent of organizational development.

The roots of OD can be traced to three "stems" that developed in the late 1940s and early 1950s: Human Behavior Laboratory Training (e.g., sensitivity training, T groups, the National Training Laboratory [NTL]); Survey Research Feedback (developed by Kurt Lewin at the MIT Center for Group Dynamics); and Open Sociotechnical Systems (developed by the Tavistock Institute of Human Relations, London).

Critics of OD maintain that it is more intuitive than systematic, that it may invade the personal rights of employees, that it is no different from scientific management in that it manipulates employees for improved productivity, that it is top-down and thus ignores bottom-up change in an organization. Although OD is more widespread in business organizations than in public or nonprofit organizations, it has nonetheless been widely and successfully applied in all types of organizations.

The more popular approaches to OD include the following:

- Team building: Helping a team of employees perform its tasks better with greater satisfaction, for the ultimate purpose of achieving improved team performance

- Conflict management: Reducing or stimulating conflict so as to improve organizational performance

- Action research: Initiating a process of change based on the theory that any organizational systemic change should involve and be managed by those employees most affected by the change

- Training interventions: Planned interventions that interrupt the functioning of an organization for the purpose of changing the way in which the organization's employees think or act

- Process consultation: Use of a consultant–facilitator to observe a work group and provide feedback to the group for the purpose of helping improve individual and group performance

- Sociotechnical changes: Finding the best match between the human social system in an organization and the technical-technology system of that organization

- Quality of work life (QWL): Efforts designed to improve the physical and psychic quality of the employee's work or organizational environment

- Job enrichment; job redesign: Making employees' jobs more satisfying so as to increase their contribution to the productivity and effectiveness of the organization

- Participative management: Sharing the process and power of organizational management with a large number of employees in order to increase their sense of commitment to organizational goals

While several of the above are appropriate for managing the change and transition to new or redesigned transorganizational systems, none is more critical than action research.

Figure 15.1 Action Research: Force-Field
Analysis and Action Planning

In every situation, there are several forces of differing intensity that maintain the status quo.

THEORY
To introduce a change, it is necessary to "unfreeze" the forces, move from the status quo (the existing state) to a new status (the desired state), at which time the forces should be "refreezed."

PROCESS
To do this, it is necessary to
- Identify the existing state.
- Define the desired state.
- Identify the helping (driving) forces, those that can move you to the desired state.
- Identify the hindering (restraining) forces, those that work to keep the status quo.
- Prepare an action plan to reduce–eliminate the hindering forces and to strengthen the helping forces. The action plan delineates each action required to achieve the ideal state—who is responsible on what time schedule and estimated resources needed.

EXAMPLE

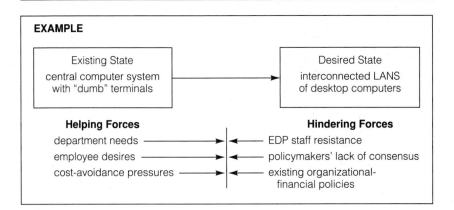

Existing State	Desired State
central computer system with "dumb" terminals	interconnected LANS of desktop computers

Helping Forces   **Hindering Forces**

department needs ⟶ ◀— EDP staff resistance

employee desires ⟶ ◀— policymakers' lack of consensus

cost-avoidance pressures ⟶ ◀— existing organizational-
financial policies

ACTION PLAN
Form a task force of department and EDP employees to prepare an action plan for centralized and decentralized uses of computers.

Action research flows out of a concept developed by Margaret Mead and Kurt Lewin that "groups of people can do a thing better when they themselves decide upon it, and also how they themselves can elect to reduce the gap between their attitudes and actions" (see Marrow 1969, 130–31). Groups of employees take a look at the existing status of work in their organizational environment, gather data, analyze the data, design changes to bring about improvements, attempt to implement such changes, and then gather more data to assess the improvement achieved by such changes.

Of the various OD techniques, action research is among the most effective and popular. Figure 15.1 provides an example of an element of action research: force-field analysis and action planning. It is a method in which a problem or an issue can be analyzed in a brief period of time and a set of activities defined so that action can be taken for improving the situation. Action planning starts with an analysis of the existing situation, a sharp definition of the desired situation to which the human services organization should aspire, the pressures or forces working to retard or aid in moving toward the improvement, and what steps would achieve significant results. The action plan document itself serves as the basis for detailed implementation, either by the task group or by one or more individuals.

Another technique of action research–oriented change management is **brainstorming**. It is based on the classic problem-solving process:

1. Accept
2. Analyze
3. Define
4. Ideate
5. Select
6. Implement
7. Evaluate

A human services manager seeks to maximize the ingenuity and creativity of employees by encouraging brainstorming and by separating the process of raising solutions from that of evaluating them to select the one that can best deal with the particular situation.

Change and Transition: Some Issues

Short-Term Versus Long-Term Benefits

For several decades, management researchers have noted what they consider an alarming trend in U.S. organizations, namely the primary focus on short-term payoff. This nearsighted approach holds true not only for the private sector but also for public and nonprofit human services organizations in the United States.

Why are short-term concerns so dominant in the United States? First, there are marketing pressures. Television has turned us into a society of consumers. This increased demand for immediate gratification places pressures on commercial, public, and nonprofit organizations to respond to short-term opportunities instead of long-term investments. This has led to the second factor, emphasis on the career-future value over the job-now value. Managers have realized that they can enhance their reputation and thus their future careers by being noted for getting immediate, dramatic payoffs through radical change and transition in organizations and systems. This generally leads to their being promoted or moving on to a better position; thus, they are not around to deal with the disastrous consequences of a transition that was superficial or limited in exploiting the full potential that can be derived from a well-conceived change.

The third reason is the difficulty of developing valid criteria for evaluating long-term benefits. It is easy to measure the short term—most generally through increased performance and productivity, which are quantifiable. But evaluating long-term benefits takes several years and is very subtle. Case 15.2 on deinstitutionalization for developmentally disabled clients illustrates the point.

Case 15.2

Court-Ordered Change and Transition

Connie Andrew always knew that a carrot or a stick were the most popular ways of implementing change, but she never realized how big a stick a court order could be. The Louisiana Association for Retarded Citizens had filed a suit, and after several years, the court ruled in favor of deinstitutionalization—mentally retarded (MR) clients were to be moved into community-based residential living arrangements. The court order was clear: The transition had to be complete in thirty months. A monitor was appointed by the judge to make sure that the state Department of Mental Retardation met the requirements and standards of the court order.

After only twelve months of the transition, the department was falling behind schedule. As head of social work for district 3, Connie was on the front line of the changeover to a community-based MR system. She knew that at today's monthly meeting, Jack Fahey, the district 3 director, was going to "get tough." Jack opened the meeting: "Let me introduce Bob Pierce, the department's new director of quality assessment."

Bob hit the ground running: "I won't beat around the bush. The department's secretary is upset. We've fallen far behind schedule and the court-appointed monitor is on our case. The secretary has put on the pressure. We need to know why the case managers are dragging their feet. Don't they realize that we're *all* under the gun?"

Jack was about to respond when Connie decided to come to his rescue. "I'm not sure the workers are dragging their feet, Bob. But if they are, could it be that they feel the department never let them share in this changeover process?"

Jack shot Connie a look that could kill; everyone knew that Bob was the secretary's hatchetman. The last thing he wanted was negative feedback to the front office.

"Come on, Connie," Bob responded quickly. "Who has time to hold the workers' hands? Maybe if this was a five-year plan initiated by the department, we could. But even then, I'm not sure; with major changes like this, the old timers just find it hard to adapt. Actually, the court may be doing us a favor."

"But there are several ways to change, Bob, beyond using a stick, in this case a *big* stick," Connie answered.

"Connie," Jack broke in hoping to deescalate the discussion, "that's all academic now. The issue now is how can we get back on track."

"Wait a second, Jack," Bob persisted. "I've been around a while and in my experience, only a carrot or a stick brings about change. What else is there?"

"Well," Connie answered, "in my experience, getting those most affected by the change involved in managing the change itself is a very effective alternative. The carrot and the stick may produce short-term results, but over the long haul, they have too many negative impacts. The proof is in the pudding. We can see that neither coercion nor extrinsic incentives are making it here. And I'm sorry if that sounds hard-headed, but we're all frustrated over the way things are going."

Bob sat rubbing his chin. "You know, Connie, you just may have a point. Let's take a long look at your idea."

Connie could see from the faces of others at the meeting that she had scored a few points for the district, even though no one was keeping score. There was only one game these days—and it was at headquarters, not in the districts.

This case illustrates that change and transition are not easy. The pressures for immediate results are very real (e.g., meeting the deadlines of the court order and the criteria set by court monitors). The critical question is, Can immediate results be achieved in a way that also enhances long-term benefits? Connie Andrew would answer yes, and I would concur.

Boundary Spanning

Transorganizational systems involve a network of organizations, which must reach beyond their own boundaries to link together for some common purpose. As Richard Scott (1987) emphasizes, the issue of **boundary spanning** is critical to this process.

A social organization is a collectivity; organizations and systems are collectivities. All collectivities have two criteria: a bounded network of relationships and a normative order that applies to all participants linked by the network. What constitutes the boundaries of a collectivity is difficult to ascertain, particularly when one views collectivities (both intraorganizational and interorganizational) from an open-systems perspective. The popular word for boundary is *turf*, a more technical term would be *domain*. In essence, an organization's domain is the claim it makes on the services provided and the population served. But whether the word *turf* or *domain* is used, both require a consensus on the part of other participants in the network of the definition of each party's boundaries.

The task environment (or organizational set) of an agency, as defined in Chapter 6, represents the agency's boundary. Because the environment is dynamic and always changing, organizations react to this turbulence in one of two ways: *buffering* and *bridging*. Strategies to buffer an organization are designed to protect its boundaries so that it can be managed in a more rational way. On the other hand, boundary-spanning strategies are designed to build bridges between the organizations and other agencies in the environment in order to enlarge its resources, influence, or mission. In response to increasing organizational interdependence and the evolution of transorganizational systems, the human services systems manager has to acquire proficiency in *bridging strategies* (Table 15.2).

There are a number of critical issues that require fundamental changes in human services systems, all of which link together a number of separate organizations. "Welfare" (AFDC) reform, at-risk children, school dropouts, the homeless, the frail elderly, and the "forgotten half" (i.e., young people who do not go on to college and who are struggling to make it) are only a few that will have to be dealt with during the decade of the 1990s. Increasingly therefore, human services managers are finding themselves involved in transorganizational systems that require different types of boundary-spanning strategies.

The Territorial Imperative

Managing change and transition to a new or redesigned transorganizational system involves devising one or more strategies for boundary spanning. But it also may have to confront a subtler but equally fundamental issue: *boundary protection*. One of the most difficult factors in the analysis, design, transition, implementation, and management of transorganizational systems will be the vigorous but often covert efforts of each participant to protect turf and boundaries.

Robert Ardery (1966) holds the view that humans have the identical imperative as animals to create and protect boundaries for the species to which they belong. This **territorial imperative** is linked to the homing tendency for the purposes of propagation with exclusive members of the species in order to

Table 15.2 Boundary-Spanning (Bridging) Strategies

Strategy	Definition
Bargaining	A prebridging strategy that defines or defends the domain of an organization prior to any effort to span its boundaries
Contracting	Negotiating an agreement for exchanges in the future, to secure some certainty in a changing future
Cooptation	Incorporating representatives of external groups into the decision-making or advisory structure of an agency
Joint venture	Two or more organizations create a new system to pursue some common purpose
Mergers	Two or more independent agencies become a single collective system to pursue ■ Vertical integration: Merging different stages of a common-service process ■ Horizontal integration: Merging to expand market or catchment area ■ Diversifying: Adding services to improve comprehensive nature of services
Association	Arrangements that permit similar organizations to work in concert to pursue mutually desired objectives

preserve the unique qualities that have helped the species survive. In effect the territorial imperative links boundary setting and protection with survival.

If the systemic manager assumes that humans also have an innate territorial imperative, then it becomes the *dependent variable* in the design and development of transorganizational systems. The best strategy for managing change and transition may become therefore one that attempts to secure the allegiance of all transorganizational-system participants to a much broader goal, mission, client, or service definition in such a way that it creates clear new boundaries for the new system. Once established, these new boundaries become the basis for a broadened definition of the territorial imperative, one that includes all members of the new systemic network and allows them to share in it.

Strategies for dealing with the territorial imperative are perhaps the most challenging task faced by the systemic human services manager who is attempting to effectively manage the transition to a new or redesigned transorganizational system.

The Transdisciplinary Approach

The environment of transorganizational systems can be characterized as interdisciplinary: that is, people from different disciplines working together, formally and informally, as teams. It is important therefore that a transdisciplinary (TD) approach be an integral element in managing the change and transition to a new or redesigned system. The term *transdisciplinary* is defined as "of, or relating to, a transfer of information, knowledge, and skills across disciplinary boundaries." It suggests a logical and consistent progression from a unidisciplinary stance, which is the outcome of basic professional education, to a multidisciplinary stance, which is the outcome of continuing education and professional development.

When working amicably within a framework of transaction, a team systematically seeks to enlarge the common core of knowledge and competency of each team member. This is accomplished through planned individual study, one-to-one instruction among team members, and by a planned team teaching–learning process.

The foundation of the TD approach is the interdisciplinary team. Many professionals view themselves as independent practitioners, and for them the **TD-team approach** involves a significant change. TD teaming is a deliberate attempt to understand the preparation and competencies of several other disciplines, through working together in areas of shared functions for the benefit of the client.

The TD approach is a deliberate pooling and exchange of information, knowledge, and skills, crossing, and recrossing traditional disciplinary boundaries by various team members. The movement toward a TD stance can be characterized in the following manner:

From a Unidisciplinary to Transdisciplinary Approach

- Unidisciplinary: Possessing a sound preparation and competency in one's own discipline
- Intradisciplinary: Working with others in your discipline believing that you can contribute to the client group
- Multidisciplinary: Recognizing that other disciplines can also make important contributions to the client group
- Interdisciplinary: Being willing and able to work with other disciplines in joint services to the client group
- Transdisciplinary: Committing to teaching–learning–working with other service providers across traditional disciplinary boundaries

The TD approach is an essential element of systemic management, both for managing the transition to a redesigned transorganizational system and for managing that system.

Creation of Settings

Seymour Sarason (1972)—who has undertaken a great deal of research in a wide range of human services, which includes mental health, mental retardation, and education—has suggested that the design, implementation, and management of transorganizational systems falls into a larger context: the creation of a new setting. The creation of settings further involves the initiation of new relationships, and settings can range in size from marriages, to new or revised programs, or to new organizational units or new systems. From this perspective, a common process can be identified to ensure the successful creating of the new setting. This process can be summarized as follows:

1. Appreciate and respect the history of the new setting—it grows out of some dissatisfaction with existing settings.
2. There may be pressure to create the new setting quickly, but it is important to take time to reach and record consensus on the underlying values that guide the new setting.
3. The leader and the core group of people who will guide the new system need more than enthusiasm and creativity to sustain the new setting beyond the initial period. Based on explicit, underlying values of the new system, they should agree in advance on the ground rules for operating the new setting.
4. "If we only had more resources" is often a myth. Even with unlimited resources, it would usually be impossible to staff new settings with only top-quality professionals. Alternate staffing strategies are necessary.
5. New settings often burden their creators with pressing mechanical activities, such as getting a new building or office ready for opening, which divert from the crucial core activities such as the nature and quality of services and the underlying service-delivery values.
6. New systems generally focus on innovations in service delivery to clients. In time the staff lose their enthusiasm as what was once new becomes generally accepted. It is important to find ways in the new setting to generate continued innovation, creativity, and enthusiasm among the staff.

These are but a few of the general concepts presented by Sarason in his analysis of the process whereby new settings (e.g., new transorganizational systems) are created and sustained successfully.

An Approach to Change and Transition

Degrees of Transition

Before delineating an approach for the change and transition to a new or redesigned transorganizational system, it is necessary to recognize the different degrees of transition. Elizabeth Loughran (1986) suggests that there is an evolving growth and developmental pattern in the transition to a new **interorganizational relationship** (IOR); this pattern involves four phases of development:

1. Identity: Establishing the identity of the interorganizational relationship: What are the superordinate goals that bind the new network, and what

concretely will it be attempting to achieve? Sharing an understanding of the worth and meaning of their new IOR and of the membership in the new IOR.

2. Empowerment: Resolving issues of power and authority to the point where members of the network, individually and collectively, feel that the IOR itself is fully empowered to accomplish its goals, whether as a voluntary or a mandated IOR.

3. Organization: Selecting a structure, from the wide range of horizontal, adhocratic structures that are available, that is appropriate to the major purpose of the IOR. Achieving a level of stability for funding the IOR.

4. Administration: Developing administrative systems and group processes that are appropriate to the IOR structure, task, and goals. Dealing with ongoing issues of creating a budget and establishing effective policies and procedures. Helping members in the IOR deal with role confusion and other group issues. Establishing a process of evaluation and feedback on the IOR's performance.

The development of an IOR is dynamic and interactive in nature. As the environment of the IOR changes, it will have to reexperience each of the four phases, most probably on a continual basis. Loughran (1986) also emphasizes the importance of selecting an organizational structure for the IOR that is appropriate to its purpose and task. For example, if the major purpose of the IOR is to raise awareness about a common problem and increase communication among the member agencies, a loose, informal network would be appropriate. On the other hand, if the task of the IOR is to operate new joint emergency services, then a more formal structure is needed.

Steps to Managing Change and Transition

For the systemic manager approaching the transition to a new or redesigned transorganizational human services system, there is a method that has proved to be very useful for creative practitioners. It is admittedly a time-consuming process that represents a significant investment by the participating agencies. It may require the involvement of experts or serious preparation on the part of the in-house "do-it-yourselfer." But because the benefits from a new transorganizational system extend over many years, the return on this investment will justify the effort by ensuring that the change and transition is managed effectively in the first instance.

Basic Principles.   This method for managing change and transition is based on some fairly straightforward basic principles, which have been discussed in other parts of the book.

- *An Interactive Organic Process:* The process that must be created should recognize that growth and improvement flow in an organic fashion: the whole can emerge over a period of time out of a series of individual actions, provided there is interaction among all parties involved and a shared consensual process.

■ *User Involvement:* The key employees (clerical, technical, professional, and administrative) must be involved in the transition process if it is to be truly interactive and organic.

■ *Integrated Set of Available Expertise:* Through a combination of in-house and consulting specialists, the process must have available expertise in all aspects of modern organizational technologies, based both in management and behavioral sciences. The key is to find specialists knowledgeable and experienced in the human services environment. These specialists need to be integrated into the process so that their major roles are to serve both as facilitators to the process and to provide technical assistance to the design, development, and implementation of the transorganizational system.

■ *Incremental Growth:* The organic approach rejects the concept of a rigid master plan; it recognizes that natural growth is evolutionary in nature, with increments of transition fashioned to meet the existing situation in a holistic fashion. This does not mean subscribing to haphazard growth; on the contrary, the involvement of all who impact on elements of the system must follow common design principles and techniques in a comprehensive and integrated fashion. Any resulting plan, rather than being engraved in stone, must be capable of reacting to this process.

■ *User Involvement:* The coordination and control over the organic transition process must involve users. In the human services environment, the user is foremost the professional employee (e.g., clerical, clinicians, administrative) at all levels of the organization. In addition, this principle recognizes the important roles played by clients and policymakers. A consensual, participative approach to transition is critical.

A Basic Approach.   The following steps describe a basic approach of which human services administrators should be aware. It is a process by which state-of-the-art transorganizational systems are designed and developed and the process by which the transition to the new system is managed.

1. *Team Formation:* A team of managers and professionals who are actively involved in developing and managing a transorganizational system participate in a four- or five-day intensive series of seminars and workshops devoted to managing change and transition. With the help of an experienced facilitator–consultant, the team begins to coalesce as a group.
2. *Systems Planning:* For the next six to eight weeks, the team–task force meets regularly on-site in the various agencies, for action planning. This process sharpens perceptions of the transorganizational system that is needed, formulates an initial plan for its development, and provides an opportunity for the team–task force to begin working together as an effec-

tively functioning group. The organization-development professional assigned to the team–task force facilitates the action planning and provides technical assistance.

3. *Systems Design:* A second four-day series of intensive "skill shops" and hands-on labs are held for the team, focusing on the transorganizational systems design and development techniques. The team develops an initial design for the new system as well as a plan for its implementation.

4. *Development:* For the next ten to twelve weeks, the team works regularly on the development of the transorganizational system. Consulting, technical assistance, and group facilitation is provided or coordinated by the professional assigned to work with them. A great amount of technical work would be undertaken, moving from the general design to the detailed systems processes. It may be necessary to set up additional work groups to finalize some of the design details and to actually develop a prototype that can be tested. Initial testing would be undertaken so that refinements and adjustments can be made in the new system.

5. *Team Management:* The teams return for their final several-day series of intensive skill shops that focus on building and sustaining transorganizational management teams and managing transorganizational systems.

6. *Managing the Installation of the New System:* For the next three to four months, the teams devote their energies to installing their transorganizational system and on beginning to work together in its management. The facilitator works with them and pulls in consultants as needed to provide the necessary technical assistance. Where necessary, on-site orientation and technical training are undertaken to strengthen the implementation and ongoing operations of the new system.

   Following the systems installation, the team can decide to what extent they need the continued assistance of the professional facilitator–technical consultant who has been working with them.

7. *Systems Implementation:* The team forms one or more action groups of employees who become actively involved in repeating the process, as they become personally involved in the transition to the new system and begin its implementation.

The planning, design, and construction of a twenty-story office building require a significant investment in time, resources, and effort. So also do the design, development, and implementation of a complex transorganizational human services system. It must be done right the first time, and that requires a significant investment in managing the change to the new system. In the long run, the benefits of the new system warrant the careful, methodical investment in the transition.

Summary

For effective systemic management, the implemention of a new or redesigned transorganizational system demands special skills in managing the change. The process of transition cannot be taken casually; it must be planned and managed with great care. It requires, first of all, understanding and appreciation of different strategies. Traditionally, the carrot and the stick have been the primary approaches to change, but these strategies may have significant disadvantages. They can result primarily in short-term benefits, accruing long-term costs that either jeopardize the change itself or severely limit its effectiveness or potential benefits. A wiser change strategy may be one that recognizes that a change is best achieved when managed by those most affected by that change.

Effectiveness in managing change and transition also requires understanding and skill in the concepts and technologies of organizational development, the transdisciplinary approach, boundary spanning, the territorial imperative, and the creation of settings. All these have contributed to our collective abilities in managing transitions. Because change has become a constant factor in a modern, complex society, the field has accumulated a body of experience from both our successes and our failures that can guide the human services manager faced with the task of managing the transition to a new transorganizational system. The human services systemic manager can benefit from a comprehensive approach to change and transition. But there must be awareness that it not only requires knowledge and skill but also time, resources, and patience.

There is too much at stake in a modern society to permit the haphazard transition to a new transorganizational human services system. Because such a system can significantly improve the quality of life of all who are involved or impacted by it, it must be carefully designed and implemented. For the human services systemic manager, skill in change and transition has become a vital necessity as we continue to strive for an improved society in the last decade of the twentieth century.

16

Managing Transorganizational Systems

Guidelines for Integrating Institutional and Systemic Management

A Shared, Interrelated Organizational Purpose
From Singular to Mutual Responsibility
The Creation of a Responsive and Supportive Community Environment
The Choice Paradigm: Creation of the Broadest Set
   of Service-Acquisition Options
Creation of a Supportive Organizational Climate

Management Repertoires: The Key to Systemic Management

Management Repertoires for Transorganizational Systems:
   Some Examples

Managing with Information

A Distinctive Set of Values for Systemic Management

Summary

Systemic (strategic) management must be executed with the same dedication and precision as institutional (organizational) management. Too often, human services managers are given the responsibility for a new transorganizational system but are expected to squeeze it in among their other duties. Such assignments are often viewed as "just another task force" that will meet periodically to talk about the assigned issue, be it the homeless, teen pregnancy, school dropouts, or community-based mental health services.

As we noted in the previous chapter, some transorganizational systems are formed primarily for improved information exchange, communications, and consciousness raising. In such situations, a cross-organizational task force for such purposes can easily be viewed as another periodic meeting that must be attended in an already over-scheduled calendar.

But increasingly, transorganizational systems are being formed to provide a new set of services or to bring about a significant improvement in the way services are now being delivered. Simple information exchange or even improved communications are not sufficient; actual implementation is necessary. It is in these situations that systemic management requires the design and implementation of the transorganizational system, with its organizational processes and tasks.

Guidelines for Integrating Institutional and Systemic Management

There are a number of general guidelines that human services managers will find helpful when integrating institutional (organizational) and systemic (strategic) management, which resonate on themes articulated in the previous chapters.

A Shared, Interrelated Organizational Purpose

Human services managers need to recognize that, because all efforts in the field can only be measured ultimately in terms of their impact on humans, all disciplines and all organizational entities share a common purpose. Education, public safety, health, social services, economic development—the myriad of human services institutions—all have a vested interest in a system where humans interact successfully with their environment.

Just as people and their environments cannot be segmented, neither can the various organizational units acting on their behalf operate totally independently of each other or claim exclusive trusteeship for the well-being and life-furthering of members of society. Society's institutions are highly interrelated; all work from a common taxonomy of human and societal needs.

For the human services manager, the fundamental value-construct for this common set of needs is the uniqueness of each person. In the individual's right to fashion her own life, the only constraint is that of participating in and protecting the common good, that is, the public interest of society. *Thus, the fundamental value for all human services professionals is neutral competence in the pursuit of the public interest.*

From Singular to Mutual Responsibilty

Traditionally, most of us are conditioned to the idea of having a single point of responsibility and accountability for the provision of a specific service to a specific client group. The modern approach to organization seeks a more dynamic notion, one that recognizes a continuous stream of processes and activities with both individual and shared responsibility prevailing.

Consider, for example, a situation where child abuse is suspected. The physician, teacher, youth services worker, police officer, and child protective social worker must team up to work in concert, each carrying out specific tasks, all of which ultimately focus on protecting the at-risk child.

This notion of mutual, collective, and cumulative responsibility—which also takes into account pinpointed responsibility for specific activities—is not new. It was first articulated by the original theorist of human services management, Mary Parker Follett. She noted that

> Authority and responsibility go with function, but . . . authority is inherent in the situation, not as attached to an official position. . . . This pluralistic responsibilty, this interlocking responsibility, makes it difficult to "fix" responsibility. . . . Instead, then, of final determination, supreme control, ultimate authority, we might perhaps think of cumulative control, cumulative responsibility. (1940, 149–55)

Modern management stresses both individual and collective mutual responsibility. There is certainly the need, on the one hand, to clearly pinpoint responsibility for specific roles and tasks at each stage of the organizational process, as well as for accountability. On the other hand, if any one part of the process is inoperative, the total system becomes inoperative. Thus, everyone also has mutual responsibility to ensure the proper functioning of all activities in a system, and for their smooth meshing. In the example of the child-abuse team, the system is inoperative unless all people involved carry out their tasks and obligations in a coordinated, shared, responsible fashion.

As transorganizational systems become more complex and involve an ever-increasing number and variety of organizations and people, the failure of even one individual to carry out a task in a timely manner will invalidate the total system. This is a profound phenomenon. It is sometimes difficult for a single professional in one organization to understand how his seemingly minor role in a system is a crucial link that has to function properly. Most transorganizational systems are dependent on concurrent, accurate performance by numerous people in many organizations, perhaps spread out geographically. For the human services manager, the design of such systems must include an ability to continuously monitor both the productive and effective performance of all individual elements of such a system, of the linkage between them, and its ultimate effectiveness in terms of client impacts.

The notion of shared, cumulative responsibility is raised to a critical requirement in the management of transorganizational systems.

The Creation of a Responsive and Supportive Community Environment

The Family Development Center envisions a community where the quality of life for each member enhances the quality of life for all. Our role is not only to provide quality, caring programs but also to make our communities more accepting and compassionate places for all people.

This is the motto of the Family Development Center (the subject of Case 4.1 presented in Chapter 4). It indicates that managers of this agency recognize the need for a strategic, integrated, conceptual base for organizing and managing human services in today's society.

When organizations and systems are viewed as strategies, then it becomes everyone's task to ensure optimum acquisition of services for the greater good of all. For the human services manager therefore, an important organizing guideline is the creation and maintenance of an environment that responds to and is supportive of all people's efforts to use their creative potential to avail themselves of services opportunities and resources in the community.

The underlying philosophy for this guideline is Ivan Illich's (1978) concept of *conviviality:* personal energy under personal control. This uses a resource that is equally distributed among all people. It implies that human services administrators should organize in such a way that their agency

1. Identifies and categorizes the collective and individual needs in a community.
2. Identifies and categorizes capabilities (resources) in the community for satisfying needs.
3. Develops a dynamic, responsive system for matching needs with needs-satisfying capabilities, for individuals and groups of citizens.
4. Monitors the responsiveness of the system to maximize services acquisition at the least expenditure of physical and psychic energy.

Figure 16.1 describes this process graphically.

In most human services situations, service provision begins with a provider

Figure 16.1   Model for a Responsive Human Services Environment

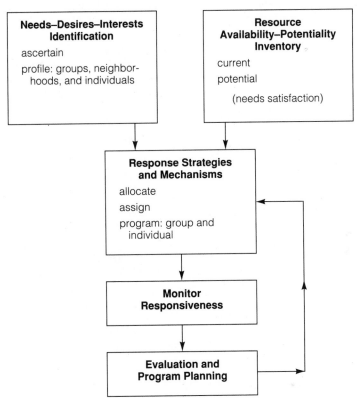

who offers a range of services in particular modes to meet client needs. A more rational approach to this might be the opposite process:

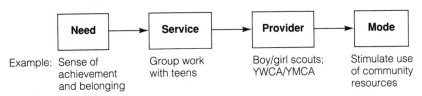

In general terms, the process of relating needs to services is as follows:

1. *A Taxonomy of Human Needs:* Establish a general taxonomy of human needs that applies to the total human services system and show, for each of the different human services functions, how it relates. (The taxonomy created by Abraham Maslow can serve in this function).
2. *Services as Needs-Satisfying Processes:* Classify the different services according to their needs-satisfying capability.

3. *Service Modes as Response Strategies–Mechanisms:* Provide a broad set
   of service-acquisition options (delivery modes) for clients.
4. *Inventory and Catalog Providers:* Identify and mobilize the (needs-satisfying) resources in the community.

The Choice Paradigm: Creation of the Broadest Set of Service-Acquisition Options

The concept that services should be laid out in a broad spectrum of alternative
modalities, with the specific choice in the hands of the recipient, is a paradigm
of human services management that is bedded in the notion of human self-
governance and autonomy. It is the heart of the responsive-environment model.
Systemically, this means that the professional manager designs and implements
flexible response strategies for service acquisition, which include a broad range
of different modes. People at different ages and stages of life exhibit varying
degrees of dependency–interdependency. Successful flexibility is when the
different modes of service options can reflect these differing situations within
the system.

A good example may be found in the approaches to food services:

- Fast-food places: Clients discover what services exist and where to find
  them. The range of choices is there, but delivery is narrow and
  prepackaged.
- Cafeteria: Availability of services is made more apparent and more accessible, but clients must acquire them independently.
- Server: Clients depend on an organizational functionary for assistance in
  ascertaining and satisfying needs.
- Force feed: Organizational employees supply services regardless of degree
  of client cooperation.

The choice paradigm assumes that human services professionals are there to
assist clients in becoming more independent and responsible for their own acquisition of community services–resources, and that clients can and should
exercise their own choice when provided service-acquisition options.

Creation of a Supportive Organizational Climate

The final guideline is directed inwardly toward the management of societal
institutions and systems. The artful balancing of institutional management and
systemic management requires the creation of an organizational climate in
which management and staff will be highly motivated to experiment, create,
and innovate. This calls for renewed attention to the three *R*s of working with

people in groups: responsibility, recognition, and reward. The human services manager needs to be sensitive to the need for maximum staff motivation in any effort that has as its goal increased effectiveness and productivity in the human services.

The supportive and responsive community environment motto of our case agency, the Family Development Center, has the following companion motto, which reflects this guideline:

> Excellence in services is a reflection of excellence in staff, and we will always strive to establish and maintain an optimal working environment— one that promotes the growth of staff as people and as professionals.

It is worth remembering that respect for human worth and dignity is always a two-way street.

Management Repertoires: The Key to Systemic Management

Are the management techniques of systemic management different than those of institutional (organizational) management? No and yes. To understand the answer to this question, let us ask another question: Is the prize-winning chocolate torte baked by a master pastry chef different from a chocolate cake you or I could bake? The answer: no and yes. The ingredients of our chocolate cakes are identical to that of a master chef; what is different is the chef's skill *and* the particular recipe for that delectable torte.

The same is true for human services managers. There is little difference between the techniques of systemic management and institutional management. Both draw on the same source of continuously evolving modern management technologies. But the two forms of management are fundamentally different in their particular recipes, that is, their *management repertoires*.

A transorganizational system made up of a large number of professionals sitting in many different agencies can administer improved, comprehensive services with the same high-level management technologies uniquely packaged for a specific system. It requires thoughtful planning and methodical, precise execution.

Systemic management consists of three highly interrelated sets of tasks. In summary, they are

1. Analyze an existing system that cuts across the boundaries of several human services organizations and design or redesign an improved system.
2. After careful planning, manage the change and transition from the existing system to the new or redesigned system.
3. Implement and administer the new or redesigned transorganizational system with a unique management repertoire.

In Chapters 14 and 15, we dealt with tasks 1 and 2 above; in this chapter, we address the final task of systemic management: managing transorganizational systems by using a uniquely fashioned management repertoire.

In Chapter 8, management repertoires were described briefly. Because they are the key to management, particularly systemic management, let us discuss them more fully. An example of transorganizational management is examined and analyzed in detail to show how their success was dependent on the ability to successfully shape management repertoires that could effectively manage transorganizational systems.

For modern human services managers, the task of management is to assemble, reassemble, and arrange clusters of applied theories and techniques in dynamic configurations that when implemented will achieve the strategic goal(s) of the organization at any given moment.

When the organization and management of institutions and systems is conceptualized in terms of repertoires or clusters of techniques, three notions emerge, which can be seen in the following example.

- Computerization. When an integrated client information system is combined with MBO, program-oriented budgeting, PERT, responsibility charting, affiliation agreements, responsibility centers, and a unique client service package, a transorganizational system can be managed on a day-to-day basis by professionals based in a number of different agencies.

From this we can deduce that:

1. The capability inherent in a specific management technique is more fully exploited when used in combination with other management techniques.
2. The same techniques (e.g., computerization) can be used in a number of repertoires with different overall results. (For institutional–organizational management, computers are vital for keeping financial accounts, maintaining client records, office automation, even diagnostic testing in medical situations. For systemic-strategic management, computers can provide the data flows that sustain the transorganizational system.)
3. Synergy is achieved when several techniques are intelligently combined. They build on each other to produce results not possible when using each technique separately or in isolation.

The last notion is particularly important. In a resource-constrained industry such as the human services, managers are continually searching for **synergy**, (i.e., when the whole equals more than the sum of its parts). The simultaneous action of separate agencies working together will have a greater total effect than the sum of their individual efforts. As human services organizations find themselves working in combined or cooperative systems with other like agencies, these systems can and should be designed and managed to exploit their synergistic potential. The concept of management repertoires is a crucial vehicle for the achievement of synergy in transorganizational human services systems.

The following example of actual management repertoires illustrates each of these notions.

Management Repertoires for Transorganizational Systems: Some Examples

The best way of illustrating management repertoires, and thus understanding systemic management, is through Case 16.1, Part 3, of River City, Inc. You may want to reread Part 1 (page 197) and Part 2 (page 275) to identify the clusters of management techniques assembled to implement what was a unique transorganizational system. It involved three prime agencies: a public school district, a social services subsidiary of a nonprofit hospital (River City, Inc.), and a proprietary group practice of pediatricians. An additional range of agencies included federal and state government agencies, Blue Cross, and federal insurance agencies administered by private corporations.

Case 16.1 _____

Part 3:* River City, Inc.

The THC (Teen Health Centers, Inc.) board meeting had just closed, and River City's executive, Jim O'Neill, came over to Nan Rogers and said, "Stick around for a few minutes if you can, Nan. Amos Thompson wants to talk to us about an idea he has." Nan thought to herself: Here go my weekends! Amos was Tucker county's dynamic superintendent of schools who had supported Jim in the formation of THC, and she knew that when those two got together, the pace would become frenetic.

Amos approached: "Hi Jim, Nan; thanks for waiting. I wanted to bounce an idea off you. Jim, refresh my memory on how THC was formed; it's important for the idea I want to toss out to you two!"

"Well, as I remember it, Amos," Jim began, "a number of us met with the idea of providing a comprehensive set of health services for teens. In the first stage, we did a lot of talking, trying to share ideas and values, to arrive at a consensus on the problem and on what needed to be done. The University of Tennessee provided consultants who collected pertinent data, facilitated our meetings, and helped us deal with tensions arising from our different professional backgrounds. They even did some training on new problem-solving techniques, remember?"

"Well, where did the idea of incorporating as Teen Health Clinics come up?" Amos asked.

"I remember that, Amos," Nan joined in. "When you told the group meeting that the State Department of Education would give a challenge grant to initiate the program, we looked at some alternative governance structures and decided on a separate corporation. The consultants then used force-field analysis and action planning to help us develop a team style of management for the new corporation. That wasn't so easy! And then we went through the process of clarifying values, different approaches to services, and the different roles each of us would play. That was even tougher, but it all worked out in the end."

"After that," Jim picked up, "with the UT consultants' help, we began to design the new system. We analyzed the teens' health needs and the way in which health services are provided now; then we came up with a new comprehensive system. Here, I still have the list of the 'actors.'" He dug around in a file folder and pulled out a piece of paper.

Participant Providers: Teen Health Services

- Administrative services: General: Tucker County School District
  Information system: City of Chatfield
  Financial: State Departments of Education, Human Resources, Health, Medicaid

- Health services: General: River Hospital's Clinics
  Pediatric: Youth Health, Inc. (a group of pediatricians in private practice)
  Pregnancy and Parenting: Visiting Health Nurses
  Family Planning: River City, Inc.
  Mental health–substance abuse counseling: River City, Inc.

"But the final stage was the most difficult, Jim," Nan added. Remember?"

"And how!" Jim grimaced. "After trying some simulations, we formed a management team to actually plan for the transition and develop the management techniques for THC. The team developed PERT and responsibility charts, set up an MBO system supported by a program-budget format, agreed on a client-service package supported by an integrated-information system, and developed a format for affiliation agreements that set outcome measures, unit costs, and cost capping. By the time it was over, we were exhausted."

"Some of us were barely talking to each other," Nan added. "We did have some start-up problems, but with some technical assistance from the UT consultants and a lot of their team-building training, it all began to work out. By the end of the second year, we had smoothed out all kinks in the system."

"And smoothed out all turf-related issues as well," Jim was quick to note. "But now it's your turn, Amos. I don't know about Nan, but I'm dying to know. What do you have in mind?"

Amos laughed. "What I have in mind will make THC seem like a cinch. But nothing succeeds like success, and I wondered if we could tackle what will be the major problem for the turn of the century—the issue of "The Forgotten Half" (Halperin, 1988).

Nan and Jim looked at each other puzzled: "The what?"

"The Forgotten Half," Amos replied. "That's the next big issue on our doorstep, and it's also the title of a new study I just encountered. It documents what we all know—that we make a solid investment in our youth who go on to higher education. We have developed a comprehensive support system to help them make it. But only about fifty percent of our young people decide to go on to college or other advanced training. What about the remainder? They are having an increasingly hard time making it in society in every way, and the study shows that matters will get worse unless there's timely intervention."

Jim whistled. "What you just did, Amos, is take our country's number-one problem—the school dropouts and the undereducated—and make it a subset of a larger societal problem. This cuts across so many of our community's education, employment, health, mental health, youth services, job-training, social services, criminal justice, and recreational agencies that it makes THC elementary. It will involve all the sectors of our economy. Do you think we dare tackle this?"

"Do we have a choice?" Amos quickly responded.

"Did I tell you about my plans to take a sabbatical next year to work on my Ph.D.?" Nan asked Jim.

Jim and Amos looked at her with frowns and then noted her Cheshire cat grin. They all laughed and took out their calendars to look for a time when they could meet with a group of key community leaders to explore the issue further.

*Parts 1 and 2 of the River City case can be found in Chapters 8 and 11, respectively.

To assist in the analysis of the management repertoires fashioned from this case, two analyses are presented: (1) a graphic representation (Figure 16.2) and (2) a tabular listing of each management repertoire and its four clusters of management techniques (Table 16.1).

At this point, we can draw three conclusions about the way in which management repertoires are fashioned for transorganizational systems management. First, there are generally four clusters in a systemic management repertoire, one that approximates each of Elizabeth Loughran's (1986) stages in the evolutionary formation of interorganizational relations: identity, empowerment, organization, and administration.

Second, historically, academics who specialize in management research separate the management sciences from the behavior sciences. Scholars tend to specialize in one or the other. In practice not only is there no such split, there also is a naturalness in their relationship for managers (see Figure 16.3). Practitioners interrelate and integrate administrative technologies from all sources.

Table 16.1 Clusters of Systemic Management Techniques Assembled

Group Formulation	System Building	Systems Design	Systems Management
Intervention–Facilitation Intervening in a process to facilitate changing the way group members think or act	**Process Consultation** Consulting with a group of organizational employees to help them identify and better understand interpersonal processes within the agency	**Systems Analysis** The systemic analysis of an issue to derive the overall strategy, with particular emphasis on interrelationships	**Team Building** A process designed to increase the abilities of a group of people to function more effectively as a team
Data Collection and Feedback Collection of data from members of an organization about their perceptions of the organization, which is then fed back to those members in summary form	**Force-Field Analysis** A group analytic process for identifying all organizational-environmental forces that help and hinder movement toward improvements	**Client-Needs Analysis** Analysis of data to more clearly identify the human services needs of a specific group of clients	**MBO** Management By Objectives
Values Clarification A process in which members of a group clarify and share their beliefs, attitudes, and values	**Action Planning** Based on force-field analysis, the delineation of each action required to change and improve an agency; an action plan becomes the basis for PERT and responsibility charts	**Systems Conceptualization** Developing a concept of a new or revised system for achieving a specific set of goals	**ProB** Program-Oriented Budgeting
Training Professional development workshops	**Governance Structuring** The process of arriving at the best policy-making structure for a new transorganizational system	**Domain Consensus** The process by which an organization achieves consensus around its claim over the services it renders to a specific set of clients	**PERT Charts** Program Evaluation and Review Technique: graphic presentation of interrelationships of all required events and activities in a project to be managed
Technical Assistance Highly specialized technical advice from consultants	**Value–Role Perceptions** A group process for clarifying members' perceptions of the role each plays in the agency	**Models and Simulation** The construction and manipulation of a mathematical expression that abstracts the real world in symbolic terms	**Responsibility Charts** A graphic representation of the roles and responsibilities of a group of managers involved in a process, project, or system
Consensus Building Defining a course of action (decisions) that represents a position that all members of the group can accept		**Team Organization** An institutional structure that vests the management of an organization or a system in a team of managers	**Client-Services Package** A set of services assembled for the unique needs of a specific client
Conflict Management Creative, constructive use of real conflicts			**Cost Centers** The aggregation of all costs for a unique, specific object, purpose, program, or client

- *Role Expectations*
  A process for developing standards of behavior that can be expected from an individual occupying a given position in an organization
- *Participative Management*
  Greater participation in the management of an organization or system by a larger number of employees of the organization or system

- *Integrated-Information System*
  A computer-based information system that interrelates its data flows, data processing, and data bases
- *Transition Planning and Management*
  The methodical planning and management of a process that involves a change in an organization or system
- *Affiliation Agreements*
  A mutual understanding, in writing, of the ways in which two or more organizations will relate to each other in a trans-organizational system
- *Unit Costs*
  A unit measure derived by dividing investments by measures of performance
- *Cost Capping*
  Placing a maximum on the costs of a service for a specific client or program
- *Outcome Measure*
  Standards or criteria for measuring the outcomes, client impacts, or results of a service

Figure 16.2 Management Repertoire for River City, Inc.

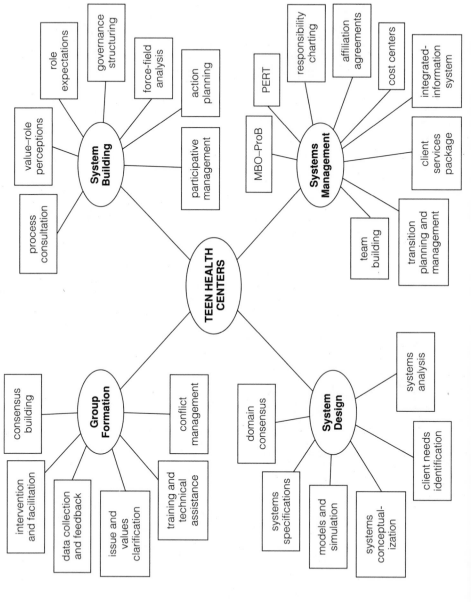

Figure 16.3   Interrelating the Management and Behavioral
            Science Administrative Sciences

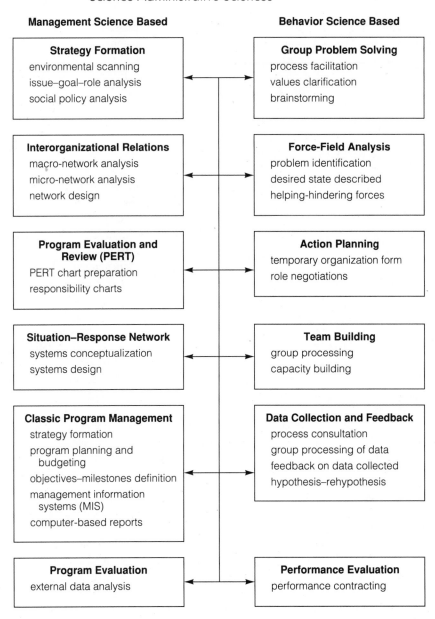

Management Science Based

Strategy Formation
environmental scanning
issue–goal–role analysis
social policy analysis

Interorganizational Relations
macro-network analysis
micro-network analysis
network design

**Program Evaluation and
Review (PERT)**
PERT chart preparation
responsibility charts

Situation–Response Network
systems conceptualization
systems design

Classic Program Management
strategy formation
program planning and
  budgeting
objectives–milestones definition
management information
  systems (MIS)
computer-based reports

Program Evaluation
external data analysis

Behavior Science Based

Group Problem Solving
process facilitation
values clarification
brainstorming

Force-Field Analysis
problem identification
desired state described
helping-hindering forces

Action Planning
temporary organization form
role negotiations

Team Building
group processing
capacity building

Data Collection and Feedback
process consultation
group processing of data
feedback on data collected
hypothesis–rehypothesis

Performance Evaluation
performance contracting

This is illustrated in the management repertoire for the River City case and follows in the other management repertoires found in this chapter. It is actually true for any management repertoire.

Third, the reader can also note that many of the management techniques used for systemic management of the new transorganizational system designed in the River City case appear to be common to any human services management situation. What is different is the unique way in which it was packaged to become a successful management repertoire for this situation.

Managing with Information

One of the consistent themes throughout this book has been that the human services manager increasingly will use two simultaneous, coexisting management functions: Institutional (organizational) and systemic (strategic) management. In attempting to differentiate the two, we have suggested that it is the particular clustering of management techniques that distinguishes one from the other because they both use essentially the same management tools. One way in which one can differentiate institutional from systemic management is its source of empowerment. Differentiated thus, *institutional management is based on authority, whereas systemic management is based on information.*

There is a second differentiation, equally important: Existing institutional structures are *dependent* variables for societal systems that cross organizational boundaries; information flows, on the other hand, are *independent* variables. In other words, one does not always have to create new organizational structures to respond to new societal problems. Instead, several organizations can be fashioned into a new transorganizational system designed to deal with the new problem or client group. It is the flow of information linking the organizations in the new system that is the critical element in keeping the new structure (network) operating. Implicit in this hypothesis are a number of corollary propositions:

1. Once an institution (i.e., organization) is created, it is difficult, if not impossible, to eliminate. This phenomenon has been recognized and accepted by sociologists for a long time.
2. Further, it is impossible to create a single institution that can deal with all aspects of a specific societal issue. For example, there are too many aspects of drug abuse to contain within one large federal department all the different professions–disciplines needed to deal with this issue. In the United States, it has in recent times even included elements of the State Department, Defense Department, Coast Guard, and FAA.
3. Even if obsolete institutions could be eliminated and replaced by new ones, it would be impossible to respond quickly enough, as societal needs and priorities change very rapidly.

4. Although changes in organizational-institutional structures can take months and even years, data and information have an opposite attribute. As noted in Chapter 13, the computer can be a general-purpose symbol manipulator. A computer-based information system can assemble, then reassemble, data literally within minutes.
5. When viewed as systems rather than organizational structures, institutions are essentially relationships of people, tasks, and technologies, working in concert according to an agreed-on plan of action, monitored and controlled by rapid communications based on modern technologies. A NASA space shuttle is one good example of such a system, as is the Medicare system.
6. One is led to the conclusion, therefore, that by building on existing organizational structures and using modern, systemic management technologies, it is possible to design and manage transorganizational systems that meet the rapidly changing needs and priorities of society.

This trend toward an information-based organization constitutes, in the mind of Peter Drucker, a "radical break" with the way in which most organizations are being managed today:

> We are entering a period of change: the shift from the command-and-control organization, the organization of departments and divisions, to the information-based organization, the organization of knowledge specialists. We can perceive, though perhaps only dimly, what this organization will look like. . . . But the job of actually building the information-based organization is still ahead of us—it is the managerial challenge of the future. (1988, 91)

In Drucker's vision of an information-based organization, there are a number of elements:

- Small task forces of specialists
- Greater diversity and number of specialists
- Clear goals and performance expectations
- Organized feedback that compares results with expectations
- A flat organization (fewer levels of management)
- Irrelevant span of control
- Collegial relationships
- Power based on responsibility, not authority
- Expectation that each team member will exercise self-control and self-discipline based on shared values and mutual respect
- Information responsibility: shared data on what is being done, what should be done, and how well it is done, for each colleague and the group

The human services manager will increasingly recognize that systemic management is founded on the conception that authority flows from information, not position. The way information is managed therefore becomes the cornerstone for systemic management.

A Distinctive Set of Values for Systemic Management

Experienced human services managers have come to recognize that more important than mastery of the complex skills required for transorganizational management is the acquisition and internalization of a set of organizational and managerial values that serve as the underpinnings of systemic management. We conclude the discussion of systemic management by briefly stating this additional set of values:

1. *The responsibility for managing rests largely with clients or client-surrogates.* Most people manage their own delivery of human services, almost out of necessity, because in this process they have to deal with a large number of different professionals, institutions, and systems. In situations where they must be dependent on others (members of family or professionals), advocates or surrogates assisted them in the process. The redefinition of the role of clients as partners in the helping process is consistent with the thinking of a large number of social work theorists who support "competence-oriented practice." Although the notion of clients as a primary resource in the helping process is widely accepted in theory, the perception of client self-management of service delivery is not so widespread. Both of these perceptions, however, are necessary values for agencies and personnel involved in transorganizational processes.
2. *Each client is a discrete organizational set.* The shift to flexible systems production of goods and services was initially conceived and operationalized in the United States but adopted quickly by world economies. Although it created a management crisis initially, it has now become commonplace in American corporations, not only for the production of goods but also in services (e.g., airline travel, health services, financial services). In human services it requires a totally new value-stance, bedded in the concept of each client being a unique organization. The notion, for example, of caseload (i.e., X number of clients for each social worker) is a necessary element of institutional management. This is not so for a transorganizational system in which each client is responsible for the self-management of her unique organizational set. Human services managers, conditioned by years of operating in a hierarchical environment and required to operate in that environment while also functioning in a transorganizational system, could experience difficulty in accepting this value,

despite its acceptance as a fundamental value of social work. Service providers need to offer systemic options that permit people to assemble services in a way that captures the uniqueness of each individual and the inherent dynamic energy that can flow from each person's pursuit of self-governance.

3. *Self-regulating, self-controlling organizations and systems are fundamental.* For those who design transorganizational networks, fashioning systems that are self-regulating and self-controlling is complicated but relatively straightforward. Acceptance of the underlying cybernetic value, however, may not be easy for social workers accustomed to institutional management in which organizations are controlled and regulated by administrators. The value that "I (the administrator) know what is best for the organization" clashes with the value that "the organization is designed to manage itself." Tom Peters contends that "the modest-sized, task-oriented, semi-autonomous, mainly self-managing team should be the basic organization building block" and that it calls for the "elimination of the traditional first-line supervisor's job" (1988, 356). He also contends that the difficulty we have in achieving more effective and efficient production of goods and services is management attitudes: "It remains a fact that W. Edwards Deming's assessment of management as 90% to blame for lack of enthusiastic participation among front-line employees applies to the public as well as the private sector" (1988, 354).

4. *The tensions of dualism must be resolved.* The shift to transorganizational management with its value base of dualism may also be difficult for a human services manager. Several authors have examined the concept of a multiple-command (e.g., two-boss) management system. The ability to manage with dual loyalties is not yet well analyzed. Dualism is inherent in transorganizational management. But it clashes head on with the concept that *no* employee can work for two bosses, a value that runs deep within anyone who has worked or managed in a traditional institutional setting. In a similar manner, organizational domain conditions any administrator to be fiercely loyal to a single agency. Dual loyalty, along with dual bosses, necessitates a totally new mind-set and value-stance for social work administrators who operate within transorganizational systems.

5. *Transdisciplinary practice responds to modern societal needs.* The concept that other specialists can practice in your discipline is as difficult to accept as the reverse—that you can practice in other disciplines. For the most part, this value is rejected out of hand as unworkable. The root of this attitude can be traced to the fact that all organizations in the United States, business and nonbusiness, fashion personnel systems on a narrow definition of specialization. This now puts us at a disadvantage when flexibility and fast response to the unique needs of individuals and situations are requirements of modern economies. Other economies, in Japan as well as in Europe, provide more latitude in the definition of the scope of work and specialization of individual workers.

There are a number of theorists who maintain that a transdiciplinary approach to practice is the only possible one for our society. This approach does not suggest that a social worker could perform brain surgery. It does anticipate, though, that a team of different disciplines can enlarge the common core of knowledge and competency of each team member, moving methodically from a unidisciplinary to a transdisciplinary approach. This shift does have a prerequisite: a shift in basic values, which accepts the notion that transdiciplinary practice can lead to more effective, individualized client services as well as more productive service delivery. For many human services managers, accepting this value may be less difficult than for their counterparts in a transorganizational system who are from other disciplines more deeply entrenched in unidisciplinary practice.

6. *Mutual-shared responsibility is fundamental.* Inherent in the institutional management principle of accountability is a subtle value as old as the Bible. (Some consider it the first recorded incident of buck-passing, when Adam blamed his eating of the forbidden fruit on Eve and the serpent.)

   Western nations' conception of management is one of singular responsibility and accountability, and implies searching the hierarchy of accountable people to find the responsible (i.e., guilty) individual when something goes wrong. But the real issue should not be placing blame; instead, energies should be focused on making the total system function more effectively. The value of mutual-shared responsibility is largely absent in institutional management. But for transorganizational management, mutual and shared responsibility by everyone is a fundamental value: If the total system is not functioning effectively, everyone is responsible. Accepting this value of mutuality in practice could prove difficult when making the transition to transorganizational management.

7. *Authority flows from roles, not position.* It is generally accepted in institutional management that the position one occupies automatically carries with it specific authority. In transorganizational management, the roles that professionals play will be different depending on the particular client and the particular situation. In each of these roles, the authority one has flows out of the role being carried out and not from one's position.

   Everyone will still have a position in their own agency and will retain, for purposes of agency management, the authority and power that comes with that position. But when participating in transorganizational arrangements, each person must learn to accept the value that authority, in a specific situation and at a specific time, is related to a specific role.

8. *Diversity of intercultural norms should be nurtured.* By far the most important value required for transorganizational management is the nurturing of a diverse range of intercultural norms. It will require a continually expanding set of knowledge and skills focusing on awareness, sensitivity, acceptance, and utilization of the diverse perceptions and behaviors of different cultures. In terms of those people who staff social work organizations and in terms of those people who are served by social work agencies,

there are two demographic changes that will impact on organizational processes. Within the next decade or two, women and people from nonwhite cultures will be the majority of the population. This has profound implications for the United States and for our profession. Because the structure of our experience is molded by our culture, cross-cultural training will be a cornerstone of professional preparation and development (see Hall 1965, 1967). Enlightened social work administrators could well provide leadership for other human services managers in reshaping institutional processes and systems that both recognize this diversity and capitalize on it.

Summary

As this text has consistently maintained, the human services manager must exert effort to become skilled in the practice of both institutional and systemic management. With experience and knowledge one succeeds at integrating the two to achieve the prize, synergy. Not only is the total effect of working jointly with other agencies greater than the sum of each agency's impact when operating separately, but also the outcome for the human services manager's own agency is greater than could be achieved if operating in isolation.

It can be difficult to shift between two different managerial environments—from managing one's own traditional organization while participating in the management of a transorganizational system. This final chapter of Part V presented some guidelines, techniques, concepts, and values to help facilitate this process. All human services managers have mutual responsibility for a shared, interrelated purpose—creating a responsive environment. The challenge is fashioning an effective, responsible organizational climate that allows all human services professionals and employees to be supportive to people with needs.

The key to managing transorganizational systems is a set of management repertoires: the assembling of carefully crafted clusters of management techniques. This chapter describes some management repertoires to show how transorganizational systems are designed and managed. Developing management repertoires for systemic management takes a serious investment of time and energy. Tacking the design and management of transorganizational systems onto managing one's own agency is inappropriate. It will result in an ill-designed system doomed to ineffectiveness.

Successful systemic management represents a move toward what Drucker heralds as a new concept of organization for the future, one bedded in knowledge and information. It calls for more than just a new style of management. It requires a new set of values. Internalizing these values is the challenge to the profession; it also represents the hope that our society will be able to fashion and manage the new transorganizational systems so vitally necessary if we are to respond to the rapidly changing needs of our populace and the inexorable demands of the decades ahead.

Epilogue

Multiple Realities and the Human Services Manager's Role Perceptions

Before concluding this book's analysis and discussion of human services management, let us look at two more themes of personal concern to the human services manager. Our discussion of these two subjects—multiple perceptions of reality and existence and the human services manager's role perceptions—will be brief. But brevity should not be mistaken for insignificance. These two themes comprise the foundation for everything that you will do to implement the theories and techniques that have been presented.

Multiple Perceptions of Reality and Existence

The heart of all human services management is each manager's own perception of human existence and reality. This seems both simple and self-evident. But the path to understanding the implications of this statement is more complex, and the reader willing to explore this subject in depth will struggle with issues that have brought both despair and elation to countless human beings through the millenia. The first prerequisite for mastery of this quest is humility, because the greatest minds of civilization have yet to produce a single set of theories that have withstood the test of time to gain universal acceptance. The compounding of wisdom in the flow of history provides us with ever-new insights and requires us to reflect on the conditions of humans. Though the path is complex, the task is vital, because by exploring the nature of being or reality we understand human services management tenets in the context of other philosophies.

Everything you do is an expression of your construction of reality and your perception of human existence. This fact of life operates so subtly that one is usually unaware of it. Let us do an exercise as an example. Which of the following constructions of reality comes closest to your own beliefs? How might each one affect the decision-making process of a human services manager?

1. While all people are to be respected, some of us can be expected to lead better lives than others. This is a reward for things done in the past.
2. We really don't have much choice in our lives. This is because most of what controls our lives is predetermined by other forces.
3. People must understand how to conduct themselves. Otherwise there is bound to be disharmony and confusion that produce human suffering.
4. All of us have important inherent rights because we are equal. No one has the power to control us without our consent.

Each of these equally valid statements is a paraphrased simplification of a pronouncement by a great thinker, whose perceptions influenced the actions of millions of the world's citizens. In case you did not readily identify the sources, the first was Mohammed, the second Buddha, the third Confucius, and the last Thomas Jefferson in the opening statement of the Declaration of Independence.

The evolution of the centrality of human individuality in western thought can be followed through both religious and mythological origins. The Levant religions stressed the notion of a one-to-one relationship between creator and created. Yehezkel Kaufman noted (1965) that this relationship to the divine, not monotheism itself, was the contribution of Judaism, and eventually Christianity, to world thought. A similar concept can be seen in the Greek myth of Prometheus who defied the gods. How revolutionary a thought: Humans could defy their creators! And from the Promethean notion of human defiance, ancient Greeks evolved Protagoras' notion (440 B.C.) that "man is the measure of all things."

What is the importance of this to you, a human services manager? It means that the determination of your actions is not imposed by someone else, because it flows ultimately from the core of your own conception of human existence and your own construct of reality. This is of great significance because it defines our approach to the management of human services organizations. Reality formation as a basis for action is the starting point of organization and management. As Peter Berger and Thomas Luckmann note (1966, 1), "reality is socially constructed." It is not, like the rain falling outside your window, something over which you have no control.

To more fully understand the implications of this idea, we need to briefly expand our discussion in Chapter 3 of the interrelationship between organizations and different perceptions and metaphors of human behavior. A new management school of thought has emerged in the past two decades known as the *interpretive* approach or paradigm. Gareth Morgan compares the interpretive paradigm with the functionalist paradigm, which has dominated organizational theory during this century:

> The *functionalist* paradigm is based upon the assumption that society has a concrete, real existence and a systemic character oriented to produce an ordered and regulated state of affairs.
>
> The *interpretive* paradigm, on the other hand, is based upon the view . . . that what passes as social reality does not exist in any concrete sense, but is the product of the subjective and inter-subjective experience of individuals. (1980, 608–9)

From the interpretive perspective, people in organizations are active participants in shaping meaning and organizational reality, not detached observers of some concrete organizational reality that is preordained. In analyzing the implication of these two perspectives, Linda Smircich (1986) notes that for the interpretive manager, "organizations are socially constructed systems of shared meaning." To deal with the multiple realities in an organization, the manager becomes a "framer of contexts, maker and shaper of interpretive schemes. Organized action does not occur through specified procedures for getting things done: it occurs through the achievement of shared meaning." Smircich concludes that for the interpretive manager:

> There is a major shift in emphasis from *managing* and *controlling* to *interpreting* and *knowing*. The major concern for an interpretive practitioner is the examination and critique of organizational realities . . . to clarify the various realities in a setting and to remove distortion in their understanding of what is going on, in order to contribute to the more informed practice of the organization. (1986, 225)

The implication for the creative, dynamic manager of human services organization is profound. She needs to recognize that the starting point of human services management is the awareness of and sensitivity to the concept that human beings in organizational settings construct their own reality, and that therefore one manages in an environment of multiple realities.

Managing is not attempting to deal with an organization as if it were an inanimate object. Instead it is a continuous flow of organizing, interpreting, and shaping meaning from the multiple realities that exist among the members of the organization. In this process, nothing is more critical for the human services manager than the final theme of this text: the human services manager's need to reflect on one's own multiple role perceptions, and of the full understanding of the dominant values that energize one's daily actions.

Early in their careers, human services managers will discover that they are engaged in a lifelong struggle devoted to participation in the shaping of human services organizations and thereby society. Without conscious and deliberate efforts by managers, other less positive forces will fashion the human services organization in ways that are counterproductive for individual clients and for society collectively. To Mary Parker Follett, the task of management is to promote the harmonious integration of individual development within a democratic conception of social progress (Michael Harmon and Richard Mayer 1986, 341.) For the human services managers, the challenge comes down to *shape or be shaped*. How human services managers deal with this struggle is related to their own self-image, their own role perception, their own driving values. As can be anticipated, self-images, role perceptions, and values are not static—they evolve in a dynamic fashion and are formed and reformed in an environment that can be characterized as kinetic.

Summary

In this Epilogue, we deviated from the textbook posture of being analytical and objective. Instead we became prescriptive with a clear bias. Even if the reader rejects the bias, it is our hope that this discussion has made the human services manager aware of the deep philosophic and metaphysic underpinnings that affect our field. If the major theme of the book is dynamic, creative management for each human services organization, then managers bring to the situation their own perception of human existence and constructions of reality, and their own role perceptions and self-images that will direct their energies. All of us therefore must examine and reflect on these perceptions. That is the crucial point of departure for creative human services management.

Your task for the rest of your career will be to exploit your personal realities, strengths, and goals, and to mediate, integrate, and orchestrate them with your skills for the improvement of our field and the betterment of all humankind.

Appendix

Office Management

The first management process that faces every human services manager responsible for running an operating agency, be it large or small, is the day-to-day mechanics of managing an office. Because it is such an elemental part of management and long preceded modern theories of organization and management, the literature on the subject is extensive. Comprehensive handbooks covering office management in detail have been published and used for most of the twentieth century (see, for example, Carl Heyel 1972.) Because good resources are readily available and the subject quite specialized and technical, this appendix provides only an introductory overview to acquaint the reader with the different aspects of the field.

Another reason for not including more extensive coverage of this topic is that often managers have little control over a major part of office management—facilities management. In public human services organizations, there are usually special general services units (either in a department of administration or a department of public works) that have responsibility for managing the physical facilities.

Increasingly, human services agencies operate in rented space; in such situations, facility management is largely the responsibility of the lessor or a rental management company and was negotiated in the lease prior to the agency acquiring the space. What is important is that human services managers be able to communicate to these agencies as to the provisions and standards they require. So, even though most human services managers may not need extreme proficiency in the minutiae of office management techniques, it is still necessary to have a good understanding of this fundamental management function to be able to interface effectively, and to take an active role in planning, when this is possible.

The basic parts of an office include provision for the building and its space, division and layout, work operations and the work environment, furnishings and aesthetics, and the basic services that any office requires. Table A.1 lists the basic aspects of office management.

In terms of the competing organizational and management paradigms, office management is the most neutral of all fundamental management processes. It can be used to support one paradigm over the others; it can also be used to balance all paradigms. Arguments can be made that because offices are the daytime home of employees, office management is primarily directed toward strengthening the staff development paradigm. A similar argument could be made for the client paradigm because the physical environment for human services provision on the whole takes place in an office.

As the human services management student and practitioner can recognize, the basic order established by office management is equally essential to the control paradigm or the mission paradigm. In essence for the creative, dynamic human services manager, office management provides a vital set of fundamental processes for establishing the smooth mechanics and an optimal environment for shaping and improving the functions of human services organization.

Image Management

There is another fundamental process: **image management,** which has become a critical function of management. It also has become so sophisticated and comprehensive that it requires much fuller treatment than can be provided in the context of this text. We can only hope to introduce the outlines of the subject to the reader, and to stress the necessity to acquire proficiency in its knowledge and skills.

In today's world, the *image* of what you do is often as important as the *substance*, perhaps even more important. And image management cannot be left to chance; it not only requires specialists who are skilled in every aspect of this fundamental management process, but it must permeate every aspect of the management of organizations, institutions, and systems. Understanding and mastering the approaches, concepts, and technologies of image management are an absolute necessity for successful management in modern societies. As for studying the underlying theory, if one thinker were to be singled out as the supreme authority on the subject it would be Marshall McLuhan. He fully understood that the medium, and the resultant image, were indeed the message, and the impact and implications of this truth.

Image management creates a tension, even conflict, in values for many of us. Most human services managers prefer to concentrate on the *substance* of their organization: the productive and effective achievement of agency mission,

Table A.1 Basic Aspects of Office Management

Building

Maintenance	Open-space design
Lighting, heating, ventilation	Noise reduction
Toilet facilities	Employees' facilities
Safety	Elevators
Flexible, ergonomic furnishings	Parking and landscape
Repairs	Safety and security

Office Machines

Typewriters, dictating machines	Calculating machines
Duplicating machines	Standardization
Centralized versus decentralized	Repairs and maintenance

Correspondence

Manuals	Use of form letters
Review of letters	Uniformity of style
Typing-steno pool	Word processing
Use of dictating machines	

Internal Communications

Telephones	Intercom
Messages (written/oral)	Messenger service
Electronic memos and mail	Electronic calendaring

External Communications

Mail (including electronic mail)	Telephones and cables
Delivery services	Telegraph
Facsimile processing	Electronic data dissemination
Desktop publishing	Electronic bulletin boards

Records-Data Management

Forms design and control	Storage of records
Forms creation	Destruction of records
Filing systems and services	Micrographics-reprographics
External electronic databases	Library services

Office Methods

Simplify-standardize procedures	Followup complaints-requests
Manuals	Work scheduling
Office automation	Office design and layout

Vehicles & Transportation

Fleet management	Use of personal vehicles
Client transportation	Preventive maintenance
Risk management	Vehicle scheduling

Figure A.1 An Overview of Image Management

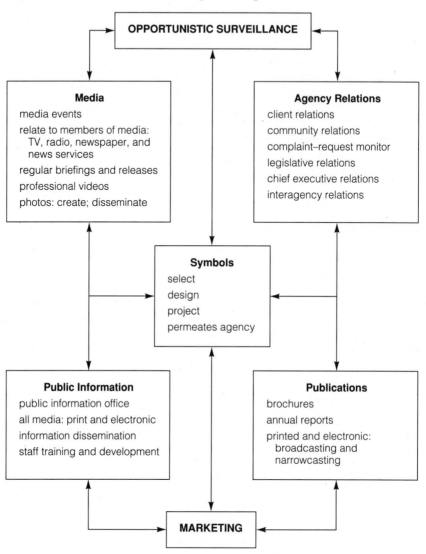

goals, and program objectives. To focus their time and energy on the *image* of their organization, something they deem superficial, represents to many a diversion of effort. Marketing experts, on the other hand, fully understand that image is as important as substance: they sell the look and the icing of the cake, or the sizzle and the aroma of the steak, not the cake or the steak itself. For them it is paramount to project the correct symbol and image: it is the icing and the sizzle that forms the reality of their product.

Table A.2 A Checklist of Do's and Don'ts for Media Relations

Do	Don't
Return all media phone calls promptly.	Overuse press releases; use more personal contacts with reporters.
Give plenty of lead time for deadlines.	
At each staff meeting, set aside time to discuss potential media events that the agency wants covered.	Go over the heads of reporters.
	Assume that the media understand your agency and your area of human services.
Maintain an active media-contact list.	Say anything "off the record."
Keep a file of all media coverage: newspaper clippings; video copies of TV news items or TV features of the agency; review and evaluate them periodically.	Withhold information that reporters can get from other sources.
Practice good TV behavior (e.g., look at the interviewer, not the camera; have comfortable, attractive surroundings).	
Help reporters (newspaper and TV) with background information on the agency and its programs—issues.	
Do your "homework"—be fully informed.	

In the global village that we now live in, the management of the image of the organization is nearly as important as the management of its substance. Both must be developed simultaneously and synergistically. This requires proficiency in a set of concepts and technologies that have become extremely sophisticated and comprehensive. Figure A.1 provides an overview of image management; it serves as a guide in pursuing further this fundamental management process that must be exploited to the fullest in today's managed image environment.

As noted earlier, image management has become sophisticated and comprehensive, requiring activities and efforts that range from the very general to the very detailed. A good starting point is to develop an image or public relations plan. The planning process requires

1. Delineation of goals and objectives.
2. Determination of current perceptions of the agency through formal or informal research and analysis of media reporting on the agency over the past two years.
3. Development of a comprehensive program: specific activities with performance targets and level of investment committed to each activity.
4. Pinpointing responsibility for the total plan.
5. Creating a partnership with the media—acquiring an understanding of their needs, objectives, and constraints.

6. Motivating staff to think and act creatively in improving the agency's image.

Managers may find the checklist in Table A.2 useful in developing good relations with the media. These are but a few examples of the many activities that the human services manager can undertake to enhance the agency's image. Practically every aspect of the agency's actions from the answering of its telephones to the impression received from its correspondence and reports, contributes to a positive or negative image. Timeliness and effectiveness of responding to clients and the pubic also shape an organization's image, as do ambience and tone, two less tangible phenomena. Many effective human services managers keep a camera handy to photograph the agency in action when they feel the picture might be newsworthy. Although this topic requires acquiring highly specialized knowledge and skills, one principle is clear: positive image management requires a plan that is proactive and gives a very high priority to this aspect of management.

Bibliography

CHAPTER 1

Becker, Ernest. 1975. *Escape from Evil*. New York: Free Press.

Bellah, Robert N., et al. 1986. *Habits of the Heart: Individualism and Commitment in American Life*. New York: Harper & Row.

Brown, Norman O. 1974. "Norman O. Brown's Body: A Conversation with Norman O. Brown" in *Voices and Visions*, edited by Sam Keen. New York: Harper & Row.

Buber, Martin. 1970. *I and Thou*. (A new translation with a prologue and noted, by Walter Kaufmann.) New York: Charles Scribner's.

Campbell, Joseph. 1968. *The Hero with a Thousand Faces*, 2d ed. Princeton, N.J.: Princeton University Press.

———. 1974. "Man and Myth: A Conversation with Joseph Campbell" in *Voices and Visions*, edited by Sam Keen. New York: Harper & Row.

———. 1976. *The Masks of God: Oriental Mythology*. New York: Penguin Books.

———. 1976. *The Masks of God: Occidential Mythology*. New York: Penguin Books.

———. 1976. *The Masks of God: Creative Mythology*. New York: Penguin Books.

———. 1976. *The Masks of God: Primitive Mythology*. New York: Penguin Books.

Drucker, Peter. 1988. "The Coming of the New Organization." *Harvard Business Review* (January/February).

Dubos, René. 1968. *So Human an Animal*. New York: Charles Scribner's.

Follett, Mary Parker. 1924. *Creative Experience.* New York: Longmans, Green.

⸺. 1940. *Dynamic Administration: The Collected Papers of Mary Parker Follett,* edited by Henry C. Metcalf and L. Urwick. New York: Harper & Row.

Frankl, Viktor E. 1962. *Man's Search for Meaning: An Introduction to Logotherapy.* Boston: Beacon Press.

Fromm, Eric. 1956. *The Art of Loving.* New York: Harper & Row.

Heschel, Abraham J. 1965. *Who Is Man?* Stanford: Stanford University Press.

Leonard, George B. 1968. *Education and Ecstasy.* New York: Delacorte Press.

Maslow, Abraham. 1954. *Motivation and Personality.* New York: Harper & Row.

Rogers, Carl. 1977. *Carl Rogers on Personal Power.* New York: Dell.

CHAPTER 2

Berry, Wendell. 1977. *The Unsettling of America.* San Francisco: Sierra Club Books.

Campbell, Joseph. 1976. *The Masks of God: Primitive Mythology.* New York: Penguin Books.

Charlesworth, James C. 1951. *Governmental Administration.* New York: Harper & Row.

Davis, Stanley M. and Lawrence, Paul R. 1977. *Matrix.* Reading, Mass.: Addison-Wesley.

Dvorin, Eugene P. and Simmons, Robert H. 1972. *From Amoral to Humane Bureaucracy.* San Francisco: Canfield.

Habermas, Jurgen. 1968. *Toward a Rational Society.* Translated by Jeremy J. Shapiro. Boston: Beacon Press.

Illich, Ivan. 1971. *Deschooling Society.* New York: Harper & Row

⸺. 1973. *Tools for Conviviality.* New York: Harper & Row.

⸺. 1976. *Medical Nemesis: The Expropriation of Health.* Toronto: Bantam Books.

⸺. 1978. *Toward a History of Needs.* New York: Pantheon Books.

Kahn, Herman, et al. 1976. *The Next 200 Years.* New York: Morrow.

Laski, Harold. 1930. "The Limitations of the Expert." *Harper's* 162 (December): 101–18.

Lehan, Edward Anthony. 1978. *The Future of the Finance Directorate.* MFOA Study No. 3. Chicago: Municipal Finance Officers Association.

May, Rollo. 1972. *Power and Innocence.* New York: W. W. Norton.

O'Toole, Laurence J. 1977. "Lineage, Continuity, Frederickson, and the New Public Administration." *Administration and Society* 9, No. 2 (August).

Rothman, Jack. 1970. "Three Models of Community Organization Practice" in *Strategies of Community Organization: A Book of Readings,* edited by Fred M. Cox et. al. Itasca, Ill.: F. E. Peacock.

Sarason, Seymour and Lorentz, Elizabeth. 1979. *The Challenge of Resource Exchange Networks*. San Francisco: Jossey-Bass.

Schroyer, Trent. 1973. *The Critique of Domination: The Origins and Development of Critical Theory*. New York: Braziller.

Thompson, Victor. 1975. *Without Sympathy or Enthusiasm: The Problem of Administrative Compassion*. University, Alabama: University of Alabama Press.

CHAPTER 3

Adler, Alfred. 1927. *Understanding Human Nature*. New York: Greenburg.

Ardrey, Robert. 1966. *The Territorial Imperative*. New York: Atheneum.

Becker, Ernest. 1968. *The Structure of Evil*. New York: Free Press.

————. 1975. *Escape from Evil*. New York: Free Press.

Beer, Stafford. 1975. *Platform for Change*. London: John Wiley.

Bellah, Robert N., et al. 1986. *Habits of the Heart: Individualism and Commitment in American Life*. New York: Harper & Row.

Campbell, Joseph. 1968. *The Hero with a Thousand Faces*, 2d ed. Princeton, N.J.: Princeton University Press.

————. 1976. *The Masks of God: Oriental Mythology*. New York: Penguin Books.

————. 1976. *The Masks of God: Occidental Mythology*. New York: Penguin Books.

————. 1976. *The Masks of God: Creative Mythology*. New York: Penguin Books.

————. 1976. *The Masks of God: Primitive Mythology*. New York: Penguin Books.

City of St. Paul, Minnesota. 1972. *A Methodology for Systems Analysis in the Human Resource Development Subsystem*. Springfield, VA: National Technical Information Service. PB211213.

Dewey, John. 1933. *How We Think*. New York: Heath.

Ellul, Jacques. 1965. *The Technological Society*. New York: Alfred A. Knopf.

Erikson, Erik. 1959. *Identity and the Life Cycle*. New York: International Universities Press.

Fromm, Eric. 1956. *The Art of Loving*. New York: Harper & Row.

Habermas, Jurgen. 1968. *Toward a Rational Society*. Translated by Jeremy J. Shapiro. Boston: Beacon Press.

Jung, C. G. 1958. *Psychology and Religion: West and East*. New York: Pantheon Books.

LeShan, Lawrence. 1976. *Alternative Realities: The Search for the Full Human Being*. New York: M. Evan.

Mannheim, Karl. 1952. *Essays on the Sociology of Knowledge*, 2d ed. New York: Oxford University Press.

Maslow, Abraham. 1952. *Motivation and Personality.* New York: Harper & Row.

McLuhan, Marshall. 1964. *Understanding Media.* New York: McGraw-Hill.

————. 1967. With Fiore, Q. *The Medium Is the Massage.* New York: Bantam Books.

Morgan, Gareth. 1980. "Paradigms, Metaphors, and Puzzle Solving in Organization Theory." *Administrative Science Quarterly* 25: 605–20.

————. 1986. *Images of Organization.* Beverly Hills, Calif.: Sage.

Nietzsche, Friedrich. 1976. *The Will to Power.* New York: Vintage.

Piaget, Jean. 1973. *The Child's Conception of the World.* London: Paladin.

Rowan, Roy. 1986. *The Intuitive Manager.* Boston: Little, Brown.

Weber, Max. 1930. *The Protestant Ethic and the Spirit of Capitalism.* Translated by Talcott Parson. London: Allen & Unwin.

White, Orion, Jr. 1973. "The Concept of Administrative Praxis." *Journal of Comparative Administration* (May): 55–86.

CHAPTER 4

Barnard, Chester I. 1938. *The Functions of the Executive.* Cambridge, Mass.: Harvard University Press.

Beer, Stafford. 1975. *Platform for Change.* London: John Wiley.

Bertalanffy, Ludwig von. 1956. "General System Theory" in *General Systems: Yearbook of the Society for the Advancement of General Systems Theory,* edited by Ludwig von Bertalanffy and Anatol Rappaport. Vol. 1, 1–10.

————. 1968. *General Systems Theory: Foundations, Development, Applications.* New York: Braziller.

Boulding, Kenneth E. 1956. "General Systems Theory—The Skeleton of Science." *Management Science* (April): 197–208.

Follett, Mary Parker. 1940. *Dynamic Administration: The Collected Papers of Mary Parker Follett,* edited by Henry C. Metcalf and L. Urwick. New York: Harper & Row.

Gulick, Luther and Urwick, L. 1937. *Papers on the Science of Administration.* New York: Institute of Public Administration.

Katz, Daniel and Kahn, Robert. 1966. *The Social Psychology of Organizations.* New York: John Wiley.

Parsons, Talcott. 1951. *The Social System.* Glencoe, Ill.: Free Press.

————. 1960. *Structure and Process in Modern Societies.* Glencoe, Ill.: Free Press.

Perrow, Charles. 1979. *Complex Organizations: A Critical Essay.* New York: Random House.

Scott, W. Richard. 1987. *Organizations: Rational, Natural, and Open Systems,* 2d ed. Englewood Cliffs, N.J.: Prentice-Hall.

Selznick, Philip. 1957. *Leadership in Administration.* New York: Harper & Row.

Simon, Herbert A. 1976. *Administrative Behavior: A Study of Decision-Making Process in Administrative Organization.* 3d ed. New York: Free Press.

Taylor, Frederick W. 1911. *The Principles of Scientific Management.* New York: Harper & Row.

Thompson, James D. 1967. *Organizations in Action.* New York: McGraw-Hill.

Thompson, Victor A. 1975. *Without Sympathy or Enthusiasm: The Problem of Administrative Compassion.* University, Al.: University of Alabama Press.

Trist, Eric L. 1981. "The Evolution of Sociotechnical Systems as a Conceptual Framework and as an Action Research Program" in *Perspectives on Organization Design and Behavior,* edited by Andrew H. Van de Ven and William F. Joyce. New York: John Wiley, 19–75.

Vroom, Victor H. 1973. "A New Look at Managerial Decision Making." *Organization Dynamics,* 1(4).

Weber, Max. 1947 (trans.). *The Theory of Social and Economic Organization,* edited by A. H. Henderson and Talcott Parsons. Glencoe, Ill.: Free Press. (First published in 1924.)

Wiener, Norbert. 1950, 1954. *The Human Use of Human Beings: Cybernetics and Society.* Boston: Houghton Mifflin.

Woodward, Joan. 1965. *Industrial Organization: Theory and Practice.* New York: Oxford University Press.

CHAPTER 5

Abramovitz, Mimi. 1988. *Regulating the Lives of Women.* Boston: South End Press.

Argyris, Chris. 1964. *Integrating the Individual and the Organization.* New York: John Wiley.

Bennis, Warren G.; Benne, Kenneth D.; Chin, Robert; and Corey, Kenneth E. (eds.). 1976. *The Planning of Change,* 3d ed. New York: Holt, Rinehart & Winston.

Follett, Mary Parker. 1924. *Creative Experience.* New York: Longmans, Green.

———. 1940. *Dynamic Administration: The Collected Papers of Mary Parker Follett,* edited by Henry C. Metcalf and L. Urwick. New York: Harper & Row.

———. 1987. *Freedom and Coordination,* edited by Arthur P. Brief. New York: Garland Publishing.

Hasenfeld, Yeheskel. 1983. *Human Service Organizations.* Englewood Cliffs, N.J.: Prentice-Hall.

Heidegger, Martin. 1969. *Discourse on Thinking.* Translated by J. M. Anderson and E. Hans Freund. New York: Harper & Row.

Hersey, Paul and Blanchard, Kenneth H. 1988. *Management of Organizational Behavior: Utilizing Human Resources,* 5th ed. Englewood Cliffs, N.J.: Prentice-Hall.

Katz, Daniel and Kahn, Robert. 1966. *The Social Psychology of Organizations.* New York: John Wiley.

Lewin, Kurt. 1948. *Resolving Social Conflicts: Selected Papers on Group Dynamics.* New York: Harper & Row.

————— 1951. *Field Theory in Social Science.* New York: Harper & Row.

Likert, Rensis. 1961. *New Patterns of Management.* New York: McGraw-Hill.

—————. 1967. *The Human Organization.* New York: McGraw-Hill.

Marrow, Alfred J. 1969. *The Practical Theorist: The Life and Work of Kurt Lewin.* New York: Basic Books.

McGregor, Douglas. 1960. *The Human Side of Enterprise.* New York: McGraw-Hill.

—————. 1967. *The Professional Manager.* New York: McGraw-Hill.

Schein, Edgar. 1985. *Organizational Culture and Leadership.* San Francisco: Jossey-Bass.

Scott, W. Richard. 1987. *Organizations: Rational, Natural, and Open Systems,* 2d ed. Englewood Cliffs, N.J.: Prentice-Hall.

Simon, Herbert A. 1966. *The New Science of Management Decision.* New York: Harper and Bros.

Vroom, Victor H. 1973. "A New Look at Managerial Decision Making." *Organization Dynamics,* 1(4).

Weber, Max. 1947 (trans.). *The Theory of Social and Economic Organization,* edited by A. H. Henderson and Talcott Parsons. Glencoe, Ill.: Free Press. (First published in 1924.)

Weissman, Harold; Epstein, Irwin; and Savage, Andrea. 1983. *Agency-Based Social Work.* Philadelphia: Temple University Press.

CHAPTER 6

Alissi, Albert S. 1980. *Perspectives on Social Group Work Practice.* New York: Free Press.

Beer, Stafford. 1975. *Platform for Change.* New York: John Wiley.

—————. 1979. *The Heart of the Enterprise.* New York: John Wiley.

Fuller, R. Buckminister. 1978. *Operating Manual for Spaceship Earth.* Boston: Dutton.

Gabor, Dennis. 1972. *The Mature Society.* New York: Praeger.

Halpern, Samuel (ed.). 1988. *The Forgotten Half: Pathways to Success for America's Youth and Young Families.* Washington, D.C.: William T. Grant Foundation Commission on Work, Family and Citizenship.

Hasenfeld, Yeheskel. 1983. *Human Service Organizations.* Englewood Cliffs, N.J.: Prentice-Hall.

Heintz, Stephen, et al. 1987. *One Child in Four: Investing in Poor Families and Their Children: A Matter of Commitment.* Washington, D.C.: American Public Welfare Association.

Illich, Ivan. 1978. *Toward a History of Needs.* New York: Pantheon Books.

Lehan, Edward Anthony. 1969. "The Municipality's Response to Changing Concepts of Public Welfare" in *The Revolution in Public Welfare: The Con-*

necticut Experience, edited by Rosaline Levenson. Storrs, Conn.: University of Connecticut, Institute of Public Service.

Maluccio, Anthony. 1981. *Promoting Client Competencies.* New York: Free Press.

McLuhan, Marshall. 1968. With Fiore, Q. *War and Peace in the Global Village.* New York: Bantam Books.

Naisbitt, John. 1983. *Megatrends: Ten New Directions Transforming Our Lives.* New York: Warner Bros.

Peters, Tom. 1987. *Thriving on Chaos: Handbook for a Management Revolution.* New York: Alfred A. Knopf.

Stoline, Anne and Weiner, Jonathan P. 1988. *The New Medical Marketplace.* Baltimore: Johns Hopkins University Press.

Thompson, James D. 1967. *Organizations in Action.* New York: McGraw-Hill.

Titmuss, Richard M. 1956. "The Role of Redistribution in Social Policy." *Social Security Bulletin* (June): 14–20.

Toffler, Alvin. 1980. *The Third Wave.* New York: Morrow.

Yankelovich, Daniel. 1981. *New Rules: Searching for Self-Fulfillment in a World Turned Upside Down.* New York: Random House.

Yessian, Mark. 1986. "The Editors Interview Robert M. Hayes." *New England Journal of Human Services* 6(4).

————. 1988. "Toward Effective Human Services Management." *Public Administration Quarterly* 12(1).

CHAPTER 7

Abramovitz, Mimi. 1988. *Regulating the Lives of Women.* Boston: South End Press.

Braiker, Harriet. 1986. "The Secret of Psychological Stamina: The Power Source Every Executive Needs." *Working Women,* (September).

Chernesky, Roslyn H. 1983. "The Sex Dimension of Organizational Processes: Its Impact on Women Managers." *Administration in Social Work* 7(3/4).

Kanter, Rosabeth Moss. 1977. *Men and Women of the Corporation.* New York: Basic Books.

————. 1983. *The Change Masters.* New York: Simon & Schuster.

Loden, Marilyn. 1985. *Feminine Leadership or How to Succeed in Business Without Being One of the Boys.* New York: Time Books.

Sargent, Alice G. 1987. *The Androgynous Manager.* New York: AMACOM.

Weil, Marie. 1981. "Southeast Asians and Service Delivery: Issues in Service Provision and Institutional Racism" in *Bridging Cultures: Southeast Asian Refugees in America.* Los Angeles: National Institute of Mental Health.

————. 1987. "Gender and Ethnic Shifts: Managing for Leadership Development and Response to Changing Client Populations" in *Social Work,* edited by Lynne Healy. West Hartford, Conn.: University of Connecticut School of Social Work.

CHAPTER 8

Drucker, Peter. 1977. *The Best of Peter Drucker.* New York: Harper & Row.
————. 1988. "The Coming of the New Organization." *Harvard Business Review* (January/February): 89–91.
Galbraith, Jay R. 1977. *Organization Design.* Reading, Mass.: Addison-Wesley.
McLuhan, Marshall. 1964. *Understanding Media.* New York: McGraw-Hill.
————. 1967. With Fiore, Q. *The Medium Is the Massage.* New York: Bantam Books.
Taylor, Frederick W. 1947. *Scientific Management.* New York: Harper & Row.
Thompson, James D. 1967. *Organizations in Action.* New York: McGraw-Hill.
Weiner, Myron E. 1988. "Designing and Executing Effective Human Services Organizations." *Public Administration Quarterly* 12(1): 32–59.

CHAPTER 9

Drucker, Peter F. 1974. *Management: Tasks, Responsibilities, Practices.* New York: Harper & Row.
Matthies, Leslie H. 1961. *The Playscript Procedure: A New Tool of Administration.* Stamford, Conn.: Office Publications.
Miller, Sara. 1980. "Program Management Versus Financial Management in a Bureaucracy." Unpublished paper. West Hartford, Conn.: University of Connecticut School of Social Work.
Patti, Rino; Poertner, John; and Rapp, Charles A. (eds.). 1987. *Managing for Services Effectiveness in Social Welfare Organizations.* Binghamton, N.Y.: Haworth Press.
Sarason, Seymour. 1971. *The Culture of the School and the Problem of Change.* Boston: Allyn and Bacon.

CHAPTER 10

Anthony, Robert N. and Young, David. 1988. *Management Control in Nonprofit Organizations.* Homewood, Ill.: Richard D. Irwin.
Chandler, Alfred D., Jr. 1962. *Strategy and Structure.* Cambridge, Mass.: MIT Press.
Drucker, Peter F. 1954. *The Practice of Management.* New York: Harper & Row.
Odiorne, George S. 1965. *Management by Objectives.* New York: G. P. Putnam's.
Peters, Tom. 1987. *Thriving on Chaos: Handbook for a Management Revolution.* New York: Alfred Knopf.

Ramanthan, Kavasseri V. 1982. *Management Control in Nonprofit Organizations*. New York: John Wiley.

Shuchman, Edward. 1968. *Evaluative Research: Principles and Practices in Service and Social Action Programs*. New York: Russell Sage Foundation.

Starling, Grover. 1979. *The Politics and Economics of Public Policy: An Introductory Analysis with Cases*. Homewood, Ill.: Dorsey Press.

Thompson, James D. 1967. *Organizations in Action*. New York: McGraw-Hill.

Wilson, Woodrow. 1887. "The Study of Public Administration." *Political Science Quarterly.*

CHAPTER 11

Anthony, Robert N. and Herzlinger, Regina E. 1980. *Management Control in Nonprofit Organizations*. Homewood, Ill.: Richard D. Irwin.

Brager, George, and Holloway, Stephen. 1978. *Changing Human Services Organizations: Politics and Practice*. New York: Free Press.

Gross, Malvern J., Jr. and Warshauer, William, Jr. 1979. *Financial and Accounting Guide for Nonprofit Organizations*, 3d ed. New York: John Wiley.

Lehan, Edward Anthony. 1978. *The Future of the Finance Directorate*. MFOA Study No. 3. Chicago: Municipal Finance Offices Association.

———. 1980. *Budgetmaking: A Workbook of Theory and Practice*. New York: St. Martin's Press.

——— 1981. *Simplified Governmental Budgeting*. Chicago: Government Finance Officers Association.

CHAPTER 12

Austin, Michael J. 1981. *Supervisory Management for the Human Services*. Englewood Cliffs, N.J.: Prentice-Hall.

Barnard, Chester I. 1938. *The Functions of the Executive*. Cambridge, Mass.: Harvard University Press.

Beer, Stafford. 1979. *The Heart of the Enterprise*. New York: John Wiley.

Cleare, Mary Jane. 1985. *The Assessment Center*. Storrs, Conn.: University of Connecticut Press.

Davis, K. 1972. *Human Behavior at Work*. New York: McGraw-Hill.

Drucker, Peter F. 1954. *The Practice of Management*. New York: Harper & Row.

Gardner, John W. 1964. *Self-Renewal*. New York: Harper & Row.

Gilbert, Dennis and Kahl, Joseph. 1987. *The American Class Structure: A New Synthesis*. Chicago, Ill.: The Dorsey Press.

Hackman, J. Richard and Oldham, G. R. 1980. *Work Redesign*. Reading, Mass.: Addison-Wesley.

Healy, Lynne Moore; Havens, Catherine M.; and Chin, Alice. 1989. "Pre-

paring Women for Social Work Administration: Building on Experience."
Administration in Social Work (Fall).

Knowles, Malcolm. 1978. *The Adult Learner: A Neglected Species,* 2d ed. Houston: Gulf Publishing.

Maluccio, Anthony N. 1979. *Learning from Clients.* New York: The Free Press.

March, James G. and Simon, Herbert A. 1958. *Organizations.* New York: John Wiley.

Milkovich, George T. and Boudreau, John W. 1988. *Personnel/Human Resource Management: A Diagnostic Approach,* 5th ed. Plano, Tex.: Business Publications.

Milkovich, George T. and Glueck, William F. 1985. *Personnel/Human Resource Management: A Diagnostic Approach,* 4th ed. Plano, Tex.: Business Publications.

Pecora, Peter J. and Austin, Michael J. 1987. *Managing Human Services Personnel.* Beverly Hills, Calif.: Sage Human Services Guide #48.

Peters, Tom. 1987. *Thriving on Chaos: Handbook for a Management Revolution.* New York: Alfred A. Knopf

Thompson, James D. 1967. *Organizations in Action.* New York: McGraw-Hill.

Van Maanen, John and Schein, Edgar H. 1977. "Career Development" in *Improving Life at Work,* edited by Hackman & Suttle, pp. 30–84. Santa Monica, CA: Goodyear Publishing.

Weiner, Myron E. 1988. "Managing People for Enhanced Performance" in *Managing for Service Effectiveness in Social Welfare Organizations,* edited by Rino J. Patti. et al. New York: Haworth.

CHAPTER 13

Butterfield, William H. (ed.). 1983. "Computers for Social Work Practitioners." *Practice Digest.* National Association of Social Workers, 6(3).

Caputo, Richard K. 1988. *Management and Information Systems in Human Services.* New York: Haworth Press.

Gingerich, Wallace J. 1988. *Expert Systems and Their Potential Uses in Social Work.* A paper presented at the Annual Program Meeting of the Council on Social Work Education, Atlanta, Ga., March 7, 1988.

Marrow, Alfred J. 1969. *The Practical Theorist: The Life and Work of Kurt Lewin.* New York: Basic Books.

Schoech, Dick. 1982. *Computer Use in Human Services: A Guide to Information Management.* New York: Human Sciences Press.

Schwartz, Marc D. (ed.). 1984. *Using Computers in Clinical Practice.* New York: Haworth Press.

Weiner, Myron E. 1971. *Public Automation: 2001.* Storrs, Conn.: University of Connecticut Press.

CHAPTER 14

Beer, Stafford. 1975. *Platform for Change*. London: John Wiley.
————. 1979. *The Heart of Enterprise*. New York: John Wiley.
Drucker, Peter F. 1974. *Management: Tasks, Responsibilities, Practices*. New York: Harper & Row.
————. 1988. "The Coming of the New Organization." *Harvard Business Review* (January/February) 89–91.
Patti, Rino J.; Poertner, John; and Rapp, Charles A. (eds.). 1987. *Managing for Service Effectiveness in Social Welfare Organizations*. New York: Haworth Press.
Stoline, Anne and Weiner, Jonathan P. 1988. *The New Medical Marketplace*. Baltimore: Johns Hopkins University Press.

CHAPTER 15

Ardery, Robert. 1966. *The Territorial Imperative*. New York: Atheneum.
Bennis, Warren and Nanus, Burt. 1985. *Leaders*. New York: Harper & Row.
Kanter, Rosabeth Moss. 1983. *The Change Masters*. New York: Simon & Schuster.
Loughran, Elizabeth Lee. 1986. *Consulting to Interorganizational Systems*. Amherst: Center for Organizational and Community Development, University of Massachusetts.
Marrow, Alfred J. 1969. *The Practical Theorist: The Life and Work of Kurt Lewin*. New York: Basic Books.
Peters, Tom. 1987. *Thriving on Chaos: Handbook for a Management Revolution*. New York: Alfred A. Knopf.
Sarason, Seymour B. 1972. *The Creation of Settings and the Future Societies*. San Francisco: Jossey-Bass.
Scott, W. Richard. 1987. *Organizations: Rational, Natural and Open Systems*, 2d ed. Englewood Cliffs, N.J.: Prentice-Hall.

CHAPTER 16

Drucker, Peter F. 1988. "The Coming of the New Organization." *Harvard Business Review* (January/February).
Follett, Mary Parker. 1940. *Dynamic Administration: The Collected Papers of Mary Parker Follett*, edited by Henry C. Metcalf and L. Urwich. New York: Harper & Row.
Hall, Edward T. 1965. *The Silent Language*. New York: Doubleday.
————. 1967. *The Hidden Dimension*. New York: Doubleday.
Halpern, Sam. 1988. *The Forgotten Half: Pathways to Success for America's*

Youth and Young Families. Washington, DC: William T. Grant Foundation Commission on Work, Family and Citizenship.

Illich, Ivan. 1978. *Toward a History of Needs*. New York: Pantheon Books.

Loughran, Elizabeth Lee. 1986. *Consulting to Interorganizational Systems*. Amherst: Center for Organizational and Community Development, University of Massachusetts.

Peters, Tom. 1987. *Thriving on Chaos: Handbook for a Management Revolution*. New York: Alfred A. Knopf.

Thompson, Victor A. 1965. *Modern Organizations: A General Theory*. New York: Alfred A. Knopf.

EPILOGUE

Berger, Peter L. and Luckmann, Thomas. 1966. *The Social Construction of Reality*. New York: Doubleday.

Campbell, Joseph. 1964. *The Masks of God: Occidental Mythology*. New York: Penguin Books.

———. 1968. *The Hero with a Thousand Faces,* 2d ed. Princeton, N.J.: Princeton University Press.

Harmon, Michael M. and Mayer, Richard T. 1986. *Organization Theory for Public Administration*. Boston: Little, Brown.

Kaufmann, Yehezkel. 1965. *The Religion of Israel*. Translated by M. Greenberg. New York: Schocken.

Morgan, Gareth. 1980. "Paradigms, Metaphors, and Puzzle Solving in Organization Theory." *Administrative Science Quarterly*. 25: 605–22.

Smircich, Linda. 1986. "Implications of the Interpretive Paradigm for Management Theory" in *Communication and Organizations,* edited by Linda Putnam and Michael Pacanowsky. Beverly Hills, Calif.: Sage.

Index